To Julie and Kate

'When one observes how here in London alone a greater quantity of manure than is produced by the whole kingdom of Saxony is poured away every day into the sea with an expenditure of enormous sums, and when one observes what colossal works are necessary in order to prevent this manure from poisoning the whole of London, then the utopian proposal to abolish the antithesis between town and country is given a peculiarly practical basis. And even comparatively insignificant Berlin has been wallowing in its own filth for at least 30 years.'

Frederick Engels, *The Housing Question*, 1872

'*The minimum dwelling* has become the *central problem of modern architecture and the battle cry of today's architectural avant-garde*. As a slogan, it is announced and promoted by modern architects, because it sheds light on a situation that has reached a point requiring the radical reform and modernization of housing; as a battle cry, it calls for answers to the question of the current crisis of housing.'

Czechoslovakian modernist architect and critic Karel Teige, *The Minimum Dwelling*, 1932; author's emphasis

'Executives often discount the value of management theory because it is associated with the term *theoretical*, which connotes *impractical*. But theory is consummately practical. The law of gravity, for example, actually is a theory – and it is useful. It allows us to predict that if we step off a cliff, we will fall.'

Harvard Business School professor Clayton Christensen and Deloitte Research director Michael Raynor, *The Innovator's Solution*, 2003

Why is construction so backward?

James Woudhuysen and Ian Abley

WILEY-ACADEMY

Published in Great Britain in 2004 by Wiley-Academy,
a division of John Wiley & Sons Ltd

Copyright © 2004   John Wiley & Sons Ltd, The Atrium, Southern Gate,
Chichester, West Sussex PO19 8SQ, England
Telephone (+44) 1243 779777

Email (for orders and customer service enquiries): cs-books@wiley.co.uk
Visit our Home Page on www.wileyeurope.com or www.wiley.com

This publication is designed to provide accurate and authoritative information in regard
to the subject matter covered. It is sold on the understanding that the Publisher is not
engaged in rendering professional services. If professional advice or other expert
assistance is required, the services of a competent professional should be sought.

ISBN 0470852895

Other Wiley Editorial Offices

John Wiley & Sons Inc., 111 River Street, Hoboken, NJ 07030, USA

Jossey-Bass, 989 Market Street, San Francisco, CA 94103–1741, USA

Wiley-VCH Verlag GmbH, Boschstr. 12, D-69469 Weinheim, Germany

John Wiley & Sons Australia Ltd, 33 Park Road, Milton, Queensland 4064, Australia

John Wiley & Sons (Asia) Pte Ltd, 2 Clementi Loop #02–01, Jin Xing Distripark,
Singapore 129809

John Wiley & Sons Canada Ltd, 22 Worcester Road, Etobicoke, Ontario, Canada
M9W 1L1

Front cover: *Les Constructeurs – définitif*, 1950, by Fernand Léger (1881–1955).
Held at the Musée National Fernand Léger, Biot, France. ©ADAGP, Paris, 2002

Typeset by Florence Production Ltd, Stoodleigh, Devon, UK

Printed and bound in Great Britain by T.J. International Ltd, Padstow, Cornwall, UK

This book is printed on acid-free paper responsibly manufactured from sustainable
forestry in which at least two trees are planted for each one used for paper production.

Acknowledgements

James Woudhuysen and Ian Abley

Special thanks go to Martin Pawley, for his Foreword, his advice and his continued encouragement.

We thank the photographers Simon Punter, Julian Dodd, Andrew Ward and Caroline Irby for the pictures reproduced here. We have also been inspired, in many aspects of the design of this book, by the designer and photographer Jonathan Schwinge. We are, finally, very grateful for the patience and professionalism of Abigail Grater, for bringing this new product to market, and of Adrian Grater for copy-editing the text.

- Simon Punter Photography, email photo@simonpunter.com
- Julian Dodd, email mail@juliandodd.com or visit www.juliandodd.com
- Andrew Ward, email andward@wards.u–net.com
- Caroline Irby, email caro@carolineirby.com
- Jonathan Schwinge may be contacted through the www.audacity.org website

Jonathan Schwinge. Photo by Jenny Back

Any and all errors in the text are the responsibility of James Woudhuysen and Ian Abley. Nevertheless, we would like to thank Kate Abley, Emeka Agbasi, Hugh Aldersey-Williams, Rami Al-Yazjee, Nic Bailey, James Barlow, Daniel Ben-Ami, Daren Brown, Nigel Davies, Garry Dobson, Jim Donoghue, Jakob Dunkl, Gail Ellement, Bridget Fidler, Peter Field, Valerie Fogleman, Gareth Griffiths, Ben Halevi, James Heartfield, Damien Hammond, Jackson Hunt, Joe Kaplinsky, Wilfried Laufs, Brian Love, Paul Markovits, Toby Marshall, Richard McWilliams, Paul Middleton, John Miles, Duncan Mitchell, Phil Mullan, Dominic Munro, Barry Murphy, John Prewer, Duncan Price, Adam Poole, Colin Porteous, Vicky Richardson, Paul Ruyssevelt, Miffa Salter, Andrew Scoones, John Stapleton, Will Stevens, Greg Stevenson, John Stewart, Alec Turner, Mick Walsh and Russ Winser.

We greatly appreciate the advice and assistance provided by Shuvro Bose at the Office of the Deputy Prime Minister, professor Paul Cheshire at the department of geography, London School of Economics, Ian Harris at the British Institute of Facilities Management, professor Ade Kearns at the department of urban studies, University of Glasgow, Clare Morris of the National Building Specification, Michael Owens, head of partnership development at the London Development Agency, Jackie Smith, senior research analyst at the Council for Mortgage Lenders, and professor Steve Wilcox at the centre for housing policy, University of York.

Contents

Boxes

Tables

Foreword

Martin Pawley

Because most of human life is conducted in buildings, everyone has an opinion about the construction industry. In recent years the housing market alone has ensured that every homeowner has become a Do It Yourself expert as well as a venture capitalist, well acquainted at some level with the 'backwardness' that is the subject of this book.

Nonetheless, despite this progressive consumerising of the issues discussed in the following pages, when it comes to answering the central question posed by the book's title we must rely on our expert authors. For as the reader will soon discover, it is a mistake to take the broad assumption of backwardness at face value when there are other questions as yet unasked that bear on the discourse of everyone concerned with building.

Questions that give pause to the entrepreneurial developer and the construction professional at the top, even as they touch the lowliest sub-contractor and site operative at the bottom.

Questions so secret that a £70 billion industry employing nearly two million people treats them as shibboleths of the world of fame and ennoblement, property, architectural genius, awards, honours, public inquiries, arbitrations, claims, toppings out, health and safety regulations, and trade disputes that altogether make up the universe of building.

Is construction really backward? Anecdotally the charge seems impossible to refute, but it is not. Even the most determined attempt to think it through soon runs into contradictions and turns back upon itself. For, in the end, who can truly say that construction is any more backward than the markets it serves? Anyone old enough to remember the labour-intensive building sites of the 1950s, with their rows of batch mixers discharging into wheelbarrows to be pushed and pulled up ramps of scaffold boards to distant formwork, would have to concede that today's tower craned and weatherproofed construction site, served by trucks making just-in-time deliveries of pre-mixed concrete and pre-engineered assemblies, represents a tremendous advance in organisation and methods.

And so of course it does, but not to the exclusion of changes of a different order that have had as great an influence. As late as the 1950s, the men employed on building sites were more likely than not to include trained craftsmen, expert in the handling of traditional materials. If the modern building site has become a model of labour-saving mechanisation since those days, it has done so at a price, leaving the traditional relationship between designer and executor far behind and adapting itself to an itinerant labour force made up of subcontractors and operatives handling precision finished assemblies and new materials.

Taken in isolation, these site and labour changes might on balance be considered favourable for fast construction, but they are not the sum of the changes made over the same 50 years.

Upstream of the improved logistics of the building site a vast bureaucracy of building regulation and statutory and advisory controls has grown up – a source of endless postponements and delays, smothering the once straightforward act of building in an impenetrable fog of overlapping responsibilities. The effect of these two levels of change, despite the industry's on- and off-site modernisation, is that construction has not yet attained an overall speed of process – from design to completion – that can keep pace with the dot com speed of global business. Still less can it match the rate of production of prefabricated houses attained in the 1940s by the public sector.

Shortcomings like this are particularly striking when one sees that, half a century ago, a disorganised and war-ravaged British building industry nonetheless contrived to produce 60,000 new prefabricated council houses; repair and refurbish 100,000 bombed dwellings; and build 34,000 new private houses, all in 15 months between April 1945 and July 1946 – a performance that can be compared to the miserable total of 130,000 new houses from all sectors that were completed in 2001, the lowest annual output since the 1920s.

Such comparisons are shocking but salutary, not least because they should remind us that the falling productivity of the housebuilding industry in recent years cannot simply be attributed to 'backwardness', but must take account of demographic and economic factors as well.

For example at the end of 2002, when it was calculated that the average mortgage debt per household in Britain stood at £40,000, a sum hypothetically secured on a modest 1952 suburban semi originally costing £1,000, that mortgage debt should have bought 40 such houses. Instead, by 2002, with each house commanding a price of £500,000 or more, it cannot pay for even one. Why has this happened? Because to have held house prices at their 1952 level for half a century would have required the sustained annual production, not of a paltry 130,000 new dwellings as at present, but of at least a million units per year.

In the tax-advantaged owner-occupier market that has dominated housing policy over the last 40 years, it would be difficult to imagine anything other than a magnificently sustained social housing programme that could have made a lower price to posterity more attractive than successive owner's capital gains. That is why, at the time of writing, an outer London suburban house can cost as much as a house in Kensington Gardens would have done in 1952. And that is why the supposed 'backwardness' of the construction industry is a more complex phenomenon than may at first appear.

What can be done to remedy the sort of institutionalised backwardness that shows up so clearly in the housing market? The celebrated German architect Cristoph Ingenhoven poses a stark choice in his book *Energies*:

We have only two alternatives in the matter of building. We can fake the past, or we can industrialise the future. The first is impossible because the past cannot be built again – certainly not when traditional craftsmanship is all but extinct. But, by the same token, industrializing the future will only work if we are able to attain a precision and complexity at least as impressive as what was achieved by the trained craftsmen of the past.[1]

These bold words, echoing Le Corbusier's *Je ferai des maisons comme on fait des voitures*, and the conclusions of Walter Gropius's comparative studies of house and car prices in the 1920s, have been paraphrased by many since Henry Ford set the world's first automobile production line in motion in 1914. But thus far the application of his basic idea to building has either been too tentative, too underfinanced or politically unacceptable – an example of the last being the concrete panel system-built apartments extensively produced in Eastern Europe prior to the end of the Cold War.

With such unhappy precedents to guide them today's prefabrication pioneers are understandably exigent about their ground rules for successful 'de-backwardisation'. John Prewer, the man behind the 1990 iteration of the microflat, a container-sized single person dwelling whose structure was based on prefabricated lift shaft components with an interior fit-out by a firm of car stylists, has distanced himself from heavy system and panel building altogether with a 30-point plan for lightness and speed in modular house construction. His emphasis is on downsizing plan areas and volumes, eliminating wet trades (including excavated foundations), reducing waste by using uncut materials in standard sizes, and (significantly) doing without contractors and construction professionals. All measures he means to employ in his current project, a new modular Peabody Trust housing development in London's Harrow Road.

When Britain's best-selling broadsheet newspaper launched a new weekly tabloid supplement on housing in the autumn of 2002 it was healthily endowed with adver-

 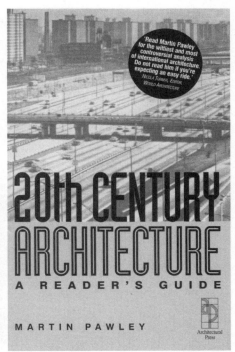

Martin Pawley gave the opening speech to the conference, held in July 2000, which inaugurated the Audacity website. His and other speeches to the conference are posted on www.audacity.org/Activity.htm. Pawley is a writer and critic best known for his weekly column in the *Architects' Journal*. He studied architecture at the Ecole Nationale Supérieure des Beaux-Arts, Paris, and the Architectural Association, London. A former editor of the weekly newspaper *Building Design*, he was later architecture critic of *The Guardian* and *The Observer*, and most recently editor of the international magazine *World Architecture*. His most recent books include *Theory and Design in the Second Machine Age*; *Buckminster Fuller: a critical biography*; *Future Systems: the story of tomorrow*; *Norman Foster: a global architecture*; *Terminal Architecture*; and *20th Century Architecture: a reader's guide*

tising. It not only carried national and local house price data, graphs of demographic and construction trends, market activity, ratios of buyers and sellers and so on, but also featured such arcane subjects as an article about the superiority of East European-trained building workers, a teach-in on using the right power tools when refurbishing an ancient manor house, how to buy a brand new apartment off the drawing board, and the usual full-page furniture ads and celebrities showing off their designer pads. In short, this supplement promised an integrated overview of the consumer end of the housing market in the 21st century.

Only one aspect of the new supplement slipped a gear and betrayed its wish-fulfilling obsolescence and that was its name – *Bricks and Mortar* – a term as antique as it is universally understood. A term that, on its own, explains why the building industry will not match the productivity of the motor industry until it is radically reformed, and the pages of every building supplement start to carry headlines like 'Inside the new Tartan 306', or 'Autohouse ships 200,000 modulars in record year'.

NOTE

1   Cristoph Ingenhoven, *Energies* (Basel, Boston, Berlin, Birkhauser, 2003) p 30.

1 An industry that barely deserves the term

1.1 Construction becomes a mainstream political issue

Infants build little towers of wooden bricks.

When the bricks fall over, little hands build them up again, but higher.

Then, as infants grow up, they may move from bricks to sandcastles and, after that, to toys like Lego.

It is human to want to extend the possibilities of building – just as human as it is to want better places to live and work. The idea is simple: to be more ingenious in construction. Of course, beavers build dams and bees build hives, but only human beings generate blueprints, improve on their designs over time, and pass down their ideas to future generations.

Ingenuity in building today commands the interest of millions. Yet the simplicity of the idea stands in sharp contrast to the real world of construction. In the early 21st century, it seems more difficult than ever to get a house or workplace built.

Construction is backward. It is atomised in industrial structure, poorly managed in practice, and endlessly weighed down by regulations. To get a kitchen or bathroom fitted, a small extension added, or a new building commissioned costs a lot of money and frequently involves recourse to the law.

Residential floor space commands more and more of a premium. On top of that, the business of buying a house can be expensive and time-consuming. Yet behind the backwardness of the whole property sector is a wider crisis of capitalist innovation. It is possible to define innovation in technological terms – in terms of *product* and *process*. Innovation also takes place when new forms of *organisation* emerge. But while some products of the construction industry are innovatory, property developers routinely bemoan the antediluvian processes and forms of organisation that surround their industry.

They are not alone in their concern. In large parts of the world, and hand in hand with transport infrastructure, *the quality and quantity of the building stock has become a mainstream political issue.*

Alex and Holly play Bob the Builder

Construction has long been important economically; in Britain, it accounts for about eight per cent of Gross Domestic Product (GDP).[1] Property has also long been important to the rich – even today, multi-millionaires in land and property make up no fewer than 150 of the top 1000 richest people in the UK.[2] But the broad social impact of the construction industry now goes further than all this. In Britain and America, millions of house-holders follow interior design. More important, millions follow the market for residential property; and they are joined in this by tens of thousands of govern-ment officials, economists and bankers.

Today the significance of property to young members of the Western middle classes is so great that estate agents even offer sexual partners to those in search of the flat that has everything.[3] In Britain, a national infatuation with property has had unexpected consequences. At 60 per cent of GDP, UK mortgage debt is well above the average for the EU. The British Medical Association has publicised the idea that such debt is bad for people's health.[4] And when Chancellor Gordon Brown declared, on 9 June 2003, that the time was not right for Britain to abandon the Pound for the Euro, the idiosyncrasies of that country's housing market, and in particular the crisis in its housing supply, formed one of the key risks in his mind.[5]

Property has also long been linked to financial speculation of a dubious char-acter. But at a time when the trustwor-thiness of financial services and financial engineering is under the spotlight, prop-erty has become a financial instrument much more central to national life. In the second quarter of 2003, General Motors earned three times as much from selling mortgages as it did from selling cars.[6] And over the much longer period 1995–2003, America's 50 top banks raised the share of their portfolios held in mortgage-backed securities from 47 per cent to 62 per cent. In so doing, they exposed them-selves to the dangers of what *Business Week* called 'refi-madness' – US con-sumers' willingness to refinance their affairs by borrowing more on their homes with the help of declining interest rates.[7]

Those financial institutions that have offered cheap loans on property have received an enormous and much-needed boost to profits. In June 2003 it was revealed that one of the largest of such institutions in the US, the Federal Home Loan Mortgage Corporation, popularly known as Freddie Mac, had indeed delib-erately understated its profits by billions of dollars. Why? It wanted to keep profit levels smooth beyond the early years of the new millennium – so fearful was it of the risk of a later *property crash* and ensuing profits collapse.

As the financial edifice erected on property has grown, so has the scale of American homes, housebuilding and house sales. The median size of an American home rose from 5.2 to 5.8 rooms in the decade before the US Census was published in August 2001. Then, 17 million US homes had eight rooms, up from 13.5 million in 1990.[8] By July 2003 the seasonally adjusted annual rate of constructing single-family homes, at 1.52 million, was the highest in 17 years and the third highest in the history of the US.[9] It was matched only by the annual rate of sales of existing single-family homes in the US. In July 2003 that reached, on a seasonally adjusted basis, no fewer than 6,120,000 units – an all time high.[10]

In China too, property is a political issue. In 2003, officials despatched from Beijing to Shanghai detained Zhou Shengyi, a property tycoon with two companies listed on the Hong Kong stock exchange, for questionable loans to the value of £166 million obtained from the local Bank of China. Scrutiny of Mr Zhou quickly acquired a national economic and political significance. Named by *Forbes* magazine in 2002 as the richest man in Shanghai, Zhou's over-rapid development of that city – he controlled its largest development site – came under the microscope as part of a wider campaign against corruption and unrestrained capitalism. With a second Shanghai developer, Qian Yongwei, also under scrutiny for loans of more than £100 million, work stopped on some of Shanghai's biggest building sites, as all big land deals in the city came under surveillance.[11]

In Russia construction is a key social issue. A country of plunging temperatures, Russia can no longer heat many of its ageing 1960s blocks of flats. Its scarce supplies of quality accommodation command the attention not just of powerful mayors, but of President Putin himself.

All over the world, then, popular interest in and expectations of property, construction and buildings are on the rise. All over the world, too, great innovations in building are still being made. But the simple idea of untrammelled progress in construction technique remains mired in wet trades. Even in modest construction projects, cost and time overruns are every bit the match of the overruns that characterise massive government projects in defence, transport and Information Technology (IT).

Popular and media enthusiasm for architecture is enormous. The contemporary art of architecture, after all, appears to bristle with breakthroughs in design and engineering. Not for nothing did the subversive, hi-tech 1960s architectural group Archigram[12] finally win, in 2002, a Gold Medal from Britain's august Royal Institute of British Architects (RIBA).[13]

Moreover as enthusiasm for architecture has grown, so have the claims made for it. Norman Foster's glassy headquarters for the Greater London Assembly (GLA), together with his Reichstag building in Berlin, are monuments to the belief that see-through forms in architecture can bring a new openness to political life.[14] When Gordon Brown proudly boasted of refurbished Treasury accommodation that 'it's open plan, it's transparent; it's no longer a maze of corridors', he was not simply celebrating the Treasury's first office make-over in almost 100 years. By spending a cool £170 million arranging clear lines of sight for staff and visitors, he and his colleagues also hoped to counter impressions of secretiveness and lack of accountability.[15]

Yet in architecture, as elsewhere, appearances can be deceptive. For every great product of the international construction industry today, such as the GLA headquarters, there are a hundred processes that remain the opaque, laborious chores they were in the 19th century. And though there have been some notable advances in process and component technology, their architectural expression often results not just in spiralling costs while projects are being completed, but also, afterwards, in heavy bills for maintenance.

The construction 'industry' barely deserves the term. After millennia of human settlement, designing and building architecture takes an unconscionable amount of time.

Norman Foster

In Britain, architects revere Norman Foster more than any other architect alive today.[16] He has lectured throughout the world and taught architecture in the US and UK. He has been vice president of the Architectural Association in London, council member of the Royal College of Art, a member of the Board of Education and visiting examiner for the RIBA, and is a trustee of the Architecture Foundation of London.

Foster graduated from Manchester University School of Architecture and City Planning in 1961, and won a Fellowship to Yale University, where he gained a master's in architecture. In 1963 he co-founded Team 4, and in 1967 established Foster Associates, now known as Foster and Partners.[17] The practice has project offices worldwide, and a main studio in London. It has won many international prizes.

Foster was awarded the RIBA Royal Gold Medal for Architecture in 1983, the Gold Medal of the French Academy of Architecture in 1991 and the American Institute of Architects Gold Medal in 1994. In the latter year, France's Ministry of Culture made him Officer of the Order of Arts and Letters. In 1999 Foster became the 21st Pritzker Architecture Prize Laureate, and was made Lord Foster of Thames Bank.

Photo by Andrew Ward

1.2 Progress, but only of a sort

Interest rates are low. The householder or the commercial client for building finds it relatively simple to finance projects. More generally, the homebuilder or property developer faces an unprecedented choice of forms and functions in construction. There are more and better designs, materials, components and technologies available than ever before.[18]

For all its exasperating backwardness since the Second World War, construction has developed a sophisticated division of labour. There has been progress; but it is progress only of a sort.

Take, just as an example, the changing technical and professional division of labour that attends the cladding of buildings with façades. Stephen Ledbetter, head of the UK's Centre for Window and

Cladding Technology (CWCT), sets the context well. Before the Victorian era, he notes, the architect was a master builder, designing buildings for construction by a contractor. Thereafter:

The advent of framed buildings in the late 19th century gave rise to the role of the structural engineer. The introduction of mechanical ventilation and air conditioning in the middle of the 20th century gave rise to the role of . . . building services engineer. By the end of the 20th century, high performance façades had become so complex that façade engineering began to emerge as a specialism.[19]

The CWCT was set up in 1989, after too many British buildings had proved ill-clad.[20] Today, its tests of prototypes regularly expose how the under-performance of a building's façade can be avoided. In

Greater London Assembly headquarters

The GLA headquarters on the Thames has a spiral ramp with faceted glazing on its exterior and interior, and a stepped façade made of triple-glazed units. The glazing contractors relied on 3D computer modelling to design both. Each glass panel, containing louvre blinds and ventilation, has a unique geometry and size. Simple but effective adjustments were achieved by concealing plates below raised floors or above suspended ceilings, and also – most impressively – by ball-and-socket joint details hidden in the final construction. The silicone-sealed glazing to the ramp had to be within the tolerances of the sealed and drained glazing sub-frame, located on steel lugs, and welded to the structure on-site.

On bespoke buildings that, like the GLA headquarters, are meant to be open to the public, it is fair enough for architects to mix intricate 3D computer modelling with lengthy and expensive time spent on site. But the further private offices behind the HQ are another matter. They try too hard to be noticed as architecture, when they might have been much more advanced simply as construction.

Testing the prototype of a façade in the manner laid out by the the UK's Centre for Window and Cladding Technology may seem crude, but it's the only effective standard there is. Positive and negative chamber pressures, smoke tests, discussions of failure and remedy, measurement of deflection and deformation, simulation of wind turbulence and rain, hose tests, destructive investigation, and checks on construction detailing all feature in the procedure. Most prototypes fail their first test, and those who install façades find the whole testing process an expensive way to develop their design details

façades, the CWCT helps specified levels of air-, water- and wind-tightness to be met, given certain levels of:

- ventilation;
- building servicing; and
- structural, thermal and acoustic excellence.

All these things can now be engineered into a building envelope together, using today's codified methods of calculation, modelling and testing.

Like other construction technologies, therefore, cladding made progress as a result of research and development (R&D). It was not cladding by itself that led to problems with façades, but the way cladding systems were both designed and installed to interface with other aspects of construction. As a result, a new discipline known as façade engineering sprang up.

Façade engineering aims to fill the gap between architectural design at planning stage and the detailing done on site: its goal is to realise the aesthetic goals that surround a building without impairing its performance. But the birth of yet another construction industry specialism, complete with a vital overview to contribute on every project, has been accompanied by familiar trends. In façades as elsewhere, architects have become less practical, leaving details to others. As a consequence, sloppy on-site workmanship has become more prevalent, and more difficult to prevent.

In short, technical and professional specialisation has often solved construction industry problems, but it has also often created new ones. Still, it is also true that, as trades have multiplied and become more specialised, so many have become simpler. Apart from structural work, highly skilled crafts, building services, or top-end façade engineering, much of construction need be little harder than an exacting DIY project.

That is good news. Yet while technical specialisation could have been a positive force among architects, they have abjured it.

Today, in construction matters, architects rely as never before on others, and especially on specialists in IT. But they never rely on each other. Apart from those large competitions that are won by a partnership of a small firm of architects with a large one, architects with expertise A are too scared of losing their clients to collaborate with architects who have expertise B.

So, as technical specialisations go, architecture has failed to develop its own division of labour. As a result, it has atrophied as a profession. Unwilling to broaden, deepen or sharpen its technical skills, architecture has preferred to retreat into a bizarrely polarised world of High Culture conceptual designs – frequently unimplemented – and Low Culture calculations of building floor areas.

Some architects retain enough influence to extract a brief or concept out of a client, and commit them to it. Yet even High Culture concepts require planning and budgetary control, though architects have relinquished these things to surveyors and project managers.

It is all rather dispiriting. Weak on specialist skills, many architects have turned themselves into irrelevant visionaries. For that they are ridiculed by other members of a project team, even though such people are themselves unable to make a good building without a clear architectural vision for it.

More than three decades ago, when architects first turned to post-modernism, they made a virtue out of their new status as a laughing-stock. In their seminal *Learning from Las Vegas*, Robert Venturi, Denise Scott Brown and Steven Izenour looked forward to the day when the architect became a jester. They favoured:

subversion through irony and the use of a joke to get to seriousness, the weapons of artists of nonauthoritarian temperament in social situations that do not agree with them.[21]

But now the joke is on the architect. In an industry full of angst, all but a few find themselves frustrated at every turn. Worse still, architects are often a source of frustration to many of the other kinds of professionals who work with them – despite, or perhaps because of, the innovations that have been made in contracts with such professionals (see Box 1).

Sir Michael Latham was a Conservative MP from 1974 to 1992. Today he is chairman of the Construction Industry Training Board; over the years he has received many awards for his services to British building and remains one of its key organising intellectuals

Box 1 INNOVATION IN CONTRACTS: ONE STEP FORWARD, TWO STEPS BACK

Never try to get anything built without a clear construction contract, setting out precisely what you want built and how you want it done. Always try to minimise the amount of design left to the contractor to coordinate in the middle of a construction programme. Contractual documentation, drawings and specifications take time and effort to produce; but they save time on site, clarify arguments, and reduce confusion if the project comes to a legal dispute.

Obvious? Perhaps so. Yet many households wander without contracts into serious construction work, only to regret doing so. That is not a risk-taking approach to business so much as a reckless or naïve reliance on contractors only too pleased to avoid contracting.

Many construction industry professionals, too, talk glibly of project teams or partnerships, based on trust, as an alternative to contracts. Clients and contractors court each other for partnerships – supposedly to share risks, but often to offload contractual liability.

Contracting, complete with a main contractor, is the conventional approach on any size of building project. In contracting, the client employs consultants in design and cost, and entrusts them with the professional duty impartially to administer a contract. A main contractor is hired and is made responsible not only for its own direct tasks, but also those aspects of the detailed design that, nowadays, it more and more delegates to subcontractors and their own consultants.

For all the flaws, pedantry and litigation that surround them, it is right that contracts predominate in construction. In 2001, no fewer than 95 per cent of UK building projects used a standard form of contract. The Joint Contracts Tribunal produced many of them.[22] JCT standard forms accounted for more than 90 per cent of all contracts and 78.9 per cent of all construction value in the UK – the highest levels in 18 years.[23]

However contracting is no panacea. The trend to avoid responsibility for shouldering risk is evident in three late 20th century innovations in the way construction has been organised and managed.

Popular from the 1980s onwards, *Design and Build* (D&B) is a *form* of main contracting, but with a greater responsibility on the main contractor to *develop the design during the contract period* – from start on site to handover of the completed building. In standard contracts, portions of the works are identified as contractor design supplements, or items for the main contractor to design during the programme.

The argument was always that the contractor was best placed to provide a practical design solution, where the design consultants were not. But this has proven to be a corrosive generalisation.

Although there has been no significant increase in D&B since 1998, its prevalence, together with the frequent use of contractor design supplements, means that *more and more UK architects and engineers detail their designs less and less*. The delegation of detailed design work is commonplace: few consultants are prepared to extend their liabilities beyond performance specifications and drawings of 'design intent'. So while there has been an increase in both the number and the value of contracts relying on specification and drawings, such specifications are not necessarily prescriptive, and the detailed content of drawings may be incomplete.

D&B has meant a shift: from fully designing a construction before it is put out to tender, to holding discussions between consultants and trade contractors on design development – discussions pursued after the tender has been won. That has enormously multiplied the number of man-hours spent in meetings. By postponing details until ground works or structure are underway on site, it is possible to shorten a building programme. But the

Site offices

Site visits

Site meetings

Site reviews

Site tolerances

number of attendees at project team meetings has exploded – and everyone around the table seeks to limit personal responsibility for the detailed design. With D&B there has been a kind of innovation in construction, but not a very productive one.

Construction Management (CM) is advocated as a distinct *alternative* to contracting with a main contractor. Fashionable on major projects, CM describes situations in which management consultants are supposed to orchestrate the activities of consultants in design and cost alongside those of trade contractors, who more and more use sub-consultants of their own to carry out detailed design work. All are directly employed by the client; the aim is to develop very buildable projects and deliver them all on time.

In his influential report of 1994, *Constructing the Team*, Britain's Sir Michael Latham noted the advantages of construction management to clients:

> The client commissions a project which involves a high degree of innovation, and many new design details. The client wants hands-on involvement and seeks strong management to produce the intended result. The best route here is construction management. It is a demanding procurement system, requiring firm leadership and team work throughout.[24]

The problems with CM, however, are threefold:

1 Consultants in design merely specify performances and indicate design intent: even assuming they retain the technical capacity to detail the construction, they don't want responsibility for items they are not being paid a fee to develop, or given the authority to determine.
2 Instead, it is the trade contractors who come up with detailed designs: but each literally makes up its designs as it goes, while trying not to take responsibility for ensuring a good fit with the designs submitted by other trade contractors. The result is often that a building's critical interfaces are ill-considered.
3 The supervisory CM consultants never want the burden of anything other than the overall programme of work to be done. That programme is invariably little more than an educated guess, since it is written at the inception of every CM project – long before the full technical issues are evident.

Given these problems, it is little wonder that CM projects often go over budget. As a result, and despite all Latham's modernising rhetoric, only the largest and most experienced clients, with the most difficult projects, have gone on to adopt CM.

With all the lawsuits that have grown up around conventional contracting, *partnering* has emerged, on top of CM, as another supposed *alternative* to contracts – or at least as a *way of making D&B and CM work better*. As early as 1998, enthusiasts at Britain's official Construction Best Practice Programme described partnering as a structured management approach to 'facilitate teamworking': the kind of teamworking that should take place 'across contractual boundaries'.[25]

That blurring of contractual liabilities is precisely why partnering should be avoided. It should not be confused with durable trading relationships, negotiated contracts or preferred supplier arrangements: all of these lack the measures that are sought in a partnering relationship. In such a relationship, the fundamental components are:

• mutual objectives that are formalised;
• methods of solving problems that are agreed; and
• an active search for continuous measurable improvements.

In partnering it is not the contract, but a partnering agreement – often, a single side of A4 paper – that drives the relationship between the parties.

It is often acknowledged that partnering is not an appropriate procurement strategy for all construction projects. It is claimed that prospective partners should seek by discussion to identify sources of risks, and then establish who can best assess and manage them. Yet fuzzy agreements to assess and manage risk are most definitely not the same thing as precise contractual liabilities.

In 2001, partnering agreements linked to standard contracts accounted, thankfully, for less than three per cent of UK construction contracts by value, while pure partnering agreements took less than two per cent. The impact of the *rhetoric* of partnering, however, is far deeper than this. Everyone in construction now prefers talk of teams to clear contractual responsibilities. People expect both design direction and design details to be sacrificed, at least in part, in the pursuit of the smooth running of a job; its adherence to budgeted costs of construction and professional fees; and – often of greater significance than costs and fees put together – its completion on time.[26]

The aim of a partnering agreement is to make inter-firm relations in the construction sector less adversarial. That sounds like a sensible thing; yet in reality the attempt to imagine away liability through a sharing of risk has led to a diffusion of clear responsibilities for getting the different parts of a construction project designed and built properly.

The moral of different attempts to innovate in forms of contract is simple. Make sure there is a construction contract; but make sure, too, that there is someone substantial to blame for the design if it turns out to be faulty.

If buildings were manufactured, rather than made on site, such blame would clearly rest with the manufacturer – end of story. Until that happens, the formal contractual methods developed by bodies such as the Joint Contracts Tribunal are likely to retain an essential role.

1.3 Local small firms do up existing homes – and always work on site

A former head of the International Council for Building Research, Studies and Documentation,[27] Gyula Sebestyén is a consultant civil engineer, architect, and part-time professor at Budapest's Technical University. Since his early interest in lightweight construction, he has been published extensively in many languages.[28] Of construction as an industry, he writes:

In an increasing number of subsectors, the most up-to-date technology is used and more of the buildings to be constructed are really high-tech products whose design requires modern scientific methods. The internal structure of the building industry is also changing.

An internationalisation of the market goes hand in hand with the emergence of construction multinationals, which themselves promote technical progress. Despite this, several publications have claimed that construction lags behind other industries, that construction technology has been the least modernised, that productivity in building has developed at a lower rate than elsewhere, and that it is still a labour-intensive economic sector with accident-prone and health-endangering work practices.[29]

Sebestyén is right. It is a mystery that construction has moved on as much as it has yet remains so backward. Some subsectors do use up-to-date technology. But the pattern of advance is terribly uneven.

Take, to begin with, what Sebestyén calls the emergence of construction multinationals – the globalisation of the construction business. It is a fact; but it has its limits, too. The table below shows the 10 companies in engineering and construction that made it into *Fortune* magazine's 2003 list of the 500 largest companies quoted on world stock markets. The final column shows the percentage of these companies' revenues that accrue from operations abroad.

The data show that:

- The size of global firms active in construction is very modest compared with other sectors. The giants are way down the *Fortune* 500 list. Even their mediocre position disguises the millions of small, inefficient enterprises that dominate the sector.
- Six of the 10 giants come from Japan. There, construction has been assisted for more than a decade by overwhelmingly national programmes of public works. Of the six, Tokyu is mainly in railway engineering, and only Kajima and Shimizu give details of the international exposure of their business. For the rest, international operations are either small, relatively weak, or both.

Gyula Sebestyén

- Three out of the other four giants are from France (Bouygues, Vinci) and Sweden (Skanska). Their globalisation is a necessity, given the limited internal markets of these nations. America's Fluor, which does have a strong performance in overseas operations, is much more an engineering than a constructional concern.

So, Europe's largest construction firms certainly are engaged in international

TABLE 1 The top 10 largest publicly quoted engineering and construction companies in the world, 2003

Rank	Company	Rank in Fortune 500	Revenues, $m	Per cent from overseas
1	Bouygues[30]	211	21,033	35
2	Vinci[31]	270	17,438	41
3	Kajima[32]	322	15,386	12.4
4	Skanska[33]	334	14,979	63
5	Taisei[34]	375	13,497	Not available
6	Shimizu[35]	398	12,718	3
7	Tokyu[36]	447	11,370	Not available
8	Obayashi[37]	460	11,005	Not available
9	Sekisui House[38]	482	10,481	less than 10
10	Fluor[39]	498	10,190	55

Source: 'The 2003 Global 500', *Fortune*[40] financial statements and annual reports on company websites

markets. Equally, America's privately-held Bechtel gained 22 per cent of its 2002 'workoff revenue' outside North America.[41] But the globalisation of industries outside the building trade is more impressive. Wal-Mart Stores, the world's largest firm, is, like construction companies, in a place-centred business. Nevertheless it has a solid 37 per cent of its outlets outside the US.[42] Britain's Tesco, a much smaller retailer, gets only 20 per cent of its turnover from overseas; but its chief, Terry Leahy, reckons that the figure could, in time, reach 50 per cent or more.[43]

Nearly all the world's construction firms can only dream of such international exposure. The construction industry acts local more than it acts global.

No other industry in the world gets by with so little capital investment as construction. Yet it is construction that underpins every other industry in the world. David Gann, professor of technology and innovation management at Imperial College, London, argues this cogently:

Construction's significance to wealth creation and quality of life extends beyond its direct economic contribution. The products and services provided by construction create an infrastructure that supports existing and newly emerging social and economic activities . . . If inadequate or inappropriate buildings and structures are produced, or they are poorly maintained and adapted, then social and economic life is compromised.[45]

The products of construction make the rest of contemporary life possible. Alternatively, the products of construction can frustrate us; despite its relevance to the wealth of the world, construction remains a retrograde affair.

In Britain it is the same story. Most construction companies have virtually no capital investment beyond their tools, some small plant and a Transit van. Many main contractors are little more than management teams employing subcontractors.

Output growth in UK building has failed to keep up with growth in GDP. Between 1968 and 1997, contractors' output barely grew by one per cent a year – well below the UK economy's long-run growth rate of about 2.5 per cent.[46] In more recent years, the comparison continues to be unflattering:[47]

Britain's construction industry is simply not strong enough to support the rate of renewal of habitat and workplace that the country needs.

Britain remains a weak economy. It fails to stretch a construction sector that has been in decline since the 1960s. Construction, always a sign of general economic circumstances, flags in output growth, and does its own bit to retard UK plc.

More than any other sector, construction remains dominated by small firms. In 1991, 94 per cent of registered firms in UK construction employed seven people or fewer, with 83 per cent employing fewer than three. By 2002 the figures were down to 89.9 and 76.5 per cent respectively. Likewise, reflecting general trends in UK employment, the proportion of building workers who are self-employed, and thus often among the better-off in their trade, fell from 45.5 per cent in the last quarter of 1995 to 36.9 per cent in the last quarter of 2001.[48]

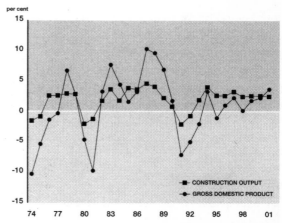

UK construction output vs GDP, 1974 to 2001, at 1995 prices[44]

Britain's building sector, then, has consolidated – but not by much. Figures for UK output published by the Building Research Establishment in 2000 tell a complementary story (see Table 2). UK media and construction industry professionals prefer to lavish most of their commentary on new-build, non-residential projects in which large firms are the key players. These are worth £7.3 billion. But at £23.8 billion, the value of total housing-related construction, repair, maintenance and refurbishment in the UK is more than three times greater. And it is in housing, and especially in housing repair, maintenance and refurbishment, that the dominion of small firms is most extensive.

With small firms go modest pay packets. Statistics show that, while some UK building operatives do well, enough do badly for average construction industry pay to be nothing special.[50] The average gross weekly pay of £393.90 earned by male manual building workers in the UK amounts to about nine per cent more than the £359.90 earned, on average, by manual male workers in all sectors of UK employment. Non-manual workers in UK construction earn about the national average. However, manual workers in UK construction do nine per cent more time on the job than their counterparts in general UK employment, and non-manual construction workers do seven per cent more hours than their counterparts outside the construction industry.[51]

In a British economy where long hours are more lamented than they are a growing trend, construction stands out as a genuinely tiring business. And, even after an April 2003 pay deal between employers and unions saw the basic pay of 600,000 craft workers rise 23 per cent, they still only received £9 an hour.[52]

British construction firms are stingy enough. But they have also failed to

TABLE 2 UK construction output, by type of work, 1997

Type of Work	£ billion	Per cent of total output
New housing	8.0	12.6
New non-housing	7.3	11.5
New work total	**15.3**	**24.1**
Refurbishment housing	7.9	12.4
Refurbishment non-housing	14.6	23.0
Refurbishment unofficial	1.7	2.7
Refurbishment total	**24.2**	**38.1**
Repair and maintenance housing	7.9	12.4
Repair and maintenance non-housing	12.7	20.0
Repair and maintenance unofficial	3.4	5.4
Repair and maintenance total	**24.0**	**37.8**
All construction total	63.5	100.0
Housing total	23.8	37.4
Non-housing total	34.6	54.5
Unofficial total	5.1	8.1

Source: Nigel Howard, *Sustainable Construction: The data*, Centre for Sustainable Construction, Building Research Establishment, 2000, and posted on www.bre.co.uk[49]

lower the price of, and universalise, high-quality environments. In the past few years, China has given a special impetus to the trend for the price of manufactured products to fall. In the US, too, growing efficiencies among IT manufacturers – most notably Dell Computer – account for much of the overall increase in productivity in manufacturing that the country has enjoyed in recent years. But UK construction? It is right up there with the National Health Service or London hotels as a sector that is predisposed to inflated prices. There are no revolutionary productivity improvements to be had here.

On a typical building site in Britain, there are Atlas Copco compressors, Ausa forklifts, Bomag rollers, Bosch power tools, Demag mobile cranes, Hydrema loaders, JCB excavators, Komatsu mini excavators and Thwaites dumpers. Caterpillar, which makes a wide range of construction machinery, also makes personal protection equipment that has become a brand in itself, while Volvo's range for building sites is narrower but equally impressive.[51]

All these machines are made in high volumes and are the subject of continuous new product development. Their manufacturers engage in fierce price competition, as well as doing battle in the field of product and vehicle design. But it is different with the process of construction. Here, volume production is relatively rare. New products are developed; yet generally they are only developed in

the sense that to put a roof over one's head is to build one anew, tile by tile. In construction there appears to be no dynamic capable of lowering costs or bringing better product designs.

Above all, *in construction pretty much everything happens on site*. While materials and components are made in volume off site, they are only put together into assemblies on site. Building frames are rarely made off site; they are put together on site. It is the same with rooms.

The failure to invest in off-site methods allows construction to carry on in the old labour-intensive, low-investment manner. This is all the more remarkable today, when demand for more and better housing, in particular, is so great.

1.4 Illegal, cursed and DIY

Go to any showroom in Britain that is in the business of selling fitted kitchens. In it there are respectable middle-class couples buying themselves kitchens in enormous quantities. The quantities are enormous because there is nearly always a sale on. But kitchens bought in such volumes can only be installed by tens of thousands of *unregistered* builders – people who earn their keep, in part, by eluding the tax collectors of the Inland Revenue, and instead contribute to the black economy. These builders are beneficiaries of Britain's boom in housing repair, maintenance and refurbishment.

More care Built in

VOLVO L330E

An extremely powerful wheel loader designed for loading shot rock, block handling, timber handling, foundry work, and feeding cargo vessels. The L330E -one of the most powerful production machines on the market.

VOLVO

The building sector in Britain has grown more atomised as its low-tech, 'informal' version has come to command more of society's resources. For, reinforcing the backwardness of official construction, unregistered building plays a prominent role in Britain's real economy. Between 1983 and 2003, average UK house prices rose by 306 per cent.[54] Home improvement through undeclared construction activity must explain some of that prodigious increase.

The expansion of black-economy building work confirms that construction is backward. This is the dark, grubby truth behind the gleaming showrooms of the UK boom in fitted kitchens. At the same time, however, the cry goes up among the British middle class that, as far as plumbers, builders and decorators are concerned, 'You can't get the staff these days'.

Ever since the emergence of the 'servant problem' in the 19th century, elites have had problems getting hold of, disciplining and retaining high quality servants. But as Joseph Losey's 1962 movie *The Servant* showed, members of Britain's moneyed classes could have problems not just with a servant like Dirk Bogarde, but also with builders. In Harold Pinter's screenplay, a neurotic Wendy Craig needs builders to fix up the house she shares with James Fox. But she cannot suppress the disgust she feels for the noisy, clumsy, white-overalled members of the working class she is forced to supervise.

It has long been an affliction of the rich that they cannot get the kind of quality staff that they deserve. And in Britain today, the specific problem of finding plumbers, builders and decorators to do a job of work has occasioned caustic comment from the *Financial Times*. Her tongue firmly in cheek, that paper's wry critic of management trends, Lucy Kellaway, wrote:

Suppose you need a plumber. You put out a message on e-mail at work asking if anyone knows one in the north London area. Perhaps you get one recommendation and 20 messages

from people saying if you have any joy, let them know; they need one too . . . You phone the number and, as the plumber is good, he is not interested in your shower. Eventually you find one who does come, though probably not at the time he said he would. He does the work after a fashion and charges about three times what you thought reasonable. I find the business so stressful that anything I know about managing people disappears as soon as I have a builder in the house. Smiling, I make them cups of tea, only to curse furiously when their backs are turned.[55]

In British homes, plumbers and decorators are cursed for their backwardness. But the same thing also happens on British building sites. There, both government officials and building workers' unions hound recent immigrants from Eastern Europe and Russia.

On major construction projects, migrants from the former Eastern bloc do indeed work without adequate clothing, training or English, and are supplied by employment agencies with no questions asked. But what defence do migrants get against all this? In May 2002, Lord Jeffrey Rooker famously attacked asylum-seekers as 'young men who have deserted their families for economic advantage'.[56] In the same month, he was appointed Minister of State at the Office of the Deputy Prime Minister for Housing, Planning and Regeneration.

It is not Polish bricklayers who drag UK construction down – rather, the sector's brutish nature makes it rely, for much of its existence, upon the almost feudal practice of *day labouring*. For many clients for buildings and their contractors, agency-based migrant labour is cheap and available by the day. It saves the employer money; and the intermediary of an agency gives him an alibi should dubious practices come to light.[57]

Construction, a retarded industry, depends on vulnerable foreign workers. It then turns round and condemns them. The tone is bigoted; but that is all that can be expected from the backward building sector.

Altogether, construction is widely performed under labour conditions that are illegal and by labourers who are hated – either for their timekeeping or for their nationality. And where construction *is* legal, the Do-It-Yourself sort, conducted by householders, has made much of the running. In 2001, expenditure on DIY goods was worth a cool £9.28 billion in UK shops.[58] Overall, growth has been enormous (see Table 3).

In DIY, construction can be pleasurable and is certainly celebrated as such on British television. But much of it persists simply because people cannot afford to pay someone else to do the work that needs doing. Expenditure on DIY is large; not just financially, but in terms of the amount of society's time that is devoted to it.

In terms of economics and technology, this very personal and inefficient kind of construction is just one more symptom of backwardness.

1.5 Arise, Sir John Egan

Sir John Egan is suave and wears a discreet purple tie. A past president of the Institute of Management, he took over as president of the Confederation of British Industry in July 2002. His early months were dominated by the sound of pneu-

Centre Point, London

matic drills brought to London's ageing – but still striking – Centre Point tower, two floors of which the CBI occupies.

The experience must have been annoying. For it was Egan, a veritable pillar of the establishment, who first really alerted people, inside and outside UK construction, to the industry's primitive character. After New Labour's success in the general election of 1997, John Prescott, Deputy Prime Minister and the man in charge of urban policy in Britain, appointed Egan as chairman of a special government enquiry into the building sector.

In his seminal *Rethinking Construction: the report of the Construction Task Force*, published in 1998, Egan expanded on Sir Michael Latham's doubts of 1994. While Latham insisted that the construction industry was too confrontational, Egan very properly saw contractual disputes as a result of the overall poor level of performance in site-based construction. He wrote:

Up to 30 per cent of construction is rework, labour is used at only 40–60 per cent of potential efficiency, accidents can account for 3–6 per cent of total project costs, and at least 10 per cent of materials are wasted. These

---

TABLE 3 Index of UK consumer expenditure on DIY goods at constant prices, 1995–2001 (1995=100)

Year	Index
1995	100
1997	115.2
1998	120.0
1999	126.2
2000	134.9
2001	143.6

Source: Key Note Ltd

John Prescott by Alex Abley, aged 3

John Prescott wonders

are probably conservative estimates . . . The message is clear – there is plenty of scope for improving efficiency and quality simply by taking waste out of construction.[59]

Egan's long years in volume car manufacturing had given him a commitment to raising productivity. Britain's backward construction sector did not escape his strictures.

Egan attacked the 'significant' costs and delays that, in the design and planning of architectural projects, were 'often incurred by the variability of enforcement of regulations, and by duplication of processes between agencies'.[60] More fundamentally, he drew a parallel between construction and volume manufacturing:

We have repeatedly heard the claim that construction is different from manufacturing because every product is unique. We do not agree. Not only are many buildings, such as houses, essentially repeat products which can be continually improved but, more importantly, the process of construction is itself repeated in its essentials from project to project. Indeed, research suggests that up to 80 per cent of inputs into buildings are repeated. Much repair and maintenance work also uses a repeat process. The parallel is not with building cars on the production line; it is with designing and planning the production of a new car model.[61]

In optimistic style, Egan set aggressive *targets* for UK construction. Year on year, he demanded:

- reductions in capital cost and construction time of 10 per cent;
- reductions in defects and accidents of 20 per cent;
- increases in project predictability of 20 per cent; and
- increases in productivity and profitability of 10 per cent.

Five key drivers which need to be in place to achieve better construction

1. Committed leadership
2. Focus on the customer
3. Integration of process & team around the project
4. A quality driven agenda
5. Commitment to people

Four key projected processes needed to achieve change

1. **Partnering the Supply Chain**
   Develop long term relationships based on continuous improvement with a supply chain
2. **Components and Parts**
   Sustained programme of improvement for the production and delivery of components
3. **Focus on End Products**
   Integration and focus on construction process on meeting the needs of the end user
4. **Construction Process**
   Elimination of waste

Seven annual targets which are capable of being achieved in improving the performance of construction projects

1. Reduce capital costs by 10%
2. Reduce construction time by 10%
3. Reduce defects by 20%
4. Reduce accidents by 20%
5. Increase predictability of projected cost and time estimates by 10%
6. Increase productivity by 10%
7. Increase turnover and profits by 10%

This total of no fewer than seven targets was to be realised, Egan hoped, by five 'drivers of change' – committed leadership, a focus on the customer, integrating the process and the team around the product, a quality-driven agenda, and a commitment to people. In turn, these were to be pursued through the four processes Egan identified as key to achieving change. Thus was born the '5-4-7' formula of *Rethinking Construction*. The formula was canonised in a 2001 report of Britain's National Audit Office, *Modernising Construction*.[62]

Since these targets were set, however, the construction industry has had little to show for itself. So in April 2003 Egan was charged with looking, not at the structural causes of backwardness in UK building, but at its educational symptoms. In a review of construction industry professions, he was to focus on:

- the skills needed by professional and technical staff in both the public and private sector, elected local authority members and members of local strategic partnerships;
- the gaps and shortcomings in professional skills and capacity;
- the implications for training and development, and how these might be better delivered through trial projects;
- the mechanisms for sharing knowledge, good practice and experience; and
- how skills can be provided countrywide, and how to develop new professional approaches.

The agenda in construction has changed and Sir John Egan with it. There are now two main priorities, both of which shift attention away from the questions of productivity with which Egan started.

First, there is a *therapeutic* perspective for construction, which focuses on respect for people, consensus, health, safety and workplace stress, training, skills, teamwork, the awarding of certificates, and an all-round increase in self-esteem in the building trade. This perspective is part of a wider social phenomenon, which Kent university professor Frank Furedi terms 'therapy culture'.[63]

Second, there is a *naturalistic* perspective for construction. In an unquestioning acceptance of the prejudices of environmentalists, 'sustainable communities' are now as sought after as sustainable buildings and interiors. In 1998, as Egan was to confess in 2002, sustainability:

did not feature as a core issue in *Rethinking Construction*, primarily because it was important at that stage to focus on the fundamental flaws in the construction procurement and delivery process.[64]

But by 2002, construction had, Egan said, to 'take responsibility for the sustainability of its products (from components to the completed structure) as well as its processes'.[65]

John Egan helped pioneer both therapeutic and naturalistic perspectives. But he did more than that. He wrapped up therapy and naturalism in the normal management language of today – the *language of measurement*. Like everything else, therapy and naturalism in construction must be made subject to market benchmarks and targets.

Therapy and naturalism distract debate from efficiency and effectiveness in building. Both perspectives reduce the ambitions that used to accompany architecture. Both also compound the backwardness of the construction sector by inviting *new government regulation*, as part of a *constantly rebranded series of government initiatives*.

There is innovation in building. But there are many more initiatives in branding and government regulation than there are in the construction industry itself.

Sir John Egan. Photo by Julian Dodd, copyright www.juliandodd.com

Sir John Egan

Born in 1939, Sir John Egan went to the London Business School, and soon became general manager of AC Delco's UK replacement parts operation. He then joined British Leyland in 1971, going on to become director of BL Parts and Service and the man responsible for the development of Unipart.

Egan next became marketing director, and subsequently corporate parts director, of Massey Ferguson's construction and machinery division in Rome. After returning to BL as chairman of Jaguar Cars in 1980, he became chairman and chief executive of Jaguar plc in 1985. He was knighted for rethinking aspects of British car manufacturing the following year.

After the take-over of Jaguar by Ford, Egan retired and was appointed to the board of directors of British Airports Authority plc in 1990. He became chief executive of BAA later that year, and held the post until 1999.

Today Egan is a non-executive chairman of several businesses, including Inchcape plc in the automotive sector, and the construction industry online procurement portal Asite plc.[66]

1.6 Backward thinking in municipal strategy

Worldwide, but especially in Europe, what economic geographers have long discussed as *inter-urban competition* has given a fresh salience to building. Since 1992, when the Single European Market was given formal force, the European Union's 200 cities with populations higher than 200,000 have vied with each other more and more for foreign direct investment, trade, tourism and EU grants. Their mutual jostling is made intense by low-cost air travel and a growing network of high-speed trains. With the enlargement of the EU on 1 May 2004, they also find themselves confronted with further rivals from the East. A city like Hamburg is now in more direct contest with a city like Prague than ever it was in the past.

Of course, different cities in Europe have always been blessed with different kinds of 'factor endowments'. Some cities are big, some small; some are ports, some old manufacturing centres, some centres of government and of the higher administrative functions of multinational corporations. In addition, different cities have different levels of administrative efficiency – levels that are dependent not just on the political complexion and economic competence of municipal regimes, but also on the geographical size of the administrative area they cover. It's easier to run a tight ship in Norwich, perhaps, than it is in Greater Manchester.

One might think, then, that the inherent differences between the world's cities would ensure that rivalry between them took the form of further distinctive innovations. Across all sectors – including the construction sector, obviously – productivity-raising innovations, particularly in processes, would do much to make cities more attractive to foreign direct investment and more powerful in terms of traded goods and services. But in fact *backward thinking surrounds overall municipal strategy as much as it does the construction of individual buildings.*

John Prescott likes to say that cities and regions in England 'sink or swim together'.[67] Yet the more they adopt the same strategy, the more Britain's cities are likely to sink.

The main innovation in urban strategy has been the advent, in London before any other of the world's capitals, of a Congestion Charge levied on users of city's roads. But this, the handiwork of the Mayor of London, Ken Livingstone, is not a productivity-raising innovation at all: it is a tax designed to limit traffic demand. Both Britain's Transport Secretary, Alasdair Darling, and the Treasury like the Congestion Charge and want it generalised to other British cities.

For the rest, however, municipal managers in Britain, like their counterparts throughout Europe, all believe the same thing. They believe that they hold, in the quality of their building, one of the principal sources of inter-urban competitiveness. To their mind, ingenious construction can bring social cohesion and bigger revenues from tourists. *The Barcelona model, in which space and architecture are seen as fundamental ingredients of culturally led urban revival, is taken seriously by mayors, speculators, leisure operators, arts administrators, geographers, town planners, architects and the broad mass of the citizenry.* Equally, Bilbao's 'Guggenheim effect' – the millions of visitors brought to the town since Frank

Ken Livingstone

Gehry's museum opened in 1997 – has been pronounced 'absolutely duplicable'.[68] Indeed it is so duplicable that, in 2003, Gehry was hired by the British seaside town of Hove to design four towers for residential and leisure use there. The aim, said the *Financial Times*, was 'to make the city look a little more like Bilbao'. The developer, Karis ING, said that its own aim was to turn Hove into Britain's architectural capital.[69]

Crowing that it is a bubbling centre for what Carnegie Mellon professor Richard Florida terms its 'creative class', every city has its own cultural strategy nowadays.[70] Indeed, such strategies are now so prevalent that:

- in September 2002, Tony Blair publicly celebrated Newcastle's ascent to *Newsweek*'s list of the world's eight 'most creative cities'. Newcastle jostled with seven other urban centres of culture, ranging from Tijuana to Kabul;[71]
- the status of EU Capital of Culture, a concept first pioneered by Melina Mercouri in the mid 1980s, will not be bestowed just upon Liverpool in 2008 (its slogan, 'The World in a City', having been adjudged superior to Birmingham's 'Many worlds, one great city'), but has already been decided for every year until 2020;
- even *within* a city such as London, local authorities engage in cultural one-upmanship against each other; and
- in the summer of 2003, Livingstone launched his own 10-year 'draft culture strategy' for London.[72]

The upshot of the cultural approach is that every city seeks to monumentalise its architectural heritage, yet at the same time confirm its modernity by commissioning new buildings designed by architects of international renown. The growing demand for culture among citizens, tourists and companies alike makes this gambit seem respectable. Britain's Minister for Europe, Denis MacShane, is on hand to suggest that if the 'renaissance' of Europe's cities is now 'the new

driving force in post-industrial Europe', European economic integration itself now depends, in large part, on 'the striking new architecture of Europe's cities': an architecture that 'is being redefined, as in the Renaissance era, by new art galleries, new space for meeting, eating and treating oneself to the best artefacts designers produce'.[69] Yet as MacShane's multiple renaissances and novelties suggest, *it is precisely around the panacea of bespoke, 'landmark' architectural developments – buildings that are visited by international tourists, nationals and locals – that thinking in municipal strategy is least innovative.*

Large-scale architectural icons, which have enjoyed a vogue as attempts to unify the identity of cities in a grandiose and self-consciously cultural way, have now become a market that is commoditised. Their claim was distinctiveness, but every minor city in Europe boasts or has plans for such an icon. And each costs a lot of money, because each is a one-off. Of course the *styles* of these buildings are highly differentiated. However, when every city tries more noisily than others to stand out from the crowd with such constructions, their *functional* impact, both on competitive advantage and on overall urban prosperity, is limited.

In September 2000 the Solomon R Guggenheim Foundation suggested that regional and metropolitan government entities everywhere should contract with it 'for a specified scope of services related to cultural interventions or cultural infrastructural projects'.[74] Since then, imitators of Gehry's Guggenheim have emerged in Britain, stretching from the ill-fated National Centre for Popular Music in Sheffield to the Turner Centre in Margate.

Though they lack Bilbao's new underground system, new bridges and new airport, the most economically deprived areas in the UK now host similarly branded and exotic architectural visitor attractions. There is Magna in Rotherham, designed by Wilkinson Eyre Architects; the Deep in Hull by Terry Farrell; and the Think Tank in Birmingham's Digbeth by

Frank Gehry. Photo by Dorothy Alexander

Rem Koolhaas. Photo by Dorothy Alexander

Nicholas Grimshaw. Richard Rogers, commissioned to design a new £130m library for the city of Birmingham at Millennium Point, Eastside, Digbeth, is reported as saying that it will 'do for Birmingham in its way what the Pompidou Centre did for Paris'.[75]

From Birmingham's International Convention Centre (1991) and its Selfridges store (2003, designed by Future Systems) to Rem Koolhaas's art museum concert hall in Porto (due to open in 2001, but only ready by 2004), what is now offered is a bespoke building-as-conversation-piece free with every city. Jean Nouvel is to design a new Guggenheim in Rio de Janeiro. In a strange alliance, St Petersberg's Hermitage Museum opened a new art gallery by Koolhaas in Las Vegas in October 2001. In Cincinnati, the Contemporary Arts Center, designed by Zaha Hadid, opened on 31 May 2003 at a cost of $20.2m. In Dallas, the Nasher Sculpture Center, designed by Renzo Piano and landscape architect Peter Walker, opened on 19 October 2003 at a cost of $70m. In Fort Worth, Texas, the Museum of Modern Art also opened in 2003, designed by Tadao Ando. All these last three museums were born despite cutbacks in government and private funding for nonprofit institutions in the US.[76]

Something similar has also happened in Spain. There, on top of Bilbao's Guggenheim, Santiago Calatrava has designed a €400 million, 350,000m² City of Arts and Sciences, comprising Europe's largest aquarium, a planetarium, a science museum and an opera house. Then, outside Santiago de Compostela, Peter Eisen-

mann has designed a €110 million, 700,000m² arts centre.

At the Wharton school of the University of Pennsylvania, Witold Rybczynski has captured much of the defects of backward thinking in urban strategy. After the collapse of the Venetian Republic at the end of the 18th century, he points out, Venice rid itself of mass begging only by eventually pioneering the idea of a *tourist destination*. Since then, not just tourism centres such as London and New York City, but the world's cities have, in Rybczynski's view, become 'all Venetians now'.[77]

Tourists expect a city to be fun and memorable. So cities will build car parks, sports facilities, retail and entertainment facilities – and they will do this downtown, and not in peripheral residential districts, which are of little interest to visitors. After Guggenheim's success, Rybczynski continues, the formula is clear:

Witold
Rybczynski

Eye-popping architecture + cultural attractions = more tourists.[78]

Rybczynski goes on:

This unprecedented wave of high-profile construction projects has been good for architects; it is less clear how good it is for cities. How often can the Bilbao effect be duplicated before it wears thin? Not only are signature buildings extremely expensive, they tend to cancel one another out, producing a sort of architectural fatigue . . .

Today's recreational cities offer essentially the same product.[79]

As Rybczynski notes, *not just museums, but also sports facilities* are part of the samey premises of urban cultural strategy. From Bolton's 28,000-seat Reebok Stadium through to the new Wembley Stadium, whose illuminated arc is set to change London's skyline, stadia are seen as a key force in municipal revival. Multipurpose sports arenas that are privately-funded have likewise spread from Vancouver (GM Place) to Helsinki (the Hartwall Areena) and Hamburg (the ColorLine Arena). Similar developments are underway all over continental Europe and, in England, Southampton plans a venue for the summer of 2005, while Croydon looks forward to a 14,500-seat arena.[80]

These ventures are no more innovative than museums designed by branded international architects. Both kinds of initiatives are largely unquestioned – for who can be against culture, museums or sport? But they can and must be questioned.

Over the past three decades, tendencies toward atrophy in Western capitalism have got the better of tendencies toward innovation. So it became possible as early as the 1980s to form the impression, as did the geographer David Harvey, that urban life in the West had moved on from industrial forms and into such services that allowed it to 'increasingly come to present itself as an "immense accumulation of spectacles"'.[81] Nearly 15 years before Rybczynski rounded on the archi-

tectural fatigue that surrounds bespoke landmark attractions in architecture and culture, Harvey presciently asked:

How many successful convention centres, sports stadia, Disney-worlds and harbour places can there be?[82]

In 1989, a radical such as Harvey could indict capitalism for commoditising culture in inter-urban competition. But Harvey did not just do this. He also exaggerated the popular benefits of cultural spectacles:

Far better that a deserted factory be turned into a community centre where the collective memory of those who lived and worked there is preserved rather than being turned into boutiques and condos.[83]

As it happens, preserving the collective memory of workers by means of a community centre was a difficult task in 1989, let alone today. But something has changed in the intervening years. *Communitarian cultural spectacles in architecture, once largely just a radical's hope, have become the main motif in official urban competitive strategy.*

Today, Rybczynski is right to suggest that there is something dishonest about trying to brighten up old towns with architectural icons:

The attraction of an urban place is in inverse proportion to its actual economic productivity. No one is interested in guided tours of Silicon Valley or Boston's Route 128; such places may be economic powerhouses, but they are too spread out, too new, too . . . well, ugly. Paradoxically, many of the very qualities that have contributed to cities' shaky position in the new economy – their density, their out-of-date buildings, their ageing infrastructure, their reliance on mass transport rather than cars – heighten their appeal to tourists and short-term visitors.[84]

The new, expensive, one-off cultural buildings boast a sparkling appearance. But they also reveal wider problems of sluggish innovation. It is hard to transform the substance of a city's apparatus for creating wealth in general and houses in particular. Instead of such a transformation of substance, therefore, capitalism veers toward changes in form. Through the architectural cosmetics of bespoke, landmark developments, the typical Western city takes the soft option. It tries not just to be a strong tourist destination for a few years – until other cities outdo it – but also to *'include' all classes in society* with a Tate Modern or a Wembley Stadium.

That is a tall order. If the new Wembley is to be inclusive, the task of explaining the 10-year leases on its corporate boxes will be almost as tricky as genuine regeneration of the Wembley area. After a year's examination of 56 British cities, 70 metropolitan boroughs and 1762 wards in Britain over a period of a year, one economist had this to say about the cockeyed priorities of UK municipal strategy:

There has been a lot of work in the right direction. But there has been too big an emphasis on physical capital and social inclusion, and not enough on the ability to create wealth. Disappointingly, cities are not becoming the economic drivers of their regions.[85]

Like bids to attract tourists, attempts at social inclusion and social engineering through architecture are preferred to the real works of engineering – in construction, manufacturing, services and government – that need to be undertaken if cities are truly to be revived. Yet even on their own terms, a succession of New Labour attempts to provoke working class interest in museums has proved fruitless: despite the introduction of free admission to museums, the proportion of museum visitors drawn from C2DE social groups in Britain only improved from 14 per cent to nearly 16 per cent between 1 April 1998 and 31 March 2002, against a C2DE presence of 51 per cent of the British population as a whole.[86] There is a similar tale to tell in British sport. There, the minister in charge has admitted that, after allowing more than £1.5 billion of taxpayer and National Lottery cash to be

spent on sport in England, Her Majesty's Government has seen an increase in popular participation so small, it is 'statistically irrelevant'.[87]

Government buildings associated with transport provide another example of how repackaging bits of a city as architectural sights is no substitute for a broader mechanisation of wealth-making. As early as 1977, the architect Christopher Alexander and his colleagues argued that the rise of inter-modal passenger behaviour gave a particular salience to transport nodes, as distinct from transport routes.[88] By 1993, forecasters at the Henley Centre, London, observed:

The significance of nodes is that central-city rail terminals, rail freight terminals and airports are becoming some of the main signals of urban competitiveness in Europe. These terminals now tie up more goods and people for longer periods than ever before. They are integral to a city's sense of place (though they often lack it themselves), and to overall image.[89]

In 1993, at a contract value of £130 million, the Eurostar International Rail Terminal at London's Waterloo station opened for business. In its vaulting excellence, Nicholas Grimshaw and Partners' design marked a key shift in the historic role of transport buildings as symbolic gateways to success.[90] With Waterloo, Grimshaw confirmed that a terminal could be a sculptured piece of engineering that deserves an audience in its own right. The lengthy makeover of New

The Eurostar International Rail Terminal at London's Waterloo station

York's Grand Central Station is part of the same pattern.

These efforts have much to commend them. But in London and New York alike, visitors soon find out about what locals know all too well – that real, functional transport snarl-ups lie beyond the terminal with glitzy added culture.

Behind every bespoke, eye-catching architectural initiative in visitor attractions, the same old problems of urban decay and limited urban productivity remain unsolved. Indeed in Britain the gap between appearance and reality has now grown so great that even zealots of cultural architecture are being forced to think again. In June 2003, Britain's Core Cities Summit, held at Newcastle with the participation of Birmingham, Bristol, Leeds, Liverpool, Manchester, Nottingham, Sheffield and John Prescott, launched a report that finally talked up old-fashioned research and development. It admonished cities:

In the UK there is a strong statistical correlation between the regional pattern of R&D (both public and private sector) and regional economic performance.[91]

In Britain for every successful Commonwealth Games (Manchester) there is a poorly performing Armouries Museum (Leeds). So now, after Newcastle's Baltic Gallery and all the other hip waterfront developments, wise heads profess to have known all along that regional and urban success is correlated not with cultural spectacles, but with technological innovation.

It is a brilliant insight, but one whose lateness confirms that municipal strategy is still in the Dark Ages.

1.7 Construction, risk and the wider crisis in capitalist innovation

How did all these things happen?

How did the effort to modernise and improve construction get diverted into avoiding interpersonal conflict on site,

protecting nature from buildings and deluding ourselves that a few funky showpieces amount to urban regeneration?

Chapter 2 explores how backward *neuroses about measurement, therapy and nature* have conspired to dumb construction down in theory.

Chapter 3 looks at the *regulation of building*, a growing habit that slows it down in practice.

Chapter 4 considers the *fear of repeating past efforts* to turn construction into manufacturing. We are particularly grateful to Miles Glendinning and Stefan Muthesius for their insight on British efforts to industrialise housing production from the 1940s to the 1970s.

Chapter 5 discusses how, learning in particular from car manufacture, *the new technologies of prefabrication, materials and energy, together with Information Technology*, could help construction finally end its historic backwardness.

Chapter 6 confronts the ways in which, *after the events of 11 September 2001, society has come to impose new and still more backward limits on construction.* The chapter lays out an alternative to those limits.

Part of the answer to 'Why is construction so backward?' is that architects have let it become so, and are holding themselves back. Architects can propel construction forward anew. The potential to do that is already available, if only resources can be politically mustered.

Yet *the failure of nerve that still surrounds construction is part of a wider decline in capitalist risk-taking – particularly as it applies to innovation.*

The *management of risk* was itself once an obscure province of corporate finance. But since its spread in the 1980s, risk management has become a mainstream business activity.[92] In November 2002, in a joint report, New York City's International Federation of Accountants and London's Chartered Institute of Management Accountants pronounced *risk management as essential to enhancing shareholder value.*[93] By contrast, however, some of America's top corporate thinkers have, since the mid 1980s, evinced *a growing disenchantment with innovation* (see Box 2).

These developments were threads in a larger tapestry. By 1999, what EU officials called the 'hampering factors' around corporate innovation in products and services were such that they started collecting data on them.[94] By 2002, the *Harvard Business Review* declared that promoting innovation was 'as much about tearing down barriers as blazing trails'.[95] Impediments to innovation today exercise specialists much more than the benefits that accrue from it.

Altogether, the failure of construction to make a real breakthrough in productivity must be seen against the background of a worldwide crisis in innovation. Today, no new product and service, for instance, is considered without the risk of it 'cannibalising' old products and services. As Benjamin Hunt has persuasively argued of corporations in general, the sensation of future risk now makes deferring investment the norm.[96]

Some are bullish about innovation. In 2002, Cap Gemini Ernst & Young remarked that US R&D spending had risen at an average of 6.1 per cent annually from 1995 through 1999, reaching $264 billion in 2000, a 7.9 per cent jump from 1999. It noted, too, that in 2001, companies had introduced 35,000 new consumer products, up from 15,000 a decade previously. But CGEY also observed that large business organisations found it hard to think about the future and innovate from within.

Like many activities that involve talent and tacit learning, reconnaissance requires an inherent feel for the work and lots or practice. Not many companies can claim that inherent strength.[97]

This was a damning indictment. While we are indeed surrounded by a world of new products, the classical corporation's capacity to innovate seems to be dwindling. As Mercer Management Consulting wrote:

Innovation has slowed in many traditional industries, resulting in products that are largely undifferentiated in performance. Think of Boeing and Airbus, Ford and General Motors, John Deere and Caterpillar. In other industries, back-and-forth jockeying occurs, as first one competitor and then another introduces a product with slightly better performance. Think of Nintendo and Sony, Intel and AMD. Product improvements aren't a source of long-term growth for any of these companies.

Furthermore, in recent years, the development of entirely new products has proven to be an unreliable source of growth . . . Our analysis of high-tech leaders' performance over recent decades reveals a disturbing pattern: they experience a couple of years of spectacular market growth followed by equally spectacular collapse.[98]

Innovative new products had, Mercer lamented, been a succession of 'bottle rockets', moving up to the heavens very quickly and then falling back to earth just as quickly.

The building sector can learn from this. *The appearance of rapid innovation in certain buildings, materials or processes is not necessarily the same as the reality of innovation.*

In 2002 the American economist William Baumol rationalised the difficulty large firms have in coming up with substantive innovations.[99] In a familiar thesis, he argued that capitalist competition took place more through innovation than through prices. However it was only to be expected that, as economies matured, multinationals should try to minimise the risks that surround innovation – minimise them by:

- outsourcing the development of the biggest innovations to entrepreneurs, and
- doing deals on their intellectual property with other firms, and even direct rivals.

In his apologia for the corporate practice of modest innovation, Baumol saw the more dynamic sort emerging from small firms. In this broad prognosis he was joined, in 2003, by Harvard's Henry Chesbrough.[100] From the University of California, Andrew Hargadon came to similar conclusions.[101] None of these experts was wrong; but their remedies are quite utopian in the big world of construction, where small firms are especially backward.

The vogue for entrepreneurialism in innovation raises big questions about the ability of large organisations, private or public, to survive. For if *large organisations insist on outsourcing innovation, or abdicate central responsibility for innovation to lower ranks*, there may be little future for them. Top decision makers in the US private sector instinctively recognise this. Writing about the February 2002 World Economic Forum, which was held in Manhattan, the distinguished economics journalist Anatole Kaletsky observed:

Not since the early 1980s have I seen America's business elite so lacking in confidence, not just about their immediate economic prospects, but about the long-term outlook for capitalism and the world.[102]

Of course, the problem of innovation does not just lie with America's business elite. In pharmaceuticals, for instance, manufacturers have hit trouble on both sides of the Atlantic. Approvals of new drugs by the US Food and Drug Administration dropped from 53 in 1996 to 16 in 2002. Applications to the European Medicines Evaluation Agency to approve new drugs fell from more than

Manntech Fassadenbefahrsysteme[103] makes powered equipment for cleaning and maintaining buildings at its factory at Mammendorf, near Munich

It is always instructive to see the records rooms of established companies in the construction industry. The thousands of drawings of mass-produced machines that hang down here attest to years and years of cumulative R&D – unlike the world of architecture, where much fewer drawings are hurriedly created out of nothing for each new one-off building comprised of never-to-be-repeated details

50 a year in 2000 and 2001 to 31 in 2002. At the end of that period, the head of EMEA testified that, in pharmaceuticals, 'Never has so much money been spent on R&D with so little result'.[104]

CBI figures show that, in the UK, innovation is as much a problem for 'support services' like building as it is for industry.[105] But it seems that not just the *capacity*, but also the *will* to innovate is in decline. As the *Financial Times* summed up sentiment in 2002:

Innovation remains a magic potion. But excessive belief causes agonising hangovers.[106]

More than two years after what it termed 'the huge technology bubble of the late 1990s', the *Financial Times* held that the problem with innovation was that there was too much enthusiasm for it.

However even a cursory analysis shows that the 'bubble' of the late 1990s was more about finance than technology. Certainly there was no technological bubble in the building trade, which meandered on through buoyant trading conditions with all its usual complacency. The real point about innovation is a different one. *The risk of 'agonising hangovers' means that few multinationals, even outside the construction industry, now wish to invest seriously in capital equipment, new products or new processes, or the new organisational forms that go with these things.* Instead, as even the gritty construction sector shows, *it is the quack remedies of quantification, corporate culture and state control that are thought to be low-risk*, and that are therefore preferred.

In mainstream companies, sensibility to risk has led to a massive shift of

'Super Rural', by Jonathan Schwinge

Box 2 AMERICAN THEORISTS RETREAT FROM INNOVATION

Nathan Rosenberg

Peter Drucker

Peter Drucker is guru to America's management gurus. In 1985 he defined innovation as the effort to create purposeful change in an enterprise's economic or social potential.[103] He believed that innovations emerged not only from unexpected occurrences, but also from incongruities within the logic or rhythm of a process, or between an industry's assumptions and its realities. Ocean freighters eventually revived not by seeking faster speeds, Drucker observed, but by being more efficient while stationary – through the roll-on, roll-off technology of container ships.

So far, so good. But what was striking about Drucker's article was that, written by a man of the right during the can-do Reagan era of Star Wars, it had a highly sceptical attitude to technology. Drucker favoured new entrant firms, or 'newcomer innovators'. He had a kind word for Club Méditerranée, since its sensitivity to demographic change was 'among the most rewarding and least risky of entrepreneurial pursuits'. Drucker admired, too, those who took advantage of changes in perception: who managed, for example, to sell more health products and services to Americans at a time when they had never been healthier. But he had stiff words for what he called knowledge-based innovations. These, he said, were 'what people usually mean when they talk of innovation, although not all innovations based on knowledge are important'. They differed from all other innovations:

> in the time that they take, in their casualty rates, and in their predictability, as well as the challenges that they pose to entrepreneurs. Like most superstars, they can be temperamental, capricious and hard to direct. They have, for instance the longest lead-time of all innovations. There is a protracted span between the emergence of all knowledge and its distillation into usable technology. Then there is another long period before this new technology appears on the market-place in products, processes, or services. Overall, the lead-time in something is like 50 years, a figure that has not shortened appreciably through history . . . [Example: the computer].

Altogether, Drucker preferred just about any kind of innovation to the knowledge-based sort – and he went further. He wrote:

> To be effective, an innovation has to be simple, and it has to be focused. It should do only one thing; otherwise it will confuse people. Indeed, the greatest praise an innovation can receive is for people to say, 'This is obvious! Why didn't I think of it? It's so simple!' Even the innovation that creates new users and new markets should be directed toward a specific, clear and carefully designed application. [Example: the electric street-car].

Drucker concluded: 'Effective innovations start small. They are not grandiose'.

By the early 1990s, the scale of ambitions in innovation narrowed as a wave of downsizing and business process re-engineering swept the West. Then, in 1995, Nathan Rosenberg, the doyen of American scholars on innovation, inspired a wave of imitators to make a knowing litany about the fundamentally unknowable impact of innovation.

In an article titled 'Innovation's uncertain terrain', Rosenberg reminded readers of the *McKinsey Quarterly* that most innovations turn out failures, and that successful ones 'typically come into the world in a primitive condition . . . with characteristics whose usefulness cannot be immediately appreciated'. Even Marconi or IBM's Thomas Watson Senior, Rosenberg remarked, had no idea how their inventions would pan out.[108] From Faraday's electromagnetic induction in 1831, through the jet (1941), the transistor (1947), the laser (1966) and the more recent discovery of the blood-thinning properties of aspirin, the uses of innovation had been both hard to predict and long in gestation.[109] This was partly because of the need to await the depreciation of existing plants, and partly because rival, established technologies might 'achieve renewed competitive vigor through continual improvement'.[110]

Rosenberg was right. But his Druckeresque, impatient attitude to innovation was coupled with real pessimism about whether it was worth the candle. 'One of the greatest uncertainties facing new technologies', he remarked, 'is the invention of yet newer ones'.[111] He went on:

> Uncertainty pervades not only basic research, where it is generally recognized, but also product design and new product development. This means that any early commitment to a specific large-scale project [in innovation] – as opposed to a more limited, exploratory approach, is likely to be risky.[112]

Yes, with innovation there has always come risk. But only by 1995 could a brilliant partisan of innovation like Nathan Rosenberg insist that risk deserved more attention than innovation.

resources away from genuine innovation, and a lowering of horizons about what innovation is. The construction industry is therefore not alone in its indecisiveness. In general management, efforts to put a number against everything have reached the status of an *idée fixe*.

Along with the management fad for measuring everything, both therapeutic and naturalistic perspectives grow out of what has been called today's *culture of fear*.[113] There is fear of conflict and social fragmentation around major building projects. That animates architecture's fad for social engineering as against real engineering. There is also the fear that mankind has over-reached itself. That animates a wider fad for sustainability.

All three fads emerge from a desire to batten down the hatches against an explosion of risk.

NOTES

1 Brian Wilson MP, 'Foreword', in Strategic Forum for Construction, *Accelerating Change* (London, Rethinking Construction, 2002) p 5.
2 Philip Beresford with Stephen Boyd, *The Sunday Times Rich List 2003*, 27 April 2003, p 10.
3 Amy Yee, 'An apartment and a partner, too', *Financial Times*, 17 May 2003, p 13.
4 Alexandra Frean, 'Mortgages are bad for your health, say doctors', *The Times*, 7 May 2003, p 1.
5 Henry Ticks, 'Shortage-hit homes market seen as still too volatile', *Financial Times*, special section on the Euro, 10 June 2003, p 3.
6 Dan Roberts, 'Depressed profits, flat demand and growing pension liabilities: the era of cheap money takes its toll on business', *Financial Times*, 21 July 2003, p 15.
7 'High anxiety for banks', *Business Week*, 9 June 2003, p 48 to 49.
8 Damian Whitworth, 'Bigger and better homes make the American Dream come true', *The Times*, 7 August 2001, p 8.
9 John Labate, 'US home construction reaches 17-year high', *Financial Times*, 20 August 2003.
10 National Association of Realtors, 'NAR: July existing homes deals smash record', *Realtor Magazine On Line*, 25 August 2003, and posted on www.realtor.org/rmoDaily.nsf/AllStories/082503
11 Richard McGregor, 'Scandal-hit Shanghai to review all big land deals', *Financial Times*, 13 June 2003, p 9.
12 www.archigram.net
13 www.architecture.com and www.riba.org
14 www.fosterandpartners.com
15 Gordon Brown, quoted in Scheherazade Daneshku, 'Treasury embraces glasnost as its Lubyanka has facelift', *Financial Times*, 26 September 2002, p 22.
16 'AJ 100 survey', *Architects' Journal*, 20 March 2003, p 63.
17 www.fosterandpartners.com
18 Gyula Sebestyén and Chris Pollington, *New Architecture and Technology* (Oxford, Architectural Press, 2003).
19 Stephen Ledbetter, 'Façade engineering: the challenge for structural engineers', *The Structural Engineer*, Volume 79, Number 11, 5 June 2001, p 13.
20 www.cwct.co.uk
21 Robert Venturi, Denise Scott Brown and Steven Izenour, *Learning from Las Vegas*, first published 1972, revised edition 1977, eigh-

teenth printing (London, MIT Press, 2001) p 161.
22 www.jctltd.co.uk
23 Davis Langdon & Everest for the Royal Institution of Chartered Surveyors Construction Faculty, *Contracts in Use: A survey of building contracts in use during 2001* (London, RICS, 2003) and posted on www.rics.org
24 Sir Michael Latham, *Constructing the Team: Joint review of procurement and contractual arrangements in the United Kingdom construction industry*, Final Report (London, HMSO, 1994) p 17.
25 Construction Best Practice Programme, *Fact Sheet on Partnering* (London, CBBP and the Construction Industry Board, 1998).
26 Daniel Lloyd and Deborah Brown, 'Architecture or Clerkitecture', chapter 16 in Ian Abley and James Heartfield, editors, *Sustaining Architecture in the Anti-Machine Age* (Chichester, Wiley-Academy, 2001) p 187 to 193.
27 Gyula Sebestyén and Chris Pollington, editors, *International Directory of Building Research, Information and Development Organisations* (London, Spon Press, 1986).
28 Gyula Sebestyén, *Lightweight Building Construction* (London, Godwin, 1978).
29 Gyula Sebestyén, Preface, *Construction: Craft to Industry* (London, E&FN Spon, 1998) p ix.
30 www.bouygues.fr/us/groupe/chiffres.asp
31 www.groupe–vinci.com/appli/vnc/vncus.nsf/web/finances.htm
32 www.kajima.co.jp/ir/finance/renketsu_153/renketsu.pdf
33 www.skanska.com/files/documents/pdf/Skanska_annual_2002.pdf
34 www.taisei.co.jp/english/
35 www.shimz.co.jp/english/pdf/ar_2002.pdf
36 www.tokyu.co.jp
37 www.obayashi.co.jp/english/
38 www.sekisuihouse.co.jp/english/page/fs2003.pdf
39 www.fluor.com
40 'Industry snapshot' for engineering and construction, in' The 2003 Global 500', *Fortune*, 21 July 2003, and posted on www.fortune.com/fortune/global500/industrysnapshot/0,15133,15,00.html
41 www.bechtel.com/pdf/2003bechtelreport.pdf
42 http://www.walmartstores.com/wmstore/wmstores/HomePage.jsp
43 Matthew Goodman, 'Tesco stays hungry for overseas growth', *The Sunday Times Business News*, 15 June 2003, p 6.

44 Construction Industry Training Board, *Construction Workforce Development Brief* (London, CITB, 2001), Chart 2, p 11.

45 David M Gann, *Building Innovation: Complex Constructs in a Changing World* (London, Thomas Telford, 2000) p 5.

46 Davis Langdon & Everest, *A Study of the UK Building Materials Sector* (London, Department of the Environment, Transport and the Regions and the Construction Products Association, 2000) p 17.

47 Construction output and gross domestic product, 1974 to 2001, yearly growth rates in 1995 prices, in *Construction Workforce Development Planning Brief 2001 to 2005* (London, CITB, 2001) p 11, and posted on www.citb.co.uk

48 Office for National Statistics and the Department of Trade and Industry, *Construction Statistics Annual 2002 Edition* (London, The Stationery Office, 2002) Tables 3.1 and 12.2, and posted on www.dti.gov.uk/construction/stats/stats20 02/pdf/constat2002.pdf

49 Nigel Howard, Centre for Sustainable Construction, *Sustainable Construction: The data* (Watford, Building Research Establishment, 2000) p 3, and posted on www.bre.co.uk

50 Office for National Statistics and the Department of Trade and Industry, *Construction Statistics Annual 2002 Edition* (London, The Stationery Office, 2002) Tables 12.3 and 12.4, and posted on www.dti.gov.uk/construction/stats/stats 2002/pdf/constat2002.pdf

51 Office for National Statistics and the Department of Trade and Industry, *Construction Statistics Annual 2002 Edition* (London, The Stationery Office, 2002) Tables 3.1 and 12.5, and posted on www.dti.gov.uk/construction/stats/stats 2002/pdf/constat2002.pdf

52 David Turner, 'Construction workers awarded 23% rise', *Financial Times*, 17 April 2003, p 3.

53 www.volvoce.com

54 Anne Spackman, 'How house prices have quadrupled in 20 years', *The Times*, 25 January 2003, p 6.

55 Lucy Kellaway, 'Why DIY flouts the rule-book', *Financial Times*, 10 November 2002, and posted on www.ft.com

56 Jeff Rooker, quoted in Phillip Johnston, 'Fury over huge asylum centres near villages', *The Daily Telegraph*, 15 May 2002, and posted on www.telegraph.co.uk

57 Tom Broughton, 'Crackdown – Construction takes on the labour agencies', *Building*, 8 November 2002, p 24.

58 *The DIY and Home Improvements Industry* (Key Note, August 2002) and posted on www.keynote.co.uk

59 *Rethinking Construction: The Report of the Construction Task Force*, (London, HMSO, 1998) p 18.

60 *Rethinking Construction: The Report of the Construction Task Force* (London, HMSO, 1998) p 31.

61 *Rethinking Construction: The Report of the Construction Task Force* (London, HMSO, 1998) p 21.

62 Report by the Comptroller and Auditor General, National Audit Office, with a foreword by Sir Michael Latham, *Modernising Construction* (London, The Stationery Office, 2001) p 21 and posted on www.nao.gov.uk

63 Frank Furedi, *Therapy culture: Cultivating Vulnerability in an Uncertain Age* (London, Routledge, 2004).

64 Strategic Forum for Construction, *Accelerating Change* (London, Rethinking Construction, 2002) p 35.

65 Strategic Forum for Construction, *Accelerating Change* (London, Rethinking Construction, 2002) p 9.

66 www.asite.com

67 Office of the Deputy Prime Minister, 'Cities and regions sink or swim together – Prescott', press release, 6 June 2003, and posted on www.odpm.gov.uk/pns

68 Ricky Burdett, quoted in Leslie Crawford, 'Guggenheim, Bilbao and the "hot banana"', *Financial Times*, 3 September 2001, and posted on www.ft.com

69 Roger Blitz, 'Grand design to bring a touch of Bilbao to Hove', *Financial Times*, 25 July 2003, p 5.

70 Richard Florida, *The Rise of the Creative Class – and How it's Transforming Work, Leisure, Community and everyday Life* (New York, Basic Books, 2002).

71 'The world's most creative cities', cover story, *Newsweek*, 2 September 2002, p 50 to 60.

72 Greater London Authority, *London: Cultural Capital – realising the potential of a world class city*, June 2003 and posted on www.london.gov.uk/mayor/strategies/culture/draft–jun03/strategy_all.pdf

73 Denis MacShane, 'Thanks, Brussels, for not meddling in culture', *Financial Times*, 20 August 2003, p 17.

74 'Guggenheim Foundation announces planning alliance with Frank O Gehry & Associates and Rem Koolhaas/AMO', Solomon R Guggenheim Foundation press release, 27 September 2000 and posted on www.guggenheim.org/press_office.html

75 Jonathan Glancey, 'Shelf life', *Guardian G2*, 10 March 2003, p12 to 13.

76 Dana Micucci, 'An expansion of museums in U.S.', *International Herald Tribune*, 14 June 2003. and posted on www.iht.com/front-page.html

77 Witold Rybczynski, 'Why we are all Venetians now', *FT Weekend*, 25 January 2003, p I.

78 Witold Rybczynski, 'Why we are all Venetians now', *FT Weekend*, 25 January 2003, p III.

79 Witold Rybczynski, 'Why we are all Venetians now', *FT Weekend*, 25 January 2003, p III.

80 Peter Stürzebecher and Sigrid Ulrich, *Architecture for Sport: New Concepts and International Projects for Sport and Leisure* (Chichester, John Wiley & Sons, 2002).

81 David Harvey, *The Urban Experience* (Oxford, Blackwell 1989) p 271.

82 David Harvey, *The Urban Experience* (Oxford, Blackwell 1989) p 273.

83 David Harvey, *The Urban Experience* (Oxford, Blackwell 1989) p 276.

84 Witold Rybczynski, 'Why we are all Venetians now', *FT Weekend*, 25 January 2003, p I.

85 Robert Huggins, quoted in Jonathan Guthrie, 'Regeneration schemes "fail to drive growth"', *Financial Times*, 28 October 2002, and posted on www.ft.com

86 House of Commons, Culture, Media and Sport Committee, *National Museums and Galleries: Funding and Free Admission*, First Report of Session 2002–2003 (London, Stationery Office, 2002) p 70 to 71.

87 Tessa Jowell, speech to *Financial Times* conference, *Business of Sport*, 9 June 2003, and posted on www.culture.gov.uk/global/press_notices/archive_2003/ft_conf_speech.htm

88 Christopher Alexander, Sara Ishikawa and Murray Silverstein, *A Pattern Language* (New York City, Oxford University Press, 1977) p 65, 93, 110 to 111.

89 Henley Centre, *EC City Futures: how British cities can make their way in Europe, 1995–1999* (London, Henley Centre, 1993) p 59.

90 www.ngrimshaw.co.uk

91 Office of the Deputy Prime Minister, *Cities, Regions and Competitiveness: second report of the Working Group of Government Departments, the Core Cities and the Regional Development Agencies*, June 2003 and posted on www.urban.odpm.gov.uk/publications/cities/pdf/cities.pdf

92 Daniel Ben-Ami, *Cowardly Capitalism: the myth of the global financial casino* (Chichester, John Wiley & Sons, 2001).

93 International Federation of Accountants and Chartered Institute of Management Accountants, *Managing Risk to Enhance Shareholder Value*, November 2002, and posted on www.cimaglobal.com/downloads/risk_management.pdf

94 Eurostat, *Community Innovation Survey 1997/8* (Luxembourg, Eurostat, 12 September 2000), posted on www.europa.eu.int/comm/eurostat/Public/datashop/print-product/EN?catalogue=Eurostat&product=KS-NS-00-002-__-I-EN&mode=download

95 Editorial, 'The innovative enterprise', *Harvard Business Review*, August 2002 special issue on the innovative enterprise, p 6.

96 Benjamin Hunt, *The Timid Corporation – Why business is terrified of taking risk* (Chichester, John Wiley & Sons, 2003) and reviewed on www.audacity.org/Books.htm

97 Christopher Meyer and Rudy Ruggles, 'Search parties', *Harvard Business Review*, August 2002, and posted on www.harvardbusinessonline.hbsp.harvard.edu/b01/en/hbr/hbr home.jhtml

98 Adrian J Slywotzky and Richard Wise, 'The growth crisis – and how to escape it', *Harvard Business Review*, July 2002, p 74 to 75.

99 William Baumol, *The Free-Market Innovation Machine: analysing the growth miracle of capitalism* (Princeton, Princeton University Press, 2002).

100 Henry Chesbrough, *Open Innovation: the new imperative for creating and profiting from technology* (Boston, Harvard Business School Press, 2003).

101 Andrew Hargadon, *How Breakthroughs Happen: the surprising truth about how companies innovate* (Boston, Harvard Business School Press, 2003).

102 Anatole Kaletsky, 'Arrogance and fear: the American paradox', *The Times*, 7 February 2002, p 18.

103 www.manntech.org

104 Geoff Dyer, 'Drought of new drugs set to continue', *Financial Times*, 30 December 2002, p 19.

105 Confederation of British Industry, The Design Council and 3M, *Innovation Potential: Results and analysis of the 2002 innovation survey*, 23 May 2002, and posted on www.cbi.org.uk

106 Martin Wolf, 'The world beyond the bubble', *Financial Times*, 22 May 2002, and posted on www.ft.com

107 Peter Drucker, 'The discipline of innovation', *Harvard Business Review*, May-June 1985; reprinted November-December 1998.

108 Nathan Rosenberg, 'Innovation's uncertain terrain', *McKinsey Quarterly*, No 3, 1995, p 172, 173.

109 Nathan Rosenberg, 'Innovation's uncertain terrain', *McKinsey Quarterly*, No 3, 1995, p 175 to 178.

110 Nathan Rosenberg, 'Innovation's uncertain terrain', *McKinsey Quarterly*, No 3, 1995, p 178, 182 to 183.

111 Nathan Rosenberg, 'Innovation's uncertain terrain', *McKinsey Quarterly*, No 3, 1995, p 183.

112 Nathan Rosenberg, 'Innovation's uncertain terrain', *McKinsey Quarterly*, No 3, 1995, p 184.

113 Frank Furedi, *Culture of Fear: Risk-taking and the morality of low expectation*, first published, Cassell, 1997 (London, Continuum, revised edition 2002).

2 Backward perspectives: measurement, therapy, naturalism

2.1 The reduction of strategy to measurement

It might seem odd that, in his final programme for revitalising UK construction, a fervent advocate of free markets like Sir John Egan should favour therapeutic and environmental alternatives to the hard-edged process of making a profit. But in his obsession with quantitative targets, Egan was once again trying to rid the industry of *risk*. His own team's Bible, *Accelerating Change*, published in 2002, was careful to argue that integrated teams were good not just for efficiency, but also because they enabled issues around the management of risk 'to be fully addressed by the whole team in an open and transparent manner'. Project insurance policies – Professional Indemnity Insurance, works contract insurance and, perhaps, 'aspects' of product liability insurance – could also assist in the management of risk. But the biggest emphasis in *Accelerating Change* was on the need for 'a culture of continuous improvement based on performance measurement'.[1]

That sounded fine. But it did not contain the possibility that continuous improvement might be based on repeated cycles of analysis, experiment, experience and further analysis – not just on repeated measurements of performance. Nor, in its emphasis on continuous improvement around performance measures that are unquestioned, does it allow

for what Harvard's Clayton Christensen famously termed *disruptive* innovations – new developments that themselves challenge the old measures (see Box 3).[2] Instead the approach of Egan, the great and the good to innovation in UK construction, is to intone: 'If it gets measured, it gets managed'.

Since the advent of New Labour, the ticking of boxes for every British government department has become such a way of life that it has even come to be regretted by Tony Blair. In the spring of 2003, for instance, Britain's minister for higher education was caught trying to distinguish between *benchmarks*, *targets* and *quotas* for working class access to UK universities.[3] It does not seem to matter that, in the old Soviet Union, Joseph Stalin had targets for everything during his five-year plans, yet succeeded in making millions of products that didn't work. From hospital waiting lists, through league tables of schools to assessments of council performance, HM Government's target mentality continues and, like the Soviet regime, often imposes a twisted logic all its own.

Of course without measurement it is hard to manage; but measurement alone is no guarantee of rational practice or successful control. Measurement can often be a kind of displacement activity to do with heightened perceptions of risk, rather than a real tool for knowledge.

Vote conservative

The
Economist

Many portraits of the Blair regime have it, more or less, as an extension of Thatcherism. In fact such portraits miss the influence that old Communist Party thinking has had on New Labour. The fondness for bureaucratic state plans and for throwing resources at national priorities recalls the old pro-Soviet days. The game of targets for everything, of endlessly rebranded and sometimes even reduced targets, and of rebranded or reduced measuring systems – this game recalls the antics of Nikita Krushchev.

The reduction of strategy to measurement is confined neither to building nor even to the UK public sector. Beginning relatively auspiciously in 1992, the management-as-measurement approach grew up being applied to private sector firms in the US. But now something new has happened. Old measures of innovation, like the number of new products developed in the past five years, or the time it takes to get them to market, still have importance. But *both inside and outside construction, the corporate mindset is now adjusted, in a Wildean manner, to knowing the price of everything and the value of nothing. From the value of brand equity to the costs of reputation, every dollar and pound must be entered into the ledger books. The number of Key Performance Indicators (KPIs) grows inexorably.*

Accelerating Change reported that Egan's original seven year-on-year percentage targets for performance improvement in UK construction had grown to 12 targets.[4] These targets, or 'Headline Key Performance Indicators',[5] can be summarised as follows:

- Client satisfaction – with both Product and Service
- Product defects
- Project safety
- Project cost predictability – in both Design and Construction
- Project time predictability – in both Design and Construction
- Project profitability
- Project productivity
- Project cost
- Project time.

Just how objectively *client satisfaction* could be *measured* was not discussed. Instead, the indicators have multiplied. In Britain there are official Design Quality Indicators, which measure quality in design and construction: these were launched in 2002 with the backing of the

Department of Trade and Industry (DTI) and come complete with two kinds of trained and registered DQI Facilitators.[6] Then, in 2003, the Strategic Forum for Construction established KPIs for payment within UK construction industry supply chains. Finally, an official website devoted to construction industry KPIs counted no fewer than 69 separate and free *sources* for indicators and a further 54 sources 'for which there may be a charge'.[7]

The end result of all these KPIs is that an enormous expenditure of effort is required to keep tracking them. In the best traditions of Frederick Winslow Taylor, the father of 'scientific' management, an army of supervisors is now required to get the real army of builders to work properly. The proof, ironically, is to be found in yet more statistics. Among those industries which the UK's Economic and Social Research Council has identified as claiming to have recruited more managers of late, the 'Manufacturing/Construction' sector is up there with banks and government (see Table 4).

Given the decline of British manufacturing employment over the period 2000–2003 and, compared with this, the relatively stable performance of construction, it seems likely that the bulk of managerial and professional staff increases reported belong to the construction sector.

That might be a good thing, marking a genuine professionalisation of the sector and a forthright recruitment drive to raise productivity. But the real dynamic in hiring more managers maybe to measure more KPIs, but take fewer risks.

That can only make more difficult the genuine breakthroughs that construction now requires.

2.2 Campaigns for safety and against cowboys

Since the Health and Safety at Work Act of 1974, Britain's Health and Safety Commission and its standard-setting Health and Safety Executive[21] have seen six times more deaths take place in construction than in any other industry. Despite the activities of the HSC and HSE, nearly 900 workers and more than 50 members of the public have been killed around building sites over the past

---

TABLE 4 UK construction expands its demand for managers

'Thinking about the proportion of managerial or professional staff at your establishment over the past three years, has it increased, decreased or stayed about the same?'

	Increase	Decrease	Stayed about the same	Approximate total
Manufacturing/Construction	22.0	8.9	68.8	100 per cent
Wholesale/Retail	19.4	11.2	68.8	100 per cent
Transport, Storage, Communications	11.1	4.3	83.3	100 per cent
Financial and Business Services	25.5	5.9	67.8	100 per cent
Public Administration, Government, Health, Education	24.7	7.4	67.6	100 per cent

Source: 30-minute telephone survey, July-September 2002, of 2000 human resource or industrial relations managers in a nationally representative stratified random sample[8]

Box 3 **THE INNOVATOR'S SOLUTION**

Clayton Christensen

In his excellent book *The innovators' dilemma: when new technologies cause great firms to fail*, Harvard Business School professor Clayton Christensen argued that, among market-leading firms:

> the logical, competent decisions of management that are critical to the success of their companies are also the reasons why they lose their positions of leadership.[9]

Through a massive study of the US computer disk drive industry and other sectors, Christensen found that giant, semi-monopoly manufacturers tended to listen to and research their existing customers too much. They sought higher prices and margins from such customers, typically overshooting their demands – being guilty of 'performance oversupply' – by giving clients more than they needed or were willing to purchase. They preferred technologies that, even if they were radically new and difficult, merely *sustained* their industry by continuing its

historical improvements in performance, as defined by how performance had historically been measured.[10]

New entrant firms, by contrast, specialised in *disruptive* technologies that led to products which were typically cheaper, simpler, smaller, and, frequently, more convenient to use. They took advantage of their elder rivals' expensive overshoots in product performance by creating 'a vacuum at lower price points'. They attacked markets that were ignored by traditional market-leading firms. Through their products, above all, disrupter firms set new and eventually industry-standard measures of performance.

Geoffrey Moore, a prestigious consultant in Silicon Valley, had earlier suggested that new business-to-business IT products, as they evolved, were given different *uses* by a succession of 'early adopters', 'early majority' customers and 'late majority' customers.[11] Christensen's focus was complementary. He concentrated on 'phase changes' in the performance measures surrounding the life cycle of a new product – changes in which the rank ordering of the criteria by which customers chose one product over another often evolved from functionality to reliability, then to convenience and, ultimately, to price.[12]

Significantly, disruptive products forged ahead in the face of multiple risks. These risks were:

- their low performance as traditionally measured;
- the lower margins associated with them because of their simplicity and cheapness;
- an initial commercialisation only in emerging or insignificant markets;
- a profile that the best of the old firms' customers generally didn't want and indeed initially couldn't use; and
- the absence of research data about the new markets at which they were launched.

However by contrast with sustaining technologies, disruptive ones conferred 'significant first-mover advantages' upon their bearers. To be first into the market with them was to establish a commanding position over later entrants. As Christensen put it:

It is in disruptive innovations, where we know least about the market, that there are such strong first-mover advantages. This is the innovator's dilemma.[13]

In the early 1980s, disrupters ensured that the game in disk drives shifted from storage capacity, cost per megabyte and speed of access inside minicomputers, toward size, weight, ruggedness, power consumption and price inside desktop computers. In the mid 1980s, small, cheap-to-buy inkjet printers began being made by Hewlett-Packard as an alternative to large, high-resolution, cheap-to-run laser printers made by Hewlett-Packard. In the early 1990s, Intuit Corporation captured the US market for small business accounting software by offering QuickBooks, which boasted less functionality but greater convenience than traditional rivals.

Interestingly, US construction in the 1970s saw disrupters have a similar influence on excavating equipment. Having spent the late 1940s and 1950s opening up a market among small residential building contractors for fast, manoeuvrable and hydraulically-actuated excavators with narrow shovels, disrupters supplanted large, long-reach, large-lift cable-actuated excavators in the mainstream construction market, particularly through their greater reliability.[14]

Published in 1997, Christensen's book was a riposte to those who stressed the need to stay close to customers,[15] develop their loyalty[16] and seek, in them, the sources of innovation.[17] A development of what had earlier been described as 'the attacker's advantage', *Dilemma* struck a chord in an America that was then ramping up to the dot.com boom.[18] Its call for a radical break from the past in supply-side technologies, and its paean to new entrant firms at the expense of old management mindsets, appealed to a generation of youthful, 'new economy' entrepreneurs for whom the average American CEO 'just didn't get it'.

Christensen was not right about everything. His focus on the low 'sticker price' of disruptive products tended to absolve them from their low performance and high cost in use.[19] In construction, to make houses and offices smaller than they are already would be a mistake.

With his most recent book, *The innovator's solution*, Christensen says that the facts refute the idea that large companies fail to sustain growth because their managers become risk averse. Yet when he points to the big bad bets corporate giants such as DuPont or Corning have been prepared to make in the past, he and his co-author, Deloitte's Michael Raynor, miss the force and scope that risk aversion has today – both inside and outside the company. Christensen and Raynor themselves, for example, vainly want to make innovation a predictable process. Yet they are right to emphasise that:

- measures of product performance *change* over time;
- radical re-conceptions of a *product's 'architecture'* are needed, often but not always in the direction of *modularity*; and
- disruptive innovations demand *new kinds* of teams and organisational structures.[20]

For those who want to mass-produce wholly new building types, rather than measure one-off architecture with the old criteria, the Christensen doctrine makes a lot of sense.

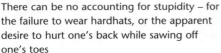

There can be no accounting for stupidity – for the failure to wear hardhats, or the apparent desire to hurt one's back while sawing off one's toes

decade. Things got so bad that an industry summit, organised by the government and the HSC in February 2001, resolved to cut the incidence of:

- fatalities and major injuries – by 40 per cent in time for 2004–2005, and by 66 per cent by 2009–2010; and
- work-related ill-health, and working days lost through injury and ill-health – first by 20 per cent and then by 50 per cent.

This was to little avail. Even though the HSE forewarns contractors whenever it is about to carry out a site inspection, conditions were so terrible in 2002 that it insisted that work had to stop on nearly half of the 1,100 sites it visited that year.[22]

In 2001 the official rate of accidents per 100,000 employees in construction was 1221, or nearly twice that for the economy as a whole.[23] If anything, that official rate underestimates the real rate. We saw in Chapter 1 how self-employment still accounts for more than a third of the jobs in UK construction, so it is worthwhile to consider what the HSE has to say on this matter:

Self-employed people are poor reporters of work-related injury. They consistently report less than one in ten reportable injuries.[24]

Some estimate that between 300,000 and 400,000 people work in UK construction's black economy.[25] For Egan and *Accelerating Change*, these hordes represented a brake on better practice within the industry.[26] In the same vein, the HSE is quick to attack what it calls 'a macho culture which thrives upon workers' belief in their own indestructibility', together with 'people who don't believe it will happen to them, or just hope that they will be lucky' and poor standards that are 'often due to ignorance (sic) of the workers, many of whom are transient'.[27]

Yet it is all too easy to indict the moonlighting builder as an untrained safety hazard to himself. Without unregistered builders, Britain would face even slower construction activity and even higher building prices. That is an unpleasant fact, but a fact all the same.

The informal sector is a symptom – not a cause – of backwardness in construction. Yet ever since a report titled *Beat the cowboys* was published in 1988, that sector has been the main object of official disgust about poor safety on site.[28] Perhaps that disgust is justified: three-quarters of those builders killed at work are self-employed or labour for a contractor employing fewer than 15 people; and half of all the deaths that occur are on sites with fewer than 15 workers.[29] However, less justified are the cynical reasons why British officialdom gives safety the exalted status it does.

For Egan and *Accelerating Change*, improved performance in health and safety matters was necessary for 'good business and ethical reasons'. Just as with their performance in relation to sustainability, clients for buildings would be judged – by financial analysts, among others – on their ethical stance in relation

to safety. Both safety and sustainability would have 'an important impact on corporate image'. Even worse, accidents on site might involve clients in legal liabilities, delays, defective work and higher prices.[30]

It was not by chance that there was concern here to *play up corporate reputation and attack cowboy practices*. After the Enron corruption crisis of January 2002, indeed, corporate reputation was made the theme of the CBI's conference in November that same year. But what are we talking about when we hear the universal complaint within the construction industry – and also in several other sectors beyond it (airlines, railways, shipping, extractive industries) – that bad on-site safety could have an important impact on reputation?

Too often, we are talking about the adoption of those safety routines and devices that make us look good and feel good in a world perceived as one of growing dangers.

Too often, too, we are talking about a safety culture that has more to do with the evasion of risk and the dispensing of bogus, bureaucratic and self-flattering therapies than it has to do with preventing injuries on site.

From time to time, such measures may genuinely reduce accidents. But that is not necessarily their purpose. It is the therapeutic burnishing of corporate image, not the lives and deaths of builders, that is the modest objective of today's drive to register everyone in the building trade. It is the fear of looking bad to the outside world, and to internal staff, which makes safety rituals so prominent in the building reformer's manifesto. At the CBI conference, Carly Fiorina, chairman and chief executive of the computer giant Hewlett-Packard, took up Egan's theme of ethical image. Like Egan, she revealed that corporate strategy and operations are now dominated by a 'safety first' ethos. It is an ethos that highlights sentimental attachments, but only because of the perceived dangers of not doing so. Fiorina said:

Managing risk across a global network involves managing reputation, and the partnerships, friendships and associations that contribute to it.[31]

Fiorina's reference to 'friendships' mirrored Egan's plea for respect for people.

When Egan was, for nearly a decade, chief executive of the British Airports Authority, he wanted a fifth terminal at Heathrow airport. During his tenure, however, he realised that, to gain government support, he had to win 'not just the legal argument but the emotional one'.[32] In the event, BAA was successful, and T5 is being built. But the primacy given to emotions in today's management canon is certainly not new.[33] Nor is it by any means without critics.[34] In construction, it must remain doubtful that the emotional, therapeutic approach to safety will really end the malpractice that manifestly exists.

So long as construction remains a backward industry, safety within it will be backward. So long as off-site manufacturing remains a footnote to general building, a lot of accidents are bound to happen in the hurly-burly rush to get on-site work completed on time. Kevin Myers, chief inspector of construction at the HSE, accepts the need to go 'designing out' health and safety risks. But in 2002, respondents to the HSE discussion document *Revitalising Health and Safety in Construction* concluded that off-site manufacturing had no role to play in the reduction of accidents. Rather, the way forward, given that only about three per cent of the UK construction industry workforce is ever in *training*, was through more training and better skills, as the chart illustrates below.

For the HSE, accidents will come down not through the re-organisation of construction but through 'cultural change', and in this change, the villain is always the stupidity of the construction operative, rather than the cynical negligence of the employer.

The focus on safety training and safety culture is an intense one. Alongside moralistic harangues, there are a multitude of go-through-the-motions procedures on safety. In their review of Design Risk Assessments which, before a building is begun, designers and then contractors are required to fill out under the Construction (Design and Management)

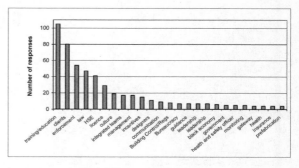

Issues around which UK construction industry respondents thought the greatest improvements could be made, 2003[36]

Source: HSE, *Revitalising Health and Safety in Construction*[35]

Regulations of 1994, the HSE recognised the widespread view that they represent:

for all practical purposes a waste of paper. Most . . . are an exercise in stating the obvious and are prepared from a generic list – and quite clearly once design is complete . . . Designers need to look at Safety on a project specific basis, not generically as they do now.[37]

Britain's Construction Skills Certification Scheme is another example of

makework in safety matters. Covering more than 90 trades and 250,000 holders of special photocards, the CSCS is one of the most recognised in UK construction.[38] Yet it is not even about employers paying immigrants for English lessons in exchange for their cheap labour. Rather, it gives employers and managers the feel-good sensation that no official will ever complain about their choice of operatives.

If a worker has a CSCS card, he will probably have a coveted National Vocational Qualification and will certainly have undergone health and safety 'awareness training or testing'.[39] So he will at all times be a paragon of safety on site. On the other hand, if a manager finds that a CSCS cardholder will not comply with a dubious instruction, the worker may then find himself maliciously unmasked as a cowboy.

A beauty of the CSCS is that, when claims for compensation for accidents are

It is now both socially accepted and legally required that designers think about how people will safely clean and maintain contemporary architecture, and rightly so. Yet clients will often not invest in adequate cleaning and maintenance equipment, even if the architect wants it. Cleaning and maintenance contractors who sign up for guaranteed maximum-price contracts on fixed programmes invariably forget to allow for enough structure to support their weighty equipment, and fail to involve the best specialists in capital- rather than labour-intensive systems

made, both employees and employers will use it to bolster their case.

In fact, across the whole of the British economy, claims for compensation from employers and the public sector are worth at least £10 billion a year, or one per cent of GDP.[40] Along with manufacturing, the building sector has made a special contribution to this state of affairs (see Table 5).

The legal duty of an employer to comply with safety regulations and take reasonable care for the health and safety of an employee is not new. What is new is the rising number of no-win, no-fee lawyers looking for every kind of injury case to bring against employers.[42]

No amount of litigation, however, will improve a backward industry.

2.3 Respecters of health, enemies of stress

Respect for People is not just an injunction in the building trade. In the UK, it is also the name of a powerful, Eganesque industry working group, chaired by Alan Crane. For many years a construction engineer with Bovis, Crane was seconded to Olympia & York to head up the development and construction at Canary Wharf, London, and was later chief

executive at the contractors Christiani & Nielsen Group.

The Respect for People Working Group is very concerned about employee health and workplace stress in the building trade. Here is what it had to say on these matters in 2002:

Health receives too little attention
Too little conscious attention is given to occupational ill health. By its nature, ill health effects are usually slow to be realised, but its costs and long-term implications are far more significant than those of accidents where there are immediate visible impacts. This is especially so in an industry reliant on hourly/weekly paid workers who often receive no benefits if they are not at work.

Stress and overwork
Stress is of increasing concern to middle managers and in particular sectors of the industry as they face ever-greater pressures and longer working hours.[43]

The remarks on occupational ill health are, hardly surprisingly, true but insufficiently explained. Manual construction workers have no continuity of employment: they move in and out of periods of self-employment, from one subcontractor to the next and from project

---

TABLE 5 Construction helps lead Britain's compensation culture

'In the past 12 months, have any of your employees taken your organisation to an employment tribunal alleging unfair dismissal?'

	Yes
Manufacturing/Construction	7.9
Wholesale/Retail	4.9
Transport, Storage, Communications	5.9
Financial and Business Services	5.9
Public Administration, Government, Health, Education	6.2
All	6.1

Source: 30-minute telephone survey, July-September 2002, of 2,000 human resource or industrial relations managers in a nationally representative stratified random sample[41]

Alan Crane

Alan Crane has spent nearly 40 years in construction, half of them with the Bovis Group, for which he eventually became main board director responsible for all international activities. He was chairman and remains a council member of the UK's Construction Confederation,[50] whose 5000 corporate members account for more than 75 per cent of the UK construction industry's turnover. An advisor to Hammond Suddards Edge, one of the UK's top construction and engineering law firms, Crane is also chairman of the engineering management board of Britain's Institute of Civil Engineers, and a member of Britain's Architects Registration Board, a body New Labour established by statute in 1997 to regulate the architects' profession in the UK.[51]

to project under different main contractors. When the client employs direct, workers again have next to no continuity of employer. *It is the site-based nature of contracts and work in the construction industry that accounts for much of both the disregard for ill health, and its incidence.*

In Britain in 2003, two building firms told their workers to protect themselves from the summertime risks of skin cancer either by adopting full dress or by slapping on protective sunblock.[44] One of the firms went as far as to mount national roadshows to make its staff aware of the issues. To avoid the sun, UK construction would rather perform such antics than entertain the possibility of building houses indoors.

The Respect for People people are a respectable lot. They are respecters of health; they are enemies of stress. They have a friendly word for:

- health screening and surveillance;
- drug and alcohol testing;
- workforce assistance programmes; and
- flexible working arrangements.[45]

Yet today's 'epidemic' of workplace stress rests on dubious foundations.[46] Of course, in construction a demanding building programme, a limited client budget or a robust engineering consultant may cause a weak manager a great deal of stress. Yet if contractual responsibilities and technical performance specifications are to be worth anything, they *ought* to induce a sense of pressure.

It is healthier to be a construction manager than it is to be a navvy, and managers enjoy some continuity of employment across a number of projects. But on top of their so-so pay and lengthy working hours, construction managers have to put up with working conditions vastly inferior to mainstream managers.

With managers, as with workers, better pay and a shift of focus from on-site to off-site work would do much to improve health and calm nerves. But such measures are not part of the Respecters' brief. They write:

Construction processes carried out in a controlled factory environment can offer real ben-

Aspects of Canary Wharf, the subject of renewed and intense financial infighting after it was put up for sale in the summer of 2003

efits to working people. Off-site manufacture can lead to on site process change, but detailed consideration of this is outside the scope of this report.[47]

To the extent that health and stress are real issues in construction, breast-beating about them will make little difference. Neither will the Respecters' nine People Performance Indicators, launched in May 2002, nor their prodigious effort to map these PPIs on to six national standards affecting people issues in construction, producing 8-column matrices with a total of 60 rows and 480 cells.[48] These number-crunching acrobatics amount only to displacement activities. The concern is less about preventing loss of life and limb and more about making sure that measurers show themselves sensitive to every kind of incident on site.

While its wider backwardness is still given a tacit nod, in the UK construction is, as the Respecters point out, 'the first industry to launch Key Performance Indicators to specifically measure (sic) human resources, people and culture issues.'[49]

Everything, even 'culture issues', must be measured. That alone is enough to give any good builder plenty of stress.

2.4 The mantra of teamwork

When they are brought together for a bespoke project, good clients, consultants, managers, and trade contractors can create more marvels than teams of mediocrities. After all, many firms are reluctant to end lucrative, if disorganised, partnerships and teams: they fear exposing their own incompetence to rivals. Specialists in construction management already work in this way, moving from job to job with preferred lists of trade contractors. Contractors avoid giving managers a hard time by acceding, no doubt in a team spirit, to their more outrageous demands. In return, they get away with work that might otherwise be condemned for its poor quality.

For Egan, however, teams that only assembled to execute one project learned on the job at the client's expense. It was 'self evident' that they would 'never be as efficient, safe, productive or profitable as those that work repeatedly on similar projects'.[52] But *if members of a building team hang together and mix disciplines over several or many projects, is that about a real division of labour and a real deepening of knowledge – or is it about something else?*

Integrated teams can work in manufacturing because products made in volume are subject to rejection in a hard-to-please market. When there is enough competition for consumers, mediocre efforts fail to sell. By contrast, in construction supply falls behind demand. Housing serves as an acute example, but the problem is more general. Builders can be much more confident than manufacturers of selling just about any design and just about any quality of finished product.

The consequence is that teams in construction have much more latitude than they do in manufacturing. As a result, *in the construction sector there is special scope for team-based therapeutic devices – devices that stroke egos more than they get real building work done.*

Outside construction, teams have a long tradition. In the 1990s they gained prominence as:

- a means by which to organise a rational division of labour;[53]
- a vehicle for learning at work – aided by a 'free flow of meaning among equals';[54] and
- a chance for conviviality, recreation and a 'circle of love'.[55]

As recent years have shown, to collaborate in a team is always to participate in a sort of post-Cold War socialist idyll within the capitalist corporation – egalitarian, dynamic, meritocratic.

Of course successful teamwork is not about equality, for the 'empowerment' of workforces is a myth.[56] It has been cogently argued that the better kinds of mainstream corporate teams rarely involve more than two disciplines, and rarely thrive on a lot of social cohesion.[57] Moreover in building there are special reasons to be wary of what Egan always refers to as 'integration'. Colin Porteous,

senior lecturer in architectural science at the Mackintosh School of Architecture, Glasgow, observes:

Once architects are no longer in full control of an aspect of architectural design, it alters the way they design . . . although there is much glib talk about successful multi-disciplinary teams and conferences, boundaries between interrelated skill tend to be distinct, and cross-disciplinary understanding is rather poor.[58]

At Britain's Design Build Foundation, operations executive Nigel Finn is also right to observe:

Bigger teams will be formed and projects will be huge. There will be a lot more projects of the size of Wembley Stadium which require people to have a tremendous grasp of business issues as well as construction knowledge.[59]

Yet the vogue for teamwork in construction has little to do with raising productivity on more Wembleys. Rather, it follows the Egan chant: 'equitably share risk and reward in a non-adversarial way'.[60] It is to do with Victorian morality: with having 'professional relationships and attitudes that result in behaviour based on mutual respect and where [sic] people treat others as they would wish to be treated'.[61] That is why, on behalf of the 80 construction firms and clients that are gathered together in the Design Build Foundation, the prestigious Henley Management College has run a pioneering programme – complete with *games* in which players slot wooden boards of different sizes into a series of interlocking squares – to end what the *Financial Times* reports as 'screaming matches' between designers and contractors, and 'horror stories' pitting architects against engineers.[62]

But the screaming and the horror will only grow worse, and the mantra of teamwork will have only a placebo effect, so long as buildings grow in size and building technique stays backward. That is not a risk to be feared, but a reality that needs to be faced.

2.5 Government buildings pioneer design as social engineering

The final aspect of the therapeutic perspective in UK construction relates to government buildings. In October 2000, New Labour published *Better Public Buildings*, insisting that buildings on the government estate must do more than just house workers. Stressing the 'design benefits' of the best Victorian schools, railway stations, post offices, and libraries, Tony Blair eulogised the strong sense of *civic pride* that Victorian public architecture embodied. He felt, too, that the built design of 100 years ago had *set an example for the private sector to emulate.*[63]

The design of public buildings, it is said nowadays, must have a measurable effect upon staff, end-users and relations with the local community.[64] For part of the function of government buildings is to arrange for *an overall sense of employee and user 'wellness', both physical and mental.* In schools, it appears that design can directly lead to better education. In its annual review for 2002, significantly entitled *Design has the power to transform every corner of our lives*, the Design Council insists:

well designed Furniture for the Future can deliver a 21st century curriculum and help teachers and learners get more out of education.[65]

But can furniture really deliver a 21st century curriculum? Are objects, and especially well-designed ones, really able to have such a therapeutic effect? Are the powers of design really so great?

In 1960, Winston Churchill told *Time* magazine:

We shape our buildings: thereafter they shape us.

Since that time, the deterministic side of Churchill's formulation – that buildings shape psychology – has come to be stressed at the expense of the side that pays attention to human activity. While Churchill appears to have had a glimmering that social psychology shapes architecture, the direction of causality that is taken for granted today is all the other way. Thus in 2003, justifying the BBC's £2.8 billion revamp of its estate of 520 buildings, John Smith, the Corporation's director of finance and property, saw its workspace as a direct impetus to broadcasting excellence: 'If we are going to be the most creative organisation in the world', he told the *Sunday Times*, 'we need the best buildings'.[66]

Nowadays, just about any organisation aspires to be the most creative in the world. But does it really follow that, to reach this goal, one needs superlative buildings? Design, it is officially believed, can perform astonishing feats of social engineering and 'culture change'. Even the relocation of the Government Communication Headquarters to two new facilities in Cheltenham is cast as a chance for spies to commune in an open-air garden at the centre of one of them. As GCHQ's chief spokesman says of the £330 million open-plan architecture:

The traditional attributes of the GCHQ person are that they are introverted and analytical. We wanted a shift . . . The aim has to be to move away from tribalism. There's now much more dialogue.[67]

Hospital design is also meant to have a measurably therapeutic effect on British hospital staff and their patients. Thus Peter Wearmouth, chief executive of NHS Estates, insists that buildings for healthcare do not just induce civic pride, but also form a *healing environment* – one in which design 'sits alongside the science of medicine'.[68]

The doctrine that building design has a contribution to make to health is an attractive one. Sweden has helped pioneer the idea, and in June 2003 Montreal played host to the third in a series of international conferences on it.[69] But building design is not the only official remedy for ill health. The Arts Council of England adds that art, too, sits alongside the science of medicine.[70]

Of course a hospital or school with well-designed furniture, good use of natural light, an easily intelligible layout and some fine paintings is better than one without these things. Yet the idea that design, architecture and art can be as physically therapeutic as surgery or powerful drugs is a New Age nonsense. What began as fear of Sick Building Syndrome has now been complemented by the desire of government, which is responsible for 40 per cent of construction orders in the UK, to lead a broader *medicalisation* of architecture.

Modern Western society has a strong inclination toward medicalising all social issues.[71] But whether architecture should join in with this trend is a moot point. We are already promised a healthier mind in a healthier office through the application, over a period of one week, of Chinese principles of design.[72] Yet British Airways' much-trumpeted Waterside headquarters, which were designed with the help of feng shui, did not prevent the airline from imposing a large number of highly stressful redundancies there in 2002.

In Britain the government would prefer construction to indulge in social and medical engineering than improve real engineering. The hopes now held in the potentially therapeutic properties of NHS property confirm this. As Wearmouth enthuses:

Not since the 18th century has there been such an impetus for investment in healthcare buildings. Within ten years we will have replaced or refurbished 25 per cent of our healthcare buildings. We have 24 million square metres of building space, of which six million will need to be replaced or refurbished within ten years. The challenge for the construction industry is immense.[73]

Taxpayers, however, might say that the challenge for the industry is to get all that building done on time and on budget. It is for doctors and nurses, not architects and builders, to deliver genuine health care.

Nowadays it is not just the function of government buildings to set an example and design in therapy. Since 2002, buildings in 17 separate central government departments, together with three from the Scottish, Welsh and Northern Ireland Offices, have also had to work within a tightly defined framework for sustainable design.[74] More broadly, it is government that has led the way in enforcing both therapeutic and naturalistic perspectives in construction.

2.6 New Labour's sustainable communities

On 5 February 2003 John Prescott was in the House of Commons and in no mood to brook argument. For 30 years, he said, government had failed to ensure that enough houses were built. But there were 70,000 privately owned homes in London and the South East lying empty. He would force their owners, and those of other homes in a similar position, to rent them out through the local council. And he was not about to start a massive programme of housebuilding now.

No, New Labour was not about to build big. It appeared to be, but it was not.

Prescott told MPs that he would spend £22 billion over three years on what he called a *programme* of housebuilding, and announced long-expected plans to build an 'extra' 200,000 homes in the South East, on top of the falling number of annual completions, in time for the year 2016. But as Table 6 shows, New Labour's programme was more for bureaucracy than for housebuilding.

Moreover, Prescott's extra homes were not much of an extra (see Box 4). In setting targets for housebuilding that could be measured, Prescott first ensured that his targets were low.

Most of the money offered by the Office of the Deputy Prime Minister (ODPM) was earmarked not for the production of houses, but rather for:

- improving parks and public space;
- the employment of planners and housing managers;
- setting up project offices to manage urban regeneration;
- the refurbishment of old public and private housing stock;
- the compulsory purchase of land; and
- the demolition of abandoned housing.

As for extra homes, these amounted to 16,000 a year – a mere 12 per cent increase on today's paltry total of 130,000 new homes built annually (see Box 4).

The ODPM's *numerical targets for the new houses actually to be built* were much more modest than they seemed. But they were not widely contested. Nor, very much, were *the methods by which new homes would be built*. All that had happened was that, before his speech, the Deputy PM had let it be known that he would fund the Housing Corporation to buy prefabricated homes, mainly in the South East.[75] These would be bought from two sources:

- those few manufacturers, such as the housebuilder Westbury,[76] experimenting in *flat-pack homes – the modular prefabrication not just of components, but of structural, loadbearing panels off-site, that are then erected on-site;* and
- Yorkon,[77] the 700-units-a-year market leader in *volumetric prefabrication*, or *the prefabrication of complete homes off site: homes that can either stand alone, or simply be stacked up, one upon another, on-site.* Yorkon is one of the few volumetric manufacturers that offer an established stackable portacabin product.

These volumetrically manufactured hotel rooms, which epr architects[78] designed specifically for the Travelodge hotel at Heathrow airport, have rightly dispensed with the portacabin approach – even if the world needs no more terracotta rainscreen cladding, nor any more of the usual suspects in plumbing and sanitary ware

TABLE 6 Home free: how funds for New Labour's February 2003 Sustainable Communities programme avoided housebuilding in the UK; £m

	2002–2003	2003–2004	2004–2005	2005–2006	2003–2006 Total	Purpose of the allocation in the headline figure of £22 billion 'for new housing'
Housing investment for affordable housing and improving housing conditions in London, the East and the South East	995	1,573	1,558	1,605	4,736	The £7,394m total comprises £4 billion to be spent on affordable housing, £1 billion on key worker housing, with the remainder on bringing council stock up to a decent standard. Most of the work to
Housing investment for affordable housing and improving housing conditions in other regions	719	852	892	914	2,658	be done is refurbishment of existing public housing stock rather than a programme of new building
To establish a new regime of Arms Length Housing Management Organisations (ALMOs)	59	323	851	820	1,994	A paper transfer of good existing council housing stock to housing associations and other approved housing managers
Regional Development Agencies	1,322	1,521	1,551	1,607	4,679	To establish a network of regional development agencies responsible for administering national and
European Regional Development Fund	210	229	229	229	687	European funding
Other housing and urban related programmes of an unspecified purpose	522	501	424	384	1,309	This residual funding of smaller initiatives operates through various overlapping quangos
Neighbourhood Renewal Fund	300	400	450	525	1,375	Community-based initiatives to tackle perceived social exclusion
New Deal for Communities	350	265	287	298	850	Promoting self-help schemes
English Partnerships	145	163	179	179	521	Reconstitution of the quango

Market Renewal Pathfinders and the problem of low demand or abandoned housing	25	60	150	290	500	Initiatives where the housing market has collapsed, including wholesale demolition and land clearance for future sale
The Thames Gateway	0	40	198	208	446	To establish tiers of agencies for planning and land acquisition
Other Growth areas	0	40	58	66	164	
Planning	27	73	153	194	420	Development control reform
Transitional funding for Housing Finance Reform	500	175	140	65	380	Changes to government funding arrangements; not new investment
Disabled Facilities Grants	97	99	99	99	297	Home modification assistance
New Ventures Fund	77	99	99	94	292	For local regeneration projects
Homelessness	90	93	83	83	259	Temporary housing relief
Local environment or 'Liveability' schemes, including skills training	13	41	79	81	201	Various schemes for teaching 'life skills' through environmental improvement projects
Total	**5,451**	**6,547**	**7,480**	**7,741**	**21,768**	**Rounded up to £22 billion**

Source: Sustainable Communities: Building for the future, London, Office of the Deputy Prime Minister, February 2003, and posted on www.odpm.gov.uk

Where the new plans were controversial was in their chosen *locations for the new homes*. David Davis, MP, described these as 'concreting the South' in the Commons;[79] but on the London *Times*, property editor Anne Spackman perceptively argued that, in the face of environmentalist and Not In My Back Yard (NIMBY) opinion, Prescott had 'chosen the line of least resistance'.[80]

The ODPM's commitment to *low housebuilding targets* was indeed calculated not to offend the naturalistic perspective. On top of that:

- in *methods of production* it was only prepared to put £200 million toward a grand total of 4000 prefabricated homes – just 2–3 per cent of a single year's UK housing output; and
- in *locational matters*, it did indeed take the line of least resistance. Instead of building new houses where shortages are greatest in Britain – around Oxford, Reading and Surrey – it planned to build in four zones up to 2016: around Milton Keynes and Stansted to the north of London (30,000 homes in each) and, to the East, in the Thames Gateway and around the town of Ashford (110,000 and 30,000 homes respectively).

New Labour's preferences in terms of location were easily explained. Prescott simply sought to minimise environmentalist and NIMBY opposition to his plans. With regard to London, Spackman observed, it was:

easier to impose housing on areas to the North and East. Not only is land, and therefore property, cheaper but also, particularly in the case of Thames Gateway, there are fewer established residents to complain.[81]

On all three counts – numbers of homes, production methods, and location – New Labour showed an unvarying commitment to the naturalistic perspective. Yet that commitment was not new: it was longstanding and fundamental.

2.7 The messianic approach

In 1999, when he announced new indicators for his Strategy for Sustainable Development for the United Kingdom, Prescott was quite explicit about what sustainability meant:

In the past, focus has centred mainly on improving labour productivity. In the future, greater emphasis will be needed on resource efficiency. We need to break the link between continued economic growth and increasing use of resources and environmental impacts.[84]

In construction as elsewhere, New Labour is now more interested in saving natural resources and minimising environmental fall-out than it is in improving productivity: this much became clear in March 2000, when the ODPM's *Planning Policy Guidance Note No 3* – known as PPG3 – on Housing established three immutable principles for sustainable residential environments:

To promote more sustainable patterns of development and *make better use of previously-developed land*, the focus for additional housing should be existing towns and cities.[85]

Local authorities should promote developments which combine a *mix of land uses*, including housing, either on a site or within individual buildings such as flats over shops. This is important not only to accommodate new households but also to bring new life into our towns and cities.[86]

New housing development in England is currently built at an average of 25 dwellings per hectare but more than half of all new housing is built at less than 20 dwellings per hectare. That represents a level of land take which is historically very high and which can no longer be sustained. Such development is also less likely to sustain local services or public transport, ultimately adding to social exclusion . . . Local planning authorities should therefore encourage housing development which makes *more efficient use of land* (between 30 and 50 dwellings per hectare net).[87]

Box 4 NEW LABOUR FUNDS A CLIPBOARD ARMY IN CONSTRUCTION

This Government's year-on-year investment in housing and regeneration is tackling the root causes of deprivation, and in towns and cities across England, the urban renaissance is taking hold . . . We are putting people first. We are determined to put an end to poor housing and bad landlords, to deliver more affordable housing, especially for key workers and young families, and to develop new sustainable communities in regions of high demand, such as the Thames Gateway.[82]

In its February 2003 plans for housing over the period 2004 to 2006, New Labour did indeed put people first. But it did not do this in the sense that Members of Parliament imagined when they were told about its intentions. The entire sustainable communities initiative was less about providing homes for people to live in, and more about establishing a salaried priesthood of experts in environmental chanting and community rectitude. Every developer will have to satisfy a new Inquisition – one that insists not just on all the right kinds of schools, health centres and transport links, but also on such imponderables as the anticipation of climate change and, inevitably, 'Design against Crime'.[83]

The headline figure of 200,000 new 'affordable homes', was deceptive. Since that target was in fact set for 2016, it meant only 16,000 extra homes a year – at a time when the overall supply of homes in Britain had for years fallen by tens of thousands each year.

The £7.4 billion described as 'housing investment' expenditure, furthermore, was not new. The figure itself was a renovation of New Labour's longstanding plans to overcome a £19 billion backlog of repair work in the social housing sector. The re-announcement that the same old money would be available for this task was made in the hopes that the whole job would be done by 2010.

It was always quite a feat to spend £22 billion over three years, bringing 48,000 (3 x 16,000) new homes on to the market, and getting more use out of the ageing existing public housing stock. The only thing that could explain such an enormously expensive figure was something that had already marked New Labour's conduct with the railways and the NHS: the engagement of thousands of professionals, consultants and managers. Their job:

- to judge the worthiness of each modest refurbishment of obsolete stock, safe in the knowledge that still more remedial work would, as is usual with old buildings, shortly be required again; and
- to mull over the handful of new schemes, consult endlessly, and procrastinate.

While the priority was refurbishment, New Labour recognised that a number of Britain's estates were beyond this. Hard-to-let or abandoned estates in Britain's regions, it announced, were to be demolished and cleared, either to provide landscaped open space or for future redevelopment. Of course, unpopular housing was not new. What was new was that fewer houses would be built than those demolished. And who, exactly, was to decide when a downbeat area should be demolished? The answer: unelected experts in urban regeneration, engaged to research the area and its context, develop plans, consider intervention options, and undertake consultation with local stakeholders.

Beyond refurbishment and demolition, officially recognised Growth Areas in Britain received £610 million, of which the Thames Gateway project took £446 million. Overall, the bulk of New Labour's £22 billion was to be spent on the coddling of paper-pushers and outdoor relief for lawyers and accountants, not new dwellings.

There was a suggestion that perhaps £150 million might go toward prefabricated homes. But the idea that homelessness, or indeed better access to accommodation for disabled people, might in large part be solved through a serious programme of mass production – this was obviously far too crude for the subtle social engineers of New Labour.

Land, land, land: New Labour's commitment to it is almost biblical.

Just weeks after the events of 11 September 2001, the Deputy PM found himself speaking about the environment in Moscow. There he argued that the same 'passion and commitment' that Britain and Russia had shown in the global coalition against terrorism should also be channelled into a wider campaign on other international problems, such as the environment. There was a real chance, he went on, that international cooperation between countries could help leave the world's environment to future generations in as good a state as it was when inherited by the current generation.[88]

For New Labour the war to preserve the environment, in the construction of housing as elsewhere, deserves the same messianic approach as the war against terrorism. It means that the rules can be changed so long as it serves the Green cause. At Ashford, 30,000 homes will be built by 2033, many by Taylor Woodrow; but to mollify the Campaign to Protect Rural England (CPRE), they will be packed in at a density of 30–40 a hectare.[89]

Increasing density means suburbs with fewer gardens and nowhere to park. Planners used to call that overcrowding; New Labour calls it sustainable. To mass-produce inexpensive homes with factory methods and site them, cheaply and with generous gardens, throughout the 88 per cent of Britain's surface area that is not urbanised – that is out of the question. Indeed it is even out of the question if Britain leaves untouched its national parks, historic buildings and their grounds, its areas of beautiful or unique countryside, and its best, most versatile farmland. The ordinary remainder is also untouchable. As Prescott put it of his building programme:

This is homes [sic] in sustainable communities to meet the shortfall in supply. Not suburban sprawl, not soulless estates, not dormitory towns.[90]

The thing that is celebrated instead of building anew is what a *Times* leader enthusiastically greeted as 'home renovations', done to high densities, on existing brownfield sites.[91]

In 1997, New Labour gave its assent to guidance on UK regional planning that provided too few homes. Then it clamped down on greenfield development through PPG3. Altogether, it has played a major part in creating the housing shortfall that now dogs Britain's South East.[92] It has shown in lurid practice how the naturalistic perspective must mean the stunting of construction and architecture.

In 2000, Friends of the Earth believed that New Labour had 'stopped short of taking the radical measures we need to promote brownfield housing'. It accused it of drowning Green policy in a well-meaning 'sea of carrots' that failed to apply Value Added Tax to greenfield development and only encouraged councils to produce strategies for dealing with empty homes, rather than making such actions mandatory.[93] But by 2003, New Labour's sustainable communities were so full of sticks, rather than carrots, that FoE, though still somewhat sceptical, could announce:

If he can pull this off, Prescott will have deserved his place in political history.[94]

In authoritarian style, the naturalistic perspective insists on a brownfield, high-density, mixed-use, car-free urbanism based on labour-intensive, on-site methods of construction. It wants to avoid being resource-intensive, and so it wants to re-use the old rather than build anew. And in this unvarying credo about the proper course of urban development, it joins forces with the therapeutic perspective.

The naturalistic perspective holds that proximity, more than anything else, guarantees political merit. Buildings that are put together cheek-by-jowl are thought not only to encourage social cohesion. If they are part of the 60 per cent of new British houses that Prescott has decreed must be built on brownfield sites, they are also deemed ecologically correct. *The smaller, the more compact, the more tightly squeezed constructions are, the more the naturalistic perspective favours them.*

Anything else is held to be neither sustainable, nor a community.

2.8 Built-up brownfields forever

We live in the era of what is called the *triple bottom line*. For governments, policymakers and corporations alike, there are the old economic KPIs, such as GDP or profitability. Then there are the two newer kinds of KPI, or indicators of what the business world terms *corporate social responsibility – CSR*. The second part of the bottom line is not about economic well-being, but social indices: health, literacy, propensity to crime, and other factors that surround a nation's population or a firm's employees. And the third part relates to environmental indicators. Altogether, the idea is that all three kinds of factors can be mutually reinforcing. Every senior person in business protests that profit is perfectly compatible with taking care of society and the environment.

In 1999, the august World Bank defined Environmental Performance Indicators,[95] and UK construction adopted them in 2001.[96] But through both architecture and rhetoric, it has been the Richard Rogers Partnership,[97] and Lord Rogers of Riverside himself, that has done most to popularise the naturalistic perspective in construction.

The purpose of architecture, Rogers proclaimed in his influential book of 1997, *Cities for a small planet*, is to safeguard the survival of *homo sapiens*. With that mixture of facile economics and doom-mongering that characterises Green thought, Rogers wrote:

The exact long-term results of current levels of consumption are not yet clear, but given the scientific uncertainty concerning their precise effects my contention is that we must apply the "precautionary principle" and ensure that

action be taken to safeguard the survival of our species on this planet.[98]

By invoking the Precautionary Principle, Rogers certainly anticipated the growth of EU regulation around that dubious premise (see Box 5). Yet in his concern for human survival, he also identified extra population with extra pollution, as well as hastened decay of the soil:

The world-wide growth of urban populations and grossly inefficient patterns of living are accelerating the rate of increase of pollution and erosion.[99]

For Rogers, safeguarding the species meant another imperative for architecture, too. *Architecture should prevent people*

In the City, the Lloyds of London building, designed by Richard Rogers and opened in 1986, was famous for its modish, inside-out aesthetics

moving around by car. In a revealing passage, Rogers wrote, of Shanghai:

Sadly, the city intends to follow the old Western model and motorise its existing 7 million cyclists.[100]

As it happens, since *Small planet* was published, the United Nations Population Division has revised its forecasts for population downward. In 2000 it estimated that world population in 2050 would amount to 9.3 billion; by 2002, its forecast for 2050 was 8.9 billion.[101] As it happens, too, Shanghai's cyclists need the help of the car if the city is ever to achieve its goal of overtaking Hong Kong as a centre of Chinese wealth. Yet despite his Malthusian and misanthropic world view, it was to Rogers that Prescott first turned when the need to accommodate four million more households in England became obvious.

Rogers duly set up what was known as the Urban Task Force. The UTF's aim was to identify causes of urban decline and to establish a vision for British cities, founded on the principles of design excellence, social well being and environmental responsibility – cities for people. Through the UTF, Rogers became the most publicly known figure within New Labour's construction elite, and Advocate General of sustainable architecture.

Rogers presented himself as a grass-roots radical, challenging the established cultures of architects, planners, and developers alike. For him urban revitalisation has to be:

owned by the people who it will affect most . . . We therefore need to promote consultation alongside more proactive mechanisms for active participation, linking people with the decision making processes which affect their own neighbourhood.[102]

Speaking more personally, he has said:

I am a natural fighter . . . So the battle's on – it's always on . . . I'd be happy to go on at this for a life-time. Just go on fighting.[103]

But as the cultural critic Geoffrey Nowell-Smith suggests in a cogent critique of this kind of management-speak, employees cannot really 'own' a company's targets.[104] Equally, people cannot really 'own' urban revitalisation. The language is inclusive and full of empowerment and fight; but the policy on the

Pitsea in Essex was built spontaneously on redundant farmland in the 1930s, so great was Britain's shortage of housing then. It still suggests that people want space to live in, even when a large building is beyond their means. Yet at the time they were built, the architectural establishment decried places like Pitsea as 'bungaloid growth'. All UK planning legislation since 1947 has outlawed development like Pitsea; but that should not rule out attempts to reinvent and mass produce spacious bungalows for today

environment is elitist and is authoritarian in effect.

Rogers knows that he shares responsibility for the future with others. But, should the great British public dare ask for spacious bungalows, gardens and car parking, the consultation that he promotes will need to be done again until the public sees sense. The reason is simple. Rogers delights in being a planning advisor to the Mayor of London because, he says, Ken Livingstone has adopted his target that *all development of land should be done at high density exclusively on brownfield sites.*[105]

In 2000, with Anne Power, professor of social policy at the London School of Economics, Rogers followed up on *Cities for a small planet* with *Cities for a small country*. There the two authors proposed something very radical.

They proposed that *all new housing in Britain must be built to London densities.* Not just greenfield sites in the process of development, but also suburbs of 20–25 dwellings a hectare and rural housing at lower figures should, as a matter of routine, be further built up. *Nothing short of a doubling of density would be required if two all-important goals were to be reached – the protection of the countryside, and the reduction of demands on greenfield sites to zero* (see Table 7).

With commuter towns and villages outside London, the naturalistic perspective in construction is, *chez* Rogers and Power, a matter of 'using small spaces, adding extra storeys, changing uses and densification'.[107] But in this schema, the relaxed, spread-out character of such towns and villages is lost. The task of construction becomes what is known as *infill* – infill in ways that planners would previously have blocked as *speculative overdevelopment*. It is the same story with Britain's suburbs which, despite all the obstacles, Rogers and Power are intent on making more built-up:

Suburbs offer many of the spare corners, underused buildings and patches of land that cry out for small additions. Renovating, man-

TABLE 7 Changing the location of new UK housing from greenfield to brownfield development: the gospel according to Rogers and Power

Capacity of land needed to handle new houses, per cent	Brownfield	Greenfield
Based on 25 houses per hectare, as typical in 1999	55	45
Increasing density by a fifth, to 30 houses per hectare	65	35
Increasing density by a half, to 37.5 houses per hectare	82	18
Doubling densities to 50 dwellings per hectare – equivalent to generalising 1999 London densities	100	0

Source: Richard Rogers and Anne Power, *Cities for a small country*[106]

Not everyone can afford to live in the Barbican, London, and architects, by themselves, can do little about that. But for all its exclusive price-bracket and for all the difficulty one has navigating it, the Barbican shows one thing. Successful urban development can rise high – far higher than the levels dictated by official efforts to save Britain's ravaged farmlands through higher urban densities

aging, diversifying and densifying suburbs so that they become neighbourhood centres in their own right and more integrated into urban patterns should be part of the renewal strategy of towns and cities.[108]

Early Learning
What the Urban Summit can teach John

John Prescott, as seen by *Building* magazine

In his speech to Prescott's Urban Summit of 2002, Rogers went further. He insisted that, through using small infill sites of less than an acre, converting and extending existing buildings, using roof spaces and exploiting air rights, Britain could produce 35–50 per cent more homes than expected without encroaching on greenfield land. In many places, there was enough brownfield land to allow 100 per cent of housing to be built on previously developed land, 'if incentives and regulations were in place and properly enforced'.[109]

Why did Rogers favour built-up brownfields forever? His answer was this:

People are voting with their feet, and leaving the cities in favour of the country. And the sad reality is that the poor are left behind . . . The challenge is to reverse the drift of people from city to country. A clear and simple target! . . . [At present] we consume what little countryside we have.[110]

Lord Rogers was very radical, but very out of date. People are no longer simply migrating out of cities. The countryside is no longer simply being used up by cities.

Lord Richard Rogers. Photo by Dan Stevens

Lord Richard Rogers

Born in Florence in 1933, Rogers attended the Architectural Association School in London before graduating from Yale University. He and his first wife, Sue, worked in a partnership with Norman and Wendy Foster as Team 4 from 1963. In 1970 Rogers established a partnership with the Italian architect Renzo Piano. After the completion of the Pompidou Center in Paris, he formed the Richard Rogers Partnership. Today, the Partnership employs 46 qualified architects who, generating a fee income of more than £11 million, make it the eighth largest practice in the UK.[111]

Rogers himself is also, among those worldwide living architects that are held in respect by British architects, the eighth most admired.[112] His very considerable skills in engineering and aesthetics have been demonstrated over many projects.

Box 5 **THE PRECAUTIONARY PRINCIPLE AS EU POLICY**

After a gestation in West German environmental law in the 1970s, the Precautionary Principle was first applied mainly to the protection of the world's oceans, beginning with the North Sea. But in 1992 the Principle came of age – it was adopted in the European Community's Treaty of Maastricht. Meanwhile, a United Nations Conference on the Environment and Development held in Rio adopted Principle 15: that, to protect the environment, a precautionary approach should be 'widely applied'. Where there were threats of serious or irreversible damage to the environment, the conference agreed, lack of full scientific certainty should not be used as a reason for postponing cost-effective measures to prevent environmental degradation.[113]

Wide application of the Principle quickly saw its use extend to every aspect of the environment, as well as to matters involving human health. In 1999, the European Environmental Agency (EEA) invoked the Precautionary Principle to permit a lower level of proof of harm to be used in policymaking whenever the consequences of waiting for higher levels of proof might be very costly and/or irreversible.[114] By that same year, however, the Principle had gained enough purchase in society for two scientists to want to draw attention to its consequences in a letter to *Nature*. They defined it as follows:

> When an activity raises threats of serious or irreversible harm to human health or the environment, precautionary measures that prevent the possibility of harm shall be taken even if the causal link between the activity and the possible harm has not been proven or the causal link is weak and the harm is unlikely to occur.[115]

The merit of this definition is that it brings out how the Precautionary Principle is a direct and conscious challenge to causality.

Sir Colin Berry, one of Britain's most eminent scientists, believes as much. Professor of morbid anatomy and histopathology, Queen Mary, University of London, Berry points out first that in the low-frequency events to which the Precautionary Principle applies, risk is bound to be very difficult to measure. The standard technique of looking for changes in rates of those events that have been documented following an intervention is therefore rarely successful. But in Berry's view the Precautionary Principle compounds this problem by deliberately eschewing the scientific method as a way of dealing with data. He writes that it:

> arbitrarily changes the weight that is given to evidence from different investigations on an uncertain basis, and represents the antithesis of science. If you decide that some data are more important than others, you are deciding that you know what is best and, in the framework we are discussing, that the outcome of particular interventions will be beneficial.[116]

The Precautionary Principle arbitrarily assumes that everything must be reorganised around even a minimal or non-existent risk since, in the case of that risk occurring, a worst-case scenario would still produce a horrendous impact. In an emotional calculus, a fractional scientific possibility is multiplied by the infinite human consequences of 'serious or irreversible harm'. That harm is also seen as eventually inevitable, unless a massive amount of society's resources is diverted into its prevention.

In 2000 the Precautionary Principle gained the backing of the European Commission, which pronounced:

> Decision-makers faced with an unacceptable risk, scientific uncertainty and public concerns have a duty to find answers.[117]

Here the odds against making a decision in favour of innovation were lengthened still further. Even a very modest risk could be multiplied not just by putative impact, but also by the amount of scientific uncertainty surrounding that risk, as well as the extent of popular or media prejudice about it. As if dimly aware of where its precautionary approach led, the Commission murmured:

> Action taken under the head of the precautionary principle must in certain cases include a clause reversing the burden of proof and placing it on the producer, manufacturer or importer, but such an obligation cannot be systematically entertained as a general principle.[118]

EU sanctions under the Precautionary Principle, then, will not be systematic. Firms can expect no consistency from Brussels, but must rather live in fear of investigation 'in certain cases'. Yet in practice, yielding to those public concerns it holds so dear, the Commission today insists that the burden of environmental proof be imposed on producers of everything from chemicals to GM crops.

In 2002 the EEA took the Precautionary Principle a stage further still. On top of risk, impact, uncertainty and popular fear, the EEA insists that mankind should be humble about its *ignorance* – about what has elsewhere been described as 'unknown unknowns'.[119]

> No matter how sophisticated knowledge is, it will always be subject to some degree of ignorance. To be alert to—and humble about—the potential gaps in those bodies of knowledge that are included in our decision making is fundamental. Surprise is inevitable . . .
>
> A key element in a precautionary approach to regulation involves a greater willingness to acknowledge the possibility of surprise. This does not mean resorting to blanket opposition to innovation. But acknowledging the inevitable limits of knowledge leads to greater humility about the status of the available science, requiring greater care and deliberation in making the ensuing decisions.[120]

It is a beguiling argument. We are forever ignorant so, without being guilty of blanket opposition to innovation, our care should be infinite; our deliberations, unending.

Of course, life is indeed full of the possibility of nasty surprises. As Henry Petroski, now professor of civil engineering and professor of history at Duke University, North Carolina, wrote two decades ago, to engineer is to be human and fallible. Yet good design minimizes the effects of surprises by anticipating troublesome details and by overdesigning for an extra measure of safety.[121]

To minimise the effects of surprises by designing in an extra measure of safety is one thing. But in construction it has long been no surprise that the force of gravity works each and every day. Moreover as Petroski points out, mechanical and structural failure in design:

is central to understanding engineering, for engineering design has as its first and foremost objective the obviation of failure. Thus the colossal disasters that do occur are ultimately failures of design, but the lessons learned from those disasters can do more to advance engineering knowledge than all the successful machines and structures in the world. Indeed, failures appear to be inevitable in the wake of prolonged success, which encourages lower margins of safety. Failures in turn lead to greater safety margins and, hence, new periods of success.[122]

We can never find all the evidence that our precautions are complete. Yet if each morning we start out mindful of all that we do not know, and are suitably humble as a consequence, we would never build another building.

Once a group leader at America's prestigious Argonne National Laboratory,[123] Henry Petroski writes the engineering column for *American Scientist* magazine

2.9 Out-of-date theories of urbanisation

Britons are not simply voting with their feet against cities and for the countryside, as Rogers laments. Like other old industrial centres – Detroit, Duisberg, Liège – a regional British city such as Liverpool is still in the process of losing people. But in Britain as elsewhere in the West, there is no overwhelming occupation of the countryside going on. For every urban exodus there is an urban influx: a Slough, a Swindon, a Wycombe. If anything, British and Western cities are swinging toward population gain.

At the London School of Economics, professor of economic geography Paul Cheshire notes that a progressive and incremental decentralisation of urban inhabitants 'ceased to be a necessary fact of urban areas in mature economies sometime during the late 1970s or early 1980s', and that this trend was recognised by some at the moment of its emergence.[124] Thus London, like Paris, has been gaining people (see Table 8).

Cheshire rightly takes the view that the contrary trend – what he calls the *recentralisation* of cities – is far from inevitable. And since the reliability of Britain's 2001 Census has been cast into some doubt, it is hard to work out exactly which cities, apart from London, have gained population in the 1990s and since the millennium. In an unpublished study, Tony Champion, professor of population geography at Newcastle university, has estimated that Birmingham, Leeds, Liverpool, Manchester, Newcastle and Sheffield lost a total of just over a quarter of a million people, or 7.1 per cent of their combined populations, between 1981 and 2001. Yet while Liverpool and Manchester lost 15 per cent of their populations, Leeds lost only 0.3 per cent – not bad, over 20 years.[125] And what, anyway, was it about Leeds that made people there choose to vote hardly at all with their feet? Was it an architectural renaissance based on the Rogers principle of high urban density? Or could it possibly have been something to do with the scale of investment in Leeds made by employers, or the city's orientation to the modern service sector?

What is certain is that, in its degree of urbanisation, Britain has long led all the other countries that account for three-quarters of the world's city dwellers. Moreover the United Nations projects that *the population of the UK, like that of much of the West, will go on concentrating in urban areas at least until 2030.* Britain and the West are still participants in exactly that worldwide growth in *urban* populations that Rogers invoked in the opening pages of *Cities for a small planet* (see Table 9).

There has been an influx of people into 'boomburbs' in America.[126] In Tokyo, people are moving back to the centre of the city 20 years after being expelled by skyrocketing property prices.[127] And as the table shows, Europe's continued rural exodus has gone hand in hand with a move into cities.

The trend in the EU reflects neither just the belated urbanisation of a hitherto largely agricultural southern Europe nor just immigration from Eastern Europe and elsewhere. Simply put, there are now fewer industrial jobs to lose from cities and more jobs to gain in financial services, IT, media, the cultural industries and – not least – government.

The city is here to stay. It is harder for people to get by outside cities, which remain the major centres for corporate and government employers. Meanwhile, the poor are hardly in a position to move out of cities. A scarcity of posts in small towns and rural environments reinforces cities in their traditional role as locations for jobs.

Rogers does see Britain's cities as 'congested'.[128] But in the past two decades, only impressionism could have allowed him to conclude that the movement of people in Britain is all toward the wasting of the countryside.

Impressions, however, are what the naturalistic perspective is based on.

TABLE 8 Population of London and Paris in millions, 1971–1997

	1971	1981	1991	1997
London				
1971 boundaries	9.78	9.05	8.76	9.04
1991 boundaries			12.52	13.21
Paris				
1971 boundaries	9.50	10.07	10.62	10.91
1991 boundaries			11.42	11.80

Source: Paul Cheshire, 'The fall and rise of cities', *LSE Magazine*, Winter 2002

TABLE 9 Countries accounting for 75 per cent of the world's urban population in 1950, 2000 and 2030, ordered by level of urbanisation

Rank	Country	Per cent national population in cities, 1950	Country	Per cent national population in cities, 2000	Country	Per cent national population in cities, 2030
1	UK	84.2	UK	89.5	Saudi Arabia	92.6
2	Netherlands	82.7	Argentina	88.2	UK	92.4
3	Germany	71.9	Germany	87.5	Argentina	91.9
4	Argentina	65.3	Republic of Korea	81.9	Venezuela	91.8
5	USA	64.2	Brazil	81.2	Germany	91.7
6	France	56.2	Japan	78.8	Republic of Korea	90.5
7	Italy	54.3	Spain	77.6	Brazil	90.5
8	Spain	51.9	USA	77.2	Colombia	84.9
9	Japan	50.3	France	75.4	Japan	84.8
10	Russian Federation	44.7	Colombia	75.0	USA	84.5
11	Mexico	42.7	Mexico	74.4	France	82.2
12	Ukraine	39.2	Russian Federation	72.9	Mexico	81.9
13	Poland	38.7	Ukraine	67.9	Iran	78.8
14	Brazil	36.5	Italy	66.9	Russian Federation	77.9
15	India	17.3	Turkey	65.8	Turkey	77.0
16	China	12.5	Iran	64.0	Italy	76.1
17	Indonesia	12.4	Philippines	58.6	Philippines	75.1
18			South Africa	56.9	Indonesia	63.7
19			Nigeria	44.1	Nigeria	63.6
20			Egypt	42.7	China	59.5
21			Indonesia	41.0	Tanzania	55.4
22			China	35.8	Egypt	54.4
23			Pakistan	33.1	Congo	49.1
24			India	27.7	Pakistan	48.9
25			Bangladesh	25.0	Bangladesh	44.3
26					Vietnam	41.3
27					India	40.9
28					Ethiopia	31.0

Source: United Nations Population Division, *World urbanisation prospects: the 2001 revision*, Table 35, p 62; www.un.org/esa/population/publications/wup2001/WUP2001_CH4.pdf

2.10 Out-of-date theories of Britain's green and pleasant land

Is the West really consuming the little countryside that remains?

In Britain, the CPRE certainly thinks so.[129] To its mind, greedy property developers merely buy land to desecrate and sell on. But since 1998, even official thinking on construction has formally accepted that land prices have a major impact on the final cost of a new building, sometimes representing up to half its total cost.[130] As Colin Cole, executive director of Westbury Homes, has noted of builders:

Our business is to buy land and get it through the planning process.[131]

For all their faults, Britain's builders earnestly try to do the latter as much as the former.

Rogers would like an end to all this. His Urban Task Force wanted to attract people back into Britain's towns and cities and put an end to greenfield construction. Yet there is no business to be had in urban flats that owner-occupiers don't want. Britain does indeed face what Paul Cheshire and Stephen Sheppard, professor of economics at Williams College, Massachussetts, call 'the long term strangulation of land supply for housing that we have lived with since the 1947 Town and Country Planning Act'.[132] All that has happened is that today's burgeoning

naturalistic perspective has tightened the strangulation still further. As a result, new UK land supply is choked off on environmental grounds, brownfield land soars in price, and urban flats built on developed land become unaffordable. A housing crisis is needlessly created in the pursuit of sustainability.

That crisis will turn out to be a disaster for Britain's construction sector. One architectural writer has described the future thus:

Private capital can – and will – tell Prescott where to get off. It will disinvest from an industry that, on the one hand, he desperately needs but, on the other, he is threatening with bankruptcy . . . If Prescott pushes housebuilders too far, their shareholders have an option that is not open to those in many other industries . . . and the Chancellor can't afford to fund a 200,000-a-year new-build programme to fill the gap.[133]

Rather than encourage private housebuilding, British planning policy could easily bring about wholesale disinvestment from the construction sector, which is already chronically underfunded and inefficient. Private investors are also unlikely to tie their capital up in off-site manufacturing unless they are allowed to build manufactured homes people want. That means large homes, with gardens and parking – to the annoyance of Prescott and Rogers.

It is just as much a myth that Britain's land is being used up as it is that there is still an unstoppable exodus from Britain's cities. Four-fifths of England's population lives in towns bigger than 10,000 people. These conurbations cover seven per cent of England's landmass.[134] Agriculture, by contrast, takes up 76 per cent.[135]

Rogers ignores all this. For him:

We should build up and intensify cities such as Birmingham before we expand Milton Keynes. Even in the north-east of England, awash with abandoned housing and land, we are still building the majority of new housing on Greenfield land.[136]

A QUALITY GATED DEVELOPMENT OF THREE BEDROOMED HOMES FINISHED TO A HIGH SPECIFICATION

Yet because British agriculture is efficient, much more land could be retired from farming than is being used up by new construction. Instead UK farmland is being diversified, used less productively, or turned over to wildlife and wilderness – anything, in fact, to prevent it from being enjoyed by people who would like to live there.

In their desire to protect the virtue of virgin soil from consumption at the hands of the human race, environmentalists do not just commit an arithmetical error about the land. Their distaste for that consumption recalls the religious tones of EF Schumacher, economist at Britain's post-war National Coal Board. In his seminal *Small is Beautiful*, first published in 1973, Schumacher argued that land and the creatures upon it:

are, of course, factors of production, that is to say, means-to-ends, but this is their secondary, not their primary nature. Before everything else, they are ends-in-themselves, and it is therefore rationally justifiable to say, as a statement of fact, that they are in a certain sense sacred.[137]

But for architects and builders, at least, land cannot be sacred: land is there as a means to an end. In saving the countryside from the city and the city from itself, the naturalistic perspective can only counsel restraint in architecture.

In the 18th century, French political economists known as the Physiocrats thought that the ability of a farm worker to create more produce than he or she could eat was a special gift, or productive power, of nature. Today many British Greens, and not a few Francophile British celebrity chefs, still think of land as the source of much of society's real wealth. But if the Physiocrats' successors, in the French Revolution, turned to tax the profitable estates of the landowners, today's environmentalist policymakers appear to want to impose a tax – or artificially high house prices, at least – on mortgage-holders and tenants in British cities.

The French Physiocrats could be forgiven, on historical grounds, for believing that agriculture was the source of value. Later on, some of the US's most respected writers – Cooper, Thoreau, Melville, Faulkner, Frost, Hemingway – wrote about retreats from a fast-developing American society into an idealised, pastoral landscape. In 1844, for example, Nathaniel Hawthorne's *Sleepy Hollow* was pierced by 'the long shriek, harsh, above all other harshness' of the locomotive.[138] But what has changed since then? Today once more, Rogers wants to stop the arrival of the machine in the garden:

Greenfield land . . . may be the easy option, but it is not cheap! The Treasury will have to subsidise roads and other services for these developments, to the tune of £40,000 per home . . . And this figure does not take into account the cost to our environment.[139]

In the naturalistic perspective, those who occupy land are eating up the sacred. They must be taxed accordingly, through high house prices. Moreover roads, which still take up little more than one per cent of the land area of the UK, together with the dispersal of construction around the countryside, are always and forever a Bad Thing, no matter how much urban house prices are inflated as a consequence.

Time to turn redundant farmland from tractors to excavators

2.11 Key worker housing and the microflat mentality

In London in early 2002, a shop window at Selfridges, Oxford Street, and the *Daily Mail* Ideal Home Show, Earls Court, gave the ultimate twist to small-is-beautiful thinking in construction. At Selfridges, the architectural firm Piercy Conner displayed its Microflat.[140] At Earls Court, the Ideal Home showed two kinds of pre-fabricated homes built by LiveIn Quarters Ltd – homes that Ken Livingstone declared 'the ideal answer to getting young professionals into London and keeping them'.[141]

Even before John Prescott's adventure into 4,000 prefabricated homes, Livingstone had insisted that no less than 50 per cent of all new developments in the capital should be reserved for housing for key workers. So a *Guardian* leader, at the same time as the Ideal Home Show, could not contain its fulsome support for this idea and pleaded for 'serious government commitment' to it.[142] Yet neither the dimensions of the Microflat nor those of the Earls Court units were at all ideal.

Piercy Conner's unit was designed for transport by container lorry. It centres on a purpose-built utility pod containing a shower room and kitchen. The usable area was 32 square metres – about a 33 per cent reduction on the size of an average one-bedroom flat in London. The 'mini suite' on show at Earls Court was even smaller: it was a 26 square metres studio flat. As for the 'home suite' that was also displayed, it was a 33 square metres studio with a double bed that folded up during the day to reveal a separate sofa. As Hugh Pearman noted in *The Sunday Times*, there is a limit to being able to design ever-smaller living spaces. That limit is reached when the resultant buildings become uninhabitable and overcrowded tenements – at a time that land values are still continuing to rise.[143]

Intended for a scheme with 200 to 300 units, Piercy Conner's design was ingenious. But beyond one architectural firm's design, in the broader world of politics, the overall logic of the micro-flat mentality is more hypocritical than ingenious. For the logic runs as follows:

1 Protect the land.
2 Stand by and watch as urban property prices soar enough to make decent accommodation unaffordable to millions.
3 Turn an artificially-created necessity into a trendy, moral, sustainable virtue: present the stylish microflat as the responsible way of life for ecologically minded, city-loving young professionals.

However in truth *it would be disastrous if construction were to be reborn as a branch of*

Prototype of a prefabricated home, once displayed in London's Ideal Home

Interior of the prototype

manufacturing, only for it to be put in the service of increasing housing densities . . . by making houses smaller.

Between the late 1940s and the early 1970s, when prefabricated housing was last deployed on any scale, government in Britain had to intervene to establish minimum space standards to prevent overcrowding and site cramming. Better known as the Parker Morris report, after the chairman of the Ministry of Housing and Local Government subcommittee that wrote it, the 1961 report *Homes for Today and Tomorrow* recommended minimum space standards that families should expect of new housing, sensibly basing these on studies of occupancy and furniture layout.[144] Before it was abandoned by a Conservative administration in the early 1980s, the Parker Morris approach was gradually applied to all new housing in the private and public sectors (see Box 6). But the basic space rations it laid down 40 years ago are now too much for New Labour. The plans of Livingstone and Prescott for key worker housing contain no minimum space standards.

If politicians really wanted to bring in a useful regulation, it would be for internal and external space minima for different kinds of housing – with minima no smaller than those specified by Parker Morris in 1961. Indeed, *ample space standards are exactly what are needed to underpin the economies that off-site manufactured housing can gain over site-based backwardness. It is only once prefabrication caters not just for single-person households, but for families of all types, that it will reach the production volumes that will be necessary to fulfil its full potential.*

Low-paid workers find it difficult to afford housing, whether or not they are officially designated as key to the economy. Indeed, almost everyone in Britain finds the cost of adequately-sized, conveniently located and high quality housing a burden relieved only by the low interest rates. But through their key worker schemes, Livingstone and Prescott have committed to building a stock of *cottages, as tiny as can be, which*

are tied to the jobs of those who live in them and for which the landlord is the state.

Some part of British officialdom will decide who is a key worker. Then, to stay in one's house, one must remain a key worker – and presumably a well-behaved one, too. Finally, the chances are that those occupying the tiny key worker flats of tomorrow will pay rent to . . . the government. Admitting that Whitehall departments sit on large quantities of unused land in London, Prescott told a Westminster conference on regeneration:

When I am told there is enough surplus public land in London for 80,000 homes, I wonder why we are selling off prime sites to the highest bidder when we could be using it for key worker housing.[145]

The naturalistic perspective in construction, then, has overtones that are strongly statist when they are not feudal. For what the key worker, like everyone else, wants today is not a grace-and-favour microflat but plenty of quality living space, financed through adequate wages. As Anthony Browne, environmental correspondent of the London *Times*, has argued:

The solution is not to extend state control of the property market, but to free up wages in the public sector: let hospitals and schools pay what is necessary.[146]

Prefabrication cannot mean miniaturisation and the hairshirt philosophy. It must mean the practical manufacture of hundreds of thousands of quality family houses and their provision with gardens – not just a media kerfuffle over a few hundred single-person-household designer flats. Nor need prefabrication mean homogeneity. When Barratt or Bovis make the same old standard homes, they neither prefabricate them, nor allow customers to specify variations around varied household talents and needs.

Arguments *for* industrial solutions to housing have been made many times before. Today it is also necessary to argue *against* people who would sacrifice space standards for architectural design. People need and are right to expect large, high-quality accommodation in adequate supply. Yet talented designers today seem willing to deliver quality only by abandoning production in quantity and in size. It is bad enough that housing shortages inflate the price of living space. It is worse still when architects respond with the naturalistic prejudice that urban space is so precious that people should have less of it.

In fact, behind the official endorsement of microflats is a subterranean love-in with Japan; not with its real, contemporary and worthwhile advances in prefabrication, but rather with a Westernised image of a pre-Hiroshima Japan. In the London *Guardian*, Adam Mornement rightly noted that, just as one in two Finns lives in houses built in factories and bolted together on site, so Japan's fashionable urban elite regards prefabricated buildings as some of the most desirable on the market.[147] In their fine report *Japanese lessons on customer-focused housebuilding*, James Barlow and Ritsuko Ozaki properly celebrate how Japanese prefabrication means choice and value:

The major housebuilders invest very substantial resources in maintaining and updating their housing products. Typically a Japanese housebuilder offers up to 300 standard designs in terms of elevations and floor plans, which can then be adapted by the customer. Although the accent is on offering a wide variety of choice in order to allow designs to be tailored, this mainly relates to floor plans and internal specification. Exteriors can be varied depending on the size and shape of the plot, along with customer needs and building and planning regulations. However exterior choices are more restricted than interior choices, so that economies of scale can be achieved in relation to cladding treatments, door and window sizes and designs, and balcony types.[148]

But the lessons popularisers of the microflat take from Japan are rarely about their desirability or the ease with which they can be customised. They are, instead, about how it's cool to follow the Japanese and live small.

Kisho Kurokawa's Nakagin Capsule Tower of 1970 in Tokyo is often cited as setting the right, miniaturised example. It is often claimed that the intention was to make residents return from the suburbs to central Tokyo,[149] or that Kurokawa was about packing people into flexible 'capsule' dwellings and offices.[150] But these colaims are entirely wrong. Kurokawa's idea was to provide Japanese employees with capsules in town *in addition* to their homes in the country. Far from a *cut* in Japanese living space, Kurokawa had in mind its *expansion*:

When residential areas in Tokyo started to shift to the suburbs, [the Kurokawa initiative] was intended to be one tactical move to restore housing units to the central part of the city and to provide those who commute to the centre from the outlying area with studios, an extra bedroom or a place for social activities.[151]

Kurokawa had no concept of urban key workers deserving just family-unfriendly accommodation. Initially, at least, his capsules were a symptom of increasing prosperity; by contrast, new-century British microflats have come into the world as *morally charged emergency housing*.

Today, reading their prejudices backwards through history, environmentally minded architects try to remould Kurokawa's old aesthetic-political movement of Metabolism into an early stab at sustainable architecture.[152] Architectural historian Charles Jencks perceives 'a thread of development, a coherent line' in Kurokawa's career.[153] But Kurokawa's early work was machine-age architecture based on geometric mega-structural forms and massive infrastructure, not the sustainable sort. Kurokawa more accurately recognises that his pursuit of what he calls a 'philosophy of symbiosis' has been elaborated through the rise and transformation of environmentalism, particularly since the mid 1980s.[154] Those who would have all Japan's explorations in design as a historic search for a kind of quietist balance between man and nature tell us a lot about themselves. They select for admiration not so much Japan's dynamic building technologies but rather those leanings that are consonant with low consumption and slow economic growth.

As late as 1996, the literary critic Ian Littlewood properly noted that, when confronted with Japan, the West was apt to find a sense of masculine superiority with which to counter the country's artistic concerns – concerns which pointed, Littlewood felt, 'to a strain of effeminacy'.[155] But by the new millennium, the rhetoric of minimalism had conquered important segments of the Western middle class. From the success of Muji's less-is-more furnishings through to John Pawson's flats for the international super-rich and his 2004 store for Marks & Spencer in Gateshead, Japan's feminine, unencumbered, downscaled, spiritual way of living in very small accommodation has received widespread support.

Ken Livingstone does not invoke Japan. But his *Draft London plan*, published in summary in June 2002, certainly betrays that precious attitude to space that the West takes to define much of Japanese psychology. An important concluding section of the *Plan* insists:

Design is an essential tool for achieving more intense use of space . . .[156]

Could this concept of design's urban role be a mite reductionist, by chance?

Kisho Kurokawa

A microflat bathroom – except there is no bath

A microflat interior

Box 6 THE SPACE STANDARDS THAT HAVE BEEN ABANDONED

The 1961 Parker Morris report was followed by three debates in Parliament in 1962 and 1963 around concern over declining housebuilding standards. In 1965 national Building Regulations replaced 19th century bye-laws;[157] but the standards drawn up were for construction quality, not for space. By 1967, in an effort to avert regulation, housebuilders began voluntarily to build to elements of the Parker Morris recommendations. In the same year all new towns were built to Parker Morris standards, and by 1969 they were mandatory for all council housebuilding.

Parker Morris standards were never generous (see Table 10). After them, slight modifications to the standards were made for the elderly, and government circulars laid down standards for single people. There was also provision for the storage, outside homes, for prams and fuel – things that might not be necessary now, even though the basic allowance made for storage would still be valuable. However eventually Parker Morris requirements proved impossible for private sector developers and public sector landlords to finance and, in 1980, the Conservatives' Local Government, Planning and Land Act abolished them for local authority housing. Private sector space standards remained voluntary and, though the space in some private houses was exceptionally roomy, in general it began very soon to fall below the former minimum.

TABLE 10 Mandatory space standards in UK public sector housing, 1969 to 1980

Number of people	7	6	5	4	3	2	1
Net floor area of habitable accommodation m²							
3 storey house	112.0	98.0	98.0				
3 storey house and garage	112.0	98.0	98.0				
2 storey centre terrace	108.0	92.5	85.0	74.5			
End terrace	108.0	92.5	82.0	72.0			
Semi-detached	108.0	92.5	82.0	72.0			
1 storey centre terrace		84.0	75.5	67.0	57.0	44.5	30.0
Maisonette	108.0	92.5	82.0	72.0			
Flat		86.5	79.0	70.0	57.0	44.5	30.0
Internal storage space m²							
Houses	6.5	4.5	4.5	4.5	4.0	4.0	3.0
Flats and maisonettes	3.5	3.5	3.5	3.5	3.0	3.0	2.5

Source: Patricia Tutt and David Adler, *New Metric Handbook*[158]

A 21st century microflat between 26 m² and 33 m² is similar in size or smaller than a one-person Parker Morris flat measuring 30 m² of living space plus 2.5 m² of storage, totalling 32.5 m². Contemporary microflats are smaller than a one-storey centre terrace, one-person Parker Morris house with 30 m² of living space plus 3 m² of storage, to a total of 33 m². However, these housing types are not really comparable at all on the question of space per person.

Today's microflats are intended to be occupied by two people, which by common sense and Parker Morris standards is definitely overcrowding. By even the 1960s minimal Parker Morris reckoning, a two-person flat should be 44.5 m² of living space plus 3 m² of storage, or a total of 47.5 m². Even when they are clever, then, current designs for microflats abandon Parker Morris space standards.

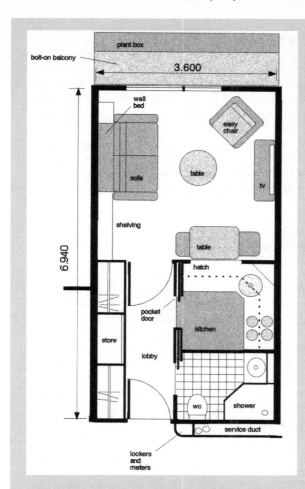

A 26 m² microflat, designed by John Prewer

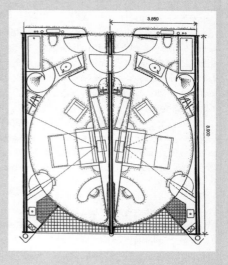

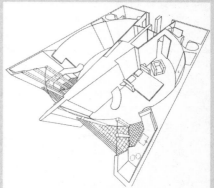

Pairs of two-person microflats, designed by John Prewer

Box 7 BUCKMINSTER FULLER'S LEGACY IN THE UK

In Martin Pawley's view the inventor, engineer, scientist, philosopher and poet Richard Buckminster Fuller (1895–1983) bequeathed more guidance to posterity than any of the great pioneers of modern architecture'.[159] Fuller taught Norman Foster. He pioneered prefabricated houses in the USA before William Levitt took them up in earnest. And when a handful of British prefab manufacturers debated their progress at the Building Research Establishment in May 2003, Fuller's ghost was present.[160]

The proceedings – titled OFFSITE 03 – testified to real advances in prefabrication. Yet Britain's off-site techniques, primarily pursued by the social housing sector, have yet to deliver value. Production runs and the general scale of investment are, as yet, too small. Three examples show this.

First, the Peabody Trust's Murray Grove scheme in Hackney, east London, relies on an expensive proto-type – complete with balconies – using Yorkon units, designed by architects Cartwright Pickard[161] and engineers Whitby Bird.[162] With the same engineers, and Alford Hall Monaghan Morris as architects, this approach was again adopted by the Peabody Trust at Raines Dairy, Stoke Newington, north London.[163] At Raines Dairy, prototypes used a modified portacabin system – not a researched and designed housing system for off-site manufacture. Nevertheless these large and well-planned flats went over budget and past the deadline for completion.[164]

Second, the Amphion Consortium of 20 housing associations has run into even bigger difficulties, despite being dubbed 'the government's great hope for boosting housing supply'.[165] Founded in 1999 to provide factory-built housing in support of the Egan agenda, Amphion sought to 'change the way in which we procure housing in Britain'. It continued its manifesto thus:

> To address housing need across Britain for years to come, Amphion is developing plans for a number of construction projects. Each will be integrated using internet based communications and knowledgebase systems developed by the Consortium to take advantage of the project management gains available from state of the art "E-commerce" technology.[166]

Amphion had 150 homes at the design stage and 70 on-site or awaiting delivery when, in April 2003, two of its off-site manufacturing suppliers went into receivership. Work on Amphion homes was merely delayed as the consortium looked for other suppliers; but the incident rattled many. What needs to be remembered, once again, is that the numbers of homes being discussed was hopelessly low.

Third, Ralph Erskine's design of off-site prefabrications for the first phase of the Greenwich Millennium Village, east London, was too wilful to be standardised as construction. The subsequent phase is being fabricated adjacent to the site. In an interesting experiment, temporary fabrication works have been built nearby – to allow a more versatile approach in which adjustments and defects are reputedly made with ease.[167] This is not necessarily a retreat from genuine off-site manufacturing; but the architecture would have to be systematised for it to afford improved productivity.

UK off-site manufacturing, then, is nascent; it has its faults, but need not be dire in the future. Indeed one of the exhibitors at OFFSITE 03, Spaceover Ltd, boasts an architect who has spent a whole career in the pursuit of off-site manufactured housing. In John Prewer, too, Spaceover has a design director who corresponded with and learnt from Fuller.

For this book, Prewer kindly formulated a work-in-progress checklist of principles necessary to optimise modular housing manufacture and construction operations. Apart from reducing costs, his advice is to cut, and sometimes to eliminate, the 30 items in Table 11.

The overall aim, Prewer insists, is to cut costs and improve quality.

It would be a fascinating exercise to develop this checklist beyond manufacturing, delivery and erection, and into servicing, operation maintenance, removal, recovery and disposal. Even more interesting is the fact that savings under one category result in, or require, savings in another. For instance, the reduction in weight makes possible savings both in transport and in the elimination of craneage. Conversely, craneage of concrete construction is costly.

Item 13, to cut 'building volume by optimising use of space before and during building occupation, is debatable. Rather, both the plan area and the height of accommodation should be maximised – something that should be possible given all the savings in time, equipment, energy and materials that industrial production is likely to afford.

Item 16, which calls for minimising energy use, is fair enough; but pursuit of this goal can become a religious obsession (see Chapter 5).

Still: *sans* Item 13, this checklist forms an excellent starting-point for progress in construction.

TABLE 11 John Prewer's list of 30 things to cut, so as to speed the construction of modular buildings

1	Building weight, so as to reduce foundation loadings
2	The need for soil excavation or movement
3	The use of cement-based products
4	Waste in labour, energy and materials
5	Transport costs; instead, containerise where appropriate
6	Operations that require skilled construction labour, such as plasterers
7	The time required for completion of each operation in the factory and on site
8	The use of components that perform only one function
9	The need for inputs from construction professionals and contractors
10	The potential for component corrosion or decay
11	The need for materials or component packaging
12	The need for scaffolding
13	Building volume – by optimising use of space before and during building occupation
14	The number of joints – by reducing the number of components
15	Construction tolerances – by improving component accuracy and surface finish
16	The use of energy, both embodied and over the lifetime of occupation
17	Fire risks – by using incombustible or low-flammability components and active controls
18	The use of wet materials and finishes at the factory and on site
19	The use of non-standard sized materials and components, such as boards
20	The need for production assembly jigs
21	The use of materials which are not labelled or electronically tagged for simple identification when they are stored, installed, serviced, replaced or recycled
22	The need to access interiors of finished modules or pods before building handover stage – for reasons of safety, security and hygiene
23	Service duct access from the interiors of finished modules
24	The wind resistance of modules in transit from the factory, and when grouped to form the completed building
25	Permanent components or features in modular buildings which are only needed during transport or handling operations and which could be reused, such as lifting eyes, spreader frames, or bracing in transit or erection
26	The need for cranes at the factory and on site
27	Noisy or hazardous factory production or site operations
28	The need for complex or expensive production facilities and equipment, such as moving assembly lines
29	The need for welding in the factory or on site
30	The need to apply finishes to materials or components once they form part of the module, so that work is carried out *on to* panels, not *into* enclosed modules

John Prewer

Born in 1939, John Prewer trained at Portsmouth Polytechnic School of Architecture from 1961 to 1967, and was awarded his diploma for his studies of both modular and volumetric methods of prefabricating student accommodation. For more than three decades, he has worked on modular and volumetric hostels, restaurants, flats, houses, student quarters and hotels, as well as on modular staircases, lift shaft systems, volumetric plant rooms and sanitary pods for offices.

Co-author of *Modular Construction using Light Steel Framing: An Architect's Guide*,[168] Prewer designed and was responsible for the manufacture of the first block of modular steel flats in Britain – one operated for the elderly in Hackney by the Greater London Council. He is currently working with the Steel Construction Institute on further guidance for lightweight volumetric housing.[169]

For a year, Prewer was design consultant to LiveIn Quarters Ltd; in that role he was responsible for the design of two modules shown by the company at the 2002 *Daily Mail* Ideal Home Exhibition. In May 2002 he joined Spaceover Ltd as design director. There, he has taken charge of developing several advanced systems in materials and components to meet the particular requirements of large-scale production methods. He has also designed a range of modular and volumetric homes.

Continues p77

Modular extensions finished in brick

Modular courtyard housing concepts developed as 'Pallisade'

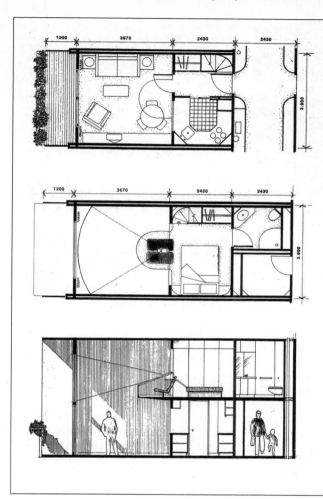

Prewer's interesting 'microloft' idea. It exploits the fact that road haulage of large items can be done without a police escort if it stays within width restrictions that are narrow, but restrictions on height that can exceed a single storey. Vehicle length exceeds building module requirements in most domestic-scale developments.

2.12 Longevity and the Royal Institute of British Architects

Toward the end of the energy crisis of 1973 to 1974, the architect Alex Gordon pioneered a naturalistic approach that, over 30 years, has become the official wisdom of Britain's august professional association, the Royal Institute of British Architects. Addressing members of the RIBA, Gordon wrote:

If we accept that new buildings are necessary, the energy that they consume in use will, no doubt, play a bigger part in influencing their form than it has in the past. But ecological thinking is not limited to energy alone: it should involve being aware of the far reaching implications of our current actions. Our predecessors left us with a stock of buildings which, in general, have been pretty adaptable and have served us for a long time. One suspects, however, that many new buildings will not be suitable for the functions for which they were designed for more than a comparatively short time.[170]

To allow for the future adaptations of buildings that he felt likely to happen over the long term, and to minimise the energy hassles around these adaptations, Gordon proposed a basic kind of modular

The Royal Institute of British Architects, 66 Portland Place, London

rules to follow in constructing a new generation of *buildings that would be so adaptable, they would all last for between 50 and 100 years*. Such a timespan, it anticipated, was likely to be the 'period of climate and resource stress' facing the world.[171] The *Rough Guide* made the following recommendations:

- Avoid functional specificity for flexibility
- Maximise access to daylight and natural ventilation through the form
- Design for simplicity for periodic upgrading
- Design for long life as a wiser investment
- Maximise access to renewable energy through correct orientation and location
- Ensure replaceability so as to make simple the upgrading of components or systems.

Now who could be against 'Design for long life as a wiser investment'? In a post-Enron world, nobody wants to be accused of making a fast buck, of thinking only for the moment. But what today begins as a vague moral injunction to environmentally-minded architects will quickly become a lot less vague, should the injunction gain legal force.

Architects already have a legal duty of care to avoid injuring people, damaging their property, or causing financial loss due to inadequate expert advice. In Britain's law of the tort of negligence, liability arises from acts or omissions breaching that duty of care. However, the inherent flexibility of the law of tort means that the duty of care can always be extended by British case law. Since few seem to disagree in principle with the idea of an *environmental* duty of care, it can only be a matter of time before the long-term claims of inanimate nature animate the immediate behaviour of architects.

The RIBA can hardly hope to assert a moral claim without the legal profession taking it at its word. Indeed, what kind of

prefabrication. A durable infrastructure of building frames, assembled on-site, should be periodically re-equipped with loosely fitting and non-structural modular panels and equally modular sub-assemblies and components.

It was Gordon's achievement to help shift architectural discussion toward *longevity*. Today it is commonplace to specify a lengthy design life for the materials, components and assemblies that make up buildings. Today, too, feeble architects often pander to excessive demands for longevity – demands that are made in the name of sustainability.

At one level Gordon was right to call for efforts to be made to minimise the energy buildings use. And even today, in areas of high urban density, designed-in scope for future long-term change may be more easily installed through Gordonesque modular prefabrications, which bear no load, than it would through more ambitious volumetric prefabrications – whole buildings, designed to plug into supporting structure-and-services networks on site, to bear loads, and to be periodically upgraded and recycled off-site.

All this can be accepted. But it is a travesty of Gordon's ideas to make longevity *the* fundamental principle of modern architecture. Yet that is what the RIBA wants to do.

Published in 2001, the RIBA's *Rough Guide to Sustainability* offered a list of

prestige would the architectural profession enjoy if the law did not take seriously pretensions to an environmental duty of care on the part of their leading institute? It is not as if architects have always enjoyed a sensibly restricted liability.

The RIBA has much to say about sustainability in general and longevity in particular. But the more it says, the more it threatens its own longevity.

2.13 Therapeutic and naturalistic perspectives meet in proximity

Too many people who should know better believe that backwardness on building sites needs measuring through clipboards and spreadsheets. That speaks of a sensibility to risk, rather than a commitment to innovation. If the main slogans for building remain emollient – 'respect for people', team-based learning, microflats for key workers – then construction will not move forward. Posed as philosophical breakthroughs for the sector, the therapeutic and naturalistic perspectives condemn construction to postpone technological advance and instead secure everyone against social and environmental disorder.

Construction is backward, in part, because the numerical, therapeutic and naturalistic concerns that now dominate the sector reinforce backwardness. But there is more. Even as social and environmental engineering, the twin programmes of therapy and naturalism will not work.

For Richard Rogers, 'brownfield first' is the policy for the location of construction.[172] By failing to obey this injunction, he says, we 'destroy any chance of a vital, compact, urban society that is eco-sustainable, based on the principles of easy human contact, the encouragement of walking, cycling and the use of public transport'.[173] He continues:

I am calling on Government to give our urban fabric the attention it must have if we are to stem the continuing flow from our congested and degraded cities . . . But I am also calling on People in every street and every neighbourhood to reclaim and stand up for their cities – to demand a better deal from their elected representatives.[174]

So, from his spacious Chelsea flat, Rogers tells us that a vital society is a compact one in which the behaviourist principles of 'easy human contact' – transport without the car – are paramount. Moreover people must 'stand up' for compact cities. But is packing people into dense urban areas the way both to re-create community and to save the planet? Does physical proximity in 21st century human habitation and patterns of work make for social and environmental success?

To answer these questions, it is worth reviewing their historical antecedents (see Box 8). But there can be no doubt that *attributing magical properties to proximity, a relatively recent phenomenon, is something done not just to cities but also to the workplace.*

In a highly influential book, the MIT researcher Thomas Allen found, as early as 1977, that the physical distances between different engineers in R&D laboratories had an enormously negative impact on communications there.[175] However it was Harvard professor and international strategy consultant Michael Porter, and his *The competitive advantage of nations* (1990), who did most to assert the relevance of geography, location and space to international political economy.[176]

For four years, Porter and more than 30 researchers studied the performance of 10 industrial countries over the period 1971 to 1985. He identified 'murderous' competition for export markets by *clusters of local firms in the same industry* as a major boost to GDP growth. For him steelmakers in Brescia, like biotechnology firms in Boston, prospered from proximity.

In fact Porter's doctrine of proximity was irrational. That is because it was strongly linked to the idea that the most

Box 8 ORIGINS OF TODAY'S DOGMA IN FAVOUR OF HIGH-DENSITY, MIXED-USE URBAN SPACE

Concern about city space has grown strongest at times when impetuous economic advance has turned sour.

The central text of British 'garden city' urban planning, Ebenezer Howard's *To-morrow: the peaceful path to real reform* (1898), had stong premonitions about the future of Victorian cities. It called for conurbations ideally limited to 30,000 people. These centres would form just one part of a rail-linked polycentric 'social city' complete with allotments, homes for waifs and 'inebriates', and farms for epileptics.

In America, Lewis Mumford's *The culture of cities* (1938) was equally a product of rocky times.[177] Depressed about the way in which US president Roosevelt's early enthusiasm for regional development plans had turned into a New Deal nightmare of high-rise housing, Mumford invoked the spectre of Megalopolis, in which space was saturated not by Athenian culture, but by Roman or Alexandrian power.

In the feeble French economy of the 1970s, leftists discovered the spatiality of capitalism. Henri Lefebvre asserted that command over space was essential to social power and control in his *La production de l'espace* (1974).[178] In 1975 the French postmodernist, Michel Foucault, reached much the same conclusions in his famous *Discipline and punish: The Birth of the Prison*.[179] Soon, too, his friend Pierre Bourdieu began, at first through a study of traditional Algerian society, a long soliloquy on the power of 'spatial structures'.[180]

While French postmodernists made the running with their conceptions of space as power, Anglo-Saxon radicals eventually took up the theme. The British architect Christoper Alexander determined that timeless patterns of building conferred community on society.[181] David Harvey wrote of *The urbanisation of capital*.[182] Edward Soja, professor of architecture and urban planning at the University of California at Los Angeles, followed that with *Postmodern geographies: the reassertion of space in critical social theory*.[183] The British sociologist Anthony Giddens, a top adviser to Tony Blair, likewise attacked conventional social theory for its neglect of the nation state's delimiting of space, of the state's surveillance of space, and of the general significance of the artificially created environment.[184] By 1999, Paul Krugman tried to systematise urban and regional economics with pages of mathematical equations. Invoking the 'extremalities' first discovered by the British economist Alfred Marshall (1842–1924), he procllaimed *The spaetial economy*.[185]

For Harvey, the urban process had 'more universal meaning than the specific analysis of any particular mode of production'. Urban form 'did not necessarily adapt to every dictate of that mode of production'.[186] Yet Harvey protested too much. To compare geography with economics and decide that the former is more important – this is to choose between the incommensurable. But generally, over the years, liberal thinking has tended to do just that.

The example of America in the 1960s shows how it is all too easy to see, in the organisation of city space, the source of much wider troubles. John F Kennedy came to power in 1961 to halt the incipient decline of America and of the Cold War system; and it is exactly at this time that we find concern about urban space growing. Thus, in a classic study published in 1961, Jean Gottman revived debate on Megalopolis in his analysis of the Boston-Washington corridor.[187] In the same year Mumford published a major attack on suburbanisation.[188] Then Morton Gabriel White and Lucia White condemned urbanisation as cancerous.[189] It began to be argued that the rise of *information* had turned the 'urban place' into the 'nonplace urban realm'.[190] By 1966 the economist and housing expert Louis Winnick called for welfare to be sent to people, not places, so great had the crisis of the American inner city become.[191] Soon European intellectuals, long fixated by Los Angeles, once more portrayed it as a nightmare. Britain's Peter Reyner Banham, for instance, accused the freeways of destroying 'any community spirit that may once have existed'.[192]

So much for different episodes of Western *concern* about urban space. What about *solutions* ? It was Jane Jacobs' book, *The death and life of great American cities*, published in 1961, that established the precedent for today's feeling that proximity can cure social ills.

Jacobs anticipated New Labour's 'Design against Crime' initiatives by more than 40 years. The first part of her book opened with a chapter titled: 'The uses of sidewalks: safety'. Then, overturning the conventional wisdom of her times, Jacobs slammed the US government's *zoning of space* for its excesses. Instead, living on Hudson Street in Greenwich Village, she called for *density and mixed-use areas*: 'a most intricate and close-grained diversity of uses that give each other constant mutual support'. For Jacobs, inability to design and provide safe streets and a civilised public life made efforts to overcome residential segregation that much more difficult.[193]

Unlike today's urban experts, however, Jacobs refused to believe that urban planning alone could overcome the problems of race, the slum and the ghetto. She ridiculed urban renewal theory as an idealist pseudoscience akin to bloodletting as medicine. In a key passage, she summed up:

> The effective breaking down of residential discrimination outside a slum, and the less dramatic self-diversification within an unslumming slum, proceed concurrently. If America has now, in the case of Negroes, reached an effective halt to this process and in general entered a stage of arrested development – a thought I find highly improbable and quite intolerable – then it may be that Negro slums cannot effectively unslum in the fashion demonstrated by slums formed by other ethnic populations and population mixtures. In this case, the damage to our cities might be the least of our worries; unslumming is a by-product of other kinds of vigor and other forms of economic and social change.[194]

Jacobs fully deserved the critical but favourable reception she later received from Marshall Berman, one of America's most brilliant cultural critics on the left.[195] Later still, she deserved the same reaction from Berman's equally acute compatriot, the writer David Brooks.[196] For she, at least, looked forward to 'other forms of economic and social change'.

How little her space-obsessed vulgarisers do that today!

Jane Jacobs

Michael Porter

important knowledge around in the world today is *tacit* knowledge – the sort that one picks up by working in the same local city or local office as someone else, rather than by reading a learned paper.

Tacit knowledge sounds fine. In their discussions of economic success, not just Porter but also AnnaLee Saxenian, now professor of city and regional planning at the University of California at Berkeley, have stressed the role of information exchange through institutions that are within easy reach – 'universities, business associations, and local governments, as well as the many less formal hobbyist clubs, professional societies and other forums that create and sustain regular patterns of social interaction in a region'.[197] But as Copenhagen Business School associate professor Anders Bordum has pointed out, managers need not justify actions and decisions if they claim that their authority is based on tacit or informal knowledge. That, he argues, is a fundamental threat to rationality.[198]

Since 1995, when Nonaka and Takeuchi published their seminal

Knowledge-creating company, the performance of the Japanese economy has tended to suggest that tacit knowledge may be an obstacle to innovation, not an aid to it.[199] Perhaps that is one of the reasons why, at the Science Policy Research Unit at Sussex university, the late Keith Pavitt, a doyen of international science and technology policy, had serious reservations about Porterian proximity:

The emphasis on tacit knowledge, and the example of either the Italian regions or Silicon Valley, has led to an excessive emphasis on regional clusters of knowledge creation and exploitation as the basis for analysis and public policy. Whilst these are clearly important, they are only part of the story. Evidence suggests that the output of basic research provides for more than the local region: in other words, Stanford University provides for more than Silicon Valley; MIT for more than Route 128; and Cambridge University for more than its Science Park. Reciprocally, successful clusters do not simply emerge from locating activities close together, and they have many important knowledge linkages outside them.[200]

For British municipal authorities and urban theorists alike, however, the impact of Porter's ideas has been immense. In the 1990s, Glasgow was keen to apply Porter's clarion call for industrial clusters: Glasgow Development Agency saw itself as an enabler of, and portfolio designer to, a Porterian cluster of inward investors in IT and related industries, together with their local suppliers. Britain's most eminent urban geographer, Peter Hall, also converted to Porter, believing that cities had a future because they encouraged the exchange of 'special privileged information', whether 'in gyms, at dinner parties, or at the pub'.[201]

By the time of the millennium, the *New Yorker* journalist Malcom Gladwell could argue that proximity was the key to innovation in the workplace as much as in the city. He wrote:

Innovation – the heart of the knowledge economy – is fundamentally social. Ideas arise as much out of casual conversations as they do out of formal meetings . . . Innovation comes from the interaction of people at a comfortable distance from one another.[202]

In hinting at the immense social significance of our old friend, the office coffee machine, Gladwell was not alone in the idea that casual communication, aided by proximity, was the key to workplace innovation.[203] Soon, in a naturalistic interpretation of Jane Jacobs's views on cities, the IT writer Steven Johnson concluded that, as small-scale activities of ants could build 'swarm logic', so local interactions between urban inhabitants were the key to a thriving neighbourhood.[204] But in offices as in cities, these ideas are highly dubious. British housing policy, after all, has moved from the construction of council homes to the doctrine that the job of local authorities is to act upon complaints made about anti-social neighbours. That alone should confirm that the fate of people living cheek-by-jowl depends on the people and the content, not just the facility, of their communications.

Innovation depends on the development of new knowledge, not just its intimate transfer. Equally, the close clustering of firms around Porter's endlessly-cited Silicon Valley has not been enough to reverse the IT slump there. So why should Rogers and Prescott believe that compactness leads to vitality and social cohesion? In the past compactness has played a role in urban riots. *Neither distance nor proximity can guarantee social progress – because progress, like innovation, is a social, not a spatial issue.*

While Gladwell was quick to add that people should be 'neither too close nor too far' from one another, environmentalists had decided that closeness was the better bet. Always repeating the brilliant insight that there is only one Earth, they popularised the feeling that there are intrinsic, immutable *limits* about cities. Cities, they insisted, had grown out of kilter with the *carrying capacity* of the land they occupied: the needs they had to

Herbert Girardet

serve outweighed their productive capacity. So they had to cut consumption, growth and transport journeys. For Herbert Girardet, a Green writer, the problem with cities was that they ingested and excreted valuable resources over longer and longer distances. Cities, having 'metabolisms' and being *parasites*, had to 'stop being centres of human self-advancement', and instead come to terms with nature.[205] Cities could grow in this perspective, but only *sustainably*. People could be allowed to move around but mobility, too, had to be sustainable.[206]

Curl up into a ball. Stay at home. Ensure that all waste is treated as close to source as possible: Ken Livingstone's *Draft London plan* says that what it calls 'the proximity principle' demands nothing less.[207] Minimise the overall footprint of each building – not only physically but also in terms of the space occupied by the people coming to it (see Box 9). Remember, too, that Porter has told the DTI that proximity brings untold benefits. The good thing about proximity, Porter avers, is that it allows firms to use:

- local goods and services suppliers – to assure low stock levels and low downtimes, and thus high productivity; and

- local educational, research, venture capital and legal institutions – to foster the capacity for innovation, productivity growth and new business formation.[208]

All this localism is wonderful – but whatever happened to the world's growing division of labour?

Whether they are formulated at the Greater London Assembly or at Porter's beloved Boston, localist politics can only cramp the future of construction. They also make no sense. As Londoners know, squeezing people together in a city can put enormous pressure on infrastructure – especially when, in today's Green age, the large-scale investments in infrastructure that are necessary are regarded with distaste. As a result, proximity alone will not curb urban demand for water, energy and other resources.

The level of urban demand for utilities and resources is established not just by the consumer needs of city dwellers but also by the needs of the firms and other bodies engaged in wealth creation. And it is wealth creation, both inside and outside the city which, at the same time, meets the wants of urban citizens.

Compact urban space has little to do with all this. For all the ambition and technological ingenuity of the individual buildings Rogers has designed, his grand social vision is not grand at all. His spatial solutions to all social problems amount to a form of determinism that is as petty as it is myopic.

2.14 The Holy Trinity in architecture

'Is this project sustainable?', Martin Pawley has observed, is:

a request not for an honest answer but for a series of passwords. Sustainability becomes another way of deciding who is in charge.[209]

The naturalistic perspective in construction, like the trend toward measuring everything in terms of therapeutic effect, is no mere passing fad. Measurement, therapy and naturalism are the new Holy Trinity in architecture. They are the creations of a new, self-appointed priesthood.

With the *therapeutic* perspective, mainstream opinion now believes that design can and should be about social engineering. The prestigious Work Foundation, which is dedicated to modernising work in Britain, believes as much. In 2002 its chief executive, Will Hutton, declared that, after Enron, the sustainability of businesses depended on trust, which in turn related to who sat where in a workplace, and to whether its layout encouraged interactivity, serendipity and cultural change. He asked whether workplaces made people 'feel good'.[210]

The Institute of Public Policy Research, New Labour's favourite think-tank, has been on a similar mission. Along with the Commission for Architecture and the Built Environment, The Design Council and the *Architects' Journal*, the IPPR in 2003 declared architects Baumann Lyons, ABK (Ahrends, Burton and Koralek) and DSDHA winners of a competition to reinvent Bradford, Stockport and North Hertfordshire town halls – as part of an effort to go about 'deepening and strengthening democracy . . . creating a new democratic space individual to the site and the character of the area'.[211]

For employees and citizens alike, therapeutic forms of construction are the order of the day. As the sports columnist Simon Kuper has written of the attitude of New Labour officials toward the construction of Olympic facilities in London in time for 2012:

They pretend the Olympics would achieve public-policy goals: it would "regenerate" poor neighbourhoods and inspire kids to play sport instead of just watch it. "Crucially", writes [Ken] Livingstone, "The Olympics will also bring much-needed new facilities: an Olympic-size swimming pool in a city that has just two Olympic pools to Berlin's 19, and a warm-up track that would be turned over to community use." (continues p91)

Box 9 **A BUILDING'S FOOTPRINT: TELEWORKING AND THE 'GHERKIN'**

Norman Foster's 40-storey, 180 metres high headquarters for the Zurich re-insurers Swiss Re, popularly described as the 'Gherkin', is an engineering triumph for structural engineers Arup and services engineers Hilson Moran, and a big success for Skanska, its builders. It is the first tall workplace to be put up in the City of London in more than 30 years; but it is also probably the last whose footprint will be considered to be a purely local affair.

In the naturalistic perspective, a workplace's footprint extends well beyond the area covered by its foundations and the immediate landscape around it. On the negative side of the Green ledger book must be counted not only the energy and materials used, over long distances, to power and build any major employer's offices, nor even the waste and emissions put out by those offices over long distances, but also the horrid human beings who insist on demanding transport, over long distances, to and from their place of work.

A monument to the importance business and society now attach to risk, the architecture of the 30 St Mary Axe building has been widely discussed, and the design critic

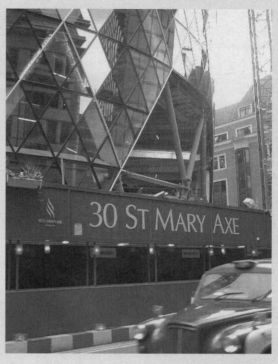

Photo by Jonathan Schwinge

Stephen Bayley has argued that its form is basically 'ludic'.[212] But there is another, more subterranean and much less exuberant discussion that the building prompts. Everything about Swiss Re, and Foster's design for it, is framed in the language of sustainability.[213] Parking spaces are not provided; instead, there are only the fashionable places to tether pushbikes and have a shower after cycling in to work. But once the naturalistic perspective is taken this far, it cannot be long before, in a misanthropic style that affects to be modern, it defines the footprint of a building in a way that calls into the question the very concept of a skyscraper.

As the architect Brian Love has pointed out, since the mid 1990s British planning regulations have upheld mixed-use development as a means of minimising popular demand for transport. More important still, any substantial development today – and this includes major leisure destinations, not just major workplaces – must, if its application for planning permission is to be at all successful, have an appraisal of its impact on local transport.

In principle this is all very sensible. But in today's naturalistic planning framework, new large office blocks are disgraced because of the commuting patterns and demand for transport they bring with them. Instead of believing that transport infrastructure must be developed to support new jobs, deterministic thinking insists that, just as building roads automatically leads to traffic jams, so building skyscrapers automatically leads to an unacceptable load on transport systems. As a result, *telework*, potentially a noble enterprise, is pressed into service as a means of evading society's responsibility for transport.

At the hoped for density of one worker for every 10 square metres, the 46,450 square metres of floor-space in the Swiss Re building will house getting on for 5000 workers. Many of these people will be coming in to work from places such as Essex. If, as official policy insists, the use of transport in Britain must at all times be reduced as far as possible, the Swiss Re example suggests that, in the future at least, no major employer can just idly erect a building and expect workers to come into it from miles around.

Swiss Re's Zurich operations already get workers to work from home as much as possible. Now British radicals and planners have taken up the argument. The public enquiry that, in 2002, allowed Kohn Pederson Fox's 37-floor, 183 metre Heron Tower, Bishopsgate to go ahead, debated the amount of telework that would surround the new building. But in fact, all the major developments planned for the City of London

Photo by Jonathan Schwinge

– the 34-storey, 144 metre Churchill Securities building at 168 Fenchurch St; Great Portland Estates' building at 80–81/104 Bishopsgate; the Sellar Property Group's 66-storey, 310 metre London Bridge Tower – are likely to face interrogation along these lines. Of the large office block, it will be asked: does it have in place transport and telecommunications policies that broadly encourage workers not to work there, if at all possible?

Workplace architecture, in short, is all too often apprehended as an inherently damaging exercise. Public and road transport infrastructure is not to be improved around new buildings so much as ridiculed for the cost that proper investment in it would involve. In a subtle twist, IT is invoked not as a means of making people working in buildings more efficient, but as a means of bringing their movements to a halt.

It is all irrational, anyway. As Love points out, teleworkers tend to come into offices and go 'hot desking' – jointly using the same workstations. Indeed one of the major economic arguments for telework is that it allows a more efficient use of office space.

The result is that if the Swiss Re building can support not 5000 normal, daily-commute workers but, say, 15,000 occasional commuters, then the demand for work-related transport by these 15,000 teleworkers may well exceed that of the original 5000. Nor is this really a surprise. IT systems tend to complement and reinforce transport use, not substitute for it.

As Love points out, planners argue that if public transport *does* exist in high-density urban areas, to site offices there is a better idea than putting them in rural areas, where road use will be necessary to get workers to and from work. But can we really agree with planners that the City of London, for example, is well served by existing public transport? So anxious is the Corporation of London to back skyscrapers full of financial services in the City against similar skyscrapers in Frankfurt, it refuses to permit the conversion of low-ceilinged, 19th century buildings into the residential uses Lord Rogers would dearly like to see. But that does not mean that the City should be allowed to get away with building tall, teleworking wide . . . and failing to build any new transport systems.

Photo by Jonathan Schwinge

Photos by Jonathan Schwinge

Photos by Jonathan Schwinge

Photos by Jonathan Schwinge

Ken Livingstone is so worried about the supposed commercial threat from Frankfurt, and so keen on high urban densities, that he and others have inaugurated a new regime of approving skyscrapers in the City. As Ian Playford, a property analyst, summed up in August 2002:

Following recent reviews of London's potential growth over the next 25 years and the continuing need to supply high quality and competitive space, a number of skyscraper development schemes have come to the fore. The London office market expects a number of these to be developed over the next five years and sentiment is generally that Central London is on the verge of a beneficial change in office composition. In particular, excitement surrounds the size of these buildings, their location and primarily their architecture.

Verdicts like that in favour of the Heron tower, Playford continued, had given property developers interested in City of London skyscrapers 'confidence that authorities are now more "pro-towers".'[214]

Livingstone has long made his gung-ho posture in favour of skyscraper City offices well known. Less well known is that, in 2001, he announced that he wanted his own staff in the Greater London Authority to engage in telework so as to set an example to London employers.[215] Nor is it well known that businesses in the Far East have proved similarly committed to telework. In a number of parts of Asia, firms and educators implemented telework, remote education and remote medicine spontaneously, in their reaction to the media-inflated Severe Acute Respiratory Syndrome (SARS) epidemic.

Altogether, reputedly dangerous and ever-widening 'footprints', alongside remote, IT-assisted ways of working round them, have begun to dominate the official and the corporate imagination. Yet once a large building is viewed as a source of peril, whether environmental or medical, there can be no limits to its malign influence. As a result, the naturalistic perspective distorts the course of architecture and IT. The focus of these two disciplines used to be on work, productivity, wealth creation and confidence in the future.

Now, the focus is on the fact that The End of the World is Nigh.

(continued from p84) But all these are just excuses. If you want to regenerate a poor neighbourhood, regenerate it. If you want an Olympic pool and warm-up track, build them. You could build pools and tracks all across London and it would still be cheaper than hosting the Olympics.[216]

From Wembley Stadium to the Olympic Games, architecture has been pressed into the service of New Labour communitarianism. The speed and expeditiousness of construction are not on this agenda. Instead, as discussion on the Olympics has revealed, *angst* is the order of the day (see Box 10).

In Britain it was the Sustainable Construction Task Group, chaired by the contractor Sir Martin Laing, which really consolidated the *naturalistic* perspective in construction through the publication of *Reputation, Risk and Reward* in 2001.[217]

That report was produced and promoted by the Centre for Sustainable Construction at the Building Research Establishment. More significantly, it was written by the environmentalist Rachel Crossley, then working for Friends Ivory & Sime.

Before it merged in 2002 with Royal & Sun Alliance Investments to manage about £60 billion as ISIS Asset Management PLC,[218] Friends Ivory & Sime had a £1.7 billion property portfolio and an interest in 300 buildings around the UK. It described itself as Europe's leading socially responsible investment manager; so it easily anticipated Sir John Egan's theme of *reputation*. In blunt style, Crossley summed up:

Ignore sustainability and your reputation is on the line.[219]

Box 10 OLYMPIC LONDON: FENCE-SITTING AS AN ENDURANCE EVENT
Vicky Richardson

In May 2003, after focus groups, hefty reports, and more than a year of deliberations, the Cabinet decided to back a bid by London for the 2012 Olympic Games. To its eyes, funding a £17 million bid for a £2.375 billion London Games was permissible, because £1.5 billion would be found from the National Lottery (complete with a new Olympic game), about £0.5 billion from a £20 increase in council taxes in London, and £250 million from the Mayor's office. But if sitting on the fence were an Olympic endurance event, Tessa Jowell, the responsible minister at the Department of Culture, Media and Sport (DCMS), would surely take gold.

The first estimate of the cost of hosting the Games appeared in a 120-page report commissioned in 2002 by a stakeholder group consisting of the Government, the British Olympic Association and the Mayor. The report, by the engineering firm Arup, estimated that, if the benefits to tourism were taken into account, a net deficit of £145 million would emerge in the worst case, with a net profit of £85 million in the best.[220]

Shortly after publishing a short summary of Arup's report, the DCMS released its own forecast of costs. That added more than £4 billion to the Arup estimate. Apart from presenting the figures in 2012 prices (unlike the Arup figures, which were in 2002 prices), the forecast costs were grossly inflated. For example, the DCMS put in £150 million to cover the entirely spurious risk of not being able to attract the right quality of administrative staff.

The release of the DCMS figures was closely followed by an ICM opinion poll which asked the public questions such as, 'do you agree the money would be better spent on school sport in communities?' and 'do you agree the majority of investment will be in London and therefore there will be no gain for the rest of the UK?' It was surprising that ICM did not also ask: 'would you like to see a repeat of the Millennium Dome saga?'

Preparing and hosting the Olympic Games is obviously a big job. There would not just be a new stadium required, but an Olympic village and housing for at least 25,000 athletes, officials and coaches; facilities for 20,000 members of the media and 63,000 operational personnel; and additional transport across London for 125,000 spectators a day. Nevertheless, the 2000 Olympics gave Sydney the most hi-tech stadium in the world, and, with 118,078 seats, the largest in Olympic history. Until then, Sydney was known for just one piece of architecture – the Opera House. Through the Olympics, it gained many others including a major railway station, a velodrome, an aquatic centre and a vast leisure park.

It is sad that the development of essential housing, transport and sports facilities in east London should rely on a one-off event such as the Olympics. But the building boom that would follow a successful Olympic bid could have a fantastic effect. The imperative to build large and fast could force British clients, architects and engineers out of conservative habits.

Yet the climate of caution and penny-pinching that surrounds the bid does not bode well. Already ministers have tried to play down the building and development work that will be necessary, suggesting that one option for a stadium is to build a temporary, dismountable one (another tent, perhaps?). Even before the bid was agreed, Transport Secretary Alasdair Darling ruled out the construction of Crossrail, running from Paddington to Liverpool Street, before 2013 at the earliest – too late for the Olympics.[221]

This minimal approach is pathetic. Yet it is official policy. The Government gives 'wholehearted' support to the Olympic bid.[222] When Tony Blair phoned Jacques Rogge about the Cabinet's decision, he told the President of the International Olympics committee that the Government would now back London's bid 'to the hilt'.[223] Having failed for months on end to feel enthusiastic about a bid, the Government now protests too much.

The lacklustre language says it all. Even when gambling will pay for most of it, to build on an Olympic scale seems too risky an enterprise to command much more than wholehearted, to-the-hilt backing. Too much social and environmental upheaval – that is the Government's continuing worry about the architecture that a successful Olympic bid would entail.

Foster's headquarters building for Swiss Re shows that the construction industry can still achieve real advances – even if backwardness remains the general rule

Here the purpose of architecture was redefined. *Architecture was now the pursuit of corporate social responsibility with regard to the environment: a responsibility that has to be upheld . . . for sound market reasons.* Because those reasons are to do with markets, this type of CSR, like the therapeutic type, must be measured. No wonder that the DTI, whose formal job it is to raise the productivity of British wealth creation, is also interested in cutting annual water consumption per DTI employee from 13 cubic litres to 7.7 cubic litres – partly by the use of water-less urinals.[224]

In fact, no sooner had Rachel Crossley instructed *builders* to be Green than she did the same to *facilities managers* – those in charge of the operation, maintenance and repair of workplaces (see Box 11). Giving an investor's perspective on Green buildings and the bottom line, Crossley spoke of what Friends Ivory & Sime had done about part of its own property portfolio: that at 100 Wood Street, London. Part of her company's achievement there was to ensure, along with everyone else since, that the office equipment it bought was thoroughly Green. But perhaps most significantly,

Box 11 FACILITIES MANAGEMENT AND THE COMING OF THE GREEN OFFICE

With the spread of more complex office facilities, salaried posts in Facilities Management (FM) at large firms and government organisations have multiplied. For more than a decade, however, managers at many large firms have also been persuaded that they themselves are unlikely to be the most professional people to handle tasks as varied as leaky plumbing or the provision of office furniture. Specialist, independent suppliers of 'contracted out' FM services have grown rapidly. The British Institute of Facilities Management says that 55 per cent of the overall potential market for FM in the UK, which is worth between £100 billion and £200 billion, is contracted out.[225] This sub-sector enjoyed a compound annual rate of growth of 15 per cent during the 1990s.[226] It includes within it the following firms as shown in Table 12. For them, the UK market breaks down as shown in Table 13.

TABLE 12   Leading independent FM suppliers active in the UK[227], by Turnover, £bn

Firm	Turnover, £ billion
Compass	3.16
Amec	1.40
Rentokil Initial	1.07
Sodexho	1.04
Amey	0.79
Serco	0.79
Capita	0.69
Land Securities Trillium	0.65
MITIE Group	0.52
OCS Group	0.40
Jarvis Facilities Management	0.35
Carillion	0.23

Table 13   Segment market shares in FM, UK[228]

Segment	Share of market, per cent
Catering	20
Cleaning	16
Security	14
Landscaping and gardening	10
Mechanical and Electrical engineering	10
Office services	9
Building fabric maintenance	8

How has this growth in FM come about? Conventionally, FM is thought to be a mix of old concerns about the management of business property with new human resources sensibilities (an office is about the people within it) and new IT capabilities. As such, FM is usually conceived as being an obvious development. In fact, however, *FM has grown up because of the narrowing ambitions of companies and government organisations*, and their desire to outsource as many goods and services as possible – not just premises-related ones, but also general IT hardware and software. In addition, *FM has grown up because of the increasing sense of risk that now surrounds property management*.

In a famous article published in 1937, the Swedish economist Ronald Coase pioneered the idea that firms organise some things themselves, as a means of minimising the costs of transactions that would be involved if they were to ask an outside organisation to do those things on its behalf.[229] In 1960 Theodore Levitt, one of the founding fathers of American post-war marketing, unwittingly appeared to fracture the kind of confidence about the corporation that Coase had exhibited. In a seminal article titled 'Marketing myopia', Levitt insisted that corporations consider much more carefully what business they were in.[230]

In 1990, in an equally seminal article, the US management gurus CK Prahalad and Gary Hamel went a step further. They suggested that the business of a corporation was not defined by its particular constellation of subsidiaries, or strategic business units, but rather by its expertise. Not the price/performance ratios of products, but 'the collective learning in the organisation' became the criterion for success.[231]

As Prahalad and Hamel grew in stature and prominence on the US scene in the 1990s, it became mainstream wisdom that companies should stick to what they had called their 'core competences'. And at one level all this made sense. Why, if the business is, say, a pharmaceutical company, should that business itself directly take on air conditioning its offices and labs? After all, a drug company cannot be expected to know any more about air conditioning than the next man.

Nevertheless, a worrying answer to this innocent question has emerged over the past decade. Experiences of outsourced FM services have been mixed. Certainly there is no guarantee that those who independently supply such services will do so more cheaply or to a higher standard than those who have to organise them themselves.

The only guarantee is that abdicating responsibility for the management of offices and pushing that responsibility outside the firm do not, as strategies, solve the everyday problems that buildings present. Also it is guaranteed that the performance of FM suppliers will be measured to death, so ambivalent are feelings about the costs of such arrangements. Finally there is a guarantee that the therapeutic and naturalistic perspectives must always apply to FM. Practitioners speak in grave tones about the human resources dimension to FM and about the need to be sensitive to those staff working with the facilities provided. As Table 13 shows, 'Jan/san' – janitorial services that chiefly revolve around *security*, and sanitary services that chiefly revolve around *hygiene* – amount to 30 per cent of the UK office market.

Meanwhile FM professionals, official regulators and less official but still influential quangos earnestly debate the ethics of of the office. Should FM professionals not worry more about their use of forest products? After all, in the US the giant paper supplier Office Depot works with GreenOrder, an environmental consulting firm, to help clients of its business services group perform 'sustainability audits'.[232] Should they not worry about their printers using too much energy? The European Commission plans a Framework Directive on what it is pleased to call the eco-design requirements for energy-using products in the workplace and elsewhere.[233] Should FM professionals not worry about electromagnetic radiation in the office? In Stockholm, TCO Development, a company owned by the Swedish Confederation of Professional Employees, will certify products and label them if they meet stringent tests. Are FM professionals sure that their office equipment suppliers will, after August 2005, take back their gear for recycling at the end of its life? Directive 2002/96/EC of the European Parliament and of the Council of the EU, which covers waste electrical and electronic equipment, insists that they do – for free.[234] And what should the world of FM do about chemicals such as lead, mercury and cadmium, or the more obscure chromium VI, PBB and PBDE? From 1 July 2006 they will be banned at the behest of Directive 2002/95/EC on the restriction of the use of certain hazardous substances in electrical and electronic equipment (RoHS).[235]

Facilities Management has become the workplace-based branch of risk management. Its main job now is to usher in a Second Coming for an old concept: the office of the future. With FM, the office of the future has already arrived, and it is Green from carpet to ceiling.

each floor of the Wood Street building was also given water and electricity meters to track usage, and a complete system of environmental reporting was instituted, providing for the collection of data, the calculation of savings, and the communication of results to management, building tenants and others.[236]

If it gets measured, it gets micro-managed. In the specialist management of facilities, a typical service provider such as France's Sodexho may offer more than 40 services. Each would be measured across perhaps eight KPIs, giving a total matrix of no fewer than 320 KPIs. In Britain the rule of micro-management by the numbers applies also to the Building Research Establishment initiative known as Managing Sustainable Construction (MaSC). To go about profiting from sustainability, as the BRE encourages people to do, one may play a five-hour MaSC Game. But the MaSC initiative also contains a self-assessment matrix which asks builders 'Where are you now?' over no fewer than 30 KPIs.[237] This is very far from professionals designing a well-tempered environment as a matter of course.

Where are we now? According to its backers, the MaSC initiative is not prescriptive: both clients for architecture and those who build it are all on different points of the journey toward sustainability.[238] But MaSC research among

large, medium and small construction service providers, from contractors to architects to housing associations, shows that *legislation* is the main thing driving them to be sustainable.[239]

Like Peter Davey, editor of *The Architectural Review*, many in British construction desire to 'remain civilised and try to live in some kind of harmony with the planet'. This, Davey tells us, we must

do 'as Europeans – the people who invented the modern city'.[240] But what do we inventive Europeans mean by 'the environment'? For Hewitt Roberts and Gary Robinson, Canadian specialists in web-based environmental management systems who operate in Lancaster, the environment encompasses everything and everybody. It is the 'surroundings in which an organization operates,

including air, water, land, natural resources, flora, fauna, humans, and their
interrelation'.[241]

But as the surveyors Allan Ashworth
and Keith Hogg have more accurately
observed:

The concept of a green building is an elusive
one. The definition is broad and being green
in a professional sense may merely come down
to a change in attitude.[242]

In naturalism as in therapy, however,
what starts as broad and romantic yearn-
ings for a world that has been lost ends
in a very definite result: state regulation
– backward perspectives on construction
put into practice.

The Building Research Establishment's new, sustainable
image

'Free Laker', by Jonathan Schwinge

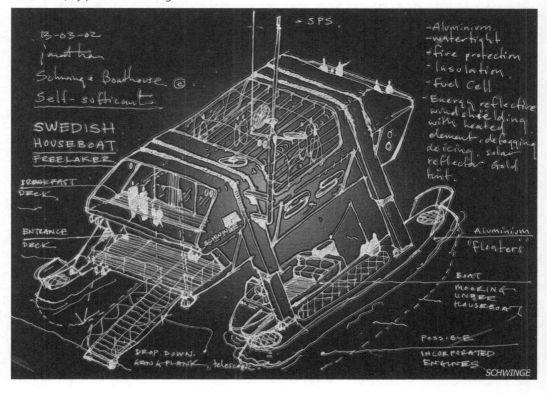

NOTES

1 Strategic Forum for Construction, *Accelerating Change* (London, Rethinking Construction, 2002) p 10.

2 Clayton Christensen, *The Innovator's Dilemma: When new technologies cause great firms to fail* (Boston, Harvard University Press, 1997).

3 Jim Kelly, 'Minister misses target amid muddle on places', *Financial Times*, 5 March 2003, p 4.

4 Strategic Forum for Construction, *Accelerating Change* (London, Rethinking Construction, 2002) p 14.

5 Strategic Forum for Construction, *Accelerating Change* (London, Rethinking Construction, 2002) p 15.

6 www.dqi.org.uk/index1.htm

7 www.kpizone.com/search

8 Robert Taylor, *Managing Workplace Change* (Swindon, Economic and Social Research Council, 2002) p 9.

9 Clayton Christensen, *The Innovator's Dilemma: When new technologies cause great firms to fail* (Boston, Harvard University Press, 1997) p xiii.

10 Clayton Christensen, *The Innovator's Dilemma: When new technologies cause great firms to fail* (Boston, Harvard University Press, 1997) p xii, xv to xvii, 165.

11 Geoff Moore, *Crossing the Chasm* (New York, HarperBusiness, 1991).

12 Clayton Christensen, *The Innovator's Dilemma: When new technologies cause great firms to fail* (Boston, Harvard University Press, 1997) p xv to xvii, xxii, xxiii, 165, 171, 172.

13 Clayton Christensen, *The Innovator's Dilemma: When new technologies cause great firms to fail* (Boston, Harvard University Press, 1997) p xv, xvii, xx, xxi.

14 Clayton Christensen, *The Innovator's Dilemma: When new technologies cause great firms to fail* (Boston, Harvard University Press, 1997) p 15, 66, 72.

15 Tom Peters, *In Search of Excellence* (New York, Basic Books, 1982).

16 Frederick F Reichheld and W Earl Sasser Jr, 'Zero defections: quality comes to services', *Harvard Business Review*, September-October 1990, and posted on http://harvardbusinessonline.hbsp.harvard.edu/b01/en/hbr/hbr_home.jhtml

17 Eric von Hippel, *The Sources of Innovation* (New York, Oxford University Press, 1988).

18 Richard J Foster, *Innovation: the attacker's advantage* (New York, Summit Books, 1986).

19 Clayton Christensen, *The Innovator's Dilemma: When new technologies cause great firms to fail* (Boston, Harvard University Press, 1997) 196.

20 Clayton M Christensen and Michael E Raynor, *The Innovator's solution: Creating and sustaining successful growth* (Harvard Business School Press, Boston, Massachusetts, 2003 p7, 13 to 17, 27, 125 to 148, 189 to 193.

21 www.hse.gov.uk

22 Kevin Myers, 'Health and Safety Performance in the Construction Industry – Progress since the February 2001 Summit', *Working Well Together*, January 2003, and posted on www.wwt.uk.com

23 Respect for People Working Group, *Respect for People: A framework for action* (London, Rethinking Construction, 2002) p 5.

24 Health and Safety Executive, *Key Facts: Injuries in the Construction Industry 1961 to 1995/96* (Bootle, HSE, 2002) p 53, and posted on www.hse.gov.uk

25 Respect for People Working Group, *Respect for People: A framework for action* (London, Rethinking Construction, 2002) p 17.

26 Strategic Forum for Construction, *Accelerating Change* (London, Rethinking Construction, 2002) p 34.

27 Summary, 'Revitalising Health and Safety in Construction', *Health and Safety Executive*, 2003, p 7, and posted on www.hse.gov.uk/consult/disdocs/dde20summary.pdf

28 David McDonald, Editor, *Beat the Cowboys: Report of the 'Beat the Cowboys' working party* (London, HMSO, 1988).

29 'UK construction accident compensation claim', *The Accident Compensation Information Service*, and posted on www.accident–compensation–information.co.uk

30 Strategic Forum for Construction, *Accelerating Change* (London, Rethinking Construction, 2002) p 21 to 22.

31 Carly Fiorina, quoted in Patience Wheatcroft, 'The human factor', *Management Today*, January 2003, p 21.

32 Patience Wheatcroft, 'The human factor', *Management Today*, January 2003, p 21.

33 Daniel Goleman, *Emotional intelligence* [1995] (London, Bloomsbury, 1996).

34 Victor Dulewicz and Malcolm Higgs, *Emotional Intelligence: Managerial Fad or Valid Construct?* (Henley-on-Thames, Henley Management College Working Paper, HWP 9813, 1998).

35 Summary, 'Revitalising Health and Safety in Construction', *Health and Safety Executive,* 2003, p 3, and posted on www.hse.gov.uk/consult/disdocs/dde20summary.pdf

36 Summary, 'Revitalising Health and Safety in Construction', *Health and Safety Executive,* 2003, p 3, and posted on www.hse.gov.uk/consult/disdocs/dde20summary.pdf

37 Summary, 'Revitalising Health and Safety in Construction', *Health and Safety Executive,* 2003, p 22, and posted on www.hse.gov.uk/consult/disdocs/dde20summary.pdf

38 Construction Skills Certification Scheme, posted on www.cscs.uk.com

39 CSCS, *Scheme profile,* posted on www.cscs.uk.com/profile.htm

40 Institute of Actuaries, *The Cost of Compensation Culture,* 17 December 2002, and posted on www.actuaries.org.uk

41 Robert Taylor, *Managing Workplace Change* (Swindon, Economic and Social Research Council, 2002) p 20.

42 'UK construction accident compensation claim', *The Accident Compensation Information Service,* and posted on www.accident–compensation–information.co.uk

43 Respect for People Working Group, *Respect for People: A framework for action* (London, Rethinking Construction, 2002) p 26.

44 Simon de Bruxelles, 'Sunburnt builders urged to turn other cheek', *The Times,* 26 June 2003, p 14.

45 Respect for People Working Group, *Respect for People: A framework for action* (London, Rethinking Construction, 2002) p 26.

46 David Wainwright and Michael Calnan, *Work Stress: The Making of a Modern Epidemic* (Maidenhead, Open University Press, 2002).

47 Respect for People Working Group, *Respect for People: A framework for action* (London, Rethinking Construction, 2002) p 13.

48 Respect for People Working Group, *Reaching the Standard* (London, Rethinking Construction, 2002).

49 Rethinking Construction, 'Industry Called To Engage In Respect For People KPIs', press release, 28 May 2002, and posted on www.rethinkingconstruction.org

50 www.constructionconfederation.co.uk

51 www.arb.org.uk

52 Sir John Egan, statement in Strategic Forum for Construction, *Accelerating Change* (London, Rethinking Construction, 2002) p 7.

53 Jon Katzenbach and Douglas Smith, *The Wisdom of Teams: Creating the high-performance organization* (Boston, Massachusetts, Harvard Business School Press, 1993).

54 Peter Senge, *The Fifth Discipline: The art and practice of the learning organization* (London, Random House Business Books, 1993).

55 Harvey Robbins and Michael Finley, *Why Teams Don't Work* (London, Texere Publishing, 2000).

56 Michael Skapinker, 'Democracy not at work', *Financial Times,* 5 March 2003, p 14.

57 Rajesh Sethi et al, 'How to kill a team's creativity', *Harvard Business Review,* September 2002, and posted on http://harvardbusinessonline.hbsp.harvard.edu/b01/en/hbr/hbr_home.jhtml

58 Colin Porteous, *The New Eco-Architecture – Alternatives from the Modern Movement* (London, Spon Press, 2002) p 143 to 145.

59 Nigel Finn, quoted in Alison Maitland, 'Raising a hard hat to all-round team players', *Financial Times,* 16 September 2002, p 17.

60 Strategic Forum for Construction, *Accelerating Change* (London, Rethinking Construction, 2002) p 10.

61 Strategic Forum for Construction, *Accelerating Change* (London, Rethinking Construction, 2002) p 10.

62 Alison Maitland, 'Raising a hard hat to all-round team players', *Financial Times,* 16 September 2002, p 17.

63 Tony Blair, Foreword, *Better Public Buildings,* October 2000, and posted on www.betterpublicbuildings.gov.uk

64 Hazel Blears, speech to Sodexho breakfast seminar on *Sustainability and Asset Management through Effective Facilities Management,* Portcullis House, 4 February 2003.

65 Design Council, *Design Has the Power to Transform Every Corner of Our Lives* (London, The Design Council, 2002) p 15.

66 John Smith, quoted in Lauren Quaintance, 'BBC plans £2,8bn building spree', *The Sunday Times,* 27 July 2003, p 9.

67 Ann Black, quoted in Mark Huband, 'GCHQ comes in from the cold', *Financial Times,* 26 February 2003, p 13.

68 Peter Wearmouth, 'Procuring Design Quality in Primary Healthcare: Working with LIFT', speech to *Primary Care: Making a Better Environment for Patients and Staff,* King's Fund and Commission for Architecture and the Built Environment conference, 1 May 2002, and posted on www.architectsforhealth.com/newsletter.html

69 Alan Dilani, *Design and Health: The Therapeutic Benefits of Design* (Stockholm, Swedish Building Council, 2001).

70 *Breaking New Ground: Annual review 2001*, Part 3 (London, Arts Council of England, 2001) p 12, and posted on www.arts council.org.uk

71 Michael Fitzpatrick, *The Tyranny of Health* (London, Routledge, 2001).

72 Graham Gunn, *Office Feng Shui in a week* (London, Hodder & Stoughton, 1999).

73 Peter Wearmouth, 'Procuring Design Quality in Primary Healthcare: Working with LIFT', speech to *Primary Care: Making a Better Environment for Patients and Staff*, King's Fund and Commission for Architecture and the Built Environment conference, 1 May 2002, and posted on www.architects forhealth.com/newsletter.html

74 *Framework for Sustainable Development on the Government Estate*, (London, Ministerial Sub-committee of Green Ministers, 2002) and posted on www.sus-tainable–development.gov.uk

75 Cathy Newman, 'Prescott to unveil prefabricated home scheme', *Financial Times*, 1 February 2003, p 2.

76 www.westbury–homes.co.uk

77 www.yorkon.com

78 www.epr.co.uk

79 David Davis, Conservative shadow to the Deputy Prime Minister, quoted in Anthony Browne, '£22bn plan "to bulldoze North and concrete South"', *The Times*, 6 February 2003, p 4.

80 Anne Spackman, 'Prescott to advance along line of least resistance', *The Times*, 6 February 2003, p 4.

81 Anne Spackman, 'Prescott to advance along line of least resistance', *The Times*, 6 February 2003, p 4.

82 John Prescott, foreword, *Sustainable Communities: Building for the future*, London, Office of the Deputy Prime Minister, February 2003, and posted on www.odpm.gov.uk

83 *Evidence: case studies on design against crime* (London, Design Council, 2003) and posted on www.crimereduction.gov.uk/secure design1.htm

84 Secretary of State for the Environment, Transport and the Regions, John Prescott MP, foreword to *Quality of Life Counts – Indicators for a Strategy for Sustainable Development for the United Kingdom: A Baseline Assessment* (London, DETR, 1999) p 4.

85 Office of the Deputy Prime Minister, *Planning Policy Guidance Note 3* – Housing, March 2000, para 1, and posted on www.planning.odpm.gov.uk/ppg3

86 Office of the Deputy Prime Minister, *Planning Policy Guidance Note 3* – Housing, March 2000, para 49, and posted on www.planning.odpm.gov.uk/ppg3

87 Office of the Deputy Prime Minister, *Planning Policy Guidance Note 3* – Housing, March 2000, para 57, and posted on www.planning.odpm.gov.uk/ppg3

88 John Prescott, Press Release, 'Win peace as well as war urges Deputy Prime Minister', *Cabinet Office*, 15 October 2001, and posted on www.nds.coi.gov.uk

89 Helen Studd, 'Green fields of Kent will vanish under red brick', *The Times*, 6 February 2003, p 4.

90 John Prescott, quoted in Anthony Browne, '£22bn plan "to bulldoze North and concrete South"', *The Times*, 6 February 2003, p 4.

91 'Home renovations', *The Times*, 6 February 2003, p 21.

92 Roger Humber, 'The truth hurts', *Building*, 8 November 2002, p 33.

93 Press Release, 'Urban White Paper: Drowning in a sea of carrots. Prescott ducks radical measures on housing and transport', *Friends of the Earth*, 16 November 2000, and posted on www.foe.co.uk/resource

94 *Friends of the Earth*, 'Prescott's wishful thinking', press release, 30 July 2003 and posted on www.foe.co.uk/resource/press_releases/presscotts_wishful_thinkin.html

95 Lisa Segnestam, World Bank Environmental Economics Series Paper 71, *Environmental Performance Indicators: a second edition note* (Washington, The World Bank, October 1999) www.worldbank.org

96 Strategic Forum for Construction, *Accelerating Change* (London, Rethinking Construction, 2002) p 16.

97 www.richardrogers.co.uk

98 Richard Rogers, *Cities for a Small Planet* (London, Faber and Faber, 1997), edited by Philip Gumuchdjian, p 3.

99 Richard Rogers, *Cities for a Small Planet* (London, Faber and Faber, 1997), edited by Philip Gumuchdjian, p 4.

100 Richard Rogers, *Cities for a Small Planet* (London, Faber and Faber, 1997), edited by Philip Gumuchdjian, p 44.

101 United Nations, 'World population prospects: the 2002 revision – Highlights',

United Nations Population Division, 26 February 2003, and posted on www.un. org/esa/population/publications/wpp2002

102 Urban Task Force, *Towards an Urban Renaissance: Final Report of the Urban Task Force* (London, DETR, E&FN Spon, 1999) p 46.

103 Richard Rogers, quoted by Robert Booth, 'Make or break time', *Building Design*, 26 April 2002, p 7.

104 Geoffrey Nowell-Smith, 'Own your own target . . . now!', *Critical Quarterly* Volume 44, Number 4, Winter 2002, p 11 to 16.

105 Richard Rogers, quoted by Mark Leftly, 'Stern Mr Prescott gives industry a real caning', *Building*, 8 November 2002, p 15.

106 Richard Rogers and Anne Power, *Cities for a Small Country* (London, Faber and Faber, 2000) p 189.

107 Richard Rogers and Anne Power, *Cities for a Small Country* (London, Faber and Faber, 2000) p 213.

108 Richard Rogers and Anne Power, *Cities for a Small Country* (London, Faber and Faber, 2000) p 249.

109 Richard Rogers, 'Cities for People', Speech to the Urban Summit, Birmingham, 31 October 2002, and posted on www.odpm. gov.uk

110 Richard Rogers, 'Cities for People', Speech to the Urban Summit, Birmingham, 31 October 2002, and posted on www.odpm. gov.uk

111 'AJ 100 survey', *Architects' Journal*, 20 March 2003, p 38, 44, 48.

112 'AJ 100 survey', *Architects' Journal*, 20 March 2003, p 63.

113 Quoted in European Environmental Agency, *EEA Multilingual Environmental Glossary*, and posted on http://glossary.eea.eu.int/EEA Glossary

114 Quoted in European Environmental Agency, *EEA multilingual environmental glossary*, and posted on http://glossary.eea.eu.int/ EEAGlossary

115 S Holm and J Harris, letter, 'Precautionary principle stifles discovery', *Nature*, 1999, Vol 400, p 398, quoted in Sir Colin Berry, 'Risk, science and society', spiked online, 1 November 2001, and posted on www.spiked-online.com/Articles/00000002D29C.htm

116 Sir Colin Berry, 'Risk, science and society', spiked online, 1 November 2001, and posted on www.spiked-online.com/Articles/ 00000002D29C.htm

117 Commission for the European Communities, *Communication from the Commission on the Precautionary Principle* (Brussels,

European Commission, 2 February 2000) p 4, and posted on http://europa.eu.int/ comm/dgs/health_consumer/library/pub/ pub07_en.pdf

118 Commission for the European Communities, *Communication from the Commission on the Precautionary Principle* (Brussels, European Commission, 2 February 2000) p 21, and posted on http://europa.eu.int/comm/dgs/ health_consumer/library/pub/pub07_en. pdf

119 Tracey Brown and Dick Taverne, 'Over-precautionary tales', *Prospect*, September 2002, p 66.

120 European Environmental Agency, *Late Lessons from Early Warnings: The precautionary principle 1896–2000*, 1 October 2002, chapter 16, p 169, and posted on http:// reports.eea.eu.int/environmental_issue_ report_2001_22/en/issue–22–part–16.pdf

121 Henry Petroski, *To Engineer is Human: The role of failure in successful design* (London, Macmillan, 1985) p 219.

122 Henry Petroski, *To Engineer is Human: The role of failure in successful design* (London, Macmillan, 1985) p x.

123 www.anl.gov.

124 Paul Cheshire, 'Postscript: Exurbia or Islington?', in Anita Summers, Paul Cheshire and Lanfranco Senn, editors, *Urban Change in the United States and Western Europe* (Washington, Urban Institute Press, second edition, 1999) p 594.

125 Quoted in Roger Blitz, 'Projects struggle to revive provinces', *Financial Times*, 28 August, p 1.

126 Christopher Parkes, 'Cities within cities', *Financial Times*, 6 August 2001, p 17.

127 David Pilling, 'Tokyo's "new Shanghai" belies a sickly economy', *Financial Times* Property, 25 January 2003, p 4.

128 Richard Rogers, 'Cities for People', Speech to the Urban Summit, Birmingham, 31 October 2002, and posted on www.odpm. gov.uk

129 www.cpre.org.uk

130 *Rethinking Construction – The report of the Construction Task Force* (London, HMSO, 1998) p 35.

131 Colin Cole, quoted by Mark Leftly, 'Housebuilders to confront Prescott over summit jibes', *Building*, 8 November 2002, p 14.

132 Paul Cheshire and Stephen Sheppard, 'Building on Brown Fields – The long term price we pay', *Planning in London*, 33, April/June 2000, p 34 to 36.

133 Roger Humber, 'The truth hurts', *Building*, 8 November 2002, p 33.

134 Office of the Deputy Prime Minister, *Our Towns and Cities: The Future – Delivering an Urban Renaissance*, November 2000, para 1.7, and posted on www.urban.odpm.gov. uk/whitepaper

135 Office for National Statistics, *Britain 2000: The official yearbook of the UK* (London, ONS, 1999) p 444.

136 Richard Rogers, letter, *Financial Times*, 6 June 2003, p 20.

137 EF Schumacher, *Small is Beautiful: Economics as if people mattered*, 1973 (London, Harper Perennial, 1989) p 113.

138 Quoted in Leo Marx, *The Machine in The Garden: Technology and the pastoral ideal in America* (New York, Oxford University Press, 1967) p 10, 13.

139 Richard Rogers, 'Cities for People', Speech to the Urban Summit, Birmingham, 31 October 2002, and posted on www.odpm. gov.uk

140 www.piercyconner.co.uk and www.themi croflatcompany.com

141 Jeevan Vasagar, 'Flat pack homes may solve crisis', *The Guardian*, 7 March 2002, and posted on www.guardian.co.uk

142 Leader, 'Homes fit for heroes – affordable housing is a policy priority', *The Guardian*, 7 March 2002, and posted on www.guardian. co.uk

143 Hugh Pearman, 'Microflats – the urban solution?', *The Sunday Times Preview*, 27 January 2002, p 4, and posted on www. hughpearman.com

144 Ministry of Housing and Local Government and the Central Housing Advisory Committee, *Homes for Today and Tomorrow*, better known as the Parker Morris Report (London, MHLG, 1961).

145 Quoted in Cathy Newman, 'Whitehall departments own enough unused land for 80,000 affordable London homes', *Financial Times*, 8 April 2003, p11.

146 Anthony Browne, '"Affordable housing" is only good for the bulldozer', *The Times*, 6 February 2003, www.timesonline.co.uk

147 Adam Mornement, 'Modular Muddle', *The Guardian*, 20 November 2002, and posted on www.guardian.co.uk

148 James Barlow and Ritsuko Ozaki, *Japanese Lessons on Customer-Focused Housebuilding – Report of a Department of Trade and Industry Expert Mission* (Brighton, Science and Technology Policy Research, University of Sussex, 2001) p 13.

149 Rosy Strati, 'Module and prefabrication – History and present-day of modular spaces', *Materia*, number 40, an issue on modular architecture, April 2003, p 96 to 107, available through www.materia.it

150 Dennis Sharp, 'Introduction', in Dennis Sharp, editor, *Kisho Kurokawa: From the Age of the Machine to the Age of Life* (London, Bookart, 1998) p 13.

151 Dennis Sharp, editor, *Kisho Kurokawa: From the Age of the Machine to the Age of Life* (London, Bookart, 1998) p 63.

152 www.cube.org.uk/exhibitions/past20.htm

153 Charles Jencks, 'Kurokawa's double vision: from Metabolism to Fractals', in Dennis Sharp, editor, *Kisho Kurokawa, From the Age of the Machine to the Age of Life* (London, Bookart, 1998) p 37.

154 Kisho Kurokawa, 'Non-Bourbakian systems', in Dennis Sharp, editor, *Kisho Kurokawa: From the Age of the Machine to the Age of Life* (London, Bookart, 1998) p 258.

155 Ian Littlewood, *The Idea of Japan – Western Images, Western Myths* (London, Secker & Warburg, 1996) p 90.

156 Greater London Authority, *The Draft London Plan: A summary* (London, GLA, June 2002) p 16.

157 Martin Gaskell, *Building Control – National legislation and the introduction of local bye-laws in Victorian England* (London, British Association for Local History, Bedford Square Press, 1983).

158 Patricia Tutt and David Adler, Editors, *New Metric Handbook* (London, Architectural Press, 1979) p 305.

159 Martin Pawley, 'Buckminster Fuller – The most farsighted man of our century', *Technopolis*, and posted on www.heise.de/ tp/english/

160 Building Research Establishment trade fair and seminar series OFFSITE 03, 19 to 23 May 2003, and posted on www.bre.co.uk and www.offsite03.co.uk

161 Josephine Smit, Interview, 'If we can make it there . . .', *Building*, 25 April 2003, p 28.

162 www.whitbybird.com

163 www.ahmm.co.uk

164 Charlie Gates and Robert Booth, 'Off-site, off-time and off-budget', *Building Design*, 2 May 2003, p 1.

165 Stuart Macdonald and Chloe Stothart, 'Off-site manufacturer hits trouble as two suppliers quit', *Housing Today*, 25 April 2003, and posted on www.housing–today. co.uk

166 www.amphion.org.uk

167 Chris Horton and Damian Arnold, 'On-site factory speeds up prefabs', *Building Design*, 23 May 2003, p 6.

168 John Prewer, RM Lawson, PJ Grubb and PJ Trebilcock, *Modular Construction using Light Steel Framing – An Architect's Guide* (Ascot, Steel Construction Institute, 1999).

169 www.steel–sci.org

170 Alex Gordon, 'Architects and Resource Conservation', *RIBA Journal*, January 1974, p 9.

171 Brian Edwards and Paul Hyett, *Rough Guide to Sustainability* (London, RIBA Publications, 2001) p 85 to 88.

172 Richard Rogers, 'Cities for People', Speech to the Urban Summit, Birmingham, 31 October 2002, and posted on www.odpm. gov.uk

173 Richard Rogers, 'Cities for People', Speech to the Urban Summit, Birmingham, 31 October 2002, and posted on www.odpm. gov.uk

174 Richard Rogers, 'Cities for People', Speech to the Urban Summit, Birmingham, 31 October 2002, and posted on www.odpm. gov.uk

175 Thomas Allen, *Managing the Flow of Technology: Technology transfer and the dissemination of technological information within the R&D organization* (Cambridge, Massachusetts, The MIT Press, 1977).

176 Michael Porter, *The Competitive Advantage of Nations* (London, Macmillan, 1990).

177 Louis Mumford, *The Culture of Cities* (London, Secker & Warburg, 1938).

178 Henri Lefebvre, *La Production de L'Espace* (Paris, Anthropos, 1974).

179 Michel Foucault, *Surveiller et Punir* (1975), published in English as *Discipline and Punish: the birth of the prison*, (London, Penguin Books, 1977).

180 Pierre Bourdieu, *Outline of a Theory of Practice* (Cambridge, Cambridge University Press, 1977).

181 Chistopher Alexander, Sara Ishikawa, Murray Silvestern, *A Pattern Language: Towns, buildings, construction* (New York, Oxford Univesity Press, 1977).

182 David Harvey, *The Urbanization of Capital: Studies in the history and theory of capitalist urbanization* (Baltimore, John Hopkins University Press, 1985).

183 Edward Soja, *Postmodern Geographies: The reassertion of space in critical social theory* (London, Verso Books, 1989).

184 Anthony Giddens, *The Consequences of Modernity* (Stanford, Stanford University Press, 1990).

185 Masahisa Fujita, Paul Krugman and Anthony J Venables, *The Spatial Economy: Cities, regions and international trade* (Cambridge, Massachusetts, The MIT Press, 1999).

186 David Harvey, *The Urban Experience* (Oxford, Blackwell, 1989) p 54.

187 Jean Gottman, *Megalopolis: The urbanized northeastern seaboard of the United States* (Boston, The MIT Press, 1961).

188 Louis Mumford, *The City in History* (London, Secker & Warburg, 1961).

189 Morton White and Lucia White, *The Intellectual Versus the City: From Thomas Jefferson to Frank Lloyd Wright* (Boston, Harvard Business School Press, 1962).

190 Melvin Webber, *Explorations into Urban Structure* (Philadelphia, University of Pennsylvania, 1964).

191 Louis Winnick, 'Place prosperity vs people prosperity: welfare considerations in the geographic redistribution of economic activity', in *Essays in Urban Land Economics in Honor of the 65th Birthday of Leo Grebler* (Los Angeles, UCLA, 1966) p 273 to 283.

192 Reyner Banham, *Los Angeles: The architecture of four ecologies* (London, Allen Lane, 1971).

193 Jane Jacobs, *The Death and Life of Great American Cities*, first published 1961 (London, Jonathan Cape, 1962), p 72.

194 Jane Jacobs, *The Death and Life of Great American Cities*, first published 1961 (London, Jonathan Cape, 1962) p 284.

195 Marshall Berman, *All That is Solid Melts into Air: The experience of modernity* (London, Verso, 1983) p 314 to 325.

196 David Brooks, *Bobos in Paradise: The new upper class and how they got there* (New York, Touchstone, 2000) p 123 to 127.

197 AnnaLee Saxenian, *Regional Advantage: Culture and competition in Silicon Valley and Route 128* (London, Harvard Univeristy Press, 1994), p 7.

198 Anders Bordum, 'From tacit knowing to tacit knowledge – emancipation or ideology?', *Critical Quarterly*, Volume 44 No 3, Autumn 2002.

199 Ikujiro Nonaka and Hirotaki Takeuchi, *The Knowledge-Creating Company* (Oxford, Oxford University Press, 1995).

200 Keith Pavitt, 'Knowledge about knowledge since Nelson & Winter: A mixed record', Science Policy Research Unit Electronic Working Paper No 83, June 2002, p 8, and posted on www.sussex.ac.uk/spru/publications

201 Peter Hall, 'Cities of people and cities of bits', *Demos Quarterly*, No 9, 1996.

202 Malcom Gladwell, 'Designs for Working', *The New Yorker*, 11 December 2000, and posted on www.gladwell.com/2000/2000_12_11_a_working.htm

203 Richard K Lester, Michael J Piore and Kamal M Malek, 'Interpretive management: what general managers can learn from design', *Harvard Business Review*, March/April 1998 and posted on http://harvardbusinessonline.hbsp.harvard.edu/b01/en/hbr/hbr_home.jhtml

204 Steven Johnson, *Emergence* (London, Allen Lane, 2001).

205 Herbert Girardet, *The Gaia Atlas of Cities: New directions for sustainable urban living* (London, Gaia Books, 1992).

206 European Commission, *The Impact of Transport on the Environment – a Community strategy for 'sustainable mobility'* (Brussels, European Commission, 1992).

207 Greater London Authority, *The Draft London Plan: A summary* (London, GLA, June 2002) p 15.

208 Michael Porter and Christian HM Ketels, *UK Competitiveness: Moving to the next stage, DTI Economics paper No 3* (London, DTI, May 2003) p 27.

209 Martin Pawley, speaking at *Building Audacity*, a conference organised by audacity.org at The Building Centre, London, 10 July 2000, and posted on www.audacity.org/Activity.htm

210 James Woudhuysen, 'Space men invade UK offices', *IT Week*, 8 July 2002, and posted on www.itweek.co.uk

211 Institute of Public Policy Research, 'Designs on Democracy – winners announced', 20 January 2003 and posted on www.ippr.org/press/index.php?release=188

212 Stephen Bayley, 'The great gherkin in the sky', *The Independent on Sunday*, Life, 13 October 2002, p 1.

213 www.swissre.com

214 Ian Playford, 'UK Property Market Overview: Markets cooling as the summer heats up . . . while buildings due to reach up for the stars', published by the financial services organisation *Credo* and posted on www.credogroup.com/news/newsAug02art8.html

215 www.london.gov.uk/mayor/mayors_report/september19_2001.jspk

216 Simon Kuper, 'Soggy brained bid would create a host of problems', *Weekend FT*, 25 January 2003, p XX.

217 Rachel Crossley, *Reputation, Risk and Reward: The Business Case for Sustainability in the UK Property Sector – A report by the Sustainable Construction Task Group* (Garston, Building Research Establishment, 2001) and posted on www.bre.co.uk

218 www.isisam.com

219 Rachel Crossley, *Reputation, Risk and Reward: The Business Case for Sustainability in the UK Property Sector – A report by the Sustainable Construction Task Group* (Garston, Building Research Establishment, 2001) p 4, and posted on www.bre.co.uk

220 Arup, in association with Richard Ellis, *London Olympics 2012 Costs and benefits*, 21 May 2002 and posted on www.arup.com/about/PDFS/Summaryreport.pdf

221 Juliette Jowitt, 'London rail project hit by 10-year build time and £15bn cost', *Financial Times*, 1 May 2003 and posted on www.ft.com

222 www.culture.gov.uk/sport/london-olympic_bid_2012/default.htm

223 Text of a statement made in the House of Commons, The Right Honourable Tessa Jowell MP, Secretary of State for Culture, Media & Sport, London 2012 Olympic Bid, posted on www.culture.gov.uk/global/press_notices/archive_2003/olympic_statement.htm

224 Chris Mill, speech to Sodexho breakfast seminar on Sustainability and Asset Management through Effective Facilities Management, Portcullis House, 4 February 2003.

225 British Institute of Facilities Management, *BIFM Fact Base*, February 2003.

226 MBD, quoted in British Institute of Facilities Management, *BIFM Fact Base*, February 2003.

227 British Institute of Facilities Management, *BIFM Fact Base*, February 2003.

228 MBD, quoted in British Institute of Facilities Management, *BIFM Fact Base*, February 2003.

229 Ronald Coase, 'The Nature of the Firm', *Economica No 4* (new series) 1937, p 386 to 405.

230 Theodore Levitt, 'Marketing myopia', *Harvard Business Review*, July-August 1960, and posted on http://harvardbusinessonline.hbsp.harvard.edu/b01/en/hbr/hbr_home.jhtml

231 CK Prahalad and Gary Hamel, 'The core competence of the corporation', *Harvard Business Review*, May-June 1990, and posted onhttp://harvardbusinessonline.hbsp.harvard.edu/b01/en/hbr/hbr_home.jhtml

232 'Depot adds to its green credentials', *Office Products International*, February 2003, p16.

233 Heinz Zourek, Deputy Director, General Directorate, *General Entreprise*, European Commission, Commission statement to the CENELEC General Assembly on 4 June 2003 Helsinki, and posted on www.ceiuni.it/presentazione/EC%20statement.pdf

234 Directive 2002/96/EC of the European Parliament and of the Council of 27 January 2003 on the restriction of the use of certain hazardous substances in electrical and electronic equipment, and posted on www.cfsd.org.uk/seeba/finalweee.pdf

235 Directive 2002/95/EC of the European Parliament and of the Council of 27 January 2003 on the restriction of the use of certain hazardous substances in electrical and electronic equipment, and posted on www.cfsd.org.uk/seeba/finalrohs.pdf

236 Rachel Crossley, 'Green Buildings & The Bottom Line: An Investor's Perspective', speech to the British Institute of Facilities Managers, 16 to 18 October 2001.

237 MaSC, *Profiting from Sustainability* (London, Building Research Establishment, 2002), and posted on www.projects.bre.co.uk/masc/index.html

238 Professor Ian Cooper, speech to Sodexho breakfast seminar on Sustainability & Asset Management through Effective Facilities Management, Portcullis House, 4 February 2003.

239 Professor Ian Cooper, speech to Sodexho breakfast seminar on Sustainability & Asset Management through Effective Facilities Management, Portcullis House, 4 February 2003.

240 Peter Davey, 'Greening the European city', flyer for a conference by *The Architectural Review*, 19 March 2003.

241 Hewitt Roberts and Gary Robinson, *ISO 14001 – Implementation Handbook*, Butterworth Heinemann, 1998, introduction p xiv.

242 Allan Ashworth and Keith Hogg, *Added Value in Design and Construction*, Pearson Education, Longman, 2000, p 31.

3 Backward practices: the regulation of urban districts, workplaces and the environment

3.1 Urban innovation as Business Improvement Districts

When they are not turning space into God, those with backward perspectives in construction would like to regulate it. In Britain the most obvious example of where therapy and naturalism end up is New Labour's enthusiasm for Business Improvement Districts, made clear in John Prescott's *Working Draft of Guidance on Business Improvement Districts*, issued in January 2003.

In a BID, a majority of businesses within a district votes to win local authority approval for the raising of a mandatory levy on all that district's property owners. The levy comes on top of existing taxes. In Britain a BID is designed to finance:

more frequent policing, installation of CCTV cameras and litter bins; remedial measures such as a rapid response to graffiti and litter; replacing street lamps, mending pavements and investment in the visual appearance of the area, such as tree planting . . . local training and employment schemes and, even (sic), more frequent local transport.[1]

Right away, the choice of 'more frequent policing, installation of CCTV cameras' as first on the list said something about New Labour's authoritarian purpose with BIDs. But Prescott's stated reason for BIDs was more revealing still.

His guidance on BIDs stated:

The Deputy Prime Minister has set out his plans for thriving, sustainable and inclusive communities in his long-term programme of action . . . But a plan just about homes would fail, as past experience shows. So these actions will be set within the overall context of creating and maintaining sustainable communities. BIDs will make a useful contribution to achieving some of these objectives.[2]

Until BIDs, UK government efforts to revive local high streets had been confined to setting limits on competing out-of-town developments. With BIDs, the British state is set to play a more direct role in high street revival. Now, through BIDs, Prescott aimed to supplement his long-established control of housing with something innovatory: a wider and more directly authoritarian regulation of sustainable communities – in other words, every last corner of urban space.

Announcing what Prescott's press office called 'New York-style schemes', local government minister Nick Raynsford upheld both localism and civic pride. In BIDs, he said:

Every scheme will be different. Each scheme will address the exclusive needs of the community. This might be about making an area safer, improving its appearance, upgrading services, or improving access . . . Today's publication of the draft BID guidance marks a significant step in our vision for making our towns and cities places that people are proud to live in, work in, and invest in.[3]

But this was not all. BIDs would help attract new businesses and 'encourage people to remain' within BIDS, so 'stemming the exodus from our towns and cities'.[4]

As a device for ensuring that people stay where they are, BIDs have been a long time coming to Britain. But as early as 1996, the distinguished urbanist Tony Travers recommended that they be adopted here.[5] In that era, BIDs won their spurs by providing practical and financial backing for New York City Republican mayor Rudolph Giuliani and his campaign against street crime. It was already clear that, for all the broad tasks they wanted to take on, *the basic idea with BIDs was that uniformed security guards, or representatives of the BID posing as 'active citizens', should operate as the eyes and ears of the police.* In the case of the Baltimore Partnership, a giant, central-area BID put uniformed guards on the streets specifically to back up local police. In Philadelphia's BID, Center City District, guides were based at the local police station.[6]

Altogether, much of the business improvement financed by owners of commercial property in US cities has long consisted of applying more law and order. In US urban circles it is *fear of crime* that has really inspired innovation. Michael Porter, indeed, favoured the corporatisation of the American inner city as early as 1995, because he found that firms in Atlanta and Boston had successfully solved their security problems by working, respectively, with local police and with neighbours disposed to call up if ever they witnessed anything amiss.[7]

All that has happened in Britain is that New Labour has brought BIDs over from the US to build a kind of giant Neighbourhood Watch for the new century. It is a Watch that involves voluntary organisations, the local community, and unspecified property owners.[8] It is also a Watch designed, as Raynsford's remarks con-

firm, to keep people away from the countryside.

From the US, Paul Levy, executive director of the Philadelphia Center City District and a former chairman of the International Downtown Association, confirms the direction in which people will be coerced. In a survey of literature on BIDs in America and Canada, he writes:

Gated or Open City?

Some opponents of BIDs have likened them to gated, defended residential enclaves. More apocalyptic critics conjure images of corporations circling the wagons to keep undesirables out. To BID leaders in once depopulated downtowns this is a curious comparison. Having hired young planners and landscape architects to restore neglected civic spaces, and having deployed cleaning and security teams, they are now funding media campaigns to draw people of all ages, incomes and races back to the center. Most BID leaders will say that their goal is, not to chase some people out, but to invite all people in.[9]

According to Lord Charles Falconer, the predecessor to Lord Jeff Rooker as Minister for Housing, Planning and Regeneration, successful legislation in Parliament's 2002/03 session would enable BIDs to come into effect in Britain from April 2004.[10] It is now anyone's guess just how many 'active citizens', dedicated to noticing deviant behaviour at pavement or at gutter, British society needs. Maybe everyone should become an upright urban sleuth. Reinforced by the events of 11 September 2001 and further buttressed by TV shows such as *Crimewatch*, the popular buy-in to the habit of being suspicious of others in Britain is already considerable.

More informing on people and more construction of 'defensible space': these are the most direct consequences of the Prescott programme for the regulation of sustainable communities in Britain's urban areas. They are consequences much more serious, and much less commented upon, than the electronic surveillance of the city (see Box 12).

Box 12 THE ELECTRONIC SURVEILLANCE OF THE CITY

Public interest in the electronic surveillance of the city has been heightened since the advent, in London, of the clever, number-plate-reading cameras brought in by Ken Livingstone to support his Congestion Charge. Equally, the electronic surveillance of the city is more and more the subject of theoretical enquiry. The opening words of *CTRL [SPACE]: rhetorics of surveillance from Bentham to Big Brother*, a 655-page doorstopper published by the MIT Press, run as follows:

> Now, more than ever, we are under surveillance.[11]

From supermarket checkouts and the credit agency Experian to intranets and tomorrow's set-top boxes for digital TV, IT-assisted surveillance is supposed to be a hidden, oppressive and growing part of every-day life.

Everyone fears surveillance. Foucault was the first to popularise Jeremy Bentham's 1787 penitentiary, or Panopticon, to an international audience. Foucault rewrote human history as the growth of power and, in particular, of that power over space given by surveillance. Ever since his *Discipline and Punish*, Western society has felt a growing and deeply Benthamite sense of always feeling watched . . . even though it might not be. In September 2002 the *Guardian* newspaper published three instalments of *Big Brother: someone somewhere is watching you*, a special series 'on you, the state, commerce and privacy'.[12]

Yet fear of surveillance has grown in the same measure as the desire to disclose very private matters. Although every senior policeman acknowledges the threat to civil liberties posed by surveillance, *CTRL [SPACE]* is right to hint that what people fear just as much, nowadays, is 'being withdrawn completely from the gaze of others'.[13] Millions want to be on television series such as *Big Brother*. Millions, too, do not mind being caught on CCTV, feeling – rightly – that they have nothing to hide. Fearful fictions about surveillance, from George Orwell's *1984* of 1948 to Philip Noyce's 1998 film *The Truman Show,* are one thing, but contemporary critics of surveillance pander to our fears, our vulnerability and our impotence.

IT-assisted urban surveillance is a disturbing trend, not because Big Brother is really tracking people everywhere they go, but because the big popular buy-in that surveillance enjoys won't, in the long run, help democracy. The critique of electronic surveillance of the city misses the point that racist conversa-tions in private, social policy, architecture, asylum-seekers and mobile-equipped policemen on the street each transfix government attention more than video cameras.

As early as 1997, Dolan Cummings presciently observed, in a pamphlet titled *Surveillance & the city*:

> Without some basis for trust, surveillance is the only guarantee of order. Measures are called for to ensure that everything is on the record and that coercive measures are available to deal with any problems. Furthermore, it is vital that everybody knows this. Such surveillance need not take the form of CCTV or of a security guard. Indeed, in most situations a kind of natural or spontaneous surveillance exists. Wherever a group of similar people gather for a particular purpose, there is the reassurance that there are rules that everyone will follow . . . Most planners prefer the implicit sur-veillance of a social environment to the crudeness of CCTV, and this is the atmosphere that they would bring to our streets and public spaces.[14]

It is our implicit willingness to distrust and subject each other to surveillance that is much more telling than Britain's international lead in installing CCTV cameras.

3.2 Innovation in the law around workplace health and business continuity

At a conference held in London in 2002, the then head of innovation at the UK high street retailers WH Smith waxed lyrical about how the company's conversion of a warehouse into a New York-style loft, complete with sofas and magazine racks, had worked wonders. No doubt, indeed, the new ambience at Smith's helps employees relax and free their minds for the playful excursions into true creativity that are now required. No doubt, too, corporate lofts allow mental freewheeling and general communing more than did the monolithic offices of the past. But refurbished offices will not necessarily bring about world-beating innovations.

Nevertheless *the workplace of the future will be a site for innovation of a sort – legal innovation.*

The workplace has been reinterpreted. It is less a site for wealth creation, and more a site for the promotion of 'wellbeing'. And in this medical matter, the state has an interest in ensuring that buildings play a full and positive part.

To read official reports on international workplace health, the world is completely overworked. Take, for example, lack of sleep. Such a deficiency, a New Zealand expert insists, 'needs to stop being regarded as a badge of honour and seen for the serious hazard that it actually is'.[15] In Japan, researchers have found that people who work for more than 60 hours a week are twice as likely to have a heart attack.[16] In Britain the Royal Society of Medicine held a conference in April 2002 titled 'Sleepless society: can we cope?'.

The broader story behind growing scares about health in the workplace goes like this:

- Globalisation leads to 24-hour, seven-day trading, which leads to physical and mental illness.
- Mergers and demergers, competition,

outsourcing and the removal of barriers to innovation make for restructuring, relocation and thus a corporate culture that is profoundly nervous and on edge.
- Traffic congestion, mobile working and email overload are also responsible for deteriorating employee health.

These fears are exaggerated. But in the UK in 2003, the Health and Safety Executive drafted *management standards for preventing stress.*[17] It is widely argued that without clear standards on factors like workload, control of the work and management support, organisations will only be able to sustain the kind of lifespan enjoyed by Enron. By 2003, too, the DTI spent £11.3 million helping nearly 400 organisations implement approved measures for aiding *work-life balance.*[18] Yet it is also lamented that, even when work-life balance policies are in place, take-up among employees is low.[19] On a European scale, a burgeoning industry of stress experts, stress auditors and stress managers will see to it that the EU innovates new laws on workplace health.

Architects and construction specialists could never have been immune from this climate. Around the workplaces of the past, they were for a long time interrogated about Sick Building Syndrome, Legionnaire's disease, the provision of ergonomic seating, and the extent of asbestos. But now the damages paid out over asbestos have grown enormous and fears of radiation through IT, of repetitive strain injury and of workplace infections have all increased.

Altogether, risk-conscious concerns about workplace health, stress management and work-life balance bring regulatory duress to the world of construction. Ever since the UK's Department of Health published its national health promotion strategy in 1999, the workplace has been identified as one of the key settings for tackling the UK's problems of heart disease, mental ill health, cancer and accidents.[20] The sports facility is also interpreted as an arena for government medical intervention. These developments can only put more pressure on architects and builders to consider their work from every health and safety angle. However, there is still more duress to come.

In 2003 the accountants Grant Thornton surveyed 100 British managing directors and finance directors. They found that the same numbers of companies were worried about their business being hit by international terrorism as were worried about being hit by a fire on their premises. In fact both terrorism and fire had, even before the events of 11 September 2001, been linked in the minds of British officialdom. *The war against terrorism that opened after 11 September 2001 only reinforced an established trend for the physical survival of companies, their buildings and their data to rise up the boardroom agenda. Like the growing body of legislation on workplace health, that around 'business continuity' will confer new and onerous responsibilities on architects and builders.*

In 1999 in the UK, the Turnbull report insisted that company boards protect shareholder value by taking responsibility for risk management – financial, operational, the lot. Thus in the event of a disaster, negligence on the part of a director could make him or her personally liable to charges of manslaughter. In the same year, the Management of Health and Safety at Work Regulations required employers to have effective arrangements in place for 'planning, organising, controlling, monitoring and reviewing preventive and protective measures'. Finally, in July 2001, the Health and Safety Commission's *Directors' responsibilities for health and safety* announced that boards should appoint a board member to be director of health and safety. The health and safety responsibilities of all board members, it argued, should be 'clearly articulated'.[21]

In the British workplace, myopic directors of FM face the same treatment as that which has been meted out by govern-ment to errant British surgeons. An army of lawyers, claimants and certificators stands ready to profit from all this. Its members salivate at tomorrow's potential burst of claims – claims that landlords knowingly failed to prepare for a building's continuity in the face of disaster, and covered up that failure.

In sum, a facility manager's failure to *guarantee* that a building is healthy for its employees, or that it incorporates all possible preventive and protective measures against disaster, invites legal revenge. In turn, reprisals will also be taken against the building's architects and builders.

It looks as though architects and builders will have to spend more and more of their time not introducing innovations into the construction process themselves, but preparing to avoid the legal innovations of others.

3.3 Innovation in the law around the environment

Tony Blair's lawyer wife, Cherie Booth, believes in innovation. In the foreword to *Environmental Law for the Built Environment*, written by the lawyer and author Jack Rostron and published in 2001, Booth noted how far environmental law had come and, even more significantly, 'how far it still needs to go'.[22]

Her Majesty's Government is right behind the wife of the prime minister. In Lisbon, in July 2002, the British Council co-organised the *International Conference on Environmental Liability*.[23] Meant as a forum for Non-Governmental Organisations, the conference was a bridge between the European Commission's February 2000 *White Paper on Environmental Liability* and the forthcoming European Directive on Environmental Liability.[24] The White Paper had already enshrined the following principles:

- the 'polluter pays' principle;
- the Precautionary Principle;

- the policy that preventive action is preferable to remedial measures;
- the principle that environmental damage should be rectified at source; and
- the practice of protection, recognising the diversity of situations of countries in the EU.

The Lisbon conference not only endorsed all this, but also acted as a preface to yet another, more massive environmental cavalcade the following month: the 2002 World Summit for Sustainable Development, held in Johannesburg. There, an Action Plan was drawn up to strengthen the framing, use and enforcement of environment-related laws. The Plan was prepared by a High Court and Supreme Court of no fewer than 100 of the world's most senior judges, appointed, without any electorate having a vote, by the United Nations Environment Programme.[25]

Among other things, the judges wanted to improve the capacity, training, funding, and education of other legal experts – particularly in developing nations. They need not have worried. In India, where hundred of millions of peasants live in little more than huts, there are likely to be eco-courts before long.[26]

All over the world, the legalisation of the environment is set to accelerate. Ironically enough, the movement looks like being led by America:

Americans are catching up with Europeans in terms of environmental performance . . . and because the USA is taking the lead in promoting green building worldwide America is setting the standard . . . State and city governments are the main driving force behind the greening of America's buildings. Cities including New York, San Francisco and Seattle have adopted green building programmes, and New York recently became the first state to grant a tax break to sustainable buildings.[27]

America faced considerable criticism at Johannesburg, but it is ahead of the world and the UK in formulating

environmental law, systems of insurance, and benchmarks of sustainability against which developments can be judged. The sinisterly named Center for a New American Dream offers a measure of how ubiquitous sustainability has become.[28] More significantly, the US Green Building Council has emerged as the foremost coalition aiming to promote buildings that are 'environmentally responsible, profitable and healthy places to live and work'.[29]

Though not a statutory body, the USGBC has developed a set of criteria by which to judge the sustainability of development. Under its initiative for *Leadership in Energy and Environmental Design*, or LEED™, it has produced a Green Building Rating System as a voluntary and consensus-based national standard. The system is said to provide

a complete framework for assessing building performance and meeting sustainability goals. Based on well-founded scientific standards, LEED™ emphasizes state of the art strategies for sustainable site development, water savings, energy efficiency, materials selection and indoor environmental quality. LEED™ recognizes achievements and promotes expertise in green building through a comprehensive system offering project certification, professional accreditation, training and practical resources.[30]

It cannot be long before such industry-wide measures of sustainability are enforced in the UK. Already, in 2001, Rachel Crossley mapped out the likely course of events by naming 15 of her favourite organisations that could help facilities managers ensure that their buildings conformed to best practice.[31] They were as follows:

1 www.greenergy.com Greenergy advises on low carbon emission fuels and CO_2 reduction strategies.
2 www.envirowise.gov.uk Envirowise is against whatever it sees as the inefficient use of raw materials, packaging and technology.

3 www.energy–efficiency.gov.uk Energy Efficiency Best Practice programme is a UK Government programme providing free information to organisations to help them cut their energy bills, and has been rebranded as www.actionenergy.org.uk.

4 www.ciria.org.uk The Construction Industry Research and Information Association is devoted to improving the performance of all involved in UK construction and the environment.

5 www.edie.net Environmental Data Interactive Exchange is a free, personalised, interactive news, information and communications service for water, waste and environmental professionals around the world.

6 www.sustainablehomes.co.uk Sustainable Homes promotes awareness of sustainable development issues and good practice, and encourages housing associations to adopt sustainable policies and practices.

7 www.business–in–environment.org.uk Business in the Environment aims to inspire businesses to work towards environmentally sustainable development as a strategic, mainstream business issue.

8 www.bre.co.uk The Building Research Establishment is the UK's leading centre of expertise on buildings, construction, energy, environment, fire and risk, providing research-based consultancy, testing and certification services.

9 www.bsria.co.uk The Building Services Research and Information Association offers independent and authoritative research, product testing, consultancy, management and market intelligence.

10 www.spongenet.org Sponge is a network of individuals who share an interest in sustainable development, working in, or associated with development of the environment. It aims to provide a focus for fresh ideas in building.

11 www.pegonline.net The Property Environment Group aims to assist its members to improve their environmental performance, providing information, tools, training, and contacts. PEG aims to start breaking down the 'vicious circle of blame' which it says has developed within the industry as a key obstacle to a more sustainable built environment.

12 www.aecb.net The Association for Environment Conscious Building is the pre-eminent environmental building trade organisation in the UK.

13 www.m4i.org.uk The Movement for Innovation was launched by the Government to be 'a dynamic, inspirational, non-institutionalised body of people who truly believe in the need for radical improvement within the construction industry'.

14 www.claire.co.uk Contaminated Land Applications in Real Environments aims to provide a link between the main players in contaminated land remediation in the UK. It facilitates the development of cost-effective methods of investigating and remediating contaminated land in a sustainable way.

15 www.ecoconstruct.com Construction Resources is Britain's first ecological building centre distributing materials and systems for sustainable construction. It has a new address at www.constructionresources.com.

Just to look at this list is to get a premonition of what the editor of the *RIBA Journal*, Amanda Baillieu, has properly described as 'a legal minefield that few architects, let alone clients, would want to enter'.[32]

The biggest innovation sought by the law is a mix of the naturalistic with the therapeutic. That mix was first defined by the World Commission on Environment in *Our Common Future*, the Brundtland report of 1987. There, sustainability is set out as the protection of the environment for future citizens; sustainable development is development that 'meets the needs of the present without compromising the ability of future generations to meet their own needs'.[33]

The naturalistic legal innovation that has grown out of Brundtland is, as Rostron points out, based on a belief that the integrity of natural ecosystems should be protected 'not simply for the pleasure of people, but as a biotic right.' By 'biotic right' is meant the idea that nature has rights because it 'has its own purpose, which should be respected as a matter of ethical principle'.[34]

The therapeutic legal innovation that has grown out of Brundtland is to sentimentalise the children of future generations and to make claims in their name – despite the fact that they are not yet born. These are claims about people in the future, but they are also claims that have personal and corporate consequences in the present.

Once these two legal principles are accepted, pretty much anything goes in environmental law. As Rostron notes, intuition triumphs with environmentalists, at the expense of reason, science and technological progress.[35] The first upshot of this freewheeling, creative and innovative posture toward environmental law is the *heightened and simultaneous growth, in the building trade as elsewhere, of both UK common law and EU statutory law on the environment.*

The phrase 'duty of care' is the legal codification of the non-contractual civil obligations that arise between citizens. An environmental duty of care based on sustainability as defined in the Brundtland report would not protect the living citizen, but the natural and built environment for anticipated future citizens. Now, some free-market environmentalists have argued for far greater reliance on individual court action under the common law,[36] while others of a more liberal persuasion have pushed for wider forms of state regulation.[37] By July 2001, however, the European Commission had overturned much of Europe's past laws on the environment and deleted all reference to civil actions for property damage and personal injury. Instead, it launched the idea of a Europe-wide statutory environmental regime enforced by national public authorities.

There are problems with both common law and EU Directive approaches. In Britain, pursuit of an environmental duty of care through the common law means, in practice, a rejection of the democratic habit of legislating for environmental issues through Acts of Parliament. It seeks to rely on unelected judges to make case law.[38] In *Cambridge Water v. Eastern Counties Leather*, Lord Goff rightly argued that it was:

more appropriate for strict liability in respect of operations of high risk to be imposed by Parliament, than by the courts. If such liability is imposed by statute, the relevant activities can be identified, and those concerned can know where they stand.[39]

Of course, Acts of Parliament are rarely perfect or fair. However, a new statute will have the best chance of being democratically contested and rationalised in the political process. It is a measure of our times that, when they come to public policy, people prefer to place it in the hands of an unelected judiciary than in those of politicians – whom they can at least change at elections.

The shift toward a European Directive on environmental law will leave national electorates in the EU unable to have any a say in the matter. Like reliance on judges to make policy through the common law courts, the consolidation of statutory powers within the EU denies democratic influence.

The problem with the legal codification of the naturalistic perspective is that, if the whole future of the planet is taken to be at risk, there can be no time or space for due process. *Ethics* are often invoked to justify innovations in both common and statutory law; but that does not mean that the innovations made are the product of political debate.

At the British Council's Lisbon conference, Valerie Fogleman gave an important speech.[40] She did so as head of the environment group at Barlow Lyde

& Gilbert, solicitors and publishers of the excellent quarterly *Pollution and Environmental Risk Digest*.[41] For her it was obvious that:

when the Directive comes into force, [EU] Member States should provide competent authorities with adequate funding to implement and enforce it and to conduct preventive, remedial and restorative measures in an emergency and when a liable operator does not have sufficient funding to do so.[42]

But who did Fogleman mean when she referred to authorities competent to enforce the EU Directive? Would such authorities include, for example, the National Trust, a charity which itches to remind the European Commission that it is 'the largest non-governmental heritage conservation organisation in Europe'? [43] Or did Fogleman mean people like herself?

After all, she is very competent to play a part in law enforcement. In a manner typical of today's mandarins of sustainability, she wears many influential hats. She:

- advises on the emerging array of environmental liabilities, claims for such liabilities, and insurance cover increasingly required against claims;
- is a member of the Council of the United Kingdom Environmental Law Association, and a convenor of its working party on insurance and liability;[44]
- sits on the Lloyd's European Environment Working Group,[45] and the City of London Law Society Planning and Environmental Law Subcommittee;[46]
- has a regular column in *Insurance Day*[47] and is a contributing author to *Commercial Environmental Law and Liability*;[48] and
- has since 1998 been named as one of the UK's leading environmental lawyers in *Legal 500, Chambers & Partners Directory and Legal Experts*,[49] and was named as one of the top 20

environmental lawyers in the world in Euromoney's *Best of the Best 2001*.[50]

Clearly Fogleman is a driving force behind innovations in law around the environment. But she, like the National Trust, is unelected.

It is possible to agree with environmental lawyers, like Jack Rostron, that development standards can and should be raised. Architects have always encouraged their clients to improve on past development practices, and have found employment because they could provide clients with a better environment than that previously experienced. It is also possible to agree with Rostron that mankind 'has the ingenuity to develop technical solutions to both remediate his past actions and, hopefully, prevent future environmental degradation'. There would not be architects and engineers if this were not the case. Yet there is no reason to accept that 'a strong and evolving legal framework is necessary'.[51]

Of course professionals should be sued for failing in a duty of care, if that is

Valerie Fogleman

limited to a restricted category of living individuals and is further based on a narrow and rational interpretation of the tests of reasonable foresight and close proximity. There are also statutory provisions for good development practice across a democratic society – provisions that are and should be thrashed out in Parliament. Yet it is a simple fact that the more consultants claim a standard of professionalism, the more the law will expand to meet those pretensions and the more designers will be sued. Worse still, the trend will be to work not in the interests of progress, but rather to reduce the perceived risk of litigation for having damaged the environment. The rigour of having to complete Environmental Impact Assessments (see Box 13) is hardly a spur to imaginative or experimental design.

Altogether, designers look set to restrain their imaginations, or to abandon technological development, for fear of building 'unsustainably'. Every innovation in law means less innovation in practice.

3.4 Quango quagmire: the ceaseless re-branding of Britain's building regulators

A good number of initiatives have been set in train and one of the problems is that the industry is experiencing initiative overload. Too many initiatives also mean that limited resources are being spread too thinly . . . The Strategic Forum believes that it is now time for the industry to take a step back and carry out a full review of all the various initiatives that are currently underway and assess the real value they are adding to making the industry an attractive sector to be employed in.[57]

The wealth of those UK official bodies in which backward perspectives on construction prevail presents itself as an immense accumulation of logotypes, its

unit being a single logo. Our investigation must therefore begin with the analysis of a logo – specifically, of the logos of quasi-autonomous non-governmental organizations.

To read any report or any website about the UK construction industry is to confront a confusing range of branded institutions, each with their own distinctive – or actually not so distinctive – marque. The realities of sponsorship ensure that every survey must be backed by a myriad of interested bodies. Furthermore, the people on these bodies invariably sit on more than one at a time. If, in the private sector, it is now regarded as a bit beneath one's dignity to be a non-executive director of too many firms, no such concerns appear to affect Britain's quagmire of building regulators.

Under New Labour, government in Britain has generated a large amount of red tape. Indeed there are many new bodies that have been created precisely to get rid of red tape. As a result, every official initiative in construction, bedecked with logos though it is, must always refer to other official initiatives, also bedecked with logos.

This represents a novel approach to social inclusion, in which the great and the good can always be guaranteed an audience – among themselves.

Such a Byzantine system of interlocking centres of authority has survived the scrutiny of the National Audit Office, and will never rationalise itself. Here is how it works. The Rethinking Construction Ministerial Steering Group provides 'strategic, overarching guidance to improving the performance of the UK construction industry'.[58] It oversees the work of Rethinking Construction Ltd,[59] a not-for-profit company that 'generates best practice and innovative ideas for improving the processes and products of the construction industry'. Rethinking Construction Ltd pursues four lines of activity:

TABLE 14 Four key quangos in the UK building trade

Quango	Responsibility	Website
Movement for Innovation (M4I)	non-housing construction in the private sector	www.m4i.org.uk.
The Housing Forum	housebuilding, refurbishment and repairs and maintenance in the public and private sectors	www.thehousingforum. org.uk.
The Local Government Task Force	best practice for local government clients	www.lgtf.org.uk
The Central Government Task Force	best practice for central government clients	www.hm–treasury.gov.uk.

These four quangos all work in partnership with three more:

TABLE 15 Three more key quangos in the UK building trade

Quango	Responsibility	Website
Construction Best Practice Programme	raising awareness of the benefits of best practice; provides the construction industry and its clients with the skills and knowledge to implement change. Has an Information Technology Construction Best Practice subsidiary	www.cbpp.org.uk www.itcbp.org.uk.
Property and Construction Panel, part of the Office of Government Commerce	considering cross-government issues that affect property and construction procurement	www.ogc.gov.uk
The Strategic Forum for Construction	the collective body of industry representatives working to deliver fundamental improvement to how the construction industry operates and to the products it produces	www.dti.gov.uk/ construction/rethink

Under Egan's chairmanship, the Strategic Forum for Construction was set up as an industry body in 2001. It maintains representation from a wide range of trade associations or bodies dealing with particular aspects of the construction process. This is structured into:

- a high-level Strategic Forum group;
- an implementation group;
- a working group on client leadership;
- a working group on integrated supply teams; and
- a working group on people issues, in which *Respect for People* is a priority campaign.[60]

Box 13 THE MITIGATION OF ARCHITECTURE: ENVIRONMENTAL IMPACT ASSESSMENTS

In 1985 the European Council enacted one of its principal pieces of environmental legislation, Directive 85/337/EEC – the requirement that, as a condition of planning approval for major development projects, public and private bodies provide not just information on the site, design and size of the project but also:

- the data required to identify and assess the main effects which the project is likely to have on the environment;
- a description of the measures envisaged in order to avoid, reduce and, if possible, remedy significant adverse effects; and
- a non-technical summary of all this.[52]

In 1997 Directive 97/11/EC widened the scope of EIAs by
- increasing the number of types of project covered;
- increasing the number of projects requiring mandatory assessment; and
- insisting that an outline of the main alternatives studied by the developer be provided, along with an indication of the main reasons for his choice, taking into account the environmental effects.[53]

In 2003 the EU published a detailed and laudatory review of the 1997 EIA Directive. It found, among other things, that the British planning and legal systems have dealt with over 500 EIAs each year since 1999. For Brussels, the 1997 Directive has been a success. But the *mitigation process* that the Directive demands – changing the design of developments 'to avoid, reduce and, if possible, remedy significant adverse effects' – means that architects must:

- provide all critics of their designs with enough timely information to allow them to mount full and timely objections; and
- revise their designs to remove any objections that are upheld, should the EIA have failed to result in a design that made sufficiently low environmental impact from the outset of the process.[54]

In line with the Precautionary Principle, the burden of proof lies with the architect. It is the architect who is charged with working out every kind of environmental objection that might ever be levelled at developments.

To demand this kind of clairvoyance is bad enough. But the demand for mitigation hurts the developer still more. Regardless of how much developers might like to take risks with a particular building design, EIAs place them under pressure to force architects, engineers and other construction industry professionals to mitigate the environmental problems that are thought to attach to that design. In his *Environmental Law for the Built Environment*, Rostron makes clear that 'the question for the developer is how far the mitigation should go?'.[55] In today's naturalistic climate, the answer is: a long way, and then some.

Most professionals already cave in to the demand for mitigation by design in the face of an unfavourable EIA procedure – even if they think the process flawed. Most comply with the determination of planning authorities that their designs be modified so that they are sustainable. Most would rather not persist with a controversial aspect of a design, possibly ending up by putting their clients in court. But the fact is that whether the environmental impact of an architectural design is, or is not, regarded as acceptable has become a matter of opinion beyond the control of architect, client or even the planner. The language of the Brussels Commission's website on environmental matters brilliantly captures the authoritarian intent of EIAs, as well as the opacity of those in charge of them:

> The EIA procedure ensures that environmental consequences of projects are identified and assessed before authorisation is given. The public can give its opinion and all results are taken into account in the authorisation procedure of the project. The public is informed of the decision afterwards.[56]

All in all, EIAs add another dimension to the difficulties facing architects who want to stay in business and avoid legal action. Moreover because sustainability is capable of such fluid definitions, EIAs ensure that every project must go through an interminable process of public and professional consultation.

With EIAs, each new piece of bespoke architecture must be accompanied by a new and yet more stringent definition of sustainability of architecture. Every building starts off having to prove that it is not a blot on the planet.

But all the different quangos are not just static. They and their logos are constantly being rebranded. Here is what was officially announced in 2002:

Directly following the launch of the *Rethinking Construction* report the Movement for Innovation was established by industry with Government to respond to the recommendation in the report for a movement for change. Whilst M4I takes the lead in general construction, the Housing Forum was established to bring together all those within the house building chain in the movement for change and innovation. Then in March 2000 the Local Government Task Force was set up to encourage and assist local authorities to adopt the principles of *Rethinking Construction*. Following some three and a half years of activity, the decision was made in April 2002 to streamline the *Rethinking Construction* initiative by bringing together the streams under the banner of Rethinking Construction Ltd which acts as the main point of co-ordination and liaison, whilst maintaining their individual focus.[61]

Here, too, is what was officially announced in 2003:

Construction Best Practice and Rethinking Construction are combining into a single organisation to be called "Constructing Excellence". Its aim will be to deliver better business improvement services to the UK construction industry for the longer term.

Peter Rogers, Chairman of the Strategic Forum for Construction has accepted the role of Chairman of "Constructing Excellence". Informally the two organisations already collaborate to make the most of their complementary services and support programmes. They both agree that now is the right time to bring the two organisations even closer together.

By any measure Rethinking Construction and Construction Best Practice have proved themselves to be remarkably effective in identifying and promoting the take-up of innovations and best practice to support business improvement. The business case for change has been proven time and time again. Thousands of construction businesses are participating in the various improvement and learning programmes.

By combining the key objective will be to create an organization that can deliver even better services and value to the industry.

"Constructing Excellence" will build on the successful services, structures and networks that have been established throughout the UK and seek to retain the expertise of the respective Teams.

The two organisations are working closely together to identify the optimum working arrangements for "Constructing Excellence" and in particular its business and management structures. A further announcement about the next steps will be made as soon as practicable once decisions have been made.[62]

In both announcements, the prose is as lucid as can be found in the quango quagmire. And who, pray, is Peter Rogers ? He is Technical Director at property developers Stanhope plc. Peter's elder brother is Richard Rogers; his business partner at Stanhope, Stuart Lipton, is chairman of the Commission for Architecture and the Built Environment (see Box 14).

Britain's quagmire is not limited to Government initiatives. There has also been an explosion of private sector umbrella bodies, advice centres, industry councils, trade associations and professional institutes. Each has its own agenda. Each has tried to cut across boundaries. Each has a therapeutic helpline. The result is that the carousel of conferences and seminars organised by earnest modernisers is so rich, it is a wonder that anyone riding on it ever gets to spend a normal working day in the office.

What does it all amount to in practice? Simon Vivian, chief executive of the giant concern Hanson Building Materials Europe, is responsible for its environmental programme. He explains what backward perspectives on construction mean in practice:

All our businesses have committed to implementing Environmental Management Systems and over 750 sites have already done so. During 2001 we devoted considerable resources to training and auditing, reflecting the need to verify that all of our operations are working to meet local regulatory requirements. We conducted over 4000 environmental audits and over 7000 of our employees received environmental training.

Our environmental programme is not driven primarily by cost benefit analysis, although financial benefits do emerge from initiatives such as concrete waste recycling, water reuse and reduced energy consumption.

I look forward to reporting to you again on the progress we have made.[63]

What used to be a matter of running an efficient business and keeping it within the law has become a display of corporate innocence to the quango quagmire. Today's ethical construction industry executives will never again utter the phrase 'it's none of your business!'. If some official sets a standard, they will comply with it (see Box 15). Yet they are right to have the premonition that compliance fuels the demand for more compliance.

The obscurantist interdependency of the quango crocodiles works against the awkward truth being told – that the construction industry is not being rethought so much as meditated upon and massaged. Yet as successive governments have contracted out policymaking on construction and the environment, the quangos' reach has grown at the same rate as their intellectual rigour has declined. They also jostle with each other for position, knowing no self-restraint in their meandering initiatives (see Box 16).

In Britain many people have bemoaned the breaking up of Prescott's Department of Environment, Transport and the Regions, itself designed as a sop to the man's ego. But if the government shows no coherent thinking on the related issues of land use, infrastructure and construction, that is not a fluke of nature, but a logical result of its preference for regulation at the expense of political accountability.

Peter Rogers

Peter Rogers is a chartered civil engineer. With Stuart Lipton, he co-founded Stanhope plc in Britain.[64] Employed by several major contractors, both internationally and in the UK, he has worked on commercial buildings in New York City using construction management, has planned dry docks and airports in the Middle East, and has designed offshore oil production platforms and roads. His clients include the Ministry of Defence, the Royal Opera House, Glyndebourne Productions and Tate Modern.

Rogers has most recently worked on several new corporate HQs in London, major business parks at Chiswick and Hemel Hempstead, the redevelopment of Selfridges, the protracted redevelopment of Paternoster Square (next to St Paul's Cathedral), and on the 60-hectare regeneration of Stratford rail lands.

Sir Stuart Lipton

Through Stanhope plc, Sir Stuart Lipton helped pioneer the use in Britain of American development and construction methods, and persuaded top British architects to design speculative office blocks to new levels of quality. He has been responsible for more than 1,115,000 m^2 of development, across more than 40 projects. His achievements include Broadgate in the City of London (418,000 m^2), Stockley Park at Heathrow (186,000 m^2 over 162 hectares), Chiswick Park (139,000 m^2), and the new Treasury building in Whitehall (93,000 m^2). Stanhope plc's pre-tax profits rose to £6.7 million in the year to March 2001 – on a turnover of £12.6 million.[65] Stanhope is also a founding partner of Asite.

Between 1985 and 1991 Lipton advised on the construction of The Sainsbury Building at The National Gallery. He was responsible for the reconstruction of the Sackler Galleries in the Royal Academy between 1988 and 1991, and between 1989 and 1994 worked with Glyndebourne Productions on a new opera house. A governor of Imperial College of Science, Technology and Medicine since 1987, he is an expert in fine art, and sits on innumerable committees.

Box 14 **THE STATE COMMISSION FOR DESIGN CORRECTION**

Chaired by Stuart Lipton, the Commission for Architecture and the Built Environment in England (CABE) was founded in 1999. The following year Lipton, a commercial developer since the late 1960s and chairman of Stanhope plc, was knighted. Since that time, New Labour has charged CABE with facilitating improvements in the quality of the whole of the built environment – not just buildings but also the spaces between them.[66]

In the three years to 2006, CABE will receive nearly £30 million in funds from Prescott's office and the Department for Culture, Media and Sport.[67] In addition, it will spend much of the £17 million set aside in New Labour's *Sustainable communities* for improving urban design skills among local authorities. CABE will teach public sector professionals and elected councillors how to avoid its disapproval over any decision they may make.

Through its Design Quality Indicators, CABE polices England's architectural taste. It is the arbiter of what is culturally acceptable in the development sector. Chief executive Jon Rouse believes that: 'well-designed homes, streets, parks, workplaces, schools and hospitals are the fundamental right of everyone'.[68]

In practice, however, this popular democratic right translates into Rouse being responsible for commenting on the plans for every significant building in England – not just on aesthetic grounds, but also in terms of what it contributes to the regeneration of an area.[69]

CABE judgments are now another determining factor whenever a 'significant' architectural design is recommended for planning approval. Of course, CABE only recommends design 'improvements'; but designers accommodate to its views like young students handing in essays to a headmaster.

The scope for CABE's intrusions can only increase. Already Debra Shipley MP, joint chair of the Architecture and Planning Associate Parliamentary Group for New Labour, wants a checklist of sustainability indicators to be included in any planning application.[70] It cannot be long before she finds her wish granted by CABE.

Jon Rouse

Jon Rouse took a degree in law before doing a masters degree in urban policy and business administration, specialising in corporate finance. Then, when he spent five years at the Department for the Environment, he did a stint as Private Secretary to the Minister for Housing and Local Government, as well as a secondment to the Energy Saving Trust. Rouse next became secretary to Richard Rogers' Urban Task Force, as well as policy and communications manager at the Government's urban regeneration agency, English Partnerships.[71] He was appointed chief executive of CABE from the quango's inception in 1999.

Box 15 **ORDEAL BY STANDARDS**

A Standard is a published specification that establishes a common language, and contains a technical specification or other precise criteria and is designed to be used consistently, as a rule, as a guideline, or as a definition. Standards are applied to many materials, products, methods and services. They help to make life simpler, and increase the reliability and the effectiveness of many goods and services we use . . . Standards are designed for voluntary use and do not impose any regulations. However, laws and regulations may refer to certain standards, making compliance with them compulsory.[72]

Here the British Standards Institution (BSI) emphasises the precision of the criteria it uses in drafting standards. But in a few short, defining sentences, it glosses over:

- the fact that its standards are arrived at out of consensus, rather than objectively. This means that a standard may be obeyed, even if it is inadequate; and
- the difference between the hard technical specifications of a product and the much more debatable quality of a service.

BSI chairman Vivian Thomas believes that 'processes as much as products now require standardisation'.[73] The ability to annex services and processes and impose standards on them accounts for much of the growing power of the BSI Group.

During the 1990s, BSI Group's turnover increased from £61 million to £232.5 million; pre-tax earnings, from just under £4 million to £21.1 million. The Group now operates in 110 countries. Staff levels have increased from 1700 in 1991 to more than 4700 in 2001, with over half of employees located outside the UK.

In 2002, recognising an opportunity to secure even more business, the BSI published a new, single standard replacing six separate ones on how to audit the quality of goods, that of services and that of the environment. In so doing, the first edition of *BS EN ISO 19011: 2002 Guidelines for quality and/or environmental management systems auditing* mixed up consensus-based verdicts on products and services with the still more subjective question of environmental 'goods' and 'bads'. The result will be that inferior products and services pass muster, so long as they are deemed environmentally beneficial.

The BSI revels in its new powers:

The cost of failing an environmental/quality management systems audit takes many forms. Companies can lose valuable contracts or prized certifications. They may have to pay for an expensive programme of improvements demanded by a client. They may see operational efficiency eroded.[74]

But to cut the mustard, builders must not only meet BS EN ISO 19011 but other standards too – a process that retains and relies upon this ever expanding list of other standards:

- *BS EN ISO 14001: 1996 Environmental management systems – specification with guidance for use;*
- *BS EN ISO 14004: 1996 Environmental management systems – general guidelines on principles and supporting techniques;*
- *BS EN ISO 14021: 1999 Environmental labels and declarations – Type II environmental labelling. Self declared environmental claims;*

- *BS EN ISO 14024: 1999 Environmental labels and declarations – Type I environmental labelling. Principles and procedures;*
- *BS EN ISO 14031: 2000 Environmental management – Environmental performance evaluation. Guidelines;*
- *BS EN ISO 14040: 1997 Environmental management – Life cycle assessment. Principles and framework;*
- *BS EN ISO 14041: 1997 Environmental management – Life cycle assessment. Goal and scope definition and inventory analysis;* and
- *BS EN ISO 14050: 1998 Environmental management – Vocabulary.*

Learn to speak sustainababble, and be tested on your environmental vocabulary! The price of tuition is available from the BSI on application, but is guaranteed to be less than the price of not enduring ordeal by standards.

Box 16 COMPETING INDICATORS OF SUSTAINABILITY

In the quango quagmire that is Britain's construction industry, every agency, research establishment and institute is in a ratings race – that is, a race to introduce new and better Environmental Performance Indicators.

The Movement for Innovation (M4I) is very clear that, whatever the faults of its own EPIs, they are the right things to have. They are 'meant to be a start for the industry, so that it can get going on the process of measuring its environmental sustainability credentials'.[75]

Here are M4I's six EPIs:

1   Operational Carbon Dioxide emissions (kg CO_2/m^2/year): the CO_2 produced as a result of the energy from fossil fuels consumed for the day-to-day operation of the building or structure. Excludes renewable energy.
2   Embodied Carbon Dioxide (kg CO_2/m^2): the CO_2 produced from the energy used in the extraction, fabrication and transportation of the materials used in the construction.
3   Water (m^3/person (equivalent)/year): analogous to operational CO_2, the amount of mains water used in the operation of the building. Excludes recovered or recycled water such as rainwater.
4   Waste in the Construction Process (measured in $m^3/100m^2$ floor area): the waste sent for disposal – that is, not specifically sent for recycling or reuse – from site operations. (This indicator is still under development – some limited data has been used to provide an initial benchmark.)
5   Biodiversity (the measure and benchmark are still to be developed): the intention is that this indicator be used as a measure of actions taken to maintain, protect and improve the flora and fauna on site. A possible basis for the measurement might be the area of wildlife habitat preserved and or created as a percentage of total site area, also taking into account the area of wildlife habitat existing prior to development, or the change in a species index per hectare site area as a result of the development.
6   Transport (the measure and benchmark are still to be developed): the purpose of this indicator is to measure the impact of the transport used to deliver materials and staff to site. Suggested measures are transport km/total on-site working hour or transport movements/total development area.

For M4I these EPIs are only the start. It expects clients and their consultants to start comparing the performance of projects against the indicators, and then move on to set targets for performance improvement. At the same time M4I wants to make its EPIs tougher. It provides a performance reporting form for industry professionals to fill in and return to the Building Research Establishment's Centre for Sustainable Construction.[76]

Members of M4I are predominantly construction managers and contractors, with a handful of design professionals. In Britain their first rivals as arbiters of sustainability therefore include the Royal Institute of Chartered Surveyors (RICS).

In 2001, the RICS developed, with the help of distinguished contributors, a *Global Manifesto* on sustainability. It was for 'enduring use, not only to RICS and the surveying profession, but to allied professions, international agencies, communities, businesses and governments throughout the world'.[77] The following year, at the Johannesburg Summit, RICS president Peter Fall established a Global Alliance for Building Sustainability with the support of the British government.

His reasons were simple. As number crunchers of building materials and experts in property market fluctuations, surveyors were better placed than anyone else to calculate the costs and benefits of sustainability:

> The global construction industry is estimated to be worth $3.2 trillion, employing 111 million people directly and accounting for 10–15 per cent of GDP. It is also estimated that each construction job generates two further jobs elsewhere, which would suggest that 20 per cent of all employment is linked to construction in some way . . . So even small percentage improvements in building efficiency would translate to many billions in savings which, if ploughed back into the industry (for example by retrofitting existing stock to make it more energy efficient) could have a beneficial "multiplier" effect on sustainability.[78]

Sustainability, then, can no longer be left to designers to explore at the client's expense. It must be properly accounted for by surveyors, or managed through neutral third parties. It may even mean more retrofittings for Greenness – tasks which, unless aggregated into larger refurbishment projects, will engage building surveyors but not architects.

The RIBA is not to be outdone. It has begun to draw up a sustainability rating system for all new buildings.[79] Meanwhile, the Construction Industry Council has published *Constructing for sustainability: a guide for clients and their professional advisors*.[80]

Mirror, mirror, on the wall, who is the most ecologically correct of them all?

3.5 Power in the building trade

In the international bestseller that first earned him his reputation as a management guru, *Competitive strategy* (1980), Michael Porter trained a generation of US bosses in ruthlessness. Beset, he said, by new market entrants, the threat of product substitution, buyer power, supplier power and direct rivals, they should make their products different, target distinct markets and strive for overall cost leadership. And he said something else besides. A corporation needed to know how to organise its *value chain*.

Ever since Porter's work, business analysts have been at pains to delineate the typical value chain – or, more recently, the trendier *value network* – in particular industries; and the construction industry is no different from any other in this regard. What, then, is the real value chain in the building trade? Where does the power lie? Does it lie with the client, the landowner, the developer, the main contractor, the trade contractor, the architect, the engineer or the surveyor?

The answer to this riddle is easy enough. In Britain at least, power, if not value, lies with other forces in the construction industry: not just with the planning system, but with the urban supervision organised by BIDs; with the workplace mandarins looking after health, safety and business continuity; with environmental lawyers and the quango quacks of sustainability. In short, *power in construction lies with the state, operating through its funded initiatives.*

Traditionally the client was seen as being the ultimate source of power in construction, on the basis of 'He who pays the piper calls the tune'. But if, in 1994, Sir Michael Latham could fairly argue that 'inexperienced clients need advice',[81] things have since changed. In Egan's later view, clients stood in need of 'objective advice free from any vested interest in a solution proposed as a result of the assistance given'.[82] Indeed by 2003, Britain's Strategic Forum planned, inevitably, to have developed a range of

techniques with which to measure construction performance – a whole 'toolkit' to help clients and suppliers 'assemble integrated teams, mobilise their value streams and promote effective team working skills'.[83]

Teamwork, it appears, is not just a good idea: it is on the order of the day. So much for freedom of contract! 'Thou shalt not use any procurement process but mine', hint the Rethinkers of Construction and the Respecters of People.

This is more than the nanny state meddling with the market. It says that the advice a client may commission from a consultant cannot be relied upon to be impartial. It implies that the provider of what it calls 'independent' advice is a consultant vetted by the state. This questioning of impartiality, which is the basis upon which contracts are supposed to be administered, is as serious an attack on professionalism as it is possible to make. It says that because fee-earning architects cannot be impartial, clients should go to someone licensed to promote the therapeutic and naturalistic perspectives in construction.

British law used to assume that customers were grown-ups. On the basis of 'buyer beware', individuals were expected to take responsibility for the commissions they offered. As Egan himself observed, clients should enter the construction process with a clear understanding of their business needs.[84] But now things are different. *In the regulatory mind, the client has become a child.* He or she must be saved by the Good Adviser from the Wicked Consultant and the Naughty Builders.

This might be pantomime, if it did not confirm, in the building trade, *the subordination of client power to that of the state.*

One of Britain's biggest clients, the British Airports Authority, shows this subordination all too clearly. Why, asked a perennially and properly curious Ruth Slavid at the *Architects' Journal*, had BAA spent such a long time worrying about

Terminal 5, only to end up with a relatively mundane building? The answer was simple:

Everything that can be measured, monitored and controlled, is . . . But it is [an approach] unlikely to generate great architecture.[85]

BAA had no choice but to accept the current level of state supervision – over both design and building. In fact clients throughout Britain's private and voluntary sectors do the same. The situation is unprecedented. *Never before in UK construction have so many people set out to check and approve what others do against so many shifting criteria.*

The result is to bring yet more paralysis to an industry that is already backward.

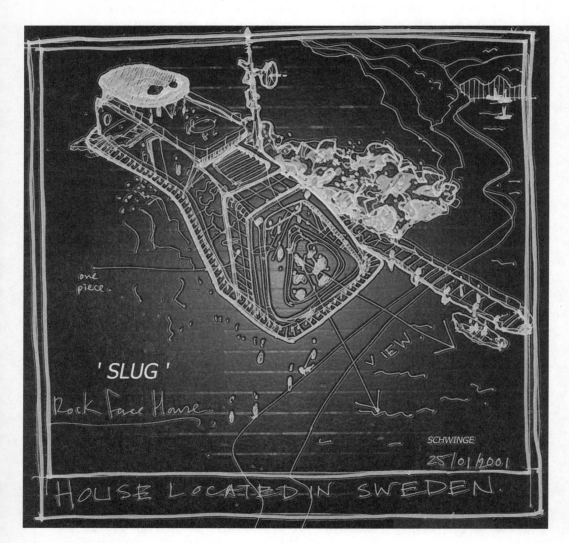

'Slug', by Jonathan Schwinge

NOTES

1 Office of the Deputy Prime Minister, *Working Draft of Guidance on Business Improvement Districts*, January 2003, p 6, and posted on www.local–regions.odpm.gov.uk/bids/index.htm

2 Office of the Deputy Prime Minister, *Working Draft of Guidance on Business Improvement Districts*, January 2003, p 7, and posted on www.local–regions.odpm.gov.uk/bids/index.htm

3 Office of the Deputy Prime Minister, 'Businesses "BID" to help communities thrive', *News Release 005*, 21 January 2003, posted on www.odpm.gov.uk

4 Office of the Deputy Prime Minister, 'Businesses "BID" to help communities thrive', *News Release 005*, 21 January 2003, posted on www.odpm.gov.uk

5 Tony Travers and Jeroen Weimar, *Business Improvement Districts New York and London* (London, Corporation of London, 1996).

6 Alan Pike, 'A private tax for cleaner streets', *Financial Times*, 9 January 1997 and posted on www.ft.com

7 Michael Porter, 'The competitive advantage of the inner city', *Harvard Business Review*, May-June 1995, p 56 to 57, 60.

8 Office of the Deputy Prime Minister, *Working Draft of Guidance on Business Improvement Districts*, January 2003, p 13 to 15, and posted on www.odpm.gov.uk/stellent/groups/odpm_localgov/documents/pdf/odpm_locgov_pdf_023522.pdf

9 Paul Levy, 'Paying for the public life', posted on www.ida–downtown.org

10 Office of the Deputy Prime Minister, 'Business Improvement Districts', *Update,* Issue 27, 11 November 2002, and posted on www.urban.odpm.gov.uk/publications/update

11 Thomas Y Levin, Ursula Frohne and Peter Weibel, editors, *CTRL [SPACE]: Rhetorics of surveillance from Bentham to Big Brother* (Cambridge, Massachusetts, The MIT Press, 2002) p 10.

12 'Special report: Big Brother', *The Guardian*, 7, 14 and 21 September 2002 and posted on www.guardian.co.uk/bigbrother/privacy/0,12377,783005,00.html

13 Thomas Y Levin, Ursula Frohne and Peter Weibel, editors, *CTRL [SPACE]: Rhetorics of surveillance from Bentham to Big Brother* (Cambridge, Massachusetts, The MIT Press, 2002) p 275.

14 Dolan Cummings, *Surveillance & the City,* Urban Research Group, 1997, p 18.

15 Anne Marie Feyer, 'Fatigue: time to recognise and deal with an old problem', *British Medical Journal*, Vol 322, 7 April 2001, p 809.

16 Y Liu and H Tanaka, 'Overtime work, insufficient sleep, and risk of non-fatal acute myocardial infection in Japanese men', *Occupational and Environmental Medicine*, 59, 2002, p 447 to 451.

17 HSE, *Management standards*, 16 June 2003 and posted on www.hse.gov.uk/stress/stresspilot/standards.htm

18 Department of Trade and Industry, Press Release, 'Major cash boost for work-life balance initiatives', DTI, 11 June 2002, available on www.nds.coi.gov.uk

19 J Kodz, H Harper, S Dench, *Work-Life Balance: Beyond the Rhetoric – IES Report 384* (Brighton, Institute of Employment Studies, 2002) and posted in summary on www.employment–studies.co.uk/summary

20 Department of Health, *Saving Lives: Our healthier nation* (London, The Stationery Office, 1999).

21 Health and Safety Commission, 'Directors' responsibilities for health and safety', booklet, HSC, July 2001, p 8 to 9.

22 Cherie Booth, Foreword in Jack Rostron, *Environmental Law for the Built Environment* (London Cavendish Publishing, 2001) page vii.

23 British Council and Ecosphere – Consultores em Ambiente e Desenvolvimento, Proceedings, International Conference on Environmental Liability, in Lisbon, 11 to 12 July 2002, and posted on www.britishcouncilpt.org/document/EnvLiabFinalProceedings.pdf

24 Commission of the European Communities, *White Paper on Environmental Liability*, COM(2000) 66 final (Brussels, EC, 2000) and posted on www.europa.eu.int

25 United Nations Environment Programme, Press Release, 'Senior Judges Adopt Ground-Breaking Action Plan to Strengthen World's Environment-Related Laws', 27 August 2002, and posted on www.unep.org

26 'Environmental courts likely in India soon', *The Times of India*, 24 January 2003, and posted on www.rupfor.org

27 Matthew Richards, 'American Dreams', *Building*, 17 January 2003, p 42 to 43.

28 www.newdream.org

29 www.usgbc.org

30 US Green Building Council, *Green Building Rating System*, first published 2002 (Washington, USGBC, version 2.1 published 2003) and posted on www.usgbc.org

31 Rachel Crossley, 'Green Buildings & The Bottom Line: An Investor's Perspective', speech to the British Institute of Facilities Managers, 16 to 18 October 2001.

32 Amanda Baillieu, editorial, 'The longer arm of the law', *The RIBA Journal*, November 2001, p 5.

33 World Commission on Environment and Development, *Our Common Future* (Oxford University Press, Oxford, 1987).

34 Jack Rostron, *Environmental Law for the Built Environment* (London, Cavendish Publishing, 2001) p 35.

35 Jack Rostron, *Environmental Law for the Built Environment* (London, Cavendish Publishing, 2001) p 35.

36 T Anderson and L Leal, *Free Market Environmentalism* (Boulder, Pacific Research Institute, Westview Press, 1991).

37 T Jewell and J Steele, *Law in Environmental Decision Making* (Oxford, Clarendon Press, 1998).

38 Jack Rostron, *Environmental Law for the Built Environment* (London, Cavendish Publishing, 2001) p 107.

39 Lord Goff, *Cambridge Water Co v. Eastern Counties Leather* (1994) 1 All ER 53 at 76.

40 British Council and Ecosphere – Consultores em Ambiente e Desenvolvimento, Proceedings, International Conference on Environmental Liability, in Lisbon, 11 to 12 July 2002, and posted on www.british councilpt.org/document/EnvLiabFinal Proceedings.pdf.

41 *Pollution and Environmental Risk Digest*, Barlow Lyde & Gilbert, and posted on www.blg.co.uk

42 Valerie Fogleman, 'A critical assessment of the legal framework of the proposed regime and the practical consequences resulting from its application', in British Council and Ecosphere – Consultores em Ambiente e Desenvolvimento, Proceedings, International Conference on Environmental Liability, in Lisbon, 11 to 12 July 2002, p 46, and posted on www.britishcouncilpt.org/ document/EnvLiabFinalProceedings.pdf

43 Press Release, 'The National Trust's initial response to the European Commission's consultation', *The National Trust*, April 2000, and posted on www.nationaltrust. org.uk

44 www.ukela.org

45 www.lr.org and www.eurolloyd.nl

46 www.citysolicitors.org.uk

47 www.insuranceday.com

48 Simon Payne, General Editor, *Commercial Environmental Law and Liability*, biannual, Sweet and Maxwell, and posted on www. smlawpub.co.uk

49 *Legal 500, Chambers & Partners Directory and Legal Experts*, and posted on www. chambersandpartners.com

50 www.euromoney.com

51 Jack Rostron, *Environmental Law for the Built Environment* (London, Cavendish Publishing, 2001) p 1.

52 *Council Directive 85/337/EEC of 27 June 1985 on the assessment of the effects of certain public and private projects on the environment*, and posted on http://europa. eu.int/comm/environment/eia/full–legal–te xt/85337.htm

53 *Council Directive 97/11/EC of 3 March 1997 amending Directive 85/337/EEC on the assessment of the effects of certain public and private projects on the environment*, and posted on http://europa.eu.int/comm/ environment/eia/full–legal–text/9711.htm

54 European Commission, *Report from the Commission to the European Parliament and the Council – On the Application and Effectiveness of the EIA Directive (Directive 85/337/EEC as amended by Directive 97/11/EC) – How successful are the Member States in implementing the EIA Directive* (Brussels, EC, 2003) p 9, and posted on www.europa.eu.int/comm/environment/ eia/report_en.pdf

55 Jack Rostron, *Environmental Law for the Built Environment* (London, Cavendish Publishing, 2001) p 71.

56 http://europa.eu.int/comm/environment/ eia/eia–legalcontext.htm

57 Strategic Forum for Construction, *Accelerating Change* (London, Rethinking Construction, 2002) p 29.

58 www.dti.gov.uk

59 www.rethinkingconstruction.org

60 Respect for People Working Group, *Respect for People: A framework for action* (London, Rethinking Construction, 2002).

61 Strategic Forum for Construction, *Accelerating Change* (London, Rethinking Construction, 2002) p 14.

62 'Combining Rethinking Construction and Construction Best Practice', *CBP-E News*, 6 February 2003, and posted on www. cbpp.org.uk

63 Simon Vivian, *Hanson Environmental Report 2001* (London, Hanson PLC, 2001) p 2, and posted on www.hansonplc.com

64 www.stanhopeplc.com

65 David Lawson, 'Stanhope Profile', February 2001, and posted on www.davidlawson.co.uk

66 www.cabe.org.uk

67 Commission for Architecture and the Built Environment, News Release, 'CABE welcomes cash boost for creating better communities across England', CABE, 15 February 2003, and posted on www.cabe.org.uk

68 Jon Rouse, 'Making good housing design our right', letter, *Financial Times*, 26 July 2003, p 12.

69 Matt Weaver, 'Rising Stars: Jon Rouse', 19 September 2001, Guardian Unlimited, and posted on http://society.guardian.co.uk/

70 David Littlefield, 'Taste powers of CABE?', *Building Design*, 28 March 2002, p 6.

71 www.englishpartnerships.gov.uk

72 British Standards Institution, *So You Want to Know About BSI* (London, BSI, 2002) p 2, and posted on www.bsi–global.com

73 Vivian Thomas, Chairman's Statement, BSI Group: Annual Review and Summary Financial Statements 2001 (London, BSI, 2001) p 3, and posted on www.bsi–global.com

74 News Release, 'BS EN ISO 19011 Guidelines for quality and environmental management systems auditing', British Standards Institution, 23 September 2002, and posted on www.bsi–global.com

75 Movement for Innovation, Sustainability Working Group, *Environmental Performance Indicators for Sustainable Construction* (London, M4i, 2002) p 1, and posted on www.m4I.org.uk

76 www.bre.co.uk

77 Peter Faulkner, Introduction, *Global Manifesto* (London, RICS, 2001) and posted on www.rics.org.uk

78 Peter Fall, 'From aspiration to reality: practical measures, values and practice', speech to the inaugural conference of the Global Alliance for Building Sustainability at the World Summit for Sustainable Development in Johannesburg, 30 August 2002, and posted on www.rics.org.uk

79 'Hyett's drive towards sustainable development "will be my legacy"', *Architects' Journal*, 22 May 2003, p 12.

80 Construction Industry Council, *Constructing For Sustainability: A basic guide for clients and their professional advisors* (London, CIC, 2003) available through www.cic.org.uk

81 *Constructing the Team: Joint review of procurement and contractual arrangements in the United Kingdom construction industry, Final Report* (London, HMSO, 1994) p 14.

82 Strategic Forum for Construction, *Accelerating Change* (London, Rethinking Construction, 2002) p 38.

83 Strategic Forum for Construction, *Accelerating Change* (London, Rethinking Construction, 2002) p 25.

84 Strategic Forum for Construction, *Accelerating Change* (London, Rethinking Construction, 2002) p 20.

85 Ruth Slavid, Editorial, 'There needs to be some letting go if airports are really going to take off', *Architects' Journal*, 29 May 2003, p 22.

4 Architecture versus Building in the 1960s housing boom

Miles Glendinning and Stefan Muthesius

To-day . . . architects are part of the building industry.[1]

> A W Cleeve Barr, chief architect,
> Ministry of Housing and Local
> Government, 1963

System building . . . was a panacea indeed – it promised the benefits of a revolution in building without a revolution actually taking place.[2]

> Brian Finnimore,
> *Houses from the factory*, 1989

4.1 Industrialisation in post-war architectural perspective

The idea that architecture is or might be an industry is as old as architecture itself. However, to consider the industrialisation of architecture as a *problem* is a recent phenomenon. It came as a by-product of the divorce of architecture as high art from building as a mechanical art – a division that took place during the Renaissance. The 19th century followed this divorce with a further subdivision of the building industry itself, separating out 'civil engineering'. In the first place that phrase meant the most demanding kind of construction, using new materials. Other kinds of building remained, in effect, with architecture, but in a subordinate position, and were thereby devalued as 'ordinary building'.

Thus *engineering* was seen as innovative, while *building* was now perceived to have remained conventional. Thereafter the situation grew yet more complex. Until about 1900, one can at least speak of a unity preserved through the overall hierarchy of cost in architecture: cheap architecture or building lacked decoration and, at the same time, was likely to be unreliably constructed. This consideration had ceased to apply in the field of pure engineering, comprised, as it mainly was, of high-profile undertakings in which the cost factor did not seem to matter.[3]

One could never conceive of a cheap work of civil engineering. Yet by the end of the 19th century, inexpensive products for houses, factories and offices had come of age: cast-iron gutters; rainwater pipes and columns; sawn structural timber and floorboards; roofing slates and tiles; processed stone, bricks and clay drainage pipes; glass and vertical sliding sash timber windows; sanitary fittings; and lead pipe and sheet lead for roofing had all somehow legitimised themselves in both architecture and 'ordinary building'. Still, this was legitimacy only in the economic field, and that within a strictly capitalist world-view.

The new legitimacy of industrial methods in construction was bound up with the emergence of mass production. Those methods served that majority of the populace that was neither poor nor rich. Naturally, the new methods largely concerned people's houses.

In the smaller English urban terraced house, there had been for some time a strong trend toward standardisation, brought about not only by the construction industry but also by the constraints set by London building regulations. The same trend toward standards applied to a lesser extent among Scottish tenement flats. It was during the late 19th century that advances in brickmaking and stone-cutting, an ever greater mechanisation in the preparing of timber, economies in transport and the rationalisation of all phases of the trading process combined to lead to an astonishing efficiency. A standard, smallish terraced house about 1900, in London as well as in the English provinces, can be said to have been very largely prefabricated and even 'industrialised' with, for instance, window frames and doors coming ready-made from Sweden. Even a certain quantity of ornament was mass-produced – in shaped or contrasting brickwork, stone bay-window features, timber doors, architraves and skirtings, or repetitive plaster ceiling mouldings for working into wet plaster applied on site.

At this earliest of stages, however, this kind of mass production of urban housing already seemed problematic. After all, the building sector's criteria of economy and efficiency were not shared generally by the world of architecture. On the other hand, members of the intellectual, middle and upper middle classes, who lived in more individualised houses, were not afraid to apply architectural judgements to mass housing: it was viewed at best with indifference, but more often with contempt. Mass-produced ornament on facades, above all, was attacked as pointless and meretricious. The detailed arguments to substantiate this contempt were provided by high architects, their associated artists and craft producers, and by some of the most revered writers, critics and opinion-formers in the land, such as William Morris.[4]

Their critiques were in turn almost immediately overtaken by the Modernist prospectus of the Deutsche Werkbund and others. Now Morris was held to be right in condemning the meretriciousness of the 19th century but wrong in overlooking the opportunities that modern, fully industrialised mass production could offer.[5] That argument prevailed until the 1960s, after which judgements began to be reversed. Thereafter Morrisians were held to be right in rejecting industrial mass production, but wrong in condemning 19th century mass-ornamented houses.[6]

What had also developed in the meantime, as a continuous movement from about 1900, was a new art and science of housing, combining architectural art with town-planning sociology. To return to a fusion of art and science, of art and industry, was one of the great projects of European Modernism. Mass building, the creation of towns, of mass housing, became the chief panacea for its implementation. Planners, architects, local and central government housing specialists, national, and particularly, local politicians all often entertained utopian visions of vast new settlements, living in greenery. Indeed, nothing short of the transformation of the whole country, or at least all major towns, would have satisfied them. Only the state – or centralised organisations, at any rate – could provide all this, and only under such a system could one hope to actually turn the vision into reality.

At first those town planner-architects would follow a largely Morrisian vision of dwellings in light, air and greenery, which was manifested in small houses and dispersed garden-cities. But from the 1920s and 1930s a few single-minded Modernist architect-planners, such as Le Corbusier and Walter Gropius, began to advocate high blocks of flats precisely as the best solution for achieving park-like greenery in equal measure for all, on relatively small plots. From the 1950s this became the dominant view of the planners in large cities – a view that lasted well into the 1960s.[7, 8, 9]

The 1960s climax of industrialised home-building in Britain was thus founded on a number of trends. Overall, the aim was a continuation of the basic Modernist, utopian vision of a welfare state building houses for all, according to certain planning ideals. High blocks saved expensive land and provided light, air and greenery for all. Crucially too, Modernist design was held to guarantee the provision of up-to-date heating and bathrooms, located for convenience. It has to be remembered that these facilities were still lacking, not only in the vast majority of small Victorian houses but also in many older middle-class dwellings.

A new kind of mass production of all these elements would make life better for members of all classes. But from the late 1950s some of these ideals changed considerably in detail, at least in advanced architectural circles. The ideal of parkland openness was transformed into a conception of *dense urbanity*. This entailed a change in the concept of the high block of flats.

The ideal of building high blocks continued during a new, more urban phase from the late 1950s until the late 1960s. In fact architects wanted to go ever higher to achieve greater densities. They also now felt that a block should not stand isolated, or form a regular group with more blocks of exactly the same shape, but should be linked to other kinds of buildings to present a more individualised and lively group. It was believed that more thought should be spent on the design of individual blocks: earlier Modernist housing now looked too monotonous.

Altogether, the built environment in 1960s Britain was a somewhat contradictory mix. In many architectural circles, especially in the large provincial conurbations and in most of Scotland, the straight Modernist preference for the widely spaced, repetitive group of blocks predominated until the late 1960s. But in the most advanced architectural circles, especially in London, these kinds of estates were increasingly disliked, and more complex groupings of high and medium-high conglomerates began to be preferred.

High blocks, of course, rely on sophisticated engineering. Their construction is much more complex than that of a house or even that of walk-ups of four or five storeys. But that was no obstacle for Modernist architects in the 1960s, as it seemed self-evident that construction formed an integral part of the art of architecture and that the most recent technical achievements should always be taken on board. Social betterment could only be achieved through harnessing technology as fully as possible. Ultimately the expertise in engineering and architecture could and should be fused again. The old breach between art and industry could be healed.

And yet the history of architecture before the Second World War showed that progress along these lines had been extremely slow. Le Corbusier, in particular, had appeared to regress in his later work: his love of *in situ* concrete, daring though it appeared in some ways, also pointed to an individualised mode of building that was, in effect, almost crafts-like.

Worse, the tasks envisaged by architects of the 1960s grew more daunting.

It was one thing to devise, in the abstract, new complex engineering solutions for a high block; it would be quite another to organise the sheer quantity of building planned in the visions of reconstruction. There were diverging views as to the best method to organise such an output. Could it be provided by the private sector – the building industry as it then existed? Or would the state have to get together with the building industry under the supervision of the Modernist architect-planner?

Naturally, most Modernists favoured the latter approach. However in the early 1920s, and then in mid 1940s, architectural perspectives of industrialisation came closer to the former view, in the concept of the 'house from the factory'. Of course, such houses were the product of close consultation with housing specialists from the state, which was, after all, the client for the accommodation. Nevertheless the house from the factory was a mass product supplied by a capitalist enterprise, drawing from experience in wartime military constructions and using plant capacity vacated by military production.

The 'prefab' concept meant literally that the whole house, mostly a bungalow except for the foundations, was factory-made and transported to sites in as few as three or four parts. Altogether more than 156,000 of such kinds of houses were built in Britain between 1945 and 1949. Many were Arcon houses, made by Taylor Woodrow Construction Ltd: 86,000 of these were commissioned in 1944.[10]

Overall, judgements on prefabs were mixed. They were certainly legitimised by the stringency of the situation in 1945: the sudden demand for dwellings after war damage, and the homecoming of young soldiers about to get married. Were they suitable? Certainly their conveniences were up to date. Yet they seemed the opposite of architecture, especially in the way they all looked exactly the same. These industrially prefabricated houses were planned to be, and by and large proved to be, strictly temporary. The development of the Arcon house had taken just over two years; to put one on the ground only took a few days.

Were prefabs cheap? This question is one of the most difficult to assess. In a way

there was no competition at that time, as conventional building materials and labour were rare. When ordinary building got fully back into its stride from the mid-1950s, virtually all interest in the prefab house was lost; it was revived under a different guise, in the 1960s, for some two-storied houses. Another crucial factor which led to the lack of sympathy for all those prefabricated individual houses was their relatively unmodern look. In fact the designers had usually attempted to make them look as much as possible like ordinary suburban houses. It was therefore doubtful whether they could be classified as modern architecture.

It was the second, statist approach that subsequently prevailed over privately made prefabs, especially during the 1950s. Instead of the capitalist producer taking the initiative, prefabrication systems were developed largely within state-designed and state-organised building projects and their architectural departments, in close collaboration with commercial manufacture. But whichever of the two approaches was dominant at any one time, what remained constant was the overwhelming reliance on the role of private industry to actually build the dwellings. By contrast with the situation in the Soviet bloc, 'direct labour' municipal building forces remained, in Britain, very much in the minority.

So, only after the immediate post-war episode of prefabs do we witness a decisive move toward the engineering-based, industrialised prefabrication of permanent buildings with a fully Modernist look. As argued for by architects, factory production meant a guarantee of ultimate control not just of production, but also – crucially – of design. Their ethos has been echoed in some historical accounts of post-war social architecture. Andrew Saint, for example, writing of the development of what he calls 'righteous' and 'responsible' design and construction in the post-war decades, observes that:

progress in the production of prefabricated building on any scale . . . could only come about by continuous interchange between design, research, manufacture and policy; and the technology of prefabrication had to be harnessed so as to combine standardised, dimensionally coordinated components in a variety of ways, not by producing complete buildings or parts of buildings'.

Otherwise, Saint insisted, prefabrication and standardisation would become 'a crushing burden'.[11]

Saint has charted the development of industrialised architecture sympathetically. He has done so through the story of English prefabricated schools during the 1950s, and of designer-led initiatives such as the Consortium of Local Authorities' Special Programme (CLASP) – a lightweight steel construction system mainly used for schools. To contemporary architects, these initiatives appeared as marvels of construction. They were light, elegant, and flexible and, above all, they seemed the opposite of monotony and repetitiveness. It was argued that the centralised efforts of architects, working in close collaboration with educationalists, had resulted in school plans of model quality.

This claim to have provided a universally valid architectural model was, in turn, attached to architect-designed public housing. Here too, the crucial task was seen as that of promoting scientifically-guaranteed construction. That led to the desire for complete *systems* of building.[12]

The system-built schools that arose in the early years after the war appeared to indicate a final break with a 200- or even 400-year old schism. Before the schools, it was held that the way to go about building was to draw up an architectural design, then hand it over to the builder to fulfil the demands of that design. The schools broke with that. They also broke with an old hierarchy which had, at the top, the expensive, one-off architectural project, requiring equally expensive one-off work by builders. At the bottom there had lurked designs that were barely architectural at all – that were already orientated toward what was cheaply available

from the building industry's normal supply. The old hierarchy praised dignified permanent buildings and denigrated cheap, temporary structures.

In contrast to all this, what was hoped for now was a seamless process which would lead from the general concept, through detailed considerations of use, down to the efficiently produced, standardised product – a process that would demand the highest quality of thinking and production throughout.

It was the high block of flats that became the building type that most interested welfare state providers, architects and engineers. In the words of one Scottish architect in 1952:

blocks with lifts are throwing their towers into the skies. They will dominate the landscape for miles around. These flats, as far as planning goes, will equal, even surpass anything that has been built . . . and in every way will probably be the finest house building achievement ever attempted.[13]

There was widespread regional variation in the spread of tower blocks. In Greater London, multi-storey blocks made up about a quarter of total new council dwellings in the three post-war decades and about half of output in the mid and late 1960s; in Glasgow, over the period 1961 to 1968, they accounted for a staggering 75 per cent of all new public housing. By the 1950s, of course, the engineering concept for a building of 15, 20 or even 30 storeys was nothing particularly novel. With its numerous high office buildings in city centres, Britain was beginning to catch up with other parts of the world. Neither was there perceived to be a problem with architectural quality and individuality. Even high blocks of council housing were regarded favourably within the prevailing climate that surrounded architecture and engineering.

The emergence of multi-storey housing in Britain highlighted what appeared to many as the most central and thorny aspect of the debate on the industrialisation of building: the relationship between the architect and the industrial producer.

Seen from an architectural perspective, the largely negative experience of the prefabs and the resounding success of the schools together suggested that the vital task was to uphold the involvement of architects, whether they worked in public housing authorities or in private practice. And it has to be remembered that small, often avant-garde private firms designed many of the most prominent examples of public housing. Yet when AW Cleeve Barr, chief architect of the Ministry of Housing and Local Government in the early 1960s, discussed the house from the factory at length, he found it impossible to reach a conclusion. He wrote:

There are some very deep questions here, involving the whole future of the status of the architect.[14]

Indeed in practice the degree of involvement of the bona fide architect in the design and building of industrialised multi-storey flats varied widely.

There were two major phases: from the late 1940s, it was architects, helped by engineers, who designed new multi-storey flats for the construction industry to build; then, in the 1960s, the balance tilted towards the building industry doing the whole job – design included.

4.2 Experiments in systems building in the 1950s and early 1960s

The story of industrialised flats in the 1950s and 1960s begins with the world of pure engineering immediately after the war. As there was little other work for engineering firms in those years, the design of experimental high blocks in the late 1940s was dominated by the most eminent practitioners of the time, such as Felix Samuely or Ove Arup. Overall, there was a spirit of experiment. In 1954, an architect-scientist, Bill Allen, and a prolific architect of houses, ED Mills, wrote

of their 'inability to settle down', and of being in a highly creative period. 'We seek', they told the RIBA's members, 'originality at every turn'.[15]

Although commentators during the later 1950s and 1960s tended to belittle some of the results of the 'architectural physics' of those decades for their lack of immediate applicability, the changes in general approach proved to be extremely influential. Take the much-valued Building Research Station handbook *Principles of Modern Building*. The 1938 edition had stood firmly in the tradition of all builders' manuals: the subject had been divided into walls, floors and other basic parts of a structure, tied in with the basic divisions of construction and trades. The 1959 edition, however, was completely different. It concentrated on the chief demands made upon a structure – namely, that water and cold should be excluded, fire prevented, and daylight admitted. It then explained how various methods of construction could help to fulfil these demands.

Primary importance was now attached to what was somewhat later called 'functional performance', and to its scientific measurement. Measurability now stood at the beginning of each constructional undertaking. Instead of the old, vaguely empirical margin of safety, achieved through the ad hoc provision of additional thickness, we now find exact performance criteria for stability and protection, with the materials allocated and the structure devised accordingly. As full air-conditioning gained growing acceptance, some theorists, such as Reyner Banham, even claimed that environmental factors were as important as the material fabric.[16] Many existing building regulations were considered to be a hindrance in these processes, and the whole system was duly changed in the 1960s.

A much closer cooperation was now demanded between the various agents of designing and building, and between architects and builders. It was felt desirable to consult the contractor at a much earlier stage; competitive or selective

Picton Street, Camberwell, London, designed and built for the London County Council (LCC) between 1953 and 1957 as a cross-wall, box-framed construction. Design was by AW Cleeve Barr; Ove Arup and Partners were the engineers and Laing the main contractor[17]

capacity. In the words of an engineer in the mid-1950s, such a modern building site was characterised by 'complete order . . . and an absence of workmen', in contrast to the traditional site, which was little more than an 'over-populated, semi-organised rubbish dump'.[18]

Within a few decades the construction of a public authority block of flats had departed radically from common traditional modes of construction. Where there had been homogenous monolithic load-bearing walls throughout and conventional roofs, there was now a plethora of materials, though usually little wood was left. Some early experimental high blocks, such as Holborn Metropolitan Borough Council's Dombey Street development, which was built between 1948 and 1949, emulated modern office construction by using steel frames.

For most public housing undertakings, however, steel frames proved far too expensive. Instead, reinforced concrete had to be used. Of course the concept of frame and in-fill went along with the concept of 'functional performance' – that is, *the separation of structure from function*. Into the basic frame would be fitted numerous smaller building elements, designed to meet multifaceted needs of different kinds of households. But it was soon realised that on-site frame construction, too, was expensive. so a large number of variations of frame construction, as well as combinations of frame- and load-bearing walls, were tried. Then, from about the mid-1950s, engineers and architects turned to a different method for construction of their slab blocks: the box-frame.

tendering, coming in at the point when the building had been fully designed, appeared too crude and inflexible. Prototype schemes such as the London County Council's Picton Street development in Camberwell were felt by many architects to hold enormous promise.

On site, new methods of construction meant a greater degree of organisation and mechanisation. Buildings of six or fewer storeys could be constructed with mobile cranes. For higher buildings, the tower crane was introduced to Britain by about 1950, so that by 1954 about 200 tower cranes were in use. Such contracts were literally centred on the crane and its

Reinforced concrete is simple in principle, but what is complicated is the casting process. The more casting of small and narrow parts and corners required, the more lengthy and costly is the process of construction, due to the complications of the formwork for casting concrete on site. Furthermore, it is notoriously hard to fit walls neatly into a frame.

Hence a method was devised which looked at a block as a kind of house of cards, consisting of a number of units or cells. The idea was to combine rigid internal dividing walls with rigid floors and other horizontal members into a kind of frame – a frame complete with ready-made internal divisions, provided only that these divisions should not need to be broken through too much.

This kind of frame system, in short, suited buildings that were rigidly divided into small units, such as blocks of small flats. Terms like 'cross-wall', 'box-frame', and 'egg-crate' were used to describe it. 'Cross-wall', however, also refers to an earlier version of this thinking. In it the whole construction of blocks of flats, of any height, had been based on solid dividing walls between sets of units and going up the whole of the building. Architects like Eric Lyons and SPAN then treated the rest of the block between the dividing walls as a lighter in-fill. In flexible style, each flat could be provided with very large windows, with large private balconies or with access balconies.

Cross-wall construction mostly proceeded with conventional brickwork, which could still not be beaten for cheapness in the mid-1950s. But among more radical London architects and engineers, such as Berthold Lubetkin before the war, Ove Arup and, from the 1950s onward, Cleeve Barr, old-fashioned brick construction was left behind in the attempt to find solutions for buildings of 10 floors or more.

By 1955 we read that a particular construction system 'lends itself to repetition and standardisation of structural as well as non-structural elements and, there-

Dombey Street Flats, Holborn   Hening & Chitty, *Architects*

HOPE'S
STEEL DOOR FRAMES

HENRY HOPE & SONS LTD., SMETHWICK, BIRMINGHAM, & 17 BERNERS ST., LONDON, W.1

Dombey Street, Holborn, London, by architects Hening and Chitty. The flats featured prefabricated sub-assemblies of doors and windows that fitted into the structural steel frame and concrete slab floors.[19] Built between 1948 and 1949, the flats show a level of coordination that, when tried today, is heralded as innovative

fore, to prefabrication and more rapid building methods.' And yet the cautionary architect maintains that 'economy is not produced by mere mass production but by a nice balance between structural strength, ease of assembly and practical convenience'.[20]

The magazine *Building* noted Spa Green estate, Rosebery Avenue, London, as a significant development in housing construction:

Wates undertook the renovation of Dombey Street estate in 2003. Overclad in profiled metal sheeting and in need of repair, the estate is situated among Holborn's town houses – see the central photo

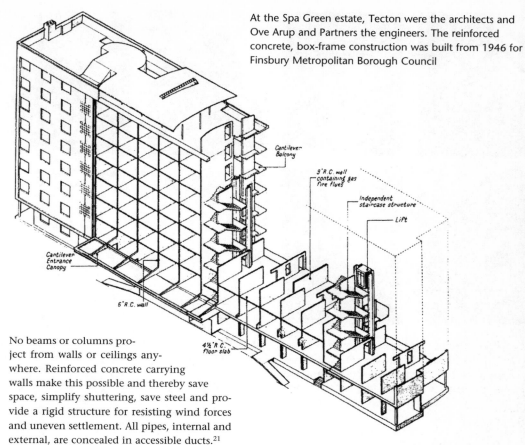

At the Spa Green estate, Tecton were the architects and Ove Arup and Partners the engineers. The reinforced concrete, box-frame construction was built from 1946 for Finsbury Metropolitan Borough Council

No beams or columns project from walls or ceilings anywhere. Reinforced concrete carrying walls make this possible and thereby save space, simplify shuttering, save steel and provide a rigid structure for resisting wind forces and uneven settlement. All pipes, internal and external, are concealed in accessible ducts.[21]

The reinforced concrete cross-wall and box-frame, too, went through numerous solutions; it was on the whole suited more to slab blocks than to point blocks. Peter Dunican, an Arup partner, and Cleeve Barr both fervently believed in the box-frame. Constructionally, their own experiment at Picton Street represented the early culmination of this development of the LCC slab block. Reinforced and unreinforced cross-walls alternate. Longitudinal strength in the box-frame 'house of cards' is provided at both ends by strong flanking walls, as well as by the grouping of stairs and lifts near the centre.

The rigid *in situ* frame, or the matrix of the box-frame, made the remainder of the components such as the in-fill or the cladding appear more flexible, and subject to a large number of attempts at optimisation: lightweight and solid, letting the light in, or keeping the cold and noise out. Scientific studies had begun to measure heat exchange between inside and outside as well as sound insulation. While for the basic structure there was a continuous narrowing-down of options, the design and technical possibilities seemed to broaden for the in-fill components, certainly during in the 1950s. A great number of materials were tried, singly or in combination. Furthermore there was the problem of joining it all together; each material and each construction method brought its own problems in that respect.

By the dawn of the 1950s, then, have we reached the threshold of the thoroughly industrialised building or of the completely prefabricated high block of flats? If we remember that as late as 1950,

Spa Green in 2003. Located opposite London's new Sadler's Wells theatre, it is in need of renovation

new LCC urban housing still largely took the form of walk-up flats that were five storeys high, built of brick, and equipped only with old-fashioned and often minimal services, the change in the following 10 years appeared radical. But did construction using a frame with in-fill or cladding really constitute a radically new approach to building? In some avant-garde architectural circles the minimal *in situ* frame and service core with interchangeable add-ons did indeed become an ideal. The British architects Cedric Price and Archigram, together with the Dutch architect Herman Hertzberger, exemplified this philosophy. User-orientation and flexibility were indeed the watchwords of the 1960s. But for mass housing, the inevitable complexity of such an undertaking made it impracticable as a general ideal. Diversity, not infinite flexibility, was the thing demanded of the design and building of flats.

The methods of constructing the prefabricated flats of the 1960s were firmly rooted in the new engineering developments of the 1950s. Replacing the term prefabrication with the term pre-casting takes us back to the beginning of the 1950s, when, in experimental LCC projects, external concrete panels began to be pre-cast on many occasions. Cleeve Barr claimed of his Picton Street scheme that it was 'perhaps the most rationalised yet. . .by maximising the use of pre-casting'.[22] The pre-casting of floors, for instance, obviated cumbersome on-site manoeuvres with horizontal shuttering. Apart from alternate cross walls, most other repetitive components of the Picton Street blocks were prefabricated too. They were dropped into position by the tower crane. Furthermore, the crane moved the floor-high shuttering for the cross-walls from one location to the next, so mechanically assisting the production of *in situ* parts.

In the new operations, there was no longer a need for any traditional scaffolding. Designers argued that speed was greatly improved, as was the standard of the concrete finishes.[23] Barr and Dunican concluded that the cross-wall system, or the box-frame, 'lends itself to repetition and standardisation of structural and non-structural elements and therefore to prefabrication and more rapid building methods'.[24] In Leeds and in London the building firm Reema offered large-panel construction techniques that formed the basis of its multi-storey work; either the

Spa Green in 2003

load-bearing wall panels were completely pre-cast or the pre-cast panels had vertical cavities filled on site to provide a kind of framework.[25]

In some ways, in terms of actual construction methods, the situation by the mid-1960s was not that different from that in the late 1940s. If anything, the overall number and diversity of solutions proposed for multi-storey flats had increased, even counting only those offered by the package dealers. Steel frames were still proposed by some firms. An entirely novel experiment was 'lift slab', a method in which all floor slabs were cast at ground level and then lifted up. Paradoxically, the most frequently applied of all the new post-war non-traditional house construction methods was called 'no-fines', a rationalised but almost totally on-site approach used chiefly by Wimpey. The term denotes, simply, the omission of fine sand from the concrete and aggregate mix, resulting in a more porous and somewhat lighter mass with good insulation qualities. Originally, everything was poured on site. In later Wimpey multi-storey blocks, complete bathrooms and kitchens were prefabricated.

Prefabrication obviates the need for scaffolding like this

New mechanised techniques – not just tower cranes, but also early use of computer programmes – achieved substantial time savings. The rest of the big British firms specialising in multi-storey systems, with practically all the construction methods derived from French and Scandinavian precedents, used methods based on panels made of reinforced concrete. The neatest solution was obviously to form the whole building out of panels and to exclude all elements of framework. Here the principle of the box-frame reigned supreme as the 'house of cards', with all its vertical components of room height. Lift cases and stair compartments could also be prefabricated.

The focus was now on:

- precision work in the production of panels;
- the exact calculation of the performance of panels in buildings – not only constructionally but also with regard to the services that could be built in to them; and
- the transportation of the panels.[26]

The same priorities applied to Soviet housing at the time.[27]

Many firms, such as France's Raymond Camus and Britain's Taylor Woodrow, publicised detailed written and pictorial descriptions of their production processes, as well as details of their jointing methods. What greatly varied was the distribution of factories up and down the country, and the distances between factory and site. As with the 1940s prefabs and other contemporary versions of the house from the factory, installation and services were usually produced or included with the main components. There was, however, great emphasis laid on the variability of dimensions as well as on the diversity of external finishes. As for internal finishes, it was usually underlined that wallpaper or paint could be applied directly to the smooth concrete surfaces of the panels. Finally, enthusiasts pointed out that, almost invisibly, a building's weight was reduced when concrete systems were substituted for conventional brickwork.

Probably the most systematic and extreme version of box-frame housing was the Bison Wall-Frame by Concrete Ltd. It was also the most prolifically used system in the UK. All parts were of the same kind, in that they all fulfil structural, load-bearing and space-dividing purposes. Non-structural internal walls were designed out. Most floors and all walls were a standard six inches thick, equating to 152.4 mm, and the external walls merely carried an additional non-load-bearing facing to provide the architectural finish. The wall panels were up to 6.4 m in length. A two-bedroom flat could thus be assembled from just 21 prefabricated components, including a completely prefabricated bathroom and toilet unit, and elements for the structure comprising the stairs. The section enclosing the lifts and stairs was assembled from pre-cast units that were three storeys in height. Not surprisingly, Bison offered only two- and three-bedroom flats. Maisonettes were not possible, and there were no balconies.

At this point, seen in constructional terms, we have reached a quiet climax to a long process. In England experiments in systems building had begun with the

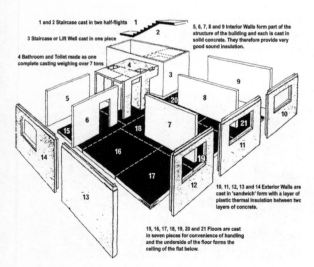

1 and 2 Staircase cast in two half-flights
3 Staircase or Lift Well cast in one piece
4 Bathroom and Toilet made as one complete casting weighing over 7 tons
5, 6, 7, 8 and 9 Interior Walls form part of the structure of the building and each is cast in solid concrete. They therefore provide very good sound insulation.
10, 11, 12, 13 and 14 Exterior Walls are cast in 'sandwich' form with a layer of plastic thermal insulation between two layers of concrete.
15, 16, 17, 18, 19, 20 and 21 Floors are cast in seven pieces for convenience of handling and the underside of the floor forms the ceiling of the flat below.

Concrete Ltd's Bison wall-frame system, 1962[28]

cross-wall constructions of Lubetkin and Tecton's high flats in the 1930s. Further experiments were then carried out through the innumerable frame, or box-frame-plus-cladding variations of the 1940s and 1950s high blocks, while at the same time in France and Scandinavia panel buildings without frames had already been developed.

Architecturally the 1960s were a transition period, in that architects began to despise regular rows of high blocks and started to favour low-rise or medium-rise high-density types. Yet at first many of those developments were built in prefabricated methods too. Perhaps the only solution that was more radical was the 'box unit construction' method, in which a whole flat was prefabricated and lifted into position. The Soviet Union built a lot of flats that way.[29]

4.3 The reality of post-war mass production

So far in this chapter we have looked at public housing from the viewpoint of the architectural profession, and of architectural and construction-design issues. From this perspective, the story is one of continuity: the architects' designs and experiments of the 1940s and 1950s mature into the systems of the 1960s.

But an essential ingredient of the definition of the welfare state after the war was, of course, the way in which all walks of life were assumed to be willing and able to work together. The UK's enormous post-war output of public housing was not the work of just a few gurus or professionals but of society as a whole. At the very least, there were architects, builders and their clients, the central state, politicians who decided how to allocate funds, and specialists on welfare, planning and housing in the Ministry of Housing and Local Government and the Department of Health for Scotland. Then there were the municipalities, whose politicians and officials administered waiting lists for housing. Last, there was the building industry.

From the point of view of all these agents, then, the story of post-war housing construction is one not of continuity but of sharp disjunction: from the architect-dominated 1950s to the industry-dominated 1960s. Although construction in some parts of the country, notably London, remained under the control of architects, the house from the factory seemed, on the whole, to have made a comeback. The old split which had dominated the story of architecture and building now once again seemed as wide as ever.

Yet the architectural discourse of the 1960s barely touched on the systems of that decade. The house from the factory was never the house from the architect's drawing board. Building and engineering science could not be turned completely into building commerce. The schism between architecture and building, between art and industry, had not been overcome; if anything, it ran deeper than ever. How did this happen? How could the building industry become so prominent, so rapidly?

The simplest answer is that it alone could provide the quantity of houses that appeared to be needed so rapidly in the early 1960s. In the politics of public housing at the time, the crucial argument was not about theory, but about numbers.

In spite of the massive amount of housing built since the war, waiting lists were still far too long. Modern conveniences were still lacking for the great majority of those living in Victorian terraces and tenements. A more rapid production seemed necessary and that, in the 1960s, was felt to be available only from an even greater degree of industrialisation. Today, 40 years later, the persistence of a north-south divide in Britain invites very different solutions to urban problems. But in the 1960s, a continuing war on slums and housing shortages still united politicians and professionals, regardless of their origins.

Through the fevered political rhetoric of 'national targets' for new homes, council housing was focused both radically and eagerly on the then novel building type of the multi-storey block. This was hoped to be a means of bringing housing output back towards the huge totals achieved in the early 1950s by low-rise housing on greenfield sites.

Let us briefly glance at some of the raw statistics of this renewed output. Overall, completions of public housing in the UK had dropped from 1,120,000 in the five years between 1951 and 1955 to 769,000 between 1956 and 1960, only to recover to 955,000 between 1966 and 1970. By the late 1960s completions in some areas, like Greater London, fully recovered to the levels of the early 1950s. Across the UK as a whole, completions of multi-storey (six or more storeys) multiplied in an unprecedented manner, from 77,000 between 1958 and 1962, to 200,000 between 1963 and 1967 – only to fall back dramatically to 66,000 between 1968 and 1972.[30]

The driving forces behind this renewed push for output, and the place of 'industrialised' building within it, were partly economic but mainly political. Public housing had to try and push costs downwards – or at least keep them under control. But in consonance with the welfarist ethos of the time, nobody believed that cheapness was an aim in itself. It appears, in fact, impossible to locate a precise judgement about the relative costs of high blocks in general, and of rationalised construction methods in particular.

Clearly much of the issue was to do with economies of scale. At the height of the mid-1960s' boom, many building firms cautiously claimed 'economy' in their production processes – for example, in factors of location and handling on-site. But there was never a stress on cost-cutting procedures in their own right; there was, in Britain, never a lobby for the fully-fledged attempts at mass construction happening in Eastern Bloc countries.[31]

The specific trigger for the radical switch into prefabricated construction for public housing in 1960 was the sudden beginning of severe national shortages of building labour and building materials, resulting from a general upsurge in construction activity. The consequences included increased prices and completion times, as firms moved out of municipal work into more profitable industrial or commercial building. By July 1964, the total volume of building work was 48 per cent higher than it was in 1958, while Britain had enough brick supplies in hand to last it just three days.

In any case, local builders had long taken municipal building – 'hospital work' – for granted; so the effect upon them of shortages of labour and materials in public housing production turned out to be devastating. In the industrial town of Oldham in September 1961, for instance, only 100 of 2000 local building workers were available to construct council houses, with the result that annual output settled at just 300 dwellings – and even that total was jeopardised by a grave shortage of bricks.[32]

The challenge of economic shortages, however, provoked political responses that were even more sharply polarised. Typically for the time, the extremes of both utopian idealism and pragmatic realism were encompassed by the overall structure of state-directed housing provision – although, as we will see, the pragmatists also drew on a substantial continuing contribution from the private building industry.

The idealist responses themselves comprised an alliance of two distinct elements, both of which built on the 1950s ethos of experiment in construction.

On the one hand, there were the technological radicals, calling above all for total modernisation of the building process. They sought this modernisation through a mix of light or heavy prefabrication technology; a more capitalistic attitude to the construction of dwelling as short-life manufactured commodities; and the ideas of Taylor and Ford – production routines optimised for efficient labour and mechanisation.

On the other hand, there was a more traditional, limited architectural concern to uphold designer control and individuality in the face of mundane production pressures.

On the whole, it was this second outlook that provided the most consistent critique of 'blind' mass housing production. Its advocates were concentrated in the architects' departments of central and local government. From 1961, in response to the building shortage crisis, there were growing calls for architectural control over prefabricated construction techniques, loosely termed 'system' or 'industrialised' building.

As noted earlier, the designers had more or less monopolised the new structural methods during their stage of R&D in the 1950s. But now they were faced with the threat that the advocates of unbridled output might grab their techniques, along with commissions for blocks of flats in general. So they counterattacked. With a vigorous burst of rhetoric, they ridiculed the bogeyman of *closed systems* – proprietary construction methods. These they branded mere vehicles for contractual control. At the same time, they upheld the ideal of *open systems*: the mass production of components suitable for use in each and every architect's idiosyncratic scheme.

These arguments were almost entirely divorced from the main thrust of housing production. This separation between argument and practice took two main forms. Both, ironically, conflicted with key elements of Modern architectural theory.

Firstly, despite their assertions that open systems would form a basis for mass production, those designers who advocated them did individualistic work that was far removed from the real world of contracting and building.

Secondly, the designers' initiatives in building organisation had little to do with solving particular housing emergencies. Instead, they were informed by general, professional ideals; these, it was

held, transcended both the perceived parochialism and myopia of housing committees, and the commercial prescriptions of the contractors.

Yet no evidence seems to have been produced at the time that the designers' blueprints and procedures were superior to those of contractors in either costs or performance. And this was a vital point. After all, the designers made rhetoric about quality and standards as if they owned the ideas, and were always out to expose the supposedly inferior results of unbridled production.

The campaign for architect-led open system building in England in the early 1960s was led by the most design-dominated public authority, the LCC, and the state's main R&D agency in the housing field, the Housing Development Group within the Ministry of Housing and Local Government (MHLG).

The LCC's involvement with prefabrication, which began in 1955 with the Picton Street project, invariably took as its starting-point the architect's design, to which structural innovations and contractors' contributions were tailored. Rather than use package deals to alleviate shortages of professional staff, the LCC chose to employ private consultancy practices, while dabbling with various limited prefabricated supplements to existing building output. These included wildly experimental systems such as the steel-framed, plastic-clad SF1 tower at Walterton Road and Watney Street Market in London – a characteristically exotic one-off that was eventually terminated after only four blocks had been built.

From its inception in 1960, the MHLG Housing Development Group was also envisaged as a vehicle for propagating architect-controlled open systems. It kept up a barrage of initiatives intended to relax the hold of closed systems on high blocks. In 1962, for example, it persuaded Oldham Borough Council to allow it to carry out a 500-dwelling experimental redevelopment project, using a large-panel prefabrication system devised by

MHLG architects, in the dilapidated St Mary's area of the town.[33]

Soon, however, it became clear that local offshoots of architect-controlled prefabrication could not be imposed on municipalities. As a result, government designers began to emphasise the idea of consortia: regional groups of municipalities, each directed by its own CLASP-like development group. The economic pretext for consortia was the emergence of big, regional lumps of demand for housing but, as the policies of the most important early consortia showed, the main intention was to advance architectural influence over Modern building.

A key example was the Yorkshire Development Group, which was formed in 1961. Initially comprised of local administrations in Leeds, Sheffield and Hull, it came increasingly under the control of a panel of city architects. Eventually, and at the instigation of its development architect, Martin

Richardson, the YDG launched into a highly experimental and complex range of 5–7 storey prefabricated deck blocks. As a result, it made only a modest impact on Yorkshire's building programmes. Yet of many other consortia that sprang up during the remainder of the 1960s, none approached even the YDG's limited level of output.[34]

In contrast to this relatively consistent and somewhat traditional pressure for architectural control over building, the more grandly utopian language of building modernisation was largely confined to the mid-1960s. In those few short years, the slogan of a 'systems revolution' took on a life of its own, adopted as it was by two key players in the housebuilding drive: contractors and government housing ministers.

To the politicians, system building was useful for two reasons. Firstly, it provided a catchphrase to justify the expanded public housing drive to the Treasury, on the tenuous grounds that it would help modernise the building industry. After all, ministers could not be seen to stand idly on the sidelines while municipalities and contractors found their own way round worsening shortages: when large sums of money were being sought from the Exchequer, politicians had to make a token show of central coordination.

Secondly, system building was a useful propaganda weapon to MHLG administrators during their brief power struggle with the Ministry of Public Building and

The Lego model of the Gibson Street, Longsight Redevelopment Area, Manchester, built between 1967 and 1969. This was one of a series of medium-rise 'spine' developments designed by an R&D group within Manchester Corporation's city architects department. Robert Stones led the group.

Envisaged as an open system and supposedly suitable for construction using any proprietary method of prefabricating large concrete panels, Gibson Street was actually built using Concrete Ltd's Bison Wall-Frame System

Works (MPBW) over control of house-building policy.

The focus of this dispute was the National Building Agency. First conceived in 1963 by the MPBW under Geoffrey Rippon, the NBA, to be overseen by the MPBW's Director-General of Research and Development, Donald Gibson, was meant to extend MPBW influence over housing by being the central agency, or super-CLASP, through which the demands of all Britain's local authorities would be coordinated. Naturally, housing would lead those demands.

When the NBA was eventually set up in March 1964, however, Dame Evelyn Sharp, the chief MHLG administrator, ensured that it was kept at several removes from local housing production process. Its only tasks were advisory and exhortatory: to certify methods of construction as constituting 'systems', and to assist the formation of local authority consortia to build such systems. In practice, architects and their advocacy of open systems served to obscure the NBA's work.[35]

4.4 State patrons of private-sector builders

Rhetorical flourishes aside, the practical implementation of the housing boom of the 1960s was quite distant from revolutionary concepts of abstract systems. Implementers responded opportunistically and somewhat conservatively to diverse municipal demands for equally diverse minor variations. While ministers and some public architects proclaimed the modernisation of the building industry, contractual negotiations and organisation, driven by the realities of local and national housing politics and the demand for production, carried on out of immediate public view.

The most powerful patrons were the municipal housing crusaders, local politicians and officials who acknowledged only a relatively elemental selection of standards – sunlight and daylight, floor-space, kitchen and bathroom provision. The previous generation of municipal flats had met these standards; but because of the multi-faceted character of the state

Part view of the Lego model produced by the R&D group led by Stones

Gibson Street empty and awaiting demolition. It was pulled down in 1991

in the housing field, they did not now result in a simple pattern of cheap and nasty building, or a penny-pinching attitude which held back modernisation. Rather, there was a complex conflict between building with the help of blank cheques, and public sector restraint.

As already noted, one of the main complications was that private contracting firms dominated the state building drive: direct labour was widely thought to be inefficient and costly. In general, then, public-private partnership in housing saw no concerted effort to modernise design and building. Since council housing was always built to order, it proved even more remote from mass production than speculative private building. Private speculative housing was akin to the manufacture of branded products for sale, whereas council housing, even if prefabricated, was more tailor-made in character. But it would be simplistic to argue that one was more advanced or backward than the other.

In English housing since the 19th century, a strong contractor tradition had, as we saw, established the use of standardised components as against hand-made building. Housing construction was thus already partly 'industrial', but technological improvements were firmly subordinated to the practical business of profitable building organisation. This was an approach that continued into the Modernist period. Overall, therefore, 1960s expectations and concepts of building quality in prefabricated dwellings stayed much the same as in their 19th and early 20th century predecessors, with precast concrete panels seen in much the same way as bricks or joinery: as components slotted into a framework.

EDLO was the building department of Edmonton (later Enfield) Borough Council, London. It ran the only public sector direct labour force to develop its own systems. In the mid- and late 1960s EDLO built a succession of massive multi-storey projects in precast concrete, using its own casting factory. This 23-storey block at Barbot Street, built in 1966, was part of its output

France had strong traditions of methodical rationalism. In England and Scotland, by contrast, prefabrication was not a general organisational and constructional aim, despite the heady rhetoric of modernisation from architects and politicians. Thus prefabrication never achieved anything near quantitative dominance in the housing programme.

The proportion of *public housing tender approvals in England* classified as 'industrialised' – using the very broad MHLG definition, which included many non-prefabricated methods – rose briefly from 28 per cent in 1965 to 42 per cent in 1967, only to fall rapidly to 19 per cent in 1970.

The proportion of *multi-storey dwellings* in England and Scotland that were prefabricated rose even more sharply. It shot up from an average of five per cent over the five-year period 1958 to 1962, through 26 per cent between 1963 and 1967 to 37 per cent between 1968 and 1972. The figures fell back to 10 per cent after 1972. The highest levels of prefabrication in the overall postwar multi-storey output of individual areas were in the East Midlands (40 per cent), Scotland (29 per cent), and North-West England (27 per cent); those of individual cities were Glasgow (26 per cent), Birmingham (24 per cent) and Greater London (20 per cent).[36]

Among Britain's large cities, these multi-storey blocks were the main response to the call for higher output, faced as they were with a proliferation of green belts, regional planning 'overspill' schemes and other drastic planning controls on land availability.[37] Whether they were designed for a contractor or a local authority, the traditional *in situ* concrete high blocks of the late 1950s and early 1960s were relatively straightforward and often very profitable to build.[38] However the urgent need to get round building industry shortages was to lead contractors away from this familiar territory and into the new and uncertain field of prefabrication.

Earlier in this chapter we touched on some of the new prefabricated techniques for constructing high flats that British contractors embarked on – a movement that, from about 1961, suddenly gained momentum. So it was a great surprise when, after 20 or even 40 years of continuous efforts in prefabricated, industrialised construction methods, it was suddenly decided to import systems from abroad. It was not only know-how that was imported, at least as far as the factory production processes was concerned, but also the prefabrications themselves.

Certainly, France and Scandinavia had instituted large-scale prefabrication between five and 10 years earlier. Cleeve Barr had toured the Continent extensively, and in late 1962 included lectures by overseas representatives at his conference Housing from the Factory in London. The French firm Raymond Camus boasted a total of 40,000 dwellings

Another EDLO development under construction in 1966 was a series of 26-storey blocks with a shopping centre at Edmonton Green

delivered since 1953; by 1963, it established a strong foothold in Liverpool.[39]

Major British building firms took on foreign methods. Taylor Woodrow adapted the Copenhagen-based Larsen and Nielsen system and used it on buildings from 1963 onward, initially for the LCC. The MHLG's R&D group modified the 12M Jespersen – a Danish system based on large panels – and licensed it to Laing. Altogether more than half a dozen foreign firms did business in Britain. In addition, at the height of the boom, there were a number of other major names which dominated the systems market, such as Laing, Wates, Wimpey, and, of course, Concrete Ltd – with its Bison system built in hybrid form in Glasgow from 1961 and in full Wall Frame form, in Birmingham and other cities, from 1963.

Advertisement for Wates's package deals of conventional on-site construction. No significant prefabrication was included[40]

But how, amid a proliferation of brand names and catchphrases about systems, was the Modern mass housing during the 1960s boom actually organised? Britain's construction industry was as atomised then as it is now. Therefore, buying from fragmented construction suppliers, Britain's largest cities had considerable power.

The market for the building of Modern flats was hierarchical. An initial demand from large authorities created and supported a complicated network of national, regional and local relations. In general, the first response of any local authority whose tender invitation during a full market was unanswered or met with excessively high quotations was to seek a negotiated contract. The contractor liked this, partly because it was more profitable, but chiefly because it made sure of the job, and thus saved trouble and expense.

With the building shortages of the early 1960s, *negotiated contracts* suddenly became of more general relevance up and down the country. A further and highly significant step beyond negotiation was the *package-deal contract*, under which the contractor both built and designed the development.

Package-deal contracts got round shortages not only of site labour, but also of professional staff such as quantity surveyors and architects. They could in turn be developed into a competitive process, in which different firms owning different designs would offer tenders based on a very general local authority brief. This was almost a mirror image of the procedures of the normal negotiated contract, in which an architect's designs were used as the basis for negotiations and briefings. By 1964, 46 per cent of all new public housing in England and Wales was accounted for by negotiated and package-deal contracts. The figure rose to 55 per cent in 1967 at the height of the housing boom, falling back again to 28 per cent in 1970.[41]

The key to the success of package-deal architecture lay not in the fact that contractors could repeatedly build the same designs, but rather in its *discipline* – a practical regime that originated in the contractors' need to maximise profits and the municipalities' requirement for reliability, punctuality and keeping to budget. Package-deal contracts represented a strictly pragmatic form of building modernisation, of course; but the response of the public sector architectural establishment was predictable. It thrust its head in the sand, and attacked the package deal for its commercialised repetitiveness.

The reality could not have been more different. Private contractors were engaged in a continuous balancing act. They had to juggle the demands of individual local authorities for small variations against their own development of more efficient and economical designs. And they had to do all this within the constraints of building regulations and Government housing standards.

In 1960, for instance, the ambitious Scottish firm of Crudens appointed its first company architect: George Bowie. He evolved type plans for blocks, incorporating ones which ran to six flats on each upper floor. Bowie's plans were loosely influenced by Edinburgh Corporation's architectural brief for the company's first multi-storey job: a negotiated contract for three 14-storey blocks. The plans were progressively refined in subsequent package-deals for other towns. Then, in the mid-1960s, there was new pressure from output-hungry authorities such as Glasgow:

Along came people looking for bigger blocks . . . The solution was obvious – make them higher, but also stick two or more together, adjust the planning of the flats for daylight and so on.[42]

The culmination of this plan-type was the 1964 Ardler development in Dundee, in which each of six 17-storey slab blocks, containing a total of 1788 flats, was comprised of three standard blocks strung end-to-end.

On each individual job, there was constant external pressure for variations of detail and finish:

There never was a standard block! No authority ever came and looked at anything we did and said, "can we have three of those?". There were always ifs and buts! Having got yourself a contract your marketing people would tell you "here's another local authority, Falkirk want a scheme, why not bash on?". We'd say "if you can come, you can see the frame coming out of the ground, if not then here's a model, and some approximate costs." Then the authority would say "start in four weeks". We'd say "here's the block". The authority would look at it and say "we do like it, but we'd like the following things, only tiny wee things, like a slightly bigger kitchen and different windows, Mr Bowie, and can we have a clothes drying area inside the block, and a play area on the ground floor?" – And so on! Also our designers and engineers were getting cleverer

Advertisement for Laing's Housing Systems, 1967

and cleverer, so we incorporated improvements. It always annoyed us – every time we got a job, another set of working drawings always had to be done![43]

Most of the largest cities fed their flat-building programmes more or less piecemeal to a range of contractors. Following a successful initial performance, a contractor could expect to negotiate repeat contracts. In some places architectural design considerations were given a high priority, but almost always within a commercial production framework.

In Birmingham, for example, under the dominant rule of city architect J A Maudsley, the council's power over the contractors secured use of its own designs in all cases. The chief local firm, Bryant, built its own *in situ* point blocks, alongside precast-concrete and timber frame low flats and cottages by Bryant Low Rise, while the firm also acted as main contractor for Bison Wall-Frame high blocks.

A different balance applied in Glasgow. There the crusades of housing convener David Gibson ensured a more single-minded focus on output. In addition, chief housing engineer Lewis Cross had the kind of negotiating experience that allowed him to keep the upper hand in managing the 77 per cent of multi-storey output allocated to contractors. Cross pursued package-deal competition in its purest form. He rigidly segregated the functions of contractor and client by assigning design to the former and leaving the latter free to concentrate on the negotiating and monitoring of contracts.

Once the Modern housing boom was underway in major centres such as Glasgow, it was necessary for firms that had invested in factories, casting moulds, and the establishment of regional offices to maximise their return by obtaining as many further contracts as possible. There were two ways of doing this. The large authorities that had already been awarded contracts were likely to remain the most prolific builders of high flats – with all the negotiating power that went with that. But if smaller towns, as we will see, could more often be drawn into the net, they represented a still peripheral part of the multi-storey market. Finally, with middle-sized or smaller towns, contractors could often recognise the influence of their own package-deal building types in the drawn shapes and dispositions – the 'profiles' – of the blocks in the design briefs sent them by local authorities.[44] Here is how George Bowie described the situation:

In the design brief, you're shown a nice layout, you'd get, say, Callendar Park, Falkirk, and you'd say "they've done our profile!" or "they've done Wimpey's profile!". It was a clue as to whose salesmen had done the best job![45]

For firms actually engaged in building thousands of houses, the utopian or rhetorical concept of system building came into focus only briefly in the mid-1960s, and then as a public relations

Bryant built the low-rise terraces of Bell's Lane, Birmingham, in 1965. Full pre-cast construction was a little unusual for two-storey houses; but Bryant, a big player in construction in the Midlands, enjoyed a succession of large negotiated contracts with Birmingham City Council. That enabled it to develop its own concrete and timber systems for low-rise accommodation, while using Bison Wall-Frame for multi-storey blocks

slogan – playing the same role that it was already fulfilling for government ministers. The contractors' use of this slogan was not systematically related to the organisation of building or even to the existing pattern of investment in prefabrication factories and plant. And with the shift towards firms as package-deal providers, 'system' labels were increasingly used as brand-names rather than as technical designations.[46] Referring to Crudens' large-panel Skarne system, originating in Sweden and licensed for UK use from 1963, Bowie candidly assessed the pressures facing the major private sector contractors:

I always took the view that there was a time when the Government, politically, was shouting about low-labour factory-made multistorey blocks, and they sent a lot of us chasing off to get some damn thing signed up on the Continent. We had to acquire one – but "systems" was and is a marketing vehicle. People would come and say "we want your system", but they didn't get it! Lots of times when we were busy we got our pre-cast elsewhere than in the Skarne factory. As the thing developed, I'd find us pre-casting ground-floor slabs in four-storey blocks, say at Whitfield in Dundee, and I'd say "that's rubbish!". Very soon we said "Skarne – so what! We won't pre-cast the floors any more, just the walls!". It became delightfully vague, even in the terms of the contracts where "Skarne" wasn't mentioned! After all, what does it really amount to? – Just casting large lumps of concrete![47]

The firms that profited most from the systems boom were those which most emphasised flexibility in response to local conditions. In the field of out-and-out prefabrication, Concrete Ltd was the only contractor to make a significant impact in all parts of Britain. Concrete's reputation as the Rolls Royce of systems had little to do with the structural attributes of its Bison Wall-Frame prefabrication. Its advantage derived from a simple organisational fact: that it was, by origin, a supplier of pre-cast concrete and a subcontractor, rather than a main contractor. The firm relentlessly exploited the fact in its marketing.

Rather than treating local authority demand for small variations from standard plans as an obstacle, Concrete Ltd instead emphasised two complementary points. In the case of authorities wanting architectural flexibility, it stressed that Bison allowed a wide variety of plan variations. Meanwhile it reassured clients worried about cost, telling them that standard plans were available – mostly worked out by the company's consultant architect, Miall Rhys Davies – and insisting that clients stick to them if they wanted genuine economies in building. Alec Mitchell, Concrete Ltd's Scottish sales director during the mid-1960s, recollected 'it was sound commercial sense for us to be seen to be all things to all men', and 'to work with the local people – local builders, local architects. Local allegiance went a long way'.[48]

Although the initial spread of Bison and the setting up of regional subsidiaries was made possible by big contracts from Birmingham, Glasgow and others, the firm's subsequent strategy was to avoid blockbusting assaults on individual localities. Instead, Concrete established footholds all over of Britain. Bison Wall-Frame was more suitable for smaller scale orders than its parent, the Larsen Nielsen system; and Concrete's sales pitch emphasised its divergence from the culture of bulk orders. Smaller developments of only 24 dwellings were possible – although it was stressed that the smaller the contract, the higher the price of each dwelling. Concrete Ltd's normal practice was to build in conjunction with main contractors in the locality of the project, which gave it the flexibility to infiltrate a region rapidly. As one architect remarked, 'any small builder could get a Bison contract!'[49]

The other big firm which really made a national success of the systems boom, Wimpey, did not use prefabrication at all, but rather a systematised and highly practical method of pouring wet concrete using coarse 'no-fines' concrete. The firm's three main selling points were:

- the regard many local authorities had for its overall reliability;
- its employment of local semi-skilled labour, with the itinerant regional pouring gang the only fixed workforce the company retained as staff from one contract to the next; and
- its flexibility of layout.

Unsurprisingly, much of Wimpey's established strength lay in cities that were half-hearted about prefabrication, such as Edinburgh, Bristol or Leeds, and in the smaller towns. Overall, Wimpey built between 20 and 35 per cent of the high flats in all parts of Britain except Greater London (only two per cent) and the North-West of England (12 per cent).

By contrast with the success that came from a flexible response to the opportu-nities of the 1960s boom, doctrinaire attempts to put into practice utopian concepts of building modernisation led to several disasters – for designers as much as for building firms. For example, municipal architects might insist on safe-guarding the flexibility of design to an extent that sacrificed their negotiating position with contractors. When West Ham Borough Council's architect, TE North, began the prefabricated high flat programme that included Ronan Point, the block which famously collapsed in May 1968, he made precisely this mistake.

North was one of the stalwarts of the English municipal-architecture establish-ment. During the 1950s, he ran West Ham's programme in the LCC manner, insisting on individual designs and com-petitive tenders. In the early 1960s, when it became clear that expanded output would require a serial contract with a big

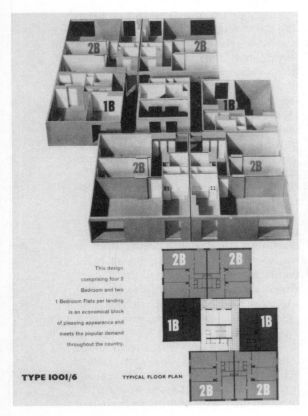

TYPE IOOI/6

This design comprising four 2 Bedroom and two 1 Bedroom Flats per landing is an economical block of pleasing appearance and meets the popular demand throughout the country.

TYPICAL FLOOR PLAN

Flats illustrated in a Wimpey brochure of 1965 show cutaway plans of, and perspectives on, the kind of package-deal block that the company built most often in the late 1960s. Put up mainly in medium-sized British towns, the block consisted of two towers with six flats on each upper floor. It was designed for construction in 'no-fines' concrete

prefabrication firm, North saw it as his first duty to ensure architectural control. Impressed by the alleged design flexibility of the Danish Larsen and Nielsen system, North became determined to use it in West Ham. This gave it a monopoly position locally so that, in the end, even North's own architects were undone by the sheer size of the commitment. North's deputy, K Lund, recalls:

We had to make so many sites available so quickly – and, because their factory could churn panels out so fast, we ended up racing and racing to get the sites ready, getting into a kind of merry-go-round![50]

But it was just as possible for building firms to come seriously unstuck. At the height of the boom, around 1964, the slogans of government and industry briefly began to react with each other in a way that was divorced from practical sense. Some firms became so intoxicated by the official rhetoric of industrialised building that they were induced to build grand pre-casting factories on a scale suited only to a vast, open-ended production stretching way into the future.

The large municipalities could only seriously trip up if, like West Ham, they insisted on narrowing their contractual options to a prefabricated bulk order with one particular firm. But the predicament of contractors reliant on large-panel concrete construction was far more serious. They soon found that there would be no sudden breakthrough to profitability. The reason for this was that the economic basis of prefabrication was somewhat unstable, given that the patronage was concentrated yet uncoordinated. Control was in the hands of powerful municipal authorities, each determined to secure its own individual housing solutions.

4.5 End of the boom

All in all, many contractors convinced themselves that system building was far quicker than it really was. They had, said

Ivy Bridge Farm, Hounslow, was a disastrous contract plagued by the strikes and contractual problems that typified the years around 1970. The development was a frame design built conventionally in reinforced concrete, without significant prefabrication. It was begun by Turriff, an inexperienced firm which went bankrupt. The photo was taken in February 1970, when the site was lying abandoned and half completed.

Mowlem eventually completed Ivy Bridge Farm. It serves as a reminder that the difficulties facing contractors in the 1960s were not just technical, to do with prefabrication, but often simply commercial

senior Wates manager Peter Lord, 'been looking through rose-tinted spectacles'.[51] In the field of large panel prefabrication, firms whose projects had enjoyed mixed success with Britain's big cities told themselves that these were simply the loss-leaders which would later bring in a deluge of orders; and they tried to spread their coverage. Sometimes they were partly successful; but most big prefabricated schemes, such as Kidbrooke or Thamesmead, either lost money or barely broke even. Losses resulted both from investments in new factories and from professional staff costs. Bowie again recalls:

To start off with, pre-casting something took a tremendous amount of work anyway . . . the volume of drawing-board staff work for pre-cast is 10 or 15 times that for *in situ*, the cost of providing documentation is enormous compared to *in situ* – and you always get mistakes! At its maximum in the late sixties, the engineering drawing-board staff in our office went up to 250 or 300 people, apportioned between various jobs. But changes multiplied this work even more – the tiniest of little changes, like changing the edge detailing, spat out all sorts of new requirements for redrawing![52]

These obstacles and contradictions were of a strictly subordinate importance, so long as the demand for output remained overwhelming: arguably, any losses made by firms on prefabrication investment were usually counterbalanced by orders for non-prefabricated mass housing. The snags only began to coalesce into real problems of profitability in the late 1960s, especially following the Ronan Point collapse in 1968 and the cuts in public expenditure on mass housing in that same year.

Government economies, however, were emphatically *not* the cause of the crisis in prefabrication. They were, rather, only a symptom of longer-term trends in Britain's mass housing market.

Earlier in the century, the Government had committed itself politically and administratively to overcoming slums and housing shortages. This would be done by continuous, open-ended construction; it would be done through the management of dwellings in accordance with political, architectural and wider social aims. That campaign formed part of a broad apparatus of state intervention that, as it turned out, had the consequence of actually worsening slums and shortages of homes. For example, rent control encouraged the spread of dilapidation.

All in all, the state grappled with so many interrelated variables that it proved unable to match the quantity of homes built with the quality required. Its open-ended, high-profile building campaign faltered as the quantitative housing shortage across the UK lost its perceived urgency and political force at varying times in the late 1960s and 1970s. This was a change that fuelled a growing left-wing critique of the quantitative, top-down provision of mass housing within the welfare state – a critique distinct from Margaret Thatcher's later hostility toward the welfare state itself.[53]

The change in political climate was most noticeable in high flats and was paralleled by a steep decline in the fortunes of prefabrication. Boom finally turned into bust, sending prices through the floor and undoing the economics of prefabrication for the contractors. The over-extension of their resources was now cruelly exposed – as Crudens found in the case of its Skarne system, which turned from a handy marketing gimmick into a very expensive liability. At Killingworth, the Longbenton local authority rescinded Phase 2 of a major contract for Skarne deck blocks without warning. George Bowie recalled:

I said "Do you know how much money has been spent on designing the second phase?". They said, "don't worry!". I said, "what the hell

The industrialised development of Killingworth, a new 'township' north of Newcastle, centred around a massive and spacious deck-access complex. Built from 1967 using the Skarne system, the cancellation of its second phase left the contractors, Crudens, with massive losses. The options for substantially refurbishing the development were rejected in favour of demolition in 1987. The investment was duly written off, the site cleared, and low-rise redevelopment of the site followed

do you think two dozen engineers have been doing for six months!"[54]

It is useful to draw some lessons from the grand adventures of the 1960s. It would tempt many, after all, to say that the systems movement failed as a result of fundamental technical deficiencies inherent in any attempt to revolutionise building.

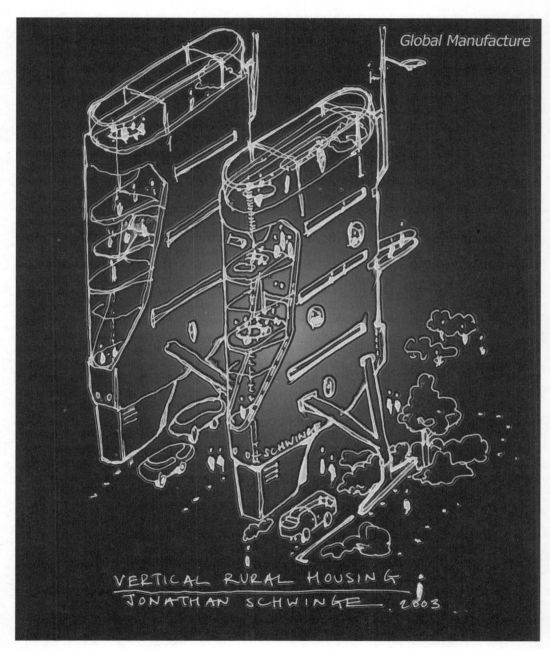

'Vertical Rural', by Jonathan Schwinge

It would be tempting, but it would be wrong. With its competing discourses and its disparity between rhetoric and realisation, the multifaceted systems boom of the 1960s was no revolution in building. Indeed, no revolution was ever seriously envisaged – still less attempted. What was most striking about it was the continuing gulf between utopian advocacy and coalface reality. Thus, it hardly represents a sensible yardstick by which to judge our efforts and aspirations today. Certainly, as regards constructional performance, there is little evidence on which to support generalised claims of failure – or indeed of success. All we know is that no prefabricated tower block since Ronan Point has suffered progressive collapse. The lesson of Ronan Point was heeded by structural engineers.

Politically, there was no demand or support for a concept of the dwelling as a manufactured commodity, in the manner of US mobile homes. A massive political commitment to Britain's housing drive was focused, instead, on numbers. Nobody of any real influence set out to actually modernise the building industry through factory-built housing, and certainly not through a grand architectural movement. People just built empirically, overlaying long-held traditions of modular component use in British homes with a new vocabulary – that of marketing.

Because of its evolutionary pragmatism and its strong roots in the practical, highly diversified world of contractors and local councillors, the 1960s systems building boom was an ad hoc movement. For these reasons, and within the politics of the day, it was effective; but in a new millennium, it is neither a guide to nor a warning against the revolution in prefabrication that is now required.

NOTES

1   AW Cleeve Barr, quoted in 'Architecture and System Building', *The Builder*, 29 March 1963, p 651.

2   Brian Finnimore, *Houses from the Factory* (London, Rivers Oram, 1989) p 371.

3   Alberto Pérez-Gomez, *Architecture and the Crisis of Modern Science* (Cambridge, Massachusetts, The MIT Press, 1984).

4   Stefan Muthesius, *The English Terraced House* (London, Yale University Press, 1984), especially chapters 17 and 19.

5   Nikolaus Pevsner, *Pioneers of Modern Design: From William Morris to Walter Gropius* (Harmondsworth, Penguin, 1960 Pelican edition).

6   Peter Reyner Banham, *Theory and Design in the First Machine Age* (London, Architectural Press, 1960).

7   Miles Glendinning and Stefan Muthesius, *Tower Block: Modern Public Housing in England, Scotland, Wales and Northern Ireland* (New Haven and London, Yale University Press, 1994).

8   Anthony Sutcliffe, *Towards the Planned City, Germany, Britain, USA, France, 1780–1914* (Oxford, Blackwell, 1981).

9   Walter Gropius, *Scope of Total Architecture* (New York, Harper & Row, 1943).

10   Brenda Vale, *Prefabs: A History of the UK Temporary Housing Programme* (London, Spon, 1995) p 6.

11   Andrew Saint, *Towards a Social Architecture: The Role of School Building in Post-war England* (New Haven and London, Yale University Press, 1987) p 27.

12   Gilbert Herbert, *The Dream of the Factory-Made House: Walter Gropius and Konrad Wachsmann* (Cambridge, Massachusetts, The MIT Press, 1984).

13   J Steel Maitland, 'Scottish housing: past and present', *Journal of the Royal Institute of British Architects*, July 1952, p 315 to 320, and quoted in Miles Glendinning and Stefan Muthesius, *Tower Block: Modern Public Housing in England, Scotland, Wales and Northern Ireland* (New Haven and London, Yale University Press, 1994) p 1, p 331 to 336.

14   Cement and Concrete Association, *Housing from the Factory conference*, Church House, London, 1962 (London, C&CA, 1962) p 5.

15   William Allen, 'Materials and Techniques', *Journal of the Royal Institute of British Architects*, June 1954, p 319, and quoted in Miles Glendinning and Stefan Muthesius, *Tower Block: Modern Public Housing in England, Scotland, Wales and Northern Ireland* (New Haven and London, Yale University Press, 1994) p 73 to 92, 386 to 387.

16   Peter Reyner Banham, *The Architecture of the Well-Tempered Environment* (London, Architectural Press, 1969).

17 AW Cleeve Barr, *Public Authority Housing* (London, Batsford, 1958).

18 'Economic Theory of Multi-Storey Flats', *Architects' Journal*, 28 January 1954, p 141.

19 Advertisement, *Architectural Review*, November 1949, p.337.

20 Peter Dunican and AW Cleeve Barr, 'Cross Walls', *Architects' Journal*, 17 March 1955, p 357 to 358.

21 *Building*, September 1946, p 276.

22 AW Cleeve Barr, *Public Authority Housing* (London, Batsford, 1958) p 110.

23 Barry Russell, *Building Systems – Industrialisation and Architecture* (Chichester, Wiley, 1981) p 212.

24 Peter Dunican and AW Cleeve Barr, 'Cross Walls', *Architects' Journal*, 17 March 1955, p 358.

25 Brian Finnimore, *Houses from the Factory* (London, Rivers Oram, 1989) p 79 to 86.

26 AFL Deeson, Editor, *The Comprehensive Buildings Annual* (London, House Publications Limited, 1965) p 117, 150 to 152. RME Diamant, *Industrialised Building – 50 International Methods, written in collaboration with The Architect and Building News* (London, Illiffe Books, 1964). Thomas Schmid and Carlo Testa, *Systems Building – An International Survey of Methods* (London, Pall Mall Press, 1969).

27 Christian Schaedlich, 'Die Industriellen Montagebauweisen im Wohnungsbau der Sowjetunion', *Wissenschaftliche Zeitschrift der Hochschule fuer Architektur und Bauwesen Weimar*, Year 9, 1962, No. 1, p 25 to 46.

28 *Architects' Journal*, 1 August 1962, p 262.

29 Miles Glendinning and Stefan Muthesius, *Tower Block: Modern Public Housing in England, Scotland, Wales and Northern Ireland* (New Haven and London, Yale University Press, 1994) p 331 to 336.

30 Miles Glendinning and Stefan Muthesius, *Tower Block: Modern Public Housing in England, Scotland, Wales and Northern Ireland* (New Haven and London, Yale University Press, 1994) p 331 to 336.

31 Cement and Concrete Association, *Housing from the Factory conference, Church House, London, 1962* (London, C&CA, 1962) p 2 to 3. RME Diamant, Preface, *Industrialised Building – 50 International Methods, written in collaboration with The Architect and Building News* (London, Illiffe Books, 1964) note 20.

32 Miles Glendinning and Stefan Muthesius, *Tower Block: Modern Public Housing in*

England, Scotland, Wales and Northern Ireland* (New Haven and London, Yale University Press, 1994) p 395 to 396, and notes 5 and 6 in chapter 24.

33 Miles Glendinning and Stefan Muthesius, *Tower Block: Modern Public Housing in England, Scotland, Wales and Northern Ireland* (New Haven and London, Yale University Press, 1994) p 394, and notes 18 and 22 in chapter 22.

34 Miles Glendinning and Stefan Muthesius, *Tower Block: Modern Public Housing in England, Scotland, Wales and Northern Ireland* (New Haven and London, Yale University Press, 1994) p 394 to 395, and notes 28 and 29 in chapter 22.

35 Miles Glendinning and Stefan Muthesius, *Tower Block: Modern Public Housing in England, Scotland, Wales and Northern Ireland* (New Haven and London, Yale University Press, 1994) p 395, and note 33 in chapter 22.

36 Miles Glendinning and Stefan Muthesius, *Tower Block: Modern Public Housing in England, Scotland, Wales and Northern Ireland* (New Haven and London, Yale University Press, 1994) p 331 to 334.

37 Miles Glendinning and Stefan Muthesius, *Tower Block: Modern Public Housing in England, Scotland, Wales and Northern Ireland* (New Haven and London, Yale University Press, 1994) p 153 to 173.

38 P Lord, Wates Ltd, interview with Miles Glendinning, 1988, in Miles Glendinning and Stefan Muthesius, *Tower Block: Modern Public Housing in England, Scotland, Wales and Northern Ireland* (New Haven and London, Yale University Press, 1994) p 203.

39 Brian Finnimore, *Houses from the Factory*, (London, Rivers Oram, 1989) p 12.

40 Advertisement, *Architect and Building News*, 13 September 1961, p 71.

41 Miles Glendinning and Stefan Muthesius, *Tower Block: Modern Public Housing in England, Scotland, Wales and Northern Ireland* (New Haven and London, Yale University Press, 1994) p 396, and notes 8 to 11 in chapter 24.

42 George Bowie, Crudens, interview with Miles Glendinning, 1987, in Miles Glendinning and Stefan Muthesius, *Tower Block: Modern Public Housing in England, Scotland, Wales and Northern Ireland* (New Haven and London, Yale University Press, 1994) p 202.

43 George Bowie, Crudens, interview with Miles Glendinning, 1987, in Miles

Glendinning and Stefan Muthesius, *Tower Block: Modern Public Housing in England, Scotland, Wales and Northern Ireland* (New Haven and London, Yale University Press, 1994) p 202.

44 Miles Glendinning and Stefan Muthesius, *Tower Block: Modern Public Housing in England, Scotland, Wales and Northern Ireland* (New Haven and London, Yale University Press, 1994) p 396, and notes 31 to 32 in chapter 24, and chapters 25 and 26.

45 George Bowie, Crudens, interview with Miles Glendinning, 1987, in Miles Glendinning and Stefan Muthesius, *Tower Block: Modern Public Housing in England, Scotland, Wales and Northern Ireland* (New Haven and London, Yale University Press, 1994) p 207.

46 Miles Glendinning and Stefan Muthesius, *Tower Block: Modern Public Housing in England, Scotland, Wales and Northern Ireland* (New Haven and London, Yale University Press, 1994) p 73 to 92 and 386 to 387.

47 George Bowie, Crudens, interview with Miles Glendinning, 1987, in Miles Glendinning and Stefan Muthesius, *Tower Block: Modern Public Housing in England, Scotland, Wales and Northern Ireland (New Haven and London*, Yale University Press, 1994) p 207.

48 Alec Mitchell, Concrete Ltd, interview with Miles Glendinning, 1987, in Miles Glendinning and Stefan Muthesius, *Tower Block: Modern Public Housing in England, Scotland, Wales and Northern Ireland* (New Haven and London, Yale University Press, 1994) p 212.

49 Tom Smyth, interview with Miles Glendinning, 1987, in Miles Glendinning and Stefan Muthesius, *Tower Block: Modern Public Housing in England, Scotland, Wales and Northern Ireland* (New Haven and London, Yale University Press, 1994) p 212.

50 K Lund, interview with Miles Glendinning, 1988, in Miles Glendinning and Stefan Muthesius, *Tower Block: Modern Public Housing in England, Scotland, Wales and Northern Ireland* (New Haven and London, Yale University Press, 1994) p 208.

51 P Lord, Wates Ltd, interview with Miles Glendinning, 1988, in Miles Glendinning and Stefan Muthesius, *Tower Block: Modern Public Housing in England, Scotland, Wales and Northern Ireland* (New Haven and London, Yale University Press, 1994) p 209.

52 George Bowie, Crudens, interview with Miles Glendinning, 1987, in Miles Glendinning and Stefan Muthesius, *Tower Block: Modern Public Housing in England, Scotland, Wales and Northern Ireland* (New Haven and London, Yale University Press, 1994) p 209.

53 Nicholas Taylor, *The Village in the City* (London, Temple Smith, 1973).

54 George Bowie, Crudens, interview with Miles Glendinning, 1987, in Miles Glendinning and Stefan Muthesius, *Tower Block: Modern Public Housing in England, Scotland, Wales and Northern Ireland* (New Haven and London, Yale University Press, 1994) p 316.

5 False innovation and real innovation

5.1 Buildings as brands

5.1.1 Investment in process lags differentiation in product

On 26 February 2003 the RICS revealed that, during 2002, UK house prices rose at twice the rate of those in Spain and Denmark, the two countries with the next highest house price inflation in the EU. At the same time, the RICS observed, no other EU country had such a poor record of housing supply.[1] Why is that?

The Office for National Statistics hinted at an answer a day earlier. The ONS revealed that, in 2002, business investment in the UK fell at its steepest rate since 1965 – by more than 10 per cent. Manufacturing led the decline, with investment in that sector falling by nearly 18 per cent to its lowest point since 1984. An economist at HSBC bank felt the fall to have been in place for five years; it was 'more likely to be structural than cyclical'.[2]

Within the same week, Deutsche Bank highlighted the very different preoccupations of China. In the second half of 2002, Chinese GDP grew by eight per cent. Over the year it was responsible for 11 per cent of the world's growth, second only to the USA. In the final quarter of 2002 Chinese factory production increased by 13 per cent, its biggest gain in five years. Exports surged 22 per cent and, significantly, investment rose by a fifth.[3]

Set against China's figures in particular, *the UK suffers from a real crisis in business and manufacturing investment. And it is that crisis which provides the context for the UK building sector's dismissive attitude toward process technologies. For if investment is held to be a risky enterprise, then process technologies, in construction as elsewhere, become merely optional extras rather than the basics of progress.*

There are many suppliers of timber- and steel-framed buildings today. But although such buildings may be bought from pattern books, they are still bespoke; they are simply prefabricated off-site as panels or frames for on-site erection. This is a step toward prefabrication, but a very small one. Broader leaps in process technologies are needed.

The 20th century has proved that components and assemblies set in a dimensionally coordinated frame offer serious advantages over site-bound building work, whether in offices or housing. America's Charles and Ray Eames revealed the economies to be had from lightweight frames coordinated with in-fill components that were continuously upgraded and available off the shelf.[4] In Britain, Walter Segal showed how a rationalised but flexible system could reduce the need for skilled tradesmen.[5] David

Walter Segal's system in Lewisham, London

Lea went on to give Segal's approach a subtler, crafted quality.[6]

The 21st century construction sector remains backward compared to these old efforts. Still, its much-expanded wealth of materials and products would allow massive improvements to be made on the modernist innovations of the Eameses and of Segal – technically, functionally and aesthetically. It is more than 30 years since, when building his own home with a tweaked version of the low-rise Segal System, the Cambridge master-planning consultant Marcial Echenique found out the hard way about unfounded hostility to architectural systems. Yet today, systems are in an even more invidious position. They:

• have none of the dominance they had in the 1960s;

• contain much more potential; and
• arouse even greater hostility.

Against even simple systems, regulators hold that preserving local architectural character is the way to preserve community. And against branded, fully serviced and finished volumetric housing – whether stand-alone or stackable – they are likely to be apoplectic.

That will be a problem. As the critic Sutherland Lyall observed long ago, the rule of custom architects and communitarian planners is ridiculous and not, in the long run, durable. Of it, he wrote:

It is easy enough to laugh up your sleeve at the seriousness with which grown men take all this . . . But the time can not be far off when the penny drops. Then developers will be calling in graphic and industrial design firms

Inspired by Segal, David Lea sought a more crafted technology and aesthetic in his homes for the Eddystone Housing Association at Churt, Surrey. Lea's work was built in two phases in 1975 and 1983

In 1972, Marcial Echenique, a master planner, took a timber-framed system developed by Walter Segal, modified it, and used it to design himself a house at 214 Chesterton Road, Cambridge.[7] More than a decade later, he noted, 'The Planning Department did not like the appearance of the house and they only accepted it after appeal. It was quite difficult to get a mortgage from a building society, but after building the house I was able to get one . . . Finally, no builders were interested in quoting a fixed price contract, so I had to contract a builder based on time and materials.'[8]

New houses, laborously and poorly built as mock-traditional

who really understand the ins and outs of large scale packaging design.[9]

It is not that there are no investments in process innovations being made today. It is rather that the aggregate pace of change is agonisingly slow. And where, as in non-residential construction, the rapid pace of building in the UK forms a real contrast with the sclerosis of residential construction, the danger of overcapacity works only as an ironic counterpoint to the nation's undersupply of homes.

The situation in *office property* throughout much of the EU, and especially in the City of London, is of soaring cranes and slumping forecasts for rents. Among the bespoke corporate offices that are being built or planned, the space on offer now looks too large for the amount of investment planned by general business. Reflecting the anarchy of the market and

the fads that go with that, builders of commercial property have overestimated the imperviousness of the financial services, media and telecommunications sectors to a downturn. Not for nothing did Canary Wharf have to agree, in 2003, that several of its tenants should be able to hand back some of their surplus space.

In 2002 Pembroke Real Estate, backed by Fidelity Investments, began to rebuild South Quay, near Canary Wharf, as London Millharbour – no fewer than 93,000 square metres of speculative development, and only the beginning of Millennium Quarter, a new 20 hectare business district south of Canary Wharf. But schemes like these are now widely criticised. It is pointed out that 223,000 square metres of speculative development were released in 2003, only slightly below the 266,000 square metres that was on the market in 1990, just before the last crash in the property market. In an acute manner, Patience Wheatcroft, business editor at *The Times*, attacks developers thus:

Last time round, the developers could at least comfort themselves with the argument that the shape of demand was changing and that the requirements for open-plan offices and vast trading floors, all provided with plentiful cabling for new technology, meant that older space was effectively redundant. But the supply has now been upgraded. There is just too much, and if the gloomier pundits are to be believed and we are headed into a Japanese-style period of prolonged stagnation, then many of the buildings now being developed could remain empty for a very long time.[10]

Of course, speculative office building has long ensured some spectacular gluts in space and disasters in the commercial property market. In the summer of 2002, about 56 per cent of all office construction in central London was speculative.[11] However, the risk-taking that surrounds speculative development is a positive thing, if only because innovation needs risk-takers. Looking at the extent to which the building of offices is already systematised (see Box 17), it ought not, in principle, to be too much of a risk for office builders to divert their energies toward the prefabrication of homes.

That has yet to happen. Instead, in the government estate, at visitor attractions and in corporate offices alike, there is now a desperate rush for *product differentiation*. As with residential housing, the backward, on-site, bespoke approach to the *process* of construction dominates.

5.1.2 *Branded landmark developments as a displacement activity*

Construction does not need to improve bespoke landmark developments, whether these are government buildings, museum or stadium attractions for mass visitors or corporate offices.

In a media-saturated world, it is facile to hold up as best practice those politically, culturally or commercially significant bespoke buildings that already enjoy the attention of the most capable architects and other professionals. This is to idolise craftwork. It is to engage in a compulsive displacement activity – one that sidelines investment and ignores the advances in process technologies achieved in sectors outside construction.

Modern society fears science and technology.[12] *What it supports, by contrast, are corporate and cultural buildings that are bespoke, highly differentiated in terms of aesthetic, and therefore one-off brands in themselves – in part, at least, because they are designed by branded, superstar architects. With the celebration of one-off branded buildings, the backwardness of the construction industry is turned into a virtue.*

That is a great pity. It reflects society's nervousness about the risks that it believes attend innovation and the future. There is nothing wrong with aesthetic differentiation. And there is nothing wrong with mass-produced branded consumer products: the Heinz brand's '57 varieties' contains a promise that the product will always reliably deliver the same high quality but variegated kinds of taste. As a result, there

would be nothing wrong with competition between branded manufacturers of different varieties of houses – houses designed, if necessary, by rival superstar architects, even hired by the same firm of manufacturers. What is sad is that such competition does not exist. Instead, there is mindless competition between architects to gain media coverage of their latest, one-off branded building. And there is a belief, on the part of clients, that the branded, landmark approach to all property is the key to success.

But is it? Throughout the world of business, people believe in the magic of brands. Giorgio Armani, the Italian fashion designer, has 200 outlets in 30 countries, but that is not enough for him: he has put hundreds of millions of dollars into 'stretching' his brand into cosmetics, shoes, jewellery and furniture. When Marks & Spencer followed its closure of 38 stores in continental Europe by opening franchise shops in the cities of Delhi and Bombay, it did so, it said, because in India, 'a lot of people know the Marks & Spencer brand'.[13] On the streets of Moscow, about 25,000 billboards advertising top brands were erected in the years 1991 to 2001 – a figure equal to the number of billboards in London. For months, a four-storey billboard dominated the entrance of Red Square.[14]

These examples of brands in urban space confirm that it is not just firms with offices that are interested in branded trophy buildings. So, too, are retailers and advertisers. As early as the 1920s, of course, commentators coined the phrase 'form follows finance' to describe the Manhattan skyline. Architecture has long been used to promote corporate values. When Chrysler commissioned William van Alen to design its New York headquarters, the Art Deco tower, completed in 1931, he advertised the company with giant radiator caps positioned like gargoyles at its corners and a frieze made up of car fenders and hubcaps.[15] But the love affair that firms now have with branded buildings is a qualitatively different phenomenon from the dalliances of the past.

Box 17 **TOWARD THE PREFABRICATION OF OFFICES**

The building firm Laing O'Rourke wants to secure a market for what it calls its 'customised office solution – where value meets choice and certainty'.[16] The venture is developed with:

- designers Geoffrey Reid Associates;[17]
- engineers Buro Happold;[18]
- cost consultants Franklin & Andrews;[19]
- property consultants FPD Savills;[20] and
- Butler & Young as the approved building inspectors.[21]

Laing O'Rourke's own new headquarters was built using its own technique. The HQ is based around a number of predesigned building elements on a 9x9m column grid subdivided into a 1.5 m x 0.5 m planning grid. It uses post-tensioned concrete slabs around a braced steel core. The intention is that, while the body of the new office type is standard, the number of storeys, the overall plan and the resultant cores, façade and building services will be bespoke for particular sites.

There is further to go here. The following features of office buildings could be standardised:

- floor-to-ceiling heights;
- raised floors and suspended ceilings with lighting and ventilation;
- stairs and lifts;
- toilet pods;
- plant rooms; and
- columns for integrated rainwater and air-conditioning drainage.

Foster and Partners relied upon modular lifts and cores in 1986 at the Hong Kong and Shanghai Bank, Hong Kong. Office prefabrications such as these could form the basis for major process innovations in house building

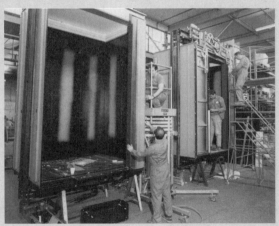

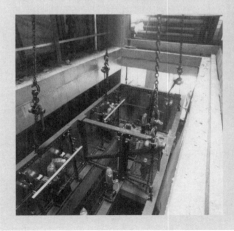

Here prefabricated lift systems are installed as part of the refurbishment of London's Old Bailey courts. Why can't such devices be applied to new buildings?

Working with lift manufacturers, John Prewer has done lengthy investigations into modular lift shafts and standardised lifts.

And so on. Predesigned façade systems and roofing solutions could also be offered. There are plenty of precedents for all of these, in better-known products that imitate innovations by Foster and Partners or the Richard Rogers Partnership, themselves influenced by the best of overseas practice.

The construction products market is awash with sub-systems and components that could be easily systematised. Indeed every newly built commercial office building has long been a tapestry of rationalised dimensional grids of services, raised floors, suspended ceilings, structure and façade. As Sebestyén writes, in the first half of the 20th century, partitions and ceilings were separated from the load-bearing structure, while new services were provided. Altogether,

> Specialisation in building components led to specialisation in the professions. The design process now called for cooperation between architects and engineers with differing professional expertise. Equally, the construction process demanded that the contractor engaged on the structure of the building should cooperate with the specialist firms responsible for the services to the building.[22]

The modularity of hierarchies of systems was extended to anticipate office layouts and furniture, which in aggregate had informed the spacing of columns and the design of floor areas. The arrangement of the plan, to achieve a form through which to impose an aesthetic, remained the specialism of the architect, thoroughly dependent on synthesising the advice of others.

The specialisation of commercial office design, begun before the war, continues to this day. So though system-built housing was rejected in the 1970s, there was no such abandonment of advance in the commercial office sector.

However, even if today's still modest approach to the prefabrication of offices were applied to British housing tomorrow, there would still be trouble. Such an approach would, first of all, demand that housebuilders make a major commitment to systems – whether low-, medium- or high-rise. Second, a further and colossal political struggle would be necessary to convince planners that mass-produced designs with a certain range of variations were, finally, preferable to costly one-offs built 'in the local vernacular'.

In new office constructions based on *in situ* reinforced concrete cores, Laing O'Rourke's Jump Shutter system pushes the limit of the productivity gains that are possible

'To weather an extended bout of distrust and instability', America's *Business Week* pronounces, 'strong brands are essential'. Brands are so important, the magazine insists, that firms will have to work 'doubly hard' to 'keep them intact'.[23] Yet *even critics of brands seem to think that they can work wonders.* Published in 2000, Naomi Klein's bestseller *No logo* indicted corporations as 'brand bullies', and accused retailer brands, in particular, of invading public space.[24] But for Klein, higher expenditure on brands ensured that some US firms, in the recession of the early 1990s, 'exited the downturn running' – 'just', she says, 'as the admen predicted'.[25]

Naomi Klein

The seriousness with which both boosters and critics of brands now regard them is inseparable from a crisis of business investment that afflicts not just the UK but the whole of the West. As Anatole Kaletsky has pointed out, in Japan and the four leading economies of Europe gross fixed capital formation as a percentage of gross domestic product was, in the 1990s, 'exceptionally low by historic standards'. Likewise, apart from corporate purchases of fast-depreciating information processing and software, every other category of US investment 'has actually been lower recently than at almost any time in the past four decades'.[26]

Since Procter & Gamble invented modern branding and marketing in the 1950s, there has been a historic tendency, in the West, to substitute these things for the much more risky and imponderable pursuit of R&D and innovation. The building sector has not been immune from this tendency.

In September 2001, P&G agreed to pay Unilever millions of dollars for using a Vietnam veteran to go 'dumpster diving' around Unilever's rubbish for secrets that would help P&G shampoo brands such as Wash & Go, Head & Shoulders, Pantene and Vidal Sassoon. As *The Times* rightly commented:

Given the fortunes that groups such as Procter & Gamble spend on product development,

having to resort to raiding rivals' dustbins is a poor reflection on their own R&D departments.[27]

Like industrial espionage, the *legal protection of brands* interests business much more than the creation of new products and services. And it is the same in architecture. In the past, a kind of gentleman's agreement between architects meant that, if a colleague reverentially mimicked a feature of a well-known building, it was the highest form of flattery. Most architects scour the glossy trade magazines and monographs for ideas to incorporate or adapt. Rem Koolhaas found himself facing accusations of *copyright infringement* over his Kunsthall in Rotterdam. British architect Gareth Pearce accused Koolhaas of copying parts of his London Docklands Town Hall plans.[28] In the same way, France's Dominique Perrault has led many other architects to *trademark* the facades of their buildings.[29]

It is important to realise that celebrating branded one-off commercial and cultural buildings runs counter to both product and process innovation. In his classic *Principles of marketing*, the doyen of marketing in the USA, Philip Kotler, held that the power of brands lay in the *intangibles* that distinguished one firm's offering from another. Kotler argued that the 'most lasting and sustainable' meanings of a brand are not its attributes (a Mercedes is well built), or even the benefits that follow from these (I am safe in the event of an accident). Firms must pay attention instead to the *values* that a brand suggests its owner holds (I own a Mercedes because I value high performance, safety and prestige), and to its *personality* (consumers might visualise a Mercedes as a middle-aged executive).[30]

Boosters of branded one-off landmark developments, then, are bound take the character traits of a building more seriously than the quality of its steel or the speed with which it – and others like it – is put up. For them, architecture will always be a matter of bespoke perceptions and associations. It could never be a matter of mass production.

5.1.3 What branded and anti-branded buildings have in common

How has the trend toward branded one-off buildings come about? At one level, as we saw in our look at inter-urban competition in Chapter 1, the relapse into branded landmark developments stands as a testament to the poverty of thinking that nowadays afflicts urban regeneration. But given the therapeutic and naturalistic trends outlined in Chapter 2 and the world's preference, just discussed, for brands over investment in product and especially over process innovations, there have been other factors at work.

As we have just seen, developers have been wrong to be so optimistic about demand for corporate offices. But they were not wrong to appreciate that, *if 1920s' clients and architects associated private capital with the dynamism of technology and urban life, today's multinational clients for architecture are desperate to create offices that reflect the supposed uniqueness of their therapeutic and naturalistic values.* That is another impetus to branded one-off buildings.

From Bloomberg's rock-and-roll Euro-

pean HQ in Finsbury Square, London EC2 through to Sainsbury's gleaming Business Centre in London EC4, the workplace must be a cultural statement.[31] It must be a statement, moreover, for staff, investors, clients, consumers, suppliers, consultants, and regulators. After Gap Inc opened a new San Francisco HQ designed by William McDonough, *Business Week* gave its glass, grass and flexibility an award because they were 'an employee's dream'.[32] Or take Toyota's new head office in Epsom, just outside London, completed in the summer of 2001. The main claim of this glassy pavilion by architect Sheppard Robson is that, through its use of natural daylight and ventilation to save energy, it speaks volumes about Toyota's commitment to general low energy use in future.[33]

The business of business has become culture, such is the crisis of investment and the fear of technological innovation in business.[34] So for firms, property is now a cultural question and one that has become more important, not less important. Of course, especially among national telecommunications carriers such as BT, France Telecom and Telecom Italia, the trend has been to outsource corporate real estate to suppliers that specialise in FM. But according to Stephen Dingle, head of the property advisory group at investment bankers NM Rothschild, 'Anglo-Saxon' corporations 'have a strong emotional attachment to property'.[35] As the *Financial Times* philosophised:

Big buildings and big trophy buildings in particular are often seen as badges of success. Companies are loathe to part with the very symbols which make them what they are.[36]

In the search for a better mission than old-fashioned shareholder value alone, every ethical corporation wants to build a one-off temple to its oh-so-idiosyncratic values – chiefly, Ethics, Goodness and Apple Pie.

Another impetus to branded one-off buildings is a more literal one – *branded*

Box 18 AMERICAN MARKETING'S HISTORIC OPT-OUT OF INNOVATION

Theodore Levitt

As late as 1959, it was still possible to write articles in the *Harvard Business Review* about the functional features of a product, as distinct from the 'values' and 'personality' evoked by it.[37] That was not surprising. GM's new 6 litre V8 Cadillac, the Eldorado Brougham, designed by Harley Earl and launched in 1957, had been plagued by reliability problems and had only sold 900 units. More notoriously the Ford Edsel, launched in 1958, showed that the world's most market-researched car was a disaster: production stopped, with a loss of $350 million, in 1960 after only 76,000 were sold.

That same year however, Theodore Levitt came to the rescue of marketing. In his key article on marketing myopia, Levitt shifted the discipline's focus from *market research* – which could at least hint at genuine improvements in features and benefits, no matter how much it had just been discredited by Ford – toward *marketing management*. Denouncing corporations for their neglect of marketing, Levitt warned of the 'dangers' of doing too much R&D. He concluded:

the organization must learn to think of itself not as producing goods or services but as *buying customers*.[38]

Business was not about what you made, but about how you marketed it. Indeed Levitt insisted that the 'genius' of Henry Ford had always been not in production, but in marketing.

Vance Packard picked up the scent quite quickly. In his famous *The wastemakers* of 1963, Packard registered marketing's turn from genuine technological improvements in products to other means of managing consumer markets that were 'saturated'. Those other means, he felt, were deliberately *planned obsolescence* in product quality and product desirability. Although there was precious little evidence for the involvement of either marketeers or designers in planned obsolescence, Packard's book emboldened consumer advocate Ralph Nader for many years.[39] It did the same for Victor Papanek, author of *Design for the Real World* in 1974 and the main post-war guru of 'survival through design'.[40] Papanek was a pioneer of therapy and naturalism if ever there was one.

It took nearly two decades for Levitt to recover from Packard. Then, in 1980, he argued that the key to commercial success was neither the enormous visibility of a company's advertising (the thing that Naomi Klein still fastens upon) nor its presumed generic product uniqueness (the thing brand boosters often like to tell us). The differentiation that was important was not in the product but in the marketing process, in the management of distributors.[41]

By 1983 Levitt's 'marketing imagination' meant remembering Charles Revson's famous slogan for Revlon: 'In the factory we make cosmetics. In the store we sell hope'. *Management was not about making a better lipstick or improving productivity in the factory. It was about marketing relationships with retailers. It was about how consumers didn't so much prefer brands as buy them to reduce risk*, or to seek 'comfort and reassurance and even flattery'.[42]

Management was about relationships with customers after the sale was over and about how ads worked wonders for people who had already bought the brand.[43] There was, said Levitt in his seminal 1983 article on globalisation, merit in 'the ideal' of innovation. But the chief merit of technology lay in 'shaping the world's preferences into homogenized commonality – into global standardisation'.[44]

Box 19 EUROPE PIONEERS THE BRANDED BUILDING

Naomi Klein's favourite brand villains are Adidas, BodyShop, Calvin Klein, Diesel, Levi's, Nike, McDonald's, Reebok, Microsoft, BurgerKing, Coke, Pepsi, Gap, Ikea, Blockbuster Video, MTV, Disney, Wal-Mart, Starbucks, Shell, Virgin and Yves St Laurent. Among these 21, only 8 – Adidas, BodyShop, Diesel, BurgerKing, Ikea, Shell, Virgin and YSL – are European brands. Of course, the prevalence of American brands in the rogues' gallery of the anticapitalists partly reflects the real domination of American brands on the world market: in the *Business Week* tables of brand equity, only 30 of the worlds' top 100 brands are European. But just as *No logo* targeted all-powerful American multinationals more than those in Europe, Europe's special expertise in branding escapes the anticapitalists.

As early as 1997, in fact, strategic management consultant Erich Joachimsthaler, together with the Global Number One Branded Academic Authority on Brands, Berkeley University's David A Aaker, insisted that, as far as brands were concerned, 'US-based companies would do well to study their counterparts in Europe'. Their reason was significant: America had entered an Internet world. Traditional mass media were a thing of the past. Thus Europe, whose manufacturers had never rested on the laurels of cheap continent-wide television commercials like their opposite numbers in the US, would 'point the way for others to succeed in the new media age'.[45]

The invasion of space that Naomi Klein detests was, Joachimsthaler and Aaker made clear, pioneered in Europe, not America. In launching Haagen-Dazs ice cream in Europe in 1989, Britain's Grand Metropolitan (now part of Diageo) eschewed television commercials, instead relying on the grooviness of new retail outlets to build the brand. By the time Britain's Cadbury chocolate makers (now part of Nestlé) opened Cadbury World in 1990, they had spent £5.8m on a theme-park history of their product and their company.

Joachimsthaler and Aaker are not alone in eulogising Europe as the proper source of branded interior design. At the *Wall Street Journal*, the right kind of kitchen must include European brands such as Bosch dishwashers (minimalist German, $780) and Dualit toasters (stainless steel British, $400). With brands such as Boffi, Bulthaup, Gaggenau and Poggenpohl, the *Journal* opines, 'Europe often sets the kitchen trends that eventually appear in upscale U.S. homes'.[46]

The historic origins of branded corporations begin with fashionable Paris in the eighteenth century. From champagne (Möet and Chandon) and luggage (Louis Vuitton) through to Versailles itself, branded luxuries and branded luxury buildings have been a decisively European contribution to world culture.

Box 20 **BRANDED ARCHITECTS**

Corporations now take branding so seriously that they prefer to outsource the magic, professional work of branding to independent *marketing services companies*: to Omnicom, WPP, Publicis. Saatchi & Saatchi first made the case for global brands in the 1980s. Since then marketing services companies have themselves become global enterprises, quoted on international stock exchanges. Their activities extend from the creative development of ads and the purchase of time and space for those ads, through public relations and investor relations, to all kinds of design. They do corporate identities, graphic design for point-of-sale display, packaging and print, Web design, retail and leisure interiors, and even product design.

Interestingly enough, the same thing has happened to *architectural services companies*. From Michael Graves's whistling teapot for Alessi onward, architects confirm their celebrity by stepping up to do everything. The trend for trophy buildings and products to be signed by celebrity architects, however, is only the most pointed signal that the building sector would prefer anything rather than engage in real process innovations. And, once again, in this it merely reflects a prevailing culture throughout industry.

In 2000, Interbrand, brand consultants within the Omnicom empire, published a collection of 25 paeans to brands. Contributors ranged from Procter & Gamble to Deepak Chopra, an internationally-renowned guru of spiritual wellbeing. Summing up the hegemony of brands within business today, Interbrand chief Rita Clifton wrote:

> Whichever way you look at it, brands today are the most demonstrably powerful and sustainable wealth creators in the world . . . just about *everything and everyone is capable of becoming a brand.*[47]

To engage in *leadership* with brands, Clifton argues, is always to be 'restless' about their 'self-renewal'.

So brands, like people, need continual life support. Like children, they need nurturing by the management if they are to lead the life they deserve. But if brands are people, people can become brands. David Beckham is a worldwide brand. But why is it that Bill Gates personifies the Microsoft brand, or Phil Knight personifies Nike?

The answer is that each represents a managerial stewardship of, and thus a partial guarantee of, future revenues. So when Bill or Phil are said to be worth billions, that is because they own titles to future revenues. When they have their health insured for squillions, that is because their ill-health is felt likely to jeopardise those revenues. It is not the intellect or charisma of CEOs that turns them into superstar brands, nor even their money, but their role as the personification of things. It is only the existence of branded products and thus brand equity that enables their owner to appear in the form of the branded leader, and to enter relations with investment bankers and others in that role.

So it is with architects. In the past, architects could be social-democratic brands – Le Corbusier, Frank Lloyd Wright, Walter Gropius, Mies van der Rohe. During the 1980s boom in US prestige property, Philip Johnson and Michael Graves, along with the developer Donald Trump, also became brands. But these names only represented a claim on future visitors or on the possibility of a building appreciating in value prior to its sale.

There is danger for architects here. *Business Week* audits corporate brand equity down to the last dollar with bizarre results: in 2003 it rated the 'brand value' of Shell ($2.98 billion) little higher than that of Smirnoff ($2.8 billion).[48] As we saw in Chapter 1, every visitor to New Labour's museums must be recorded, even if the statistics report little improvement. It is only a matter of time, then, before the revenue-earning merits and demerits of branded buildings, and branded architects, are measured and consolidated into performance league tables.

one-off buildings can be sold entirely on their own merits, as brands in themselves. Along with others, Frank Gehry, author of the Walt Disney concert Hall in Los Angeles, the Jimi Hendrix Music Project in Seattle and the Museum of Tolerance in Jerusalem, has pioneered a broad and somewhat unprecedented trend for *branded one-off visitor attractions that set their own, highly differentiated agenda rather than taking their cue from local conditions.* Like huge pieces of sculpture, his works demand to be experienced as objects rather than as extensions of the existing urban fabric. Not for nothing, then, have Gehry buildings been reproduced as iconic images on paper bags, key-rings and – inevitably – as logos.

The third and final impetus to branded buildings comes from Rem Koolhaas, who has become somewhat of an apostle of *anti-branding as itself a branding strategy.*

The retailer Prada has moved into many outlets. Describing the problem confronting Prada, his client, Koolhaas says:

Indefinite expansion represents a crisis: in the typical case it spells the end of the brand as a

creative enterprise and the beginning of the brand as a purely financial enterprise.[49]

The Koolhaas solution to what he perceives as Prada's problem is to create a series of 'epicenter' stores that redefine the brand as a 'conceptual window: a medium to broadcast future directions that positively charges the larger mass of typical stores'. The Prada brand should be reflected in 'anti-flagship stores' that are not identical, and in cultural events that are hosted in stores.[50]

In effect, Koolhaas proposes to turn a few key Prada stores into spaces that mimic museums, since, as he puts it:

in a world where everything is shopping . . . and shopping is everything . . . what is luxury? Luxury is NOT shopping.[51]

Yet Koolhaas is not alone in his disgust with trophy architecture and his desire to mix in with his surroundings.

The new millennium opened with critics of globalisation attacking architecture's attachment to branded corporate homogeneity. Taking a leaf from the book of anti-capitalist protesters, Ole Bouman, editor of the Dutch architectural magazine *Archis*, looked forward to what he called 'architecture's Battle of Seattle'.[52] From Manhattan, the editor in chief of *Metropolis* magazine focused its first issue of 2000 on 'design vs global blanding', asking architects and designers to choose buildings, objects and graphics that represented 'the local, the individual design in a global culture'.[53]

What pro- and anti-branding strategies share is a fixation, once more, on the differentiated *products* of construction, and an almost complete disregard for its *processes*. Of course, the exteriors of branded one-off visitor attractions can impress tourists, just like anti-branded one-off corporate interiors can impress commercial visitors. But neither gambit is innovative enough, by itself, to revive a city or improve a firm's bottom line. For that, something more substantial than product differentiation is required.

Yacht designer Nic Bailey, also known for the pods he designed for the British Airways millennium wheel, has applied his talent to an iconic American brand – the Airstream mobile home, dating from the 1930s. The cutaway shows the familiar sleek exterior, but the standard wood-panelled interior is generally something of a let-down. Bailey wanted to fit out a Classic Airstream in keeping with its bodywork, improving on comfort and optimising the living space in the process

ORIGINAL INTERIOR PLAN

NEW INTERIOR PLAN

Rectilinear furniture sits uneasily in rounded space

No sense of inside being related to outside

A set of small spaces each trying to ape a 'proper' house

All sense of space sacrificed to a surfeit of oversized convenience appliances

Biggest possible multi-use space

Minimal but adequate bathroom

Furniture fitted in band around perimeter, with no sacrifice of amenities

LIVING

Seating area fitted to shape of fuselage and designed for optimal seating......not as a sofa-bed

EATING

A table big enough for four comfortable dining chairs

SLEEPING

Full size double bed that when folded away completely disappears

Concept

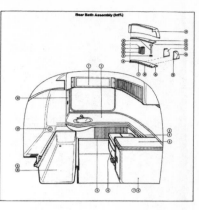

Bathroom

Interior design

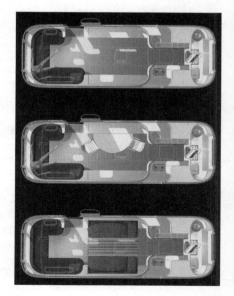

Plans

Interior views. No doubt this interpretation of the Airstream brand can be improved upon. That should always be true in the branded houses-as-products of the future. For more information, visit Nic Bailey Design at www.nic.bailey.bt internet.co.uk

5.2 The new prefabrication

5.2.1 From Paxton and Brunel to modern Japan

Prefabrication can be traced back throughout history, but most notably to Joseph Paxton's Crystal Palace of 1851,[54] and to Isambard Kingdom Brunel's prefabricated Renkioi Hospital for the Crimean War, built about 1855.

In his insightful *Building Innovation*, David Gann hails Paxton's Crystal Palace

as a landmark in the history of industrialised construction in a way that the Millennium Dome was not. The Palace typified 'the transformation of the construction site from a place where craft skills honed materials, to a place of assembly of standardised, prefabricated, mass-produced components'.[55]

The valley-guttered glass roof of the Crystal Palace was one of the inspirations for James Sterling and James Gowan's influential Engineering Building at the University of Leicester, completed in 1963. But the Leicester Engineering Building also highlights an important distinction to make about the phrase 'mass produced'. In *Building Innovation*, Gann distinguishes between two types of prefabricated components:

- *Production to order*, where components are prefabricated for a particular building design and never repeated; and
- *Production to stock*, where components are prefabricated without prior knowledge of the design or type of building in which they are to be used.[56]

The Crystal Palace represented production to order. In most regards, the Engineering Building was not prefabricated at all, but site-built. Yet in its use of patent glazing, the Engineering Building was also an example of production-to-stock, albeit that the stock extrusions had to be worked up on site, making the sizes of the glass panels tend to vary as a consequence. Nevertheless, it was the ability of the product manufacturers to produce their sub-system in bulk *for stock* that made it both innovative and an economy.

Many building developments today are so large that they offer significant economies of scale on the production *to order* of castings, extrusions and worked fabrications – almost regardless of the material used. Yet it is the *stock range* of prefabricated parts that best serves both large and smaller developments, which are sophisticated over time. However, as Gann observes, the construction industry often has a parasitical relationship to the other industrial sectors in which new materials are being developed. Yet developing construction applications out of innovations elsewhere – transferring technology into construction – is a haphazard affair:

Many materials used in construction are produced for general application across a range of industries for which construction may form only a small part of total demand: for example, aluminium or plastics. Producers of these materials may not necessarily focus their attention on improving existing products or developing new ones specifically for construction, unless they have a particular construction products division.[57]

For 21st century building, then, prefabrication of sub-systems for stock and the advancing use of old and new materials alike are more than possibilities.

More systematised than Sterling and Gowan's Leicester Engineering Building, and built a century earlier, the example of Brunel's Renkioi Hospital confirms the point. Prefabrication was not a new idea to Brunel and his peers: the concept had begun to win serious adherents as early as the 1830s.[58] But in prefabricating a hospital, Brunel took the best of the existing ideas, developed them and produced a combination that was startling, practical and successful.[59] As the Architectural Association lecturer Jane Wernick notes, the economic advantages of prefabrication ensured that, with Renkioi, Brunel:

achieved the almost unbelievable task of taking the project from the initial inception of the idea to completion, including shipping, in a period of just five months. He received the commission on 16 February 1855 and by 12 July Renkioi was ready to accept 300 patients. By the end of March 1856 it could have accommodated 2,200 patients.[60]

Of course, individual creative genius cannot always overcome objective frustrations. But Brunel was determined to make a real difference in construction,

David Gann

saw the need to prefabricate common types of building such as hospitals and houses, and had the presence of mind and the steely nerve to fulfil that need. So where are the Brunels today? Brunel fully deserved being voted, in a poll held around the BBC's 2002 series *Great Britons*, second only to Winston Churchill (see Table 16).

Yet while popular support for Brunel's achievements is strong, a systematic

The University of Leicester Engineering Building, 1963, designed by James Sterling and James Gowan, was a triumph of hand-calculated engineering by FJ Samuely and Partners. The firm's origins date back to 1933, when Felix Samuely came to Britain and worked on a number of well known and innovative structures, including the De La Warr Pavilion at Bexhill, Simpsons Piccadilly (now Waterstones) and the Skylon for the Festival of Britain. FJ Samuely and Partners was formed in 1956 and Frank Newby became senior partner in 1959 when Felix Samuely died prematurely. Newby presided over the Engineering Building. Further details are at www.samuely.demon.co.uk

approach to prefabrication is almost nowhere to be seen – except as a history lesson.

Bricks and nails were among the first and most standardised parts to be used in construction: they were produced in batch, and later, in volume.[62] Today, despite atrophy in craft-based construction practices, Gann is right to add that the forces for technical change are particularly strong among materials and component manufacturers, who are often able to invest in long-term R&D. He stresses:

Many major technological changes aimed at improving construction processes take place away from construction sites and seek to reduce skill requirements on-site. Value-added in construction is increasingly being produced upstream in the supply chain, by component manufacturers.[63]

However, most of the formal R&D carried out in construction products is orientated towards developing better ones, not to systematising the construction process itself.[64]

Neither building contractors nor contracting as a practice are necessarily to blame for technological backwardness. Gann accurately insists that contractors have always displayed a capability for innovation: 'The site-based nature of production, increasing numbers of different specialisms, relative uniqueness and the changing use of final products, and variety of production processes, constantly throw up problems which firms have to solve in a variety of ways.' Yet it is also true that much contractor-originated innovation reflects a reactive need to solve problems that, as Gann says, are often needlessly created elsewhere in the production process. As a result, contractor-based innovation generally lacks direction and can result in further problems that others have to rectify. What are needed are systematic reductions in the costs and durations associated with processes, as well as improved quality and functionality in products.[65]

As Gann points out, it is Japanese experience that exemplifies such progress – even if, as we saw with the microflats of Chapter 2, it is Japan's real or imagined repudiation of technology that attracts the Green Western architect today.

TABLE 16 Great Britons: how an architect/engineer nearly beat Winston Churchill in a popular vote, by rank, votes cast and percentages of total vote[61]

Rank	Great Briton	Votes	Percentage
1	Churchill	456,498	28.1
2	Brunel	398,526	24.6
3	Diana	225,584	13.9
4	Darwin	112,496	6.9
5	Shakespeare	109,919	6.8
6	Newton	84,628	5.2
7	Elizabeth 1	71,928	4.4
8	Lennon	68,445	4.2
9	Nelson	49,171	3.0
10	Cromwell	45,053	2.8

In the 1950s and 1960s, Japan's major cities grew furiously and with little planning. In the 20 years up to the 1980s the area of densely inhabited districts increased 2.6 times; the population of these districts, 1.7 times. By the 1980s land was scarcer than ever in Tokyo and Osaka. Land costs were high, but began to fall after the early 1990s – despite continuing urbanisation.[66]

In the face of all this, the Japanese continually developed their housing industry to achieve better land use while satisfying customer demands. Their prowess can be traced through the fascinating website www.jusoken.or.jp, which comes complete with an English translation.[67] As Gann observes, much of the achievement was a consequence of applying IT to prefabrication:

Evidence from Japanese industrialized housing production, where expert systems were used to coordinate millions of variables in component choice, indicated one way in which databases of standardised parts might be used . . . to improve the capabilities of designers and production engineers in delivering customised solutions.[68]

There are both similarities and differences between Japan's production of houses and its production of cars.[69] But there can be no doubt that Japanese construction has drawn lessons from vehicle assembly – and not the least of those lessons is that *prefabrication can be consistent with a degree of customisation.*

5.2.2 The example set by the car industry

Customisation is not an easy thing to achieve. Sebestyén hits the proper chord: brochures or catalogues promoting particular systems of building prefabrication often claim to illustrate the great variety of design solutions possible, but frequently 'demonstrate the opposite, that there is in fact only a limited range of alternatives'.[70] So when buying an Audi TT in prefabricated housing, say, one is likely to hear a salesman say 'You can have any colour you like, as long as it's silver' – a Germanic translation of Henry Ford's famous adage. However, that does not sound unendurable.

To mass-produce shiny TT-like buildings will be tough. But the task will not

Standard windows don't coordinate with standard bricks, so bricklayers have to cut brickwork to form the apertures for windows. That means brickwork often doesn't line up vertically alongside windows

be helped by the post-dotcom lurch from what Alan Greenspan, the head of the US Federal Reserve Bank, termed 'irrational exuberance' to what might now be accurately described as 'irrational pessimism' about the prospects facing IT. McKinsey, once the most zealous in promoting IT, now holds that even electronic versions of customisation – 'personalization' – are beyond the reach of most firms. It writes:

the path of effective personalization is open to relatively few companies, because of its complexity and the demands of mining lots of data . . . Sophisticated personalization is a nice-to-have, not a need-to-have.[71]

What Amazon.com can do, McKinsey would contend, is not something that housebuilders can do. But to assess this theory of what McKinsey self-consciously styles 'rational exuberance', the achievements of the car industry need to be borne in mind.

Over the past 20 years, the West has shifted much of its production to the East. Finance and electronic imagery have tended to grab its attention at the expense of mechanical engineering.

Despite the change in emphasis, however, automotive suppliers such as Unipart in Britain and Johnson Controls in America have made great strides in prefabricated components and sub-assemblies. Aided by IT, their responsiveness to clients such as Jaguar is much improved.

By contrast with construction, the automotive industry has developed enormously over the past decades. Yet the physical and chemical laws upon which both industries are founded are the same. There are no intrinsic, technical reasons why the building industry should not be as automated as the car industry.

The improvements in quality and design that have taken place in cars over the past two decades suggest that the mass production of architecture has serious prospects. The exterior and interior finishes on cars are often a delight to the eye and to the touch. Aesthetics are varied, while product ranges boast better

performance characteristics. Automotive industry products are, as Pawley has written, 'better than any building ever built, and we know it'.[72]

There is a simple reason for that, which the architect Michael Trudgeon has identified. Time is the key to quality, and takes investment in repetitive productive capacity to realise:

A totally new Japanese car requires 1.7 million hours of research and development time from blank sheet of paper to the first customer delivery. With an average run of one million cars, the design cost amortized across the production run comes in at only $425 per car, but each car has the benefit of 1.7 million hours of design thought. By comparison a new office building, costing $50 million with design consultancy fees running at 5 per cent of cost, has the benefit of only 10,000 hours of design thought. The worst case of all is a three-bedroomed architect-designed family home, with fees running at 11 per cent of cost. This will have only 1,750 hours of design thought. Under these conditions it is ridiculous to talk about "smart buildings".[73]

Automotive industry practice confirms that, since the pioneering interwar era of Harley Earl's Cadillacs and Raymond Loewy's Coldspot fridges, industrial design has proved a match for the continual modernisation of the assembly line. By contrast, architecture remains a craft affair – despite the fact that, as a profession, architecture long predates industrial design.

For years now, lean production, a generic version of the Toyota Production System, has been recognised as the most efficient production system in the world today. In *The machine that changed the world* (1990), James P Womack, Daniel T Jones and Daniel Roos showed what high-tech automation, good links with suppliers, the early removal of defects, their solution at source and design for manufacturability had done for the Japanese car industry.[74] In their subsequent *Lean thinking* of 1996, Womack and Jones generalised their observations across 50 Japanese, American and European firms in a range of industries.[75] Of one firm in construction, they observed:

five-sixths of the typical construction schedule for a custom-built home was occupied with two activities: *waiting* for the next set of specialists (architects, cost estimators, bill-of-material drafters, landscape architects, roofers, sheetrockers, plumbers, electricians, landscapers) to work a particular job into their complex schedules, and *rework* to rip out and correct the work just done that was either incorrect from a technical standpoint or failed to meet the needs and expectations of the home buyer.

As the buyer at the end of the process, you pay for all the waiting and rework – grumbling, of course – but it is a custom product, after all, and you've heard many stories from your friends about even worse problems with their homes, so you tend to accept the predominant system and its problems as unavoidable and inherent to the nature of the activity.

In fact, all of these activities – the creation, ordering, and provision of any good or any service – can be made to flow.[76]

The starting point in lean production is to recognise that only a small part of the total time and effort in any organisation actually adds value for the end-user. By clearly defining value for a specific product or service from the end-user's perspective, all valueless activities – often as much as 95 per cent of the total – can be targeted for removal step by step.

Because products or services are rarely provided by one organisation alone nowadays, the removal of waste is best pursued throughout the entire set of activities that are jointly undertaken by firms delivering the product or service in question. New relationships are required to eliminate inter-firm waste and to manage the value stream as a whole. Instead of managing *batch-and-queue* workloads through successive departments, processes are reorganised so that the product flows continuously through all the value-adding steps without interruption. Activities across each firm are synchronised by pulling the product or design from upstream steps *just in time* to meet the demand from the end customer.

Removing wasted time and effort represents the biggest opportunity for performance improvement. Creating flow and pull starts with radically reorganising individual process steps, but the gains become truly significant as all steps link together. As this happens, more and more layers of waste become visible and the process continues towards the theoretical end-point of perfection, where every asset and every action adds value for the end-user. Summing up their simple rules of thumb, Womack and Jones write:

Converting a classic batch-and-queue production system to continuous flow with effective pull by the customer will double labor productivity all the way through the system (for direct, managerial, and technical workers, from raw materials to delivered product) while cutting production throughput times by 90 per cent and reducing inventories in the system by 90 per cent as well. Errors reaching the customer and scrap within the production process are typically cut in half, as are job-related injuries. Time-to-market for new products will be halved and a wider variety of products, within product families, can be offered at very modest additional cost. What's more, the capital investments required will be very modest, even negative, if facilities and equipment can be freed and sold.

And this is just to get started. This is the *kaikaku* [translated as radical improvement] bonus released by the initial, radical realignment of the value stream. What follows is continuous improvements by means of *kaizen* [translated as continuous incremental improvement] en route to perfection. Firms having completed the radical realignment can typically double productivity again through incremental improvements within two to three years and halve again inventories, errors and lead times.[77]

There are problems with lean thinking. The emphasis on customer pull can, in the wrong hands, lead to a loss of corporate initiative in innovation – even though it provides a useful framework for the pursuit of customisation. The employer-employee relations upon which lean thinking is founded are not as harmonious as Womack and Jones make out. Finally the 'transparency' of such relations, and that which is required between firms, is not as unproblematical as they suggest. Nevertheless the lean approach has much to recommend it.

Back in 1998, with his background in the car industry, Egan was clear that the lean approach represented a path of sustained performance improvement, not a one-off programme.[78] But even then he was cautious about what lessons could be drawn from the automotive sector. Egan wrote:

the parallel is not with building cars on the production line; it is with designing and planning the production of a new car model.[79]

This was a half-hearted commitment to pre-fabrication. Egan's concept flattered the architect, but his approach would not turn out the low-cost, high-volume homes that Britain needs. It is worth clarifying what kind of prefabrication is now required.

In terms of components, *the biggest cost savings are to be made in production to stock rather than production to order. Prefabrication should aspire to complete a full, customised homemade in a lean production facility*. After all their worldwide researches, Womack and Jones were confident about this:

Imagine . . . a lean system in which the buyer can visit the homebuilder, modify the structure on the screen, pick the desired options, perform a credit check, arrange insurance, and sign the contract in one sitting. Then imagine assembling the finished house in less than a week from the moment of the order until time to move in, by use of factory-made components. Imagine further that none of the components needed for this home – windows, doors, hardware, appliances – are made until a day or two before they are needed . . . This should slash costs further and in the process create a revolution in a massive business with stagnant productivity.

The same concepts could be applied to construction in general. That it's possible is not in question. The real question is who will rationalise the value stream and when.[80]

Yes: who will rationalise construction, and when? For that process has already happened in the automotive sector, and there is no reason why it cannot be applied to building.

When Flexible Manufacturing Systems and robots first arrived in vehicle assembly in the early 1980s, many commentators had visions of consumers customising products to their individual tastes. It was obvious then that these visions were overblown. Celebrated Fiat television commercials of the period, which portrayed the company's cars as 'handbuilt by robots', are forgotten today. But in two decades, some of the promise of FMS and robots has been achieved (see Boxes 21 and 22).

It is true that the international motor industry, like the international IT industry, has started the 21st century in some straits. Daewoo is a case in point: bankrupted by the new millennium, it did more than most to bring touch-screen computers to British car showrooms, so that motorists could specify the model

Nar Nagoya, Japan, Toyota's factory at Kasugai prefabricated 3500 homes in 2002. The plant is one of three owned by the company; the house is a Toyota model issue in 2003

details they wanted. US assemblers, parts manufacturers, tyre makers, dealers and others face enormous pressures. But there are successes in cars as much as there are in IT:

- In the all-important US market, highly mechanised Japanese manufacturers, aided by a strong dollar, are able to make cars so reliable that they account for one in three of those bought. Across cars and, more recently, pick-up trucks and Sports Utility Vehicles, they make operating profit margins higher than 10 per cent.[81]
- Beleaguered Ford Motor Company hopes to save $1.5 to $2 billion over the next decade from its belated move to flexible production.
- General Motors, the world's largest producer, has saved $1.5 billion (£960 million) a year over four or more years from its Global Manufacturing System, converting 17 of the group's 29 North American plants to flexible production this way. A model changeover in a plant now takes three days, down from six weeks.[82]

Nor is the car industry alone:

- In giant airliners, Boeing's Lean Global Enterprise initiative has meant that its plant at Long Beach, California, which makes 717s, and its factory at Renton, Washington, which makes 737s and 757s, have gone from multiple 'slant' production lines to a continuous single-flow line that moves planes along at half an inch per minute. Assembly times dropped by half;[83] around 737s, inventory fell by 64 per cent and work in process by 52. Boeing's new 737 monolithic bulk-heads are easier to install than their forerunners, seven per cent lighter, nine per cent cheaper, and have 49 per cent fewer parts. Boeing hopes the moving line concept can be applied to all of its models by 2005–6.[84]
- In humble utensils, Bialetti, based at Brescia, northern Italy, uses flexible production systems to make aluminium pans worth £100 million, in 2,500 variants, a year. Most are based on standard designs, with changes to such details as the pan's dimensions or the type of handle. Automatic press machines make perhaps 5,000 items a batch, and can switch to making a different kind of product within minutes.[85]

Since the Egan report, British construction's interest in advances like these has largely waned. For example: the process for the design, production and installation of *windows*, which cries out for prefabrication, remains in Version 0.0 (see Box 23). There is, however, one commendable exception to all this backwardness: debate, at least, on what, in Britain, the Building Centre Trust called the Pre-Fabulous Home.[86]

5.2.3 The Pre-Fabulous Home

In a perceptive report titled *Homing in on Excellence*, John Miles, chairman of The Housing Forum and a main board director of engineers Arup Group, exposed just how Britain's planning system rewards backwardness in construction:

Currently the rate of production of houses is largely governed by the ability of the planning system to deliver sites capable of development. The planning system effectively 'rations' the production of new houses, and the traditional construction industry is structured to build the number of houses permitted. If the number of planning permissions increased, in a move towards meeting demand, the industry as it stands at the moment would be hard pressed to cope.[95]

Miles also identified the key context that is lacking for innovation in construction today:

New products will not appear without high capital investment. Innovation can be costly, and so long as there goes on being relatively

Box 21 **TIME TO NOTICE ROBOTS AGAIN**

Apart from experiments in the early 1990s by corporations like Shimizu and the Obayashi Company in Japan, Sebestyén is hard-pushed to find examples of the use of robotics in construction, either on or off site.[87] Yet growth in the world robotics market is predicted to continue until 2006 at an annual rate of 7.4 per cent.[88] Some of the detailed figures and forecasts are given below:

Assembling frames by hand in a factory is an advance on site-based practice, but shouldn't a machine be doing this?

TABLE 17 Installations and operational stock of multipurpose industrial robots in 2001 and 2002, and forecasts for 2006; leading economies

Area	Yearly installations			Operational stock		
	2001	2002	2006	2001	2002	2006
Japan	28,369	25,373	31,100	361,232	350,169	333,400
United States	10,813	9,955	14,500	97,257	103,515	135,200
European Union	30,735	25,866	31,800	219,515	239,139	303,500
Germany	12,706	11,867	13,900	99,195	105,217	136,400
Italy	6,373	5,470	6,600	43,911	46,881	62,000
France	3,484	3,012	2,900	22,753	24,277	31,700
United Kingdom	1,941	750	1,100	13,411	13,651	14,400

Source: *World Robotics 2003*, United Nations Economic Commission for Europe[89]

On top of the relative buoyancy of industrial robots, perhaps 500,000 robot vacuum cleaners and lawn mowers could be in operation, worldwide, by 2006.[90] Already Friendly Robotics offers Robomower, a battery-powered machine, for £1400.[91]

Given these impressive growth figures, it might be thought that robots would retain their capacity to inspire – even in construction where, for the moment, the United Nations Economic Commission for Europe has no statistics. Yet, in today's labour-intensive, full-employment world, where machines are reviled more than they are revered, the opposite is the case. In car production, a pessimistic article in the *Financial Times* argues, 'robots lose out to the human touch': they are now deemed to cost too much in terms of maintenance, downtime and adaptability.[92] In construction the emphasis on what incremental mechanisation does occur is on improving site productivity, not in creating brand-new off-site production facilities.

Japanese production line for modular housing

Box 22 TIME TO NOTICE FMS AGAIN, AS WELL AS ERP AND MES

A Flexible Manufacturing System is an IT-based integrated group of machining centres; automated handling systems for jobs and tools; automated storage and retrieval systems; auxiliary processing facilities; and set-up stations. A typical FMS costs $5 to 10 million. With an FMS, batches of products or single items can be produced at much lower costs than would normally be the case.

Usually, an FMS works alongside an Enterprise Resource Planning system. ERP software systems, supplied by firms such as Germany's SAP, automate and integrate data inside and across the functions of the firm. In the 1970s and 1980s they grew up first as materials requirement planning systems for controlling inventory. They now allow those handling inventory, for example, to share data with other back-office functions: customer service, distribution, finance, project management and human resources.

A typical ERP system costs $3 to 5 million and takes perhaps two years to implement: training, integration, data conversion and consulting fees see to that. A typical application is for a salesperson to enter a customer order. The system then updates the firm's inventory of parts and supplies automatically and worldwide, if needed. Production schedules and balance sheets are adjusted, employees are briefed, the salesperson can name a delivery date, and the management can oversee the whole process. The whole thing works not in real time, but through cycle updates.

Already ERP systems have been extended to sales force automation, data warehousing, document management, after-sales service and support, CAD, and product data management systems. To get FMS to work with ERP, however, a new type of software – Manufacturing Execution System – had to be developed over the 1990s. Especially advanced in the semiconductor industry, an MES handles scheduling, order release, quality control and data acquisition.[93]

Box 23 GOING BEYOND WINDOWS VERSION 0.0

The amount of design effort, testing and technological sophistication that automotive manufacturers can invest in repetitively produced and routinely installed car windows stands in stark contrast to that available on a bespoke building project. There is nothing more architectural than a window; but with site-based construction it will underperform unless it is designed, manufactured and installed with practically superhuman care.

With windows, who is in charge? In the first place it is likely to be the architect, perhaps under the influence of a client or a planner who decides, primarily on aesthetic grounds, on fenestration, the type of openings and the frame section size. Then the quantity surveyor may unilaterally place a cost per square metre on the glazing, taking no account of fenestration, operation, performance or detailing. After that, the construction manager may have 'partnered' with window or curtain wall fabricators and installers, each of which will have its own deals with system extruders. Then a planning supervisor may ask for windows to open inwards rather than outwards, for easy cleaning or to avoid projections. The client, letting agent and building manager might hate the consequent drop in usable floor area and inconvenience for the occupant – let alone the effect on blinds. Finally the building services engineer will worry about the uniformity of ventilation and light distribution provided.

All these conflicting criteria need to be reconciled on every bespoke, site-based job in good time to avoid disaster. A façade engineer may be inserted into the mix of professionals to provide a performance specification; but unless contractors coordinate window design, prototyping, testing and retesting prior to manufacture, performance will be less than required.

The *testing* of windows is particularly expensive, especially on bespoke projects that are modest in scope:

> It is evident that project-specific testing on a sample which is representative of the particular application will give the most realistic assessment of the system performance, provided the same or better quality of fabrication and installation is then used on site. However, the cost of such testing can be significant, particularly for small projects, and many façade suppliers would prefer to use existing test data to prove their system.[94]

Yet, just as much as ease of installation, it is at the interfaces with other construction – where the window goes into a brick reveal, for example – that site workmanship is tested. So if a trade contract includes many window types, each with a multitude of interface details, project-specific testing can never be afforded across all the permutations. But if tests sometimes lie beyond the budgets of even the dearest bespoke buildings, a product manufacturer could still spread their cost over volume runs.

In windows, levels of weathertightness and ease of operation could be researched and developed to suit the widest ranges of users in a broad spectrum of climatic conditions. As better sealing technologies are developed and different forms of hardware introduced – particularly those geared and electrically-operated windows that suffer from few limitations on operating forces – opening joints could become more predictably air-tight. But all this would require architecture to be like automotive design.

In a windows factory, or a door factory, or a factory making any architectural component, quality control would be a natural discipline from one run to the next. As volume suppliers, window manufacturers could plan their production. That would introduce predictability and simplification – a process familiar to manufacturing, if not to construction.

On large bespoke buildings, structure and envelope are engineered down to suit the exposure of each construction to its particular location. Site-specific tests, such as those conducted here with wind tunnels, are needed; but budgets are usually big enough to be able to carry the cost of such tests. Smaller bespoke developments, by contrast, have to rely for their design on generalised rules of thumb, often written into British Standards. With mass-produced architecture things will be different again. The cost of repeated laboratory tests, modifications and improvements of buildings-as-products will be spread across entire production runs. Over time, buildings will see as much improvement in their performance as cars

little sharing of research and development costs between manufacturers and suppliers, it will continue to be difficult to recoup initial investment. In the current climate, bespoke products are often a design requirement, undermining the affordability that can be ensured by moving towards ranges of standardised products and systems. Product availability will accelerate when house designs are tailored to the requirements of manufacturing processes.[96]

Miles's message was that designers needed to be subsumed into a capitalised manufacturing industry. The understandable and welcome popular demand for design must be rescued from the popular illusion that every home must always be a uniquely designed work of art. Choice was good for Miles, and there to be had, but he wanted to understand how choice and quality could be affordably realised.

In the old days of product manufacturing, people often relied first on a designer's sketch to secure R&D funding. Then various phases of physical prototyping would approximate the original design intent. As in site-based construction, big efforts were made to retain the original clarity of design against the exigencies of production. But today product design is different. Designers can move an electronic model from initial presentation to replication in reality, spreading the cost of IT-enhanced R&D across whole production runs.

Meanwhile architects, and the other specialised construction industry design consultants on whom they rely, persist in demanding a single fee for a one-off 'architectural concept'. Then *the concept is re-interpreted and made diffuse by everyone else, down to the sub-contractor having to solve the practical problem with whatever standard of drawn information manages to get issued in time.*

IT and CAD in manufacturing, Miles insisted, was the only way designers could reassert their control over production. Control was not really about the

John Miles

type of contract, as many in construction believe; it was an issue of reaping economies of scale through digitally assisted manufacturing. For Miles, *volume site-built housing* was not too dissimilar from what was required, except that:

- choice of form, function and finish was too narrow and too low in quality; and
- product stock was not sufficiently abundant.

However in volume site-built housing, the selections of components are assembled in the open air, often in no particularly sensible order and to hopeless degrees of inaccuracy and wastage. As Miles said, a limited choice of designs cannot be built on site to a consistently high quality, and certainly not to any degree of complex curvature of form:

In a mature manufactured product, the closer and closer you get to it, the better and better it looks. If you look at a well engineered car today, go closer and you will see that the detail is better. Because it is made to be manufactured efficiently, it is made to be durable, every single element on the whole vehicle is individually engineered to a very high standard, the curvature is continuous across the join, and we expect it to work.

It took me a long time to realise why the building industry is the way it is. I look at a building site and the closer and closer I get the worse it looks. But actually it is optimised, and that's the way it will stay forever unless something makes us change.[97]

Miles is right to say that quality depends on investing in the way choice can be repeatedly delivered. The idea of bespoke site-built architecture flatters the architect; but the effect of flattery is more than outweighed by the architect's recurring anger with construction managers and site labour – ire that is inevitable given the lack of capital investment in economies of scale in production. *Homing in on Excellence* is worth quoting at length on this point:

The industry is very fragmented. There are only 36 companies building 500 or more dwellings per year and, whilst the largest of these delivers around 11,000 units pa, only six companies build more than 5000 units pa. The aggregate of annual construction by the companies is 95,000 units. The balance (55,000) is delivered through a great number of small housebuilders. The largest single producer category in the country is actually self-build, with around 15,000 units pa being delivered at the latest count.

Even the large companies may be quickly disaggregated. Very little direct labour is employed: most companies operate as management contractors, passing the majority of site-based work to a wide variety of sub-contractors and self-employed individuals. With the exception of land-banks (most significant builders hold more than a year's stock of plots), investment in fixed assets is very low. As to supply, only the largest builders have begun to address supply chain management as a key discipline. Most of the rest operate loose supply chains with little in the way of formalised management and committed volumes.

If all this sounds antiquated and outmoded, don't be fooled. It follows from decades of free-market response to a demand that fluctuates quite widely from location to location and year to year, and is focused obsessively on first cost (rather than running costs, quality, reliability or any of those other classic manufacturing mantras). The result is a highly elastic, extremely low-cost delivery system that makes no demands on risk capital.[98]

For Miles, the construction industry often benefits from investment at the level of individual building components, and many manufactured products that go into buildings are advanced and advancing. Yet construction must still be capitalised at the level of whole house units if the industry is ever to integrate already specialist designers into a more sophisticated division of labour. This would provide employment in which design time is afforded by economies of scale in repeat production, and the product improved as the design team's knowledge is consolidated through cycles of manufacturing and after-sales experience.

Design Quality Indicators are no substitute for capital investment in manufactured architecture. If Miles is right, even complete houses should be volume-buildable to a high degree of customisation.

There are fantastic people working in construction. There are wonderful technologies, brilliant software programmes, great designs and superb products. But there are also colleagues who are fools, drawings that are completely uncoordinated, whole structures that ooze ugliness and details that are awful. In its backwardness, construction reflects a poverty of imagination, will and professionalism. Yet, as the off-site manufacturing consultant Darren Richards observes, if current demand for housing cannot be met using traditional methods, and it is not possible for traditional housebuilding methods to produce zero-defect houses, the good news is that UK volume housebuilders now want seriously to look at off-site manufacturing – because they too realise that 'the best products haven't been invented yet'.[99]

What should really be meant by 'best products'? Off-site prefabrication must and can extend beyond components and sub-assemblies, going on to complete homes – and on, too, to other buildings where repetition demands a new approach.

5.3 Not fearing materials, but doing more with them

5.3.1 Bring in the new – and fix the old, too

In the controversy over the fabric of Britain's Millennium Dome, environmentalists greeted the use of an innocuous 'old' material – polyvinyl chloride, or PVC – with derision, arguing that it was carcinogenic. In construction, scare stories about materials abound. In contracts and specifications, blacklists of what are called deleterious materials grow longer and longer.

In the naturalistic perspective, architecture should look towards more natural materials, but in lower quantities. It should avoid any extractive industry, and should eschew cement. So influential is the naturalistic perspective on materials that the range of those still deemed politically correct would be shorter than the list of materials now thought harmful. All this has happened, ironically enough, when the chances of moving to mechanised construction have been vastly improved by highly artificial materials.

Steel was always important to Modernist architecture. The main thing that has happened is that it has become very much cheaper than it was. When George W Bush imposed tariffs on overseas steel producers in March 2002, his main targets were low-cost East European producers. But already, China and Asia account not only for a quarter and half, respectively, of the world's consumption of steel, but also for the same fractions of world steel production. As with her car industry, China's steel mills are poised to begin deflationary exporting.

Nevertheless the significance, to architecture, of metals such as steel and aluminium is gradually decreasing. This is not because natural resources are being exhausted but because these most widely used metals, in the words of Delft University's Adrian Beukers, 'are no longer capable of meeting long term requirements of price and performance'. The long-term future of construction belongs to high-modulus and now high-temperature polymers and elastomers, composites (metal and ceramics-based), and tough engineering ceramics.[100]

Genetically engineered biological materials should also not be ruled out. Today's renewed interest among scientists in the different means – hooks, hairs, pads, glues – by which insects walk upside-down on ceilings suggests that, one day, such materials may have much to offer construction.

Proteins are polymers with 20 different possible amino acid monomers attached. As a result, construction should take an interest in the proteins in spiders' webs, because it may be able to benefit from them. In Montreal, and in association with the quaintly-named US Army Soldier Biological Chemical Command in Massachusetts, a firm named Nexia Biotechnologies has inserted the genes of spiders into cells of cows and hamsters, and then spun the resulting proteins of spider silk into threads which have nearly the strength and flexibility of a spider's web. From the genes for the different kinds of silks produced by a spider, Nexia hopes to make new synthetic silks: not in the cells of cows and hamsters, but by extruding them, through a very fine opening, from the milk of genetically engineered goats – goats the company breeds in upstate New York.[101] If it can match dragline silk, which is the sort used in the radial spokes of a spider's web, its BioSteel® will be three times tougher than a bullet-proof vest, and five times stronger, by weight, than steel.

Biotechnologists Juming Yao and Tetsuo Asakura, based at Tokyo's University of Agriculture and Technology, sum up recent developments in the field as follows:

Box 24 GETTING TO THE FOUNDATIONS OF ON-SITE MECHANISATION

Critics of off-site prefabrication will point to the fact that every site still needs to be prepared for super-structure. They will say that off-site prefabrication cannot allow for the need for foundations, or the necessary utilities. But this is to misunderstand the potential that exists to advance on-site production as much as the off-site sort. In upholding prefabrication, it is also necessary to advocate progress in just those aspects of construction that are inescapably muddy, but avoidably laborious.

Speaking at The Prefabulous Home seminar, Stephen Rogers, chief geotechnical engineer at the foundations specialists Roger Bullivant, described how it has proved possible to 'drive down the cost of piling'. One of Bullivant's new methods is the Continual Helical Displacement Pile: it is like a woodscrew that, as it is driven into the earth, is followed down with concrete without displacing soil to the surface. CHD allows a few skilled operatives to work productively, with little waste and a minimum of physical effort.

Such site innovations are very necessary. All building needs foundations, or holding down systems, and Bullivant has brought in new methods for good and bad ground alike. If off-site manufactured architecture is to be successful, urban, accurate, stable, low-cost footings and below-ground services will have to be built on poor ground, and will have to guard against contamination. Moreover as Rogers notes, such poor ground exists not just in urban locations but on greeenfield sites as well. Yet at the seminar, Rogers was able to point to innovative machinery that has been engineered to deal with these problems.

On-site mechanisation is vital if off-site fabrication is to succeed. In the preparation of a site, interfaces from off-site prefabrication are forced to confront ground of variable quality. Any misfits cause delay and lose the advantages of off-site production. Ground works for such production should adopt the best practice available, so that false economies are robustly rejected. Below ground, after all, is where the achievements of construction tend to remain uncertain.

Across a range of different ground conditions, advanced foundation systems work well with off-site prefabrication. Rogers showed how easy it would be to package a stand-alone prefabricated house on adjustable legs with innovative and minimal holding-down systems.

It might also be much safer. With prefabrications, modules should be the structure and should come as pre-finished as possible. Scaffolding, the reason behind so many on-site accidents, should become the exception rather than the rule.

In the past decade, the design and synthesis of artificial proteins have been an emerging area of research with important implications for structural biology, materials science, and biomedical engineering. Significant progress has been reported in the design of fibrous proteins that adopt predictable secondary structures and have higher order protein folding. With virtually absolute control of sequence, chain length, and stereochemical purity, the artificial proteins can be designed to represent a new class of macromolecular materials, with properties potentially quite different from those of the synthetic polymers currently available and in widespread use.[102]

Humanity is in command of more and better materials than at any time in its entire history. Every ordinary builder's merchant is full of materials and products that our forebears would have considered astonishing; the shelves in every architect's office groan with literature about the latest advances. Yet at the same time construction still struggles to know how to handle materials that are literally ancient. For innovation to proceed in materials, there is a need to do more with old ones just as much as to invent new ones.

In steel, R&D-based improvements are made difficult by price-gouging and low margins. But even in concrete there is much to be done. When sand reacts with cement, heat is dissipated unevenly and gases form cavities and pores. However, the St Petersburg State Institute of Technology has learnt how to put the resulting problems of brittleness and durability right. If, while still in the mould, concrete is placed in an antenna-like metal barrel and hit with short pulses of alternating current, blocks vibrate at ultrasound frequencies. In that way they cool uniformly and also shake out bubbles.[103]

Concrete is one example where the prospects for established materials have never been better. Stone is another. How stoney is any particular stone? There is plenty of guidance;[104] but tests for the durability of natural building stones are not generally understood. Anyway, most architects remain fixated on appearance. They remain vulnerable to stone sales-manship and stone branding.

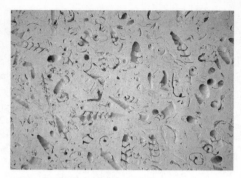

This is a particularly beautiful 'natural' limestone from Albion Stone Quarries, Portland, cut and laid with the natural geological bed vertical and parallel to the face of the wall. However the quarrying and processing of it is far from natural

5.3.2 Tablets of stone that are relatively rational

In the 21st century, the brand names for different kinds of stone still tell architects nothing about the construction materials that are actually going to be delivered on-site. Stone salesmen back their brands by waving favourable laboratory test results next to each, even though labs carrying out such tests often state that 'no certifi-cate of sampling was received' – that they had no way of knowing which quarry, and where within it, the stone they tested was first extracted.

The stone delivered on-site may, there-fore, not be the stone that was certified by a lab as sufficiently strong, dense, porous and salt-, water- and frost-resis-tant. When geologists and stone consul-tants accompany architects to quarries and oversee testing both before and after the production of workable stone, we will have the kind of unsentimental but genuine respect for the properties of nature that would, for once, be rational.

After some years of constant wrangling amongst the international authors, a draft EU standard on the testing of stone has come into force across the European construction industry. *prEn 1469 Natural Stone: Finished products, slabs for cladding*

– *Specifications* provides for the closer involvement of geologists in ensuring that architectural stone delivers every-thing that was asked of it.[105] While there is some carping that such standards could be improved through the tests and checks on quality that they require, this is in principle a clear instance of a standard that represents progress.

In industries like quarrying and slate roofing, the process of selection is criti-cal. There is a tendency for the quarry to see volumes of excavated materials dese-lected not as inferior, but as lost sales volume. What should be waste – and, in slate, waste is enormous – can be prof-itably sold to the unsuspecting public or the professionally naïve and negligent.

First, there is the need to remove the quarry over-burden to reach the useful rock

Mining may be a way round having to remove the over-burden

Quarry plant is essential

Diamond chainsaws and hydraulic wedges avoid the waste of material that happens when explosives are deployed

Architectural selection starts with the block, guided by the quarrymen

Each block is individually numbered and tracked throughout its processing

Quarries get worked out; new ones are needed

The better quarries should offer ranges of stone complete with recent and representative historic test data

Selecting stone from the available range at the quarry, before tenders are drawn up

Stocks of slabbed stone

Defining the range of acceptable characteristics from slabbed stone before processing

After tenders are completed, there is a need to programme in enough time to consider the characteristics of the quarried stone

Reversing slabs may bring more quarried material into the accepted range

Checking the appearance of stone, both dry and wet, is essential

Defining the range of acceptable characteristics from processed stone components

Several projects go through the processing works at the same time

Signing the range samples, to be divided into sets for distribution to all trade contractors and to site as a benchmark

Signing the range of processed stone for distribution either to handset stone installers or as cast-on facings to manufacturers of precast panels

Travelling saws block and slab the stone

Processing saws can wire-cut 3D curved details from stone on a turntable

Computer-controlled 3D processing saws improve productivity

Details cut with high levels of wastage

Finishing may be by hand, but with the help of tools that use compressed air

Hand-finishing mouldings where necessary   Processed stone is checked for quality and
                                                  then palleted for shipping

Box 25 THE RIGHT DIRECTION IN CONSTRUCTION PRODUCTS

The great thing about an industry-wide standard like *prEN 1469* is that it is a move toward checking construction materials *before* they have a chance to ruin a particular project, jeopardised by defective or just inferior materials. It is true that the effects of poor materials are hard to separate out from those of poor workmanship. It is also true that both materials complainants and materials culprits are understandably reluctant to advertise their construction problems. Nevertheless, someone will one day determine the annual costs of:

- *latent defects which many years later* reveal their defect and have to be replaced;
- *latent defects which within the contract defects liability period* reveal their defect and have to be replaced;
- *patent defects*, which have to be replaced within the contract;
- *patently inferior works which come to be seen as defects* in terms of design or specification but which, on the advice of his consultants that these are non-hazardous, structurally sound part of the works, the client accepts so that the building contract may be practically completed and the development occupied;
- *patently inferior works which contravene the specification* but which the design team are practically forced to advise their client to accept as an unfortunate but irredeemable, non-hazardous, structurally sound compromise forced on them by an unscrupulous contractor; and
- *latent inferior works*, which the contractor manages to cover up and pockets the cost saving, taking a calculated risk that they will never become defects of consequence.

To this might be added the cost each year of:

- the additional site attendance, testing, investigation, expert opinion, litigation, adjudication, arbitration, mediation and general management that surrounds defects in materials;

- the proportion of professional fees that are lost to rectifying the problems;
- the wasted effort in drafting contracts, writing specification and meeting about design development – only for all the work done to be ignored on site; and
- consequential losses to the client or tenant, such as the need to relocate during remedial works.

Broader than a trade or technology specific standard like *prEN 1469*, the European Construction Products Directive 89/106/EEC (CPD) is intended to stop all this, and instead flush out those producers of construction materials, components and products that are charlatans.[106] The CPD has been implemented in UK law by the Construction Products Regulations 1991,[107] explained in Department of the Environment Circular 13/91,[108] amended by the Construction Products (Amendment) Regulations 1994,[109] and again explained in Department of the Environment Circular 1/95.[110] The CPD applies to construction products which are placed on the market and produced for incorporating in a permanent manner in building and civil engineering works. Its six essential requirements are:

1 Mechanical resistance and stability
2 Safety in case of fire
3 Hygiene, health and environment
4 Safety in use
5 Protection against noise
6 Energy economy and heat retention

The essential requirements apply to the performance of the works for which the product is intended, rather than to the product itself. The products must be fit for their intended use and satisfy the essential requirements. So, for example, roofing slate would need to satisfy the requirement for mechanical resistance and stability, and resist frost.

Sensibly, the CPD groups together hygiene, health and environment not for reasons of sustainability, but simply because it is concerned with effects of pollutants reaching individuals, whether indoors or outdoors. In the same way the CPD's sixth requirement – energy-efficiency and conservation – is practical and economic in character. It means that the works must be energy-efficient in use, having regard to the climatic conditions of the location and the intended use of the works. Energy economy provisions may be related to the following energy uses:

- space heating;
- space cooling;
- humidity control;
- sanitary hot water productions; and
- ventilation.

As drafted, the CPD is more an aspiration to achieve well-tempered environments than it is an obsessional drive to save energy. How long it stays in this relatively rational guise remains to be seen.

Interminable meetings and design development often don't translate to buildable construction on site

5.3.3 Say yes to nanotubes and radio frequency ID tags

Materials are likely to become more sophisticated and more electronic in their make-up, and will link into IT-based Building Management Systems. Yet both nanomaterials and the electronic tagging of materials are already felt to constitute an unacceptable risk.

In nanotechnology, materials are worked at tolerances between 0.1 nm to 100 nm. The field became the subject of a national initiative in America in 2000: it received $700 million in R&D support in 2003. Nanotechnology will also get $1.2 billion from the EU in 2003 to 2004, and a similar amount from Japan.[111] The first international symposium on nanotechnology in construction, held in June 2003 at the Scottish Centre for Nanotechnology in Construction Materials, University of Paisley, reviewed the fabrication, properties, applications, surface finishes, tests and computer models of nanomaterials in cement, concrete, steel, ceramics, composites, natural roofing materials and photovoltaic façades.[112]

Of particular interest to architects are *nanotubes*. These are similar to the spherical carbon molecules known as *fullerenes*, but take the form of cylinders. The most basic fullerene, which can be found in normal candle soot and can be made by sending a large current between two graphite electrodes in an inert atmosphere, is C_{60}. Harold Kroto, the man who first co-synthesised the molecule, called it *Buckminsterfullerene*.

Fuller's geodesic domes were an inspiration to Kroto. Conversely, Kroto's work should inspire architects to defend 'pure' science and uphold research in nanomaterials. The reason is simple. Nanotubes can be used to:

- strengthen composite materials;
- build flat-screen devices;
- store hydrogen fuel at room temperature; and
- act, when turned into useable construction product, as a sink for the planet's carbon.

Despite all the excitement about nanotechnology, however, gradual advance

Sir Harry Kroto

Sir Harry Kroto is Royal Society Research Professor at the School of Chemistry, Physics and Environmental Science at the University of Sussex. He shared a Nobel prize in chemistry in 1996 for his synthesis, with two collaborators in 1984, of the C_{60} molecule. Today variants of that molecule have been made artificially to form nanotubes.

In the 1970s, Kroto launched a research program at Sussex to look for carbon chains in interstellar space. Alternating the search for spectral signals of a series of these chain molecules with experiments to synthesise them in the lab, Kroto found that his ambition grew with each success. Eventually, when trying to synthesise some very long carbon chains, Kroto realised that he had accidentally made a molecule that could only be spherical – shaped like one of Buckminster Fuller's geodesic domes. Kroto duly named his molecule buckminsterfullerene. Today, nanotubes are often called buckytubes.

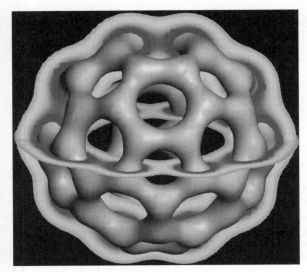

The C$_{60}$ molecule; image courtesy of Accelrys[113]

Richard Buckminster Fuller's 50 metre diameter geodesic dome. Prefabricated in aluminium, it was assembled by 38 men in 20 hours – in Honolulu, for a classical concert with an audience of 18,000

in it is already fully outrun by irrational fears.[114] In a notorious article published in the April 2000 issue of *Wired*, Bill Joy, then still chief scientist at Sun Micro-systems, used the prospect of intelligent, genetically self-replicating 'nanobots' to issue a call to 'limit the development of the technologies that are too dangerous, by limiting our pursuit of certain kinds of knowledge'.[115] Then the novelist Michael Crighton warmed to the paranoiac theme in his *Prey*,[116] while the *Sunday Times*

philosopher Bryan Appleyard, in a survey of the '10 main threats to life on Earth', warned of an Earth whose surface could be 'reduced to a grey goo of nanobots'.[117]

The irony is that, for all his reservations about nanotechnology, Joy is an unabashed admirer of another advance: radio frequency identification (RFID) tags that can be built into building components as much as anything else. He has said:

We will label every individual object as opposed to just the type of object. Your milk will know how old it is and maybe even what temperature it has been stored at. You can see the advantage to a company taking inventory.[118]

It is not necessary to share Joy's vision of electronic dairy products to recognise the benefits to construction of RFID readers and tags. The tags are tiny chips, each carrying a serial number as ID, a radio frequency transponder and a metal or carbon coil antenna, and all at a cost of as little as five cents or less by 2005 to 2006. Over a couple of metres, but without recourse to line of sight radio signals, they give out a call sign based on their ID and reveal their whereabouts.

RFID tags that are both read- and write-capable will become commonplace in construction:[119]

- by using them during manufacture and installation, it will be possible to track components into the building. Once handheld computing devices come complete with displays of CAD drawings and instructions on how and where to install each component safely, tagged components could work with them to update handheld images automatically as progress develops on-site; and

- by incorporating them into asset management systems. RFID tags can be updated throughout the life of an asset item, while tags linked to scanners running on Internet Protocols could provide those handling particular components additional real-time information on health and safety requirements or maintenance inspection.

Despite numerous software developments, however, the rate of adoption of tags by the UK building industry is rather slow. At the Information Technology Construction Best Practice subsidiary of the Construction Best Practice programme, Anna McCrea perceptively observes that applications available to potential handheld users in construction are not tailored to that industry.[120] Tags, however, have already incurred the wrath of US protesters. They will 'enslave humanity', says Katherine Albrecht, who runs Consumers Against Supermarket Privacy Invasion and Numbering (Caspian), a group that opposes data collection by retailers on privacy grounds.[121] More seriously, Chris Hoofnagle, of the Electronic Privacy Information Center (Epic), a Washington-based watchdog, calls for a US government-backed data protection commission to look at the privacy implications of RFID.

Yet tags, like privacy-invading mobile phones, can always be switched off. A tag specification drawn up by the Auto-ID Center, an industry leader based at the Massachusetts Institute of Technology, already specifies a 'self-destruct' command, allowing a tagged product to be deactivated by its owner.[122]

According to IBM, tagged products may allow firms to shrink inventories by between five and 25 per cent. Gillette, which has bought half a billion tags, already uses them to track products on the move.[123] The example of tags highlights just what the application of IT can do to 'improve asset productivity, and reduce waste and delay in the supply chain'.[124]

5.4 Not fearing energy use, but getting it in proportion

5.4.1 Reason thrown to the winds

Giving a government lead to the adoption of the naturalistic perspective, the

Bill Joy

Ministry of Defence is very proud of its energy-efficient buildings. It favours the following principles:

- Lightweight panel technology
- High levels of insulation
- Solar screening to reduce discomfort
- Orientation – to maximise and control solar energy gain
- The use of atria and intermediate zones to reduce energy demands
- Whole-life calculations 'to reduce the energy used in manufacturing components'.[126]

Perhaps it is not by chance that the British military wants the buildings from which it runs wars to be as self-sufficient in energy as possible. For UK national independence in energy is what the February 2003 White Paper *Our energy future – creating a low carbon economy* sought.[127] Renewable sources of energy, it said, would help Britain avoid over-dependence on energy imports and make the country 'less vulnerable to a security threat'.[128]

Altogether, the naturalistic perspective on UK energy holds that the country must be *autarchic*. In construction, that means that *each building must fuel itself, locally, as far as possible*. At the same time, the naturalistic perspective wants to reduce requirements for energy. Less burning of fossil fuels, it believes, will

Box 26 HOW MATERIALS CAN HELP SKYSCRAPERS BEAT EARTHQUAKES

Suspend micron-sized soft particles of carbonyl iron in water, silicone oil or hydrocarbon oil, put a magnet on the resulting fluid, and it will turn solid: a useful means of damping down shocks on cars, washing machines and exercise equipment. So Lord Corporation, of Cary, North Carolina, which specialises in such magnetorheological (MR) fluids, has put them to use against earthquakes, hurricanes and other disasters.

Lord's Rheonetic seismic dampers are metre-long pistons. Each can deliver 20 tons (200,000 N) of force using the MR principle. The piston sits in a cylinder containing five litres of MR fluid surrounded by an electromagnet. Energise the magnet and the fluid solidifies; turn off the current and it reverts to liquid. Perform the on-off operation several thousand times a second, and the damping is more effective than conventional means allow.

In the Lord set-up, sensors tell computers to charge the coils in the event of a shock. The dampers then forcefully counteract motion, but in a controlled style. Put several dampers on each floor of a multi-storey building and it is likely to withstand violent tremors.

Miraikan, Japan's National Museum of Emerging Science and Innovation, Tokyo has Lord dampers – both as protection and as exhibit.[125]

Miraikan, Japan's National Museum of Emerging Science and Innovation, Tokyo

reduce the amount of carbon and other greenhouse-effect gases emitted into the atmosphere, and so hold global warming in check.

Over the past 30 years, the White Paper concedes, the British economy has doubled in size, while energy use has hardly increased. In other words, Britain does a whole lot more than it used to, for the same energy expended. Perhaps these facts might occasion some daring in energy policy; but, *even more than energy supply, the government sees energy demand as risky and problematical. Every building must therefore play its part in saving a planet at risk from overheating and consequent* *floods.* 'Today's homes', the White Paper insightfully observed, 'contain more household appliances than our grandparents ever dreamed of . . . Not only are these new gadgets energy-hungry, but as users most of us are energy-lazy'.[129] It argued, 'The cheapest, cleanest and safest way of addressing all our goals is to use less energy'.[130]

Lower energy use might suit the Ministry of Defence and indeed the government in general, but what about the rest of us? Even by the irrational norms of the naturalistic perspective, the neglect of supply considerations in energy matters relative to those of demand is remarkable.

The EU, for example, plans to make energy producers trade different levels of carbon emissions in 2005, such is its concern about energy use; liberalisation of energy supply will only be completed in 2007.[131] In Britain it is a similar story.

Wind power is not only highly inefficient, from the point of view of physics and engineering; it is also *not dependable* because, like solar power, it is *intermittent*. The Royal Academy of Engineering (RAE) warned those drafting the White Paper that the stability of the electricity grid could be jeopardised once intermittent renewables took as much as 15 per cent of capacity. At the Cabinet Office, the Performance and Innovation Unit's *Energy Review* had earlier placed great faith in wind energy, proposing that 22 gigawatts (GW) of turbine capacity be installed by 2020.

The RAE felt that the most likely power output in real life would be much reduced when winds turned out to be light or absent. It argued that, to ensure supply, wind turbines would have to be backed up by a further 16–19 GW of conventional generation plant, adding an extra £1 billion to overall costs.[132] To no avail. The White Paper:

- acknowledged that renewable sources of energy met just three per cent of current demand;
- sought to raise this to 10 per cent, or 10 GW, by 2010, and to 20 per cent by 2020; and
- ruled out constructing new nuclear power stations, at the specific behest of Tony Blair.[133]

Just a few months after publication, three things happened to indicate just how cavalier British officialdom is about energy supply.

First, despite all the talk about carbon-free renewables and security of supply, Blair signed a bilateral energy pact with President Putin in June 2003, in which the UK and Russia agreed to cooperate on the construction of a £3.5 billion gas pipeline from Russia to Europe. On the occasion of Putin's state visit to London, BP also signed, in the presence of the two leaders, a detailed agreement for the creation of a $14 billion joint venture with the Russian oil group TNK.[134]

Blair had little choice but to make plans for possible Russian support in oil and gas in the future. Currently the UK is, with Canada, one of the world's only two net energy exporters: it still does well from significant domestic oil reserves. But nuclear power provides for a quarter of UK's energy needs, and most nuclear power stations are scheduled for decommissioning by 2010. Even before the White Paper, Britain was set to be a net importer of gas by 2006, and of oil by 2010.

Second, just before his departure from office as minister for energy and for construction, Brian Wilson admitted something important. On top of the White Paper's demand that power suppliers buy more renewables and trade carbon emissions, the electricity grid would have to be rewired so that new, remote wind farms – on top of the miniscule four megawatts of wind capacity already installed – could play their part. Together, these effects could raise electricity prices by 10 per cent by 2010.[135]

To make energy more expensive in today's economic context is quite an achievement. Yet the messianic desire to prevent the death of the planet is great. So here was the third development: in 2003 New Labour, to rapturous acclaim from environmentalists, announced proposals to build offshore wind farms consisting of hundreds of turbines.[136] As the *Financial Times* noted:

Studies produced by National Grid and Scottish Power network operators estimate it could cost up to £1.5 billion to strengthen networks in addition to the estimated £6 billion cost of building the new windfarms.

The latest proposals call for the construction of about 1500 wind turbines, each more than 100 metres high, producing up to 6000 megawatts – enough to power 3.5 million homes.

The plans represent a quadrupling of the government's previous proposals for offshore wind power and would make Britain the world's biggest offshore wind energy developer.[137]

At such a scale and at 100 metre heights, the new acreage of UK wind farms had already provoked some caustic comments: one scientist, indeed, used them to satirise the Precautionary Principle:

Unless such farms can be shown to be absolutely safe they should never be built. At the very least, there should be a five-year freeze on such developments while more research is undertaken to prove their safety for human, animal and plant life.[138]

Yet British architects and construction industry professionals will be anxious to go along with wind farms. They want to fit in socially and participate in cleansing rituals. In energy policy Britain is, after all, the world's biggest enthusiast for throwing Reason to the winds.

5.4.2 Just what can buildings do to save the planet?

When sunlit for just a day, the earth gains energy that current levels of human usage could make last for decades. If today's photovoltaic cells were laid as solar panels over a 400 x 400 kilometre square expanse of, say, Iraq, they would make enough energy for mankind's daily needs – for the moment, at least.

Energy is not in short supply and never will be. Instead, we lack the means to capture, store and transmit energy supply in an efficient manner. So why do architects try to lower demand for energy through their designs?

At her useless levels of building output, what absorbs Britain's energy is not the *operation of new buildings*. Still less do the *components and construction* of new buildings use a lot of energy. Rather, it is the *operation of Britain's decrepit building stock* that is supremely wasteful. The energy required to build anew is dwarfed by the

energy required to run inefficient buildings over their serviceable lives.

Nick Baker and Koen Steemers note that, in 1991, 35 per cent of annual UK energy supply was used in the construction and operation of domestic buildings, and 18 per cent in non-domestic, totalling 53 per cent.[139] Of that total, Brian Edwards considers that about 10 per cent is energy used in construction – whether newbuild or refurbishment – and 90 per cent is energy used in the operation of all building stock.[140] In 2001 the Office for National Statistics reckoned that about 55 per cent of all construction was newbuild, and 45 per cent repair and maintenance.[141] Taken together, of the energy used annually in the UK:

- only 2.915 per cent goes into new construction;
- only 2.385 per cent goes into the refurbishment of existing stock; but
- a full 47.7 per cent goes on the operation of the country's current building stock – stock that is, from the point of view of energy use, highly inefficient.

New houses are more energy-efficient than old ones. If more of the UK's existing stock were replaced by a serious programme of investment in prefabricated, energy-efficient homes, the efficiency of the national stock would rise.

Of course, in the quest for better quality construction, architects have a proper professional interest in producing energy-efficient new buildings. That is one thing. But what the architectural establishment does is quite another. Architects like to kid themselves that their new buildings can make a discernible dent in both energy resource usage and in terms of carbon emissions.

New buildings should indeed boast improved energy performance. 'Active' systems – modern boilers and air conditioning units – are more efficient today than in the past, so they can help here. They would only get better if they were integrated into mass-produced buildings.

'Passive' systems, that use a building's arrangement and fabric to manage performance, can also have a place. In offices, heat gained from glassy exteriors, office equipment and occupants can be handled without air-conditioning. However, successful examples of the passive approach are always complemented by investment in both heat recovery devices and IT-based building management systems. Whether through active or passive systems, or hybrid versions of the two, heat gain in many buildings is a problem, not something to be conserved. What is often required is cooling (which takes passive chimneys and the 'stack effect', in which warm air rises), cross ventilation, or, most manageable of all, mechanical methods.

Of course, airtightness to prevent draughts and heat loss, together with general insulation standards, also need to improve. Here again, though, it is worth noting that prefabrication would be a better guarantee of these qualities of construction than on-site methods.

All these things are fair enough. But it flies in the face of the facts to believe that professional duties in relation to energy can mean anything more than an effort to bring about lower operational costs in new buildings. New building is not the problem that governs the built environment's use of energy resources.

What buildings do with energy needs to be understood in context. First, *transport and industrial processes* use nearly as much UK energy as the built environment. Also, more specifically:

- if the *energy supply infrastructure were more efficient*, that would reduce the volume of energy used in supplying the built environment;
- only *those buildings that are connected to fossil fuel-burning power plants* use non-renewable sources of energy and emit carbon as a consequence. And for the moment, a quarter of Britain's overall demand for energy is met by nuclear power, not fossil fuels;
- within *offices*, much could be done to save energy by making low-energy-in-use PCs, servers and other IT products. That would be easier than designing

buildings with systems to cool high-energy-in-use IT products; and
- within *homes*, more could be done by making low-energy-in-use fridges, water boilers, washing machines, dishwashers, tumble driers and lighting than by avoiding every draught. It is these products, which lie beyond the province of the architect, that lead to bigger energy expenditures than central heating.

The UK's *Building Regulations* cannot improve its power-generating infrastructure, its office IT or its domestic appliances.[142]

What about *carbon emissions*? Compared to the carbon emitted through natural processes, man-made carbon emissions amount to only a very small proportion of the overall total carbon put out by the planet. Moreover while houses in Britain put 20 million tonnes of carbon into the atmosphere each year, energy suppliers, in the shape of coal, gas and oil-fired power stations, account for 40 million – as does each of transport and industry. The only buildings that figure as direct sources of carbon are those in which hot water and central heating, and to a lesser extent cooking, are powered by gas. It is true that three-quarters of British homes are powered this way; but the carbon they put out is modest compared with that emitted by power stations and the general apparatus of wealth production.

How modest? The Energy Savings Trust urges those who visit its Energy Efficiency website to:

find out exactly how badly your home is behaving and discover a wealth of information designed to help your home mend its disgraceful ways.[143]

But this fingerwagging technique, which targets the home and its occupants as conspirators in global warming, obscures much.

If we accept that the effects of global warming are best dealt with by reducing carbon emissions, what is at issue for the

UK construction industry is how much architects can do to cut the contribution made by Britain to the four per cent of global emissions that are anthropogenic. Yet to the very limited extent that the architect can lower carbon emissions, it is mostly by reducing the seasonal requirement that occupiers of new houses have for central heating powered by fossil fuels. To cut the much larger carbon emissions made by the daily requirement that occupiers of new houses have for washing and drying – this is something architects can affect, but only be specifying more efficient boilers and related building services.

In 2002, Part L of the UK's *Building Regulations*, which concerns the conservation of fuel and power was revised, to become Part L1 for domestic,[144] and Part L2 for non-domestic construction.[145] The revisions aimed to:

- introduce criteria for performance in airtightness;
- improve overall levels of performance in building operations; and
- allow for calculations of carbon emissions to be aggregated together – in pursuit of government targets for reduced emissions.

Yet while any improvements in construction quality on-site are welcome, even an author of the revised Part L, Ted King, from the Building Regulations Division of the Office of the Deputy Prime Minister, expects these changes, *over both newbuild and refurbishment*, to deliver less than 10 per cent of the total cut in carbon emissions called for by the government, as well as typically adding nearly two per cent to the costs of a building.[146] That may prove to be an over-estimation of emissions reductions and an under-estimation of on-costs. It seems, rather, that the revisions were about *being seen to be doing something*, rather than any concern to work out the facts of the matter. What Helene Guldberg and Peter Sammonds ridiculed as *design tokenism* holds full sway.[147]

For all the (energy-efficient) haloes they light up around their heads, British construction industry professionals are fooling themselves. Through their undersupply of new buildings, they can have little discernible effect either on the country's energy efficiency or on its carbon emissions.

Yet that will not, for long, stop organisations, modelled on the Climate Justice Programme, from suing all those – including, no doubt, architects – whom they deem responsible for climate change. The CJP is an unprecedented alliance of 70 environmental organisations, lawyers, academics and individuals in 29 countries. In July 2003 it announced its backing for legal cases to combat climate change. Under the umbrella of the CJP, these self-appointed reformers want to see existing laws enforced 'for the benefit of present and future generations', and to hold the 'perpetrators' of climate change accountable and liable for the consequences of their actions.'[148]

5.4.3 Photovoltaics, solar chimneys and hydrogen

Prefabricated photovoltaic materials have much to recommend them within a wider programme of prefabricated houses. Patrick Bellow, a founding director of the consulting environmental and building services engineers Atelier Ten,[149] observes:

A new generation of responsive cladding materials must emerge, integrating some photovoltaic or generating capability, which will herald a new breed of intelligent building that absorbs less and produces more, while achieving its prime objective – comfort and facilities for the humans within.[150]

At high volumes of production and as part of prefabricated homes, prefabricated photovoltaic materials would become inexpensive much more rapidly than they are currently set to do. The market for them, in potential at least, could also be huge: just like anyone else, buyers of new houses want cheaper heating and power bills, and comfort. Yet despite these facts there is little discussion, from either environmentalists or architects, about the mass production of photovoltaics. Perhaps it is thought too ambitious an enterprise for the environment to bear.

In principle, architects can only favour the development of renewable sources of energy – provided only that they make a real difference in a cost-effective manner. In Stuttgart, structural engineering professor Jörg Schlaich hopes to build the world's tallest structure as a solar-driven power station. His plans for a steel-reinforced concrete tower one kilometre high are exciting; but as with all new tech-

nologies that are proposed, their merits are worth keeping in proportion.

In warmer latitudes, conventional solar plants, based on parabolic mirrors, can concentrate light to the temperature of a furnace – but only with direct sunlight. Now Schlaich, a founding partner of Schlaich Bergermann und Partners, has suggested combining turbines and sun with a concrete chimney in a way that generates 200 megawatts of electricity even when the sky is overcast.[151]

Place a giant, circular glass roof two to six metres above ground, with its circumference unimpeded. Affix an airtight chimney to the slightly taller centre of the roof and, at its base, install pressure-staged wind turbines to catch the resulting updraught of warm air. Result: an efficient greenhouse-chimney-windmill

Solar Chimney proposed for Manzanares, Spain

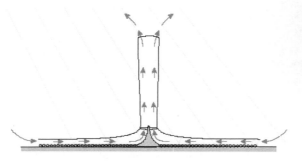

Impression of the concrete Solar Chimney by Schlaich Bergermann and Partners

The principle of the greenhouse roof and the Solar Chimney

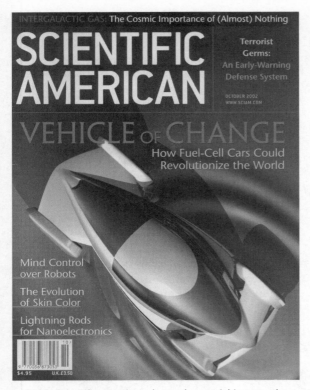

INTERGALACTIC GAS: The Cosmic Importance of (Almost) Nothing

SCIENTIFIC AMERICAN

OCTOBER 2002
WWW.SCIAM.COM

Terrorist Germs:
An Early-Warning
Defense System

VEHICLE OF CHANGE
How Fuel-Cell Cars Could
Revolutionize the World

Mind Control
over Robots

The Evolution
of Skin Color

Lightning Rods
for Nanoelectronics

$4.95   U.K. £3.50

In 2002, Scientific American devoted a special issue to the future of the hydrogen fuel cell in a cleaner and leaner generation of automotive design

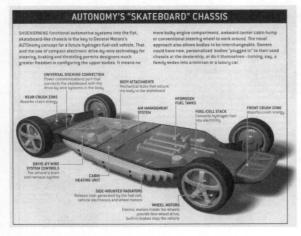

AUTONOMY'S "SKATEBOARD" CHASSIS

GM's AUTOnomy concept. Hydrogen fuel cell plus drive-by-wire electronic steering and braking systems are all contained in a 'skateboard' chassis less than 30 cm thick. That allows both for easy worldwide standardisation, and for a variety of body types – beginning with the Hy-Wire sedan

that is nevertheless easy and cheap to build where land prices are low, and that should require little maintenance. Tight water-filled tubes, placed underneath the roof, keep hold of the heat captured in the day for use during the night.

The technology has been licensed to EnviroMission, a firm in Australia intent on supplying 200,000 homes there with electricity. This energy output will represent an annual saving of more than 750,000 tonnes of CO_2. In Manzanares, Spain, a pilot plant consistently generated 50 kilowatts between 1982 and 1989; the opening, in Mildura, Australia, of the world's full-scale solar thermal power station is set for 2005.

Schlaich's initiative will be a first and will have its place, but each chimney will cost a hefty $800 million. As energy technologies go, the collection, storage, distribution and burning of hydrogen will have a more universal future.

Hydrogen, like Schlaich's tower, solves the intermittency problems that plague wind and conventional solar power. As the environmentalist architect Peter Smith points out:

The US Department of Energy plans to power two to four million households with hydrogen and fuel cells by 2010 and ten million by 2030. If the hydrogen is obtained from sewage, livestock waste, underground methane or water split by photovoltaic electrolysis then this programme will certainly be one to be emulated by all industrialized countries.[152]

In January 2003 US President George Bush offered $1.7 billion to boost hydrogen technologies. In transport alone, General Motors talks of having its four-door, 100mph Hy-Wire sedan, silently powered by a hydrogen fuel cell and currently priced at $5 million, in showrooms by 2010 – and of having sold a million vehicles by 2015.[153] According to the *Scientific American*, people might one day plug hydrogen fuel cell cars into photovoltaic houses so that the hydrogen fuel

GM's Hy-Wire car. The interior is spacious, given the absence of conventional steering and brakes

cell works like an electricity generator and the house generates hydrogen during the day.[154]

Hydrogen technologies are coming. Construction would take itself much more seriously if it invested in them, and not in sustainababble.

5.4.4 Less energy = more therapy, more bureaucracy

Architects' fears are misdirected. They should not fear energy use, but get it in proportion. But instead, they spend an inordinate amount of time and effort:

- imagining that they are doing their bit to save energy; and
- creating a new layer of jobs, done by professional evaluators of sustainable energy, complete with Environmental Performance Indicators.

When they are not flattering themselves in Green matters, architects prefer the therapy of bureaucratic flagellation by their peers, feeling that they are not doing enough. But given all their efforts, it is surprising that so few have read the 28 Articles and two Annexes of the 11 December 1997 Protocol to the United Nations Framework Convention on Climate Change – the Kyoto Protocol, which insisted that industrialised nations cut their carbon emissions.[155]

Bjørn Lomborg, associate professor of statistics in the department of political science at Denmark's University of Aarhus, has read the Protocol. In his landmark bestseller, *The Skeptical Environmentalist*, published in 2001, he suggested that there was 'no risk of running out of fossil fuels anytime soon, even if some sources might be getting more expensive'.[156] Moreover, he attacked the naturalistic perspective on what he called its 'trump card': global warming. Adhering to the Kyoto Protocol on emission cuts would, he said:

Bjørn Lomborg

- most likely postpone a 1.92° rise in global temperatures, reached in 2094, only to 2010: a total of six years;
- equivalently, bring down the rise in temperatures reached in 2100 by 0.15°;
- bring down the rise in sea levels reached in 2100 by 2.5 centimetres;[157] and
- cost, by 2050, two per cent of the GDP of nations belonging to the Organisation of Economic and Commercial Development, or more than £900 billion annually – and about four per cent of such GDP in 2100.[158]

Lomborg argued that, despite our intuition that we naturally need to do something about global warming:

it will be far more expensive to cut CO_2 emissions radically than to pay the costs of adaptation to the increased temperatures.[159]

By 'adaptation', Lomborg meant doing work with 'the same money directly in the Third World' and with its present inhabitants, so giving the future, richer inhabitants of those countries 'a much better future position in terms of resources and infrastructure from which to manage a future global warming'.[160]

For suggesting that the best solution to global warming might, among other things, be direct investment in architecture and construction in the Third World, Lomborg was accused of denying the existence of global warming. For doing that, some writers compared him with those who would deny the Holocaust.[161] [162] But as he said of naturalistic opponents of that putative source of cheap and clean energy, cold nuclear fusion:

Essentially, the criticism points to other values, arguing for a change to a decentralised society which is less resource oriented, less industrialised, less commercialised, less production-oriented. Such an agenda is entirely valid, but it is important to realise that the discussion is no longer primarily about energy.[163]

In creating a new priesthood around the naturalistic perspective in general and sustainable energy in particular, construction says much more about itself than it does about the fate of the planet. Architects in particular are unsure of themselves; they want to connect to society, their children and the future. But that is no reason for them to rush, like lemmings, to restrict energy demand. They should be thinking about how the new technologies of energy supply can work with new prefabricated buildings.

5.5 Face time, playing with virtual space, and monkeying with CAD

5.5.1 Critics of IT revive 'face time' and real space

The fetishistic view of space that we encountered in Chapter 2 tends to get still sillier once IT is introduced into it. *First, face-to-face contact in real space is upheld against the electronic, remote sort, which is thought to contain risks. Next, grandiose claims are made for virtual space and, more recently, for the wireless space of mobile devices. Last, risk-free cruising in virtual space is preferred to the dodgy and dirty business of actually improving the real built environment. This section begins with 'face time' in real space.*

One of the appealing myths about IT was that its growth would be complemented by social trends that work against society's fragmentation and alienation. In this concept, the growth of IT was accompanied by a renewed growth of intercourse in the real world. There would always be physical *offices* because we would always need to commune with each other. Local *shops* could boost their trade by becoming collection points for on-line shoppers.[164]

No sooner had the dotcom boom ended in the spring of 2000, however, than virtual space began to lose prestige against the real sort. In his famous *Neuromancer* (1984), the novelist William Gibson had turned a fictional analogy between the physical world and the world of networks into a much more all-embracing – and much more dubious – description of the latter.[165] But now the popular and genial US architectural critic, Bill Mitchell, Dean of the School of Architecture and Planning at the Massachusetts Institute of Technology, had this point to make:

Place-based enterprises will compete for our presence, attention, and dollars in a digitally mediated world by attempting to add as much value as possible to the face-to-face experiences that they offer.

Local food shops that want to compete with online supermarkets will pitch themselves to the senses, through foodie-magnet displays of produce, nostril tickling aromas of coffee, spices and baked goods, and tempting tasting stations at every aisle. Those very same shoppers who save time during the week by ordering their detergent and toothpaste from an online supermarket may allocate some of their weekend leisure time to visiting a sophisticated wine and cheese store.[166]

At one level this made common sense: there is little fun to be had in buying detergent and toothpaste in the flesh. However, the sentimentality that attached to 'face-to-face experiences' in retailing went further than just Mitchell. In 2000 Jeremy Rifkin, a best-selling US management guru and feelgood apostle of the information age, experiences and 'cultural capital', also upheld old-fashioned place:

the more connected people become in a range of multifaceted global networks, the less time they have available for the kinds of intimate social relations that can take place only in real time and by way of face-to-face engagement. In a new century dominated by electronically mediated environments, the challenge in every country will be to create new opportunities for direct participation with our fellow human beings in geographic based communities.

All real cultures exist in geography because that's where intimacy takes place, and without intimacy it is not possible to create bonds of social trust and engender true feelings of empathy. Resurrecting and revitalising culture, then, means paying at least as much attention to geography as to cyberspace and to participation in real communities as to computer interfacing inside electronic chat rooms.[167]

Joel Kotkin, another public policy specialist, also rushed to rehabilitate place. Quoting but distorting Mitchell, he gave him the profound riposte that 'the importance of geography is not dwindling to nothing in the digital era: in fact, quite the opposite'.[168]

By the spring of 2001 and the collapse of irrational exuberance, discussion of the future of the workplace had turned quite hostile to IT. In Britain, Charles Handy said what many had thought: that verbal expression, body language and eye

William J Mitchell. Photo by Donna Coveney

contact were preferable to telework, 'hot desking' in the office, mobile work, or teams working together by email.[169] In America, even the subtle David Brooks attacked what he called 'Wireless Man' as a multi-tasking speed freak and 'info junkie', ready to react to a prompt every 15 seconds.[170]

The argument about the value of space-based 'experience' retailing and interpersonal office work appeared as an argument against IT. However, while it caricatured the fragmentary and alienating aspects of IT, the argument was not really about IT or space at all. When people enthuse about communion in real space, they speak to our sense of loss. They give a sense of what lies behind that sense of loss – the social corrosion caused by the past two decades of sharpening market forces. And they exhibit a misplaced desire to seek redress for that social corrosion in a sometimes playful but always ultimately unfulfilling round of see-and-be-seen rituals.

In America, there are now fewer retail banks; but they have more and more physical outlets. Yet this may say little about how space becomes more precious as IT is valued more highly. After all, the expansion of retail banking space has not been accompanied by big successes in IT. Ventures in internet banking have rarely proved profitable. What is more likely is that both banks and their customers seek,

in 'face time', that recognition and legitimacy both sides feel they have lost over the past decade or more of financial scandals and consumer indebtedness.

Altogether, those who seek refuge from the negative social aspects of IT by recourse to real space have things the wrong way round. It is not IT that is anti-social, but those human beings who programme and use it to anti-social ends. Nevertheless, *the communitarian instinct in favour of real space and against the virtual sort is something that tells against the professional application of IT to architecture and construction. By coquetting, in postmodern style, with the supposed interplay between real and virtual space, it diminishes what IT can do. Nor will urban space itself benefit from such an attitude.*

5.5.2 The claims made for virtual space

The man who has done most to apply doctrines of virtual space to public policy is the urbanist Manuel Castells. As early as 1985 he proclaimed the advent of the 'informational city', arguing:

New technologies allow the emergence of a *space of flows*, substituting for a space of places, whose meaning is largely determined by their position in a network of exchanges in our cities.[171]

This was always an exaggeration. Whatever a space of informational flows is, it does not substitute for normal space. Nor is the meaning of normal space largely determined by its position in the putative virtual stuff. Nevertheless, Castells's enthusiasm for what he believes is a new era – that of the 'network society' – was and remains infectious, especially in universities and among urban policymakers. There is, indeed, what the technology expert James Crabtree has termed a 'cult of Castells'.[172] And in construction, Castells's hyping up of IT has been accompanied by an equally unbalanced resort, on the part of architects, to the expensive, if investment-free delights of 'virtual' space – a realm where buildings and cities can be navigated on screen, but realised in bricks and mortar all too rarely.

Like his followers, Castells is guilty of outdated theories of society.

These theories naïvely dismiss the importance, to society, of agriculture, construction, energy, transport, manufacturing and services. They dismiss, in a word, the realm of *production*, and action – including political action – on the real world. Instead, they privilege *communications, language, dialogue, media, identity and interactions*. That is why Castells invokes Marshal McLuhan's *The Gutenberg Galaxy* and *The medium is the message* in the titles both of his 18th book, *The Internet Galaxy*, and of that book's opening chapter, 'The network is the message'.[173] It is not the unrivalled changes that human beings wreak on nature that occupy the central place in these theories. Rather, it is insisted, *speech* is the characteristic that makes us human. As Castells puts it:

Conscious communication (human language) is what makes the biological specificity of the human species.[174]

This is an understandable mistake for Castells to make. The power and weight of telecommunications in society has, it can be argued, grown even faster than that of computers. But *for all the great advances achieved by telecoms, they do not justify the laziness of seeing the world and its cities merely as one big IT network of interpersonal interactions*. The Platonists erred when they took the hand-crafted vessel as a model for an ordered universe, or *kosmos*. Given what has happened to nuclear power, it is arguable whether we ever entered what was known in the 1950s as the 'atomic era'. To define the world in the image of the currently prevalent technology is an error that has been made for a long time now.[175] To inflate the significance of IT to society will do neither any good.

Manuel Castells was born in Barcelona in 1942 and is professor of sociology and planning at Berkeley University

Castells does this. For him 'core economic, social, political, and cultural activities throughout the planet are being structured by and around the Internet, and other computer networks'.[176] However Table 18 shows how old and one-dimensional are the hopes that information and communication technologies inherently, and in a deterministic manner, bring about a new era or a new society.

Whatever Castells would like us to think, the internet is *not* structuring a whole number of core economic, social, political, and cultural activities. It has done little for European productivity. It has, as yet, a very modest economic and social impact on the Third World, and the outsourcing of Western jobs to the East, which it assists, is also still modest. Its role as a durable and dynamic organiser of anti-globalisation protest has been overstated; and its record in the arts milieu is esoteric, to say the least.

The internet has barely penetrated construction. But the Castellsian Galaxy has had a big influence on thinking there. For by suggesting a future in which the Internet conquers everything, Castells is bound to downplay building things on Earth. In 1996, he wrote:

We are just entering a new stage in which Culture refers to Culture, having superseded

TABLE 18 Just a selection of technological-determinist theories of the future

Published	Author(s)	Key concept around Information	Key concept around Communication
1962	Machlup	Knowledge economy	
	McLuhan		Gutenberg Galaxy
	McLuhan and Fiore		Medium is the message
1971	Touraine, Bell, Toffler	Post- or super-industrial society	
1982	Naisbitt		Integrated information and communication system
1990	Gilder	Global quantum economy	
1996	Castells		Network society
1997	Mulgan		Connexity
1999	Leadbeater	Living on thin air	
2000	Cairncross		Death of distance
	Rifkin		Age of access
	Bard and Söderqvist		Netocracy
	Kopomaa	Mobile information society	
2001	Castells		Internet Galaxy
2002	Capra		Hidden connections
2003	Rheingold		Smart mobs

Nature . . . Because of the convergence of historical evolution and technological change we have entered a purely cultural pattern of social interaction and social organisation. This is why information is the key ingredient of our social organisation and why flows of messages and images between networks constitute the basic thread of our social structure. This is not to say that history has ended in a happy reconciliation of Humankind with itself. It is in fact quite the opposite: history is just beginning, if by history we understand the moment when, after millennia of a prehistoric battle with Nature, first to survive, then to conquer it, our species has reached the level of knowledge and social organisation that will allow us to live in a predominantly social world. It is the beginning of a new existence, and indeed the beginning of a new age, the information age, marked by the autonomy of culture *vis-à-vis* the material bases of our existence.[177]

Whether or not they have read him, too many architects believe in the Castellsian utopia of a 'new existence'. They want to get right away from what Castells calls 'the material bases' of existence. They want to dabble forever in virtual space.

In virtual space architects appear to recover that sense of creative control which today so often eludes them in the real world. The most talented digital architects, indeed, do push out the boundaries of the human imagination. But the problem with virtual space is that, so long as they lark around in it, architects need no longer ask why real-life construction is so backward in every regard. Instead, they can imagine that bricks and mortar are an irrelevance, and that unidentified hewers of wood and drawers of water can always be relied upon to build and maintain the material world.

The virtual architect simply *plays* in virtual space. Equally, IT-supported collaborative teamwork is regarded as *Playing Together*.[178] Yet in fact there is no refuge in virtual space from the backwardness of site-based construction. The tendency of architects to want to show off fly-throughs of their virtual work has plenty in common with the immortal computer game Sim City, but little with real architecture. It is akin to art about art.

Even purely digital architecture has its place. But set even the most delightful weightless fantasies of virtual space against the burdensome reality of how most architects actually have to spend their time with IT, and those fantasies become rather tragic.

5.5.3 The claims made for mobile IT

In the summer of 2003, after swingeing cuts in tariffs, the mobile network operator Hutchison began selling thousands of third-generation (3G), internet-equipped mobile phones on the British market. At the same time the London policy expert James Harkin usefully drew attention to the many opportunities for the modern city that lie with 3G, and especially with the location-tracking services that 3G handsets would bring.[179] As we have already seen in our treatment of RFID tags in the building supply chain and will shortly see again in our treatment of Tablet PCs on site, *the potential of mobile IT is considerable for architects and the construction industry. That is one thing. It is quite another to put Castells' claims for virtual space on mobile wheels.*

To talk up the consumption patterns and even the citizen protests that emerge around the use of mobile IT as fundamentally transformative – this is an error. Greater, more sophisticated use of mobile IT in the street sounds like a relatively cheap, investment-light way of saving our cities. But the difference mobile IT can make to building and to house buyers in Britain lies elsewhere. While the building sector obviously has a responsibility

Real space is much more of a challenge than the virtual sort

to smooth the integration of mobile IT facilities into the urban fabric, its first task is to make the right large-scale investments in mobile IT around the building process.

In 1997, the City Council of Helsinki, the city's University of Art and Design, Finland's Ministry of Trade and Industry and local landowners and developers formed Art and Design City Helsinki (ADC Helsinki), to transform Arabianranta (Arabian Shore), the waterfront area where the city was founded in 1550, as a residential neighbourhood. Today the fastest telecommunications area network in Finland is located in Arabianranta. With data transfer in the area's backbone network running at 1 Gigabite per second, residents enjoy connections of a corporate standard. The Helsinki authorities' wider hope is that:

The birthplace of the city, as well as the manifestation of technical and industrial culture, art and music, [will] make altogether a unique synergy.[180]

Arabianranta is yet another unique, synergistic urban cultural renaissance – except that it is at least being established in the capital of the country that gave the world the Nokia mobile phone. It was not many years after Arabianranta's revival, then, that America's *Wired* magazine was concluding that life with a Nokia handset in Arabianranta was what life itself would be like in future. In March 2001 and in

Howard Rheingold: exaggerated claims for mobile IT

its best breathless style, *Wired* wrote that, in Arabianranta:

your cell phone is a broadband browser, a smart wallet, and a passport to the wireless community of the future. And your fellow citizens are the content, 24 hours a day.[181]

Howard Rheingold, author of hip classics of the fixed-line era – *Virtual Reality*,[182] *The Virtual Community*[183] – reached similar conclusions. For him the mobile phone could, for good or ill, empower groups of people, or 'thumb tribes', to press their case. These 'smart mobs', were, as the blurb to his book of the same name related, 'a fundamentally new form of social connectivity, where the physical and virtual worlds meet, and where people can communicate across space and time to engage in collective action on a scale never before achieved'. They were 'the brave new convergence of pop culture, cutting-edge technology, and social activism'.[184] In an endlessly cited example smart mobs, exchanging text messages, had been responsible for the overthrow of Philippine President Joseph Estrada in January 2001.

Naturally enough, Rheingold's book became a bestseller in Helsinki and, in America and worldwide, a key populariser of the idea that mobile IT can transform urban space. *What Castells had trumpeted as a space of flows and architects had meandered into as virtual space, Rheingold now promoted as a kind of mobile space.* For Rheingold, pedestrians around Shibuya railway station in Tokyo, once equipped with mobile devices, now divided their attention:

among three places at the same time. There's the physical world where pedestrians are expected to avoid walking into each other. Surrounding the crowd is an artificial but concrete world, the city as the all-encompassing environment of commercial propaganda . . . Less garish but no less influential than the neon and video of the twenty-first-century metropolis are the private channels of the texting tribes, a third sphere in which bursts of terse communications link people in real time and physical space.[185]

Was Rheingold right? Did video-carrying handsets that people stare at really Change Everything about the modern city? With the downturn in telecommunications after the collapse of the dotcom boom, the development of the mobile Internet was, at first, a phenomenon confined to the Japan that Rheingold celebrated. But by 2003 real, live smart mobs pulled off prank gatherings in Macy's department store in Manhattan, celebrating their collective power at a specially chosen urban location and, inevitably, in the annals of *Wired*.

Rheingold was joined by distinguished comrades-in-arms. Bill Mitchell also concluded that mobile IT had brought about something really new: not just the part-man, part-machine *cyborg self* but also – wait for it! – the *networked city*.[186] Meanwhile, as 'wireless fidelity' Local Area Networks (LANs), or *WiFi hotspots*, emerged as a modest public alternative to third generation (3G) mobile networks, new scholars came forward to discover that *installing a wireless base station, or access point, and advertising its presence could bring, in effect, a warm cloud of mobile riches to different urban spaces.*

At New York University's Taub Urban Research Center, research scientist

Anthony Townsend joined with Terry Schmidt, co-founder of the non-profit organisation NYCwireless, to explain 'Why WiFi wants to be free'. Of the spread of wireless hotspots in the US in the years beginning the new millennium, they wrote:

Property owners and building managers moved quickly to provide the valuable amenity of wireless connectivity within their spaces. Like the internet a decade earlier, the idea of a "wireless cloud" spread from [the campuses of] universities into the broader market. Once it reached homes and business, taking it outdoors was the next step. This would be the province of the free wireless movement.[187]

Activists and hackers in the free wireless movement, Townsend and Schmidt suggested, had 'established beachheads' worldwide – pressure points that would ensure that public spaces would increasingly be expected to provide hassle-free wireless bandwidth. The authors wrote of the 'intrinsic value that a wireless "cloud" brings to the place in which it is located', especially given the inexpensive nature of bandwidth.[188] And they made another discovery too:

The Persistence of Place. Widespread open hotspots will reinforce existing face-to-face communities by allowing people to go the places where they want to be rather than seeking out deskbound terminals. Location-based services will augment the value of interesting places.[189]

Despite all their shallow thinking and over-familiar points, there is something in what the apostles of mobile IT say. Many street emporia are now equipped with WiFi facilities, and will shortly go broadcasting information about themselves to anyone who comes near with mobile IT. Rheingold is probably right to say:

With a ubiquity of knowledge about crime, restaurants, neighbourhoods, the flow of people through cities will change and change

faster. Cities need to be prepared for faster oscillations.

What Rheingold calls the 'swarming' of owners of mobile IT to different locations may also increase. So, if we are forced to use Townsend's terms, may the 'metabolism' of what becomes the 'real-time city'.[190] All this is all very well. But the fewer bogus metaphors architects borrow from biology and computer science, the faster they will get down to the job of using mobile IT *in the construction process*. If we really want the fabric of cities to make the most of mobile IT facilities, we must look to technologies such as Tablet PCs and mobile intranets.

5.5.4 Architects as CAD monkeys

If architecture became serious about manufacturing and IT, it would become more powerful.

Until that time architects will continue to console themselves with the idea that they are, if not powerful, then certainly creative. They will flatter themselves about – and continue to work cheaply on – the minority of culturally significant buildings that society wishes to lavish resources upon.

Many rightly consider Computer Aided Design (CAD) a tool with which architects can and should work creatively with colleagues and other professional disciplines. Many know that it would be easy to borrow or originate ideas from once source and collectively develop them, with the aid of IT, into built form. Yet the reality of teamworking in offices today reduces junior architects and, episodically, quite a few middleweights to the role of being 'CAD monkeys'.

Instead of CAD living up to its promise of freeing users from stupid, repetitive tasks so that they can perform creative ones, hundreds of young architects, trained over a period of seven years, spend up to a decade of their careers as keyboard-and-mouse jockeys who constantly re-invent the most mundane items. Worse, they are without access to the technical support they need in the preliminary stages of design, when the exigencies of project management constrain budgets. Many architects complain that they spend too much time on mindless details and not enough on grand design, but the fact that so many young architects spend so long crouched over hot computer screens speaks more of twisted priorities on the part of their employers than it does of any inherent flaws in IT.

Yet the principals of many architectural firms, for all their ethical commitment to social responsibility and having employees as 'stakeholders' in their business, are preoccupied not with innovation in studio processes and organisation, but with getting their one-off branded buildings and their personal brands into the public eye. The web is used as a means of advertising, or as a means of saving money, but not – yet – as a means of open access to professional architectural knowledge or the knowledge of related disciplines. Anna McCrea recognises the dynamic in her treatment of the architectural software applications that could become available on demand:

Instead of paying large sums for software and licences, a company can rent the use of applications from Application Service Providers and access them over the Net. It is an attractive concept, as businesses would not have to invest in expensive hardware, staff with IT expertise or pay for upgrades. Instead they will just have to pay the third party ASP for the use of software they particularly require. As a result, more and more small to medium size companies are turning to ASP services, especially when a professional level of security is included in the package. Market researchers are predicting a surge in the uptake of project collaboration software, accounts packages and customer relationship management tools. So, has your company signed up for the broadband yet?[191]

IT is often adopted grudgingly, as a threat rather than for its promise. The conventional wisdom among architects' practices is that 'those companies that do not embrace IT will miss out on new business to those that do'.[192] But letting staff have free rein with IT is another matter. In *Building* magazine, Marcus Fairs has observed, of architects' studios:

the IT revolution is not about flashy gizmos but information – and information is made for sharing. Now, hands up all those firms who haven't given all their employees access to email and the internet?[193]

Perhaps the internet exposes boardroom rhetoric about empowering employees as somewhat unlikely. Perhaps it also challenges the culture of *copyright protection* that has come to dominate business life, and especially the world of IT, over the past decade – a culture so obsessively legalistic that the accent in intellectual property is much more on the property than on the intellectual side. For the moment, however, such progress in knowledge that is made within individual architects' offices is kept proprietary. To take advantage of the chief characteristic of software – that, once built, it can be easily duplicated and spread over the Internet at little cost – is to invite disaster in the courts.

Architects could make their own life a lot easier by relying on each other more – electronically.

But the underuse of IT in architecture needs explaining. After all, they are not averse to plagiarism: most get a lot of their ideas from the same stream of glossy architectural magazines. So why won't architects share ideas through IT? Why do they insist on turning CAD into a mindless bore?

There is of course some ineptitude and cowardice at work. This is concealed in the mystique that surrounds architectural design, which is supposed to shift attention from the large- to the small-scale only over a protracted period. As a result it is easy for ignorance and indecisiveness to lead the devil of details to be delegated to juniors at the last moment – or worse still, abdicated to contractors and further to a multiplicity of trade contractors as 'the practical experts'.

A more basic problem is simply an unwillingness to grapple with the truth head-on. On a development it is vital, at the start of the project, to identify the most complicated *architectural interfaces* and *hand-over points* between the different trade contractors present. Clients should always summarily dismiss a project architect who fails to do this. They should always ask the awkward question of where architectural integration is most difficult and should always insist that talent is directed to resolving integration issues at the beginning. It is not difficult to compile a list (see Box 27).

The discipline to *work with CAD to minimise construction interfaces in number and variety* frequently eludes architects. It is just not fashionable to repeat details. Contemporary architecture is often gratuitously complex, regardless of the technical ability to deal with the explosion of variables. It seems that architects always want to express themselves not by assigning a special merit to a few really great components and technologies but rather by expanding the already lengthy menu at their disposal. Indeed, it is often mediocre environmentally-minded practitioners who most wastefully indulge in the excess of 21st century bells and whistles that is available to them.

The non-standard, bespoke, novel and never-to-be-repeated is the real and wilful architectural motif of our present anti-machine age. This gratuitous aesthetic makes a virtue out of the chaos of on-site construction. It increases the number of drawings that are required to coordinate critical interfaces and thus diminishes the time the architect can devote to perfecting and testing each interface.

The outcome is obvious. Buildings have errors designed in, and the reputation of architects declines. In a vicious circle, clients retaliate by insisting on contracts that reduce, to a bare minimum, all fees for the production drawings, coordination and testing that are so essential to the success of their building. Then, relieved by angry or doubtful clients of its responsibility for buildable interfaces, the architectural practice loses technical ability over time. Finally, reduced to the status of a 'concept' designer, it can smugly accuse the trade contractor of ruining the beauty of his or her creations. The architect can remain blissfully unaware of how hard it might be to reconcile design intent with site-built weathertightness. For their part, contractors can more and more make the riposte that architects don't know how to detail.

In the end, weighed down by technically clueless and counter-productive schemes, the conceptual architect is likely to escape into computer visualisation, probably teaching an expanding brood of students the mysteries of spatial design without gravity, weather, construction operatives and the building user. As a result, the profession further brims with:

- bored junior CAD monkeys who dream of their promotion to concept design; and
- directors and associates who have lost more and more of the will and ability to force their visions into buildable form and to train juniors accordingly.

As fees evaporate in a crisis of disrespect, typical architectural practices pay their monkeys peanuts. Even if left to an eternity, a studio full of CAD monkeys will never design a good building. Yet despite the peanuts, the drawings are always required tomorrow.

Clear design leadership is required and, to support that, a firm technical knowledge base. If they were properly thought about and managed, CAD and the Internet could play a part in laying out that knowledge base. At present, however, the IT that is around in construction is used at only a fraction of its potential.

Box 27 **THE LOO'S THE THING – FOR BACKWARDNESS**

A good project architect should draw red rings around critical construction interfaces on sectional drawings as the design develops. It is too late if the contractor does this when the design is submitted for tender or construction. In an office, say, the critical interfaces to consider include:

- slab edges – where ceiling void perimeter detail, structural downstands, toleranced slab and raised floor meet the façade zone. Slab edges need to be fire-compartmented and protected, require servicing, and must not clash with any window heads on the elevation;
- columns – these need to be accessible and capable of taking diameters of roof drainage and condensation pipework from air-conditioning units vertically through the building. They must also be fire-protected as structure, and fine finished;
- lift motor overruns or plant rooms – these should be within the planning height restriction when all the floor to floor heights are considered with adequate raised floor, slab and ceiling void depths for structure and services;
- stairs – these should be of adequate location, width, length and standard floor to floor heights, working with sufficiently sized service risers orientated the right way for accommodation;
- eaves details – where structure may be exposed or penetrate a façade,need to be related back to a viable roof parapet, upstands, drainage, balustrading and the façade maintenance cradle equipment;
- the entrance door threshold – must be set relative to paving levels and waterproofed, and should be related to any basements in need of waterproofing or smoke venting;
- lift shafts – consideration should be given to the capacity and door widths for occupancy, along with the need for periodic fit-out;
- fire control panel and switches – where they should be located and their size; and
- refuse stores – drainage and finishes for hosing down, room size and door widths to install a compactor.

Such lists should be easy to compile with experience. Decisive answers are essential to each of these critical interfaces, and all to meet statutory and specified performances. Yet often *top managers in architectural studios are content interminably to rework the finishes in dozens of lavatories in a building rather than grapple with the fundamentals of the complete structure's design. Those leading designers and clients who make a mountain out of these molehills deserve their projects to fail spectacularly.*

Loos are important. People need them, and they are invariably a key feature in the letting or selling of a building as an attractive proposition. But loos are not the difficult bit of architecture that top architects should agonise over.

Beyond some basic strategic decisions on the palette of finishes and fittings that are possible within a certain budget, the design of features like loos, fire doors or skirtings should be routine. But when a senior architect fiddles with loos at the last moment, and finds that they fail in some practical regard, that is all because they have not been deliberately perfected over time in a properly managed way. After all, architectural practices tend to last a good few years, so their iterative improvements could easily solve the repeated design problems that loos represent.

These problems, therefore, should be delegated to junior staff and overseen by the project architect as part of the professional development of those juniors. Similarly, wannabe architects should be dismissed if they don't treat the challenge of yet another package of toilet drawings, door schedules or joinery details as an important discipline to repeatedly get right in their early careers.

Yet many architectural offices often maintain 'standard' details that would best be put in the bin. These are often details that are known to have been dismal failures; it is just that many managers lack the self-discipline to tell a junior where he or she has gone wrong. In a profession denuded of technicians, the habit has become disastrous.

Today architects sit in front of terminals that could connect them not only to each other but to the best designers among them. Instead, the critical interfaces are ignored or avoided by talented but listless youth, misled by their seniors tinkering with the toilets. In the ritual, all conspire to waste everyone's time, producing or reproducing concept drawings for trade contractors to work up as practical propositions.

When the critical details finally turn out, on-site, to look appalling, or when a loo fails to work properly, architects blame either the trade contractor or the cost-conscious client – or both. But, if anything, architects should blame themselves. Poor detailing of mundane aspects of a project has always been to the shame of the mediocrities in the architectural profession; but with CAD such serial derelictions of duty are unforgivable.

Details that are worth repeating should be falling out of the internet – details, indeed, that go further than merely internal finishes and fittings. The resources of architectural studios should be devoted to sifting these details, maintaining libraries of the best, developing them in practice and reposting the improved versions on the web to return the favour. The best studios should take a lead in this, in the spirit of a free competition.

5.6 Organising wider aspects of IT to live up to their full potential

5.6.1 Supplier relationship management

Neil Yule is managing director of Waterloo Air Management, suppliers of air conditioning and ventilation products. About the construction industry's handling of suppliers like himself, he argues:

The way people buy has to change. In exchange for higher volumes and a long-term contract, we can cut prices. When we know a customer's annual requirements, volumes and costs we can immediately start saving them money. But better still, we can deliver further saving year on year if they work with us to tackle waste in both our processes.

I see an awful lot of waste in design. Consultants tell us how to make the system as opposed to what they want the system to do. This creates ridiculous specifications. We had one design that required almost 200 individually designed grilles that we rationalised to just two!

Often our production team has worked round the clock to get the delivery to site only for it to sit for weeks, waiting for the contractor to install them. We need to have access to the real construction schedule so that we can get the products to site when and where they are needed. This also helps us control production cost which, in turn, gets fed back into lower prices for our partners.

Then we have disputes. In the old days, we'd get a complaint about faulty parts. We would argue that they were not faulty and the customer would argue they were. The first thing the customer did was to stop payment. Then if it got nasty we would both file a claim for damages. When it got really nasty the lawyers piled in. Eventually we agreed a settlement, paid the lawyers and lost the customer. Often it is simpler to replace the part, allow the job to continue and agree the settlement later and without the lawyers. The dispute culture in the construction industry has to change. We are all wasting too much money, time and effort arguing and not enough solving the ultimate problem.

My top three changes – move to annual supply contracts, get suppliers involved in the design and share the construction schedule with everyone.[194]

Construction is often a nightmare for building systems suppliers like Yule. *But if the problems that suppliers to builders face today will only partly find their solution with IT, IT will nonetheless be a growing part of those solutions.*

What, after all, has been the main way in which IT has been applied in business, and especially in private sector manufacturing and retailing? And what single field of application of IT has probably done most to cut costs, as well as to boost US productivity since 1995? To a large degree, the answer is what has become known as *supply chain management.* From vehicle manufacturers through Dell Computer to Wal-Mart, it is the reconfiguring of supply that has been perhaps IT's biggest success over the past decade.

Of course, boosters of IT have often overstated the contribution it has made to supply chain management. Here as elsewhere, after all, IT is a tool, and no substitute for well-founded strategy and process. Nevertheless, in today's supply chain management, there is more and more of an effort to get software to act in real time on:

- logistics links;
- handovers; and
- e-commerce and partnership arrangements between suppliers, manufacturers and distributors.

The aim is to make these activities more cost-effective and more geared to the uncertainties of market demand (see Box 28).

The discipline of supply chain management covers timely information sharing in, and the synchronisation of, the whole production process of any item, from supplier processes, raw materials and manufacturing processes through to post-production and retailing. In fact, the chain is best managed from the standpoint of reducing lead-times and late deliveries for customers right at the end of the chain. In a study of what they term 'customer-oriented cost cutting' at Volvo, Susanne Hertz, Johny Johansson and Flip de Jager highlight the methodology behind the Swedish carmaker's attack on wasteful supply sub-processes. They write that 'the key criteria used to identify a separate sub-process involve the importance of the activity to the business, the amount of money involved, and whether the task is repetitive'. As one Volvo interviewee explained to them:

Take the maintenance that is taking place at the [car] dealers. It is very repetitious. It's very important to have good customer satisfaction. So what do we do as a company? We do process management because we are sending service bulletins to all the dealers which say, this is the way you should do it. It's a perfect example of [IT-assisted] process management. We don't say to each dealer, you find out how to solve each and every problem yourself. No, we do it centrally and we do it together with technicians who know what they are talking about.[195]

The same disciplined, client-conscious methodology, the same standardising attack on repetitive work and the same judicious use of telecommunications and

IT tools are all required in the construction supply chain.

However there are fewer simply linear supply chains nowadays, and more supply networks, of considerably greater complexity. In supplier *relationship* management, moreover, the issues are not just about moving goods, information and money around in an efficient manner between one firm and the next. Deliveries, schedules and inventories are still important; but when a car manufacturer, say, manages a relationship with a parts supplier, the issues are also about remuneration, insurance and appointment. They are about contracts, law and the exchange of detailed product designs. In what has become known as e-sourcing, the work is about electronic tendering, e-auctions, advanced project management and the tracking of supplier performance against (usually over-demanding) 'service level agreements'.

These are all the highly vexatious things that Yule so poignantly dissects. *It is high time that the construction industry took supplier relationship management, and the IT within it, as seriously as manufacturers and retailers.*

In general commerce, private online business-to-business exchanges, prefaced by a long era of Electronic Data Interchange, have made real progress. Moreover as early as 2000, it was clear that the successes of supplier relationship management among private manufacturers and retailers during the 1990s made *government* – as we have seen, a key source of construction industry contracts – the obvious place for what the *Economist* termed 'the next revolution' in the internet. If IT were applied to the state's procurement of buildings, the news-paper implied, things could be very different:

The starting point for most e-government projects is the desire to reduce costs and make tax revenues go further. The potential for savings comes from the sheer scale of public-sector spending and from the opportunities to make internal processes more efficient. American federal, state and local procurement spending on materials and services this year will be around $550 billion. Some big private-sector companies are now achieving annual savings in the region of 20 per cent by putting their supply chains on the web. If government services in the United States could replicate that, they could save $110 billion a year. In the European Union, where the member states' combined procurement spending is about €720 billion ($778 billion), savings could be of a similar order. As with commercial businesses, the benefits come from the way the web can slash purchasing and fulfilment cycles, lower administrative costs by up to 75 per cent and halve stocks.[196]

But the 'next' revolution trumpeted by the *Economist* has not happened. Government supplier relationship management, in construction as elsewhere, is still in the dark ages.[197] In fact supplier relationship management throughout construction, public sector or private sector, is in the dark ages.

Supplier relationship management should have revolutionised the way that construction professionals conduct their business.[198] But while few contractors buy *building materials* online, the tendering and procurement of *building services* over the internet has become much more prevalent. Fearing a fee war, architects hate on-line bidding. Yet supplier relationship management does more than cut costs:

The bidding process, whether electronic, paper based, or undertaken through negotiations is usually the zenith of a highly complex procurement process. It is the point at which price is matched to scope, risk, demand and supply and many other dynamics present at that particular moment. On-line bidding is simply the ability to submit prices in an open and transparent electronic environment. The underlying issue is that many goods and services in the construction industry are complex purchases and it is not just the price that is important. Detailed market intelligence and expert construction procurement knowledge is no less important whether an on-line bidding tool is used or not.[199]

Site-based construction, however, is far from the ideal domain in which to begin supplier relationship management. It means:

- performance-specifying and design-ing-in all but the details before a tender is issued;
- getting 'guesstimate' prices from specialist subcontractors who have only a fraction of the overall project information;
- asking those specialist subcontractors to form committees to design the variously interfacing parts in an afternoon;
- having the client change the brief;
- expecting everything to come together in the rain; and
- expecting everything to function when the building is switched on.

Nobody would buy anything in that way in any other walk of life. It is madness made into a contract – the only thing that might protect those involved from the further nightmare of confused legal liabilities. To blame that contract is to make a mistake. To try to manage site-based contracting through cyberspace is to compound that mistake.

Supplier relationship management will eventually help construction. Through it, IT will allow clients and main contractors to be more able to:

- get involved in property development early, and so ensure that specifications are improved;
- forecast demand and so ensure that inventories are minimised;
- balance the ordering of supplies between centralised and decentralised buying units; and
- specify the global and local places where orders should be both assembled and delivered.

Supplier relationship management will more and more merge with flexible manufacturing systems, enterprise resource planning and business-to-

business e-commerce. It will make the mass production and supply of buildings much easier in years to come, based on clear specifications that should read like an excellent instruction manual.

Supplier relationship management will mean that clients for buildings will want to get more intimate with all their suppliers. Architects must ask themselves if they are ready for that intimacy and for the role that IT can play in achieving it. If 'partnering' means architects understanding clients' concerns earlier and better, that will allow them to regain a measure of control over building and end some of their subordination to clients. But if they are not to be undone by overbearing clients, architects must have about them enough rational sense of purpose, authority, character and command of detail to enforce execution in a robust manner on-site. And, critically, they must be ready to specify what they want in a tightly defined manner, with a set of production data that is not only coordinated but also reflects the very latest best practice.

A tight specification, robustly enforced on site, is one of the best ways of serving the client's interests. Sadly, it is all too rare an occurrence.

5.6.2 What IT can do for building specification and project information

Clare Morris

The *specification* of a building, as part of a wider panoply of *project information*, is at the heart of any newly constructed edifice. Building specification details the quality of the materials to be used, the standards of workmanship to be applied, and – outside the form of contract – the conditions under which work is to be done. Good specifications help make projects run smoothly. In a comprehensive manner, they define quality standards and facilitate communications, resulting in more effective management, and fewer problems on-site.

Box 28 THE DIFFERENCE LOGISTICS COULD MAKE

Even car makers, for all their lean factories, produce cars that sit idle for up to 100 days.[200]

Minimising inventories of coming parts and outgoing goods means taking an axe to as much as 10 per cent of a company's costs. McKinsey estimates that the European market for third party logistics will move from $155 billion in 1999 to $213 billion by 2005. The world's largest logistics firms, Exel and TPG (under the TNT Logistics brand) do enormous business. TPG's contract with Ford to service its factory in Toronto, which makes 1500 Windstar mini-vans a day on a near 24-hour basis, shows what IT-based supply chain management could do for the construction industry:

TPG has to organise 800 deliveries a day from 300 different parts makers. Its software must be tied into Ford's computerized production system. Loads have to arrive at 12 different points along the assembly lines without ever being more than 10 minutes late. Parts must be loaded into trucks in a pre-arranged sequence to speed unloading at the assembly line. To make all this run like clockwork takes a team of ten computer-wielding operations planners and 200 unskilled workers, who make up the loads in the right sequence at a warehouse down the road. The vehicles involved are mostly owner-operated, but under contract to TPG. It is a seven-year contract, and TPG has to lower its price by 2 per cent a year.[201]

The fact is, however, that *specifications frequently fall short. They often contain either too little or too much information, ambiguous statements and additional material that does not belong in them at all. IT cannot help much here. Where it can and must help is in ensuring that, in an on-line world, specifications are fully up-to-date.*

Based in Newcastle upon Tyne and, by 2003, in operation for 30 years, the National Building Specification is a library of pre-written specification clauses for selection and editing by the designer.[202] These clauses, and associated guidance, are written and reviewed by a team of technical authors: architects, surveyors and engineers each have specific areas of responsibility. Their job is to ensure that the NBS keeps up-to-date with the latest changes in legislation, regulation, standards, technology and working practice. Importantly, they also maintain close contact with manufacturer trade associations, and they offer in-depth knowledge about current construction practice.

Problems can arise when architects re-use old specifications. Pressed for time, architects are often tempted to take those from an old project and adapt them for a new one. But unless great care is taken, this can lead to the use of dated and irrelevant information. And *if the specifications drafted for a building are actually obsolete, they are worthless as tools in the construction process. That is why IT is so vital to the whole endeavour that is specification – let alone to the wider business of project information.*

Thankfully, since 1987, the NBS has collaborated with the Construction Project Information Committee (CPIC), which is formed from representatives of the RIBA, the RICS and other institutions in construction and engineering.[203] Because the NBS now follows the CPIC's *Common Arrangement of Work Sections*, cross-referencing between drawings, specifications and bills of quantities is easy.[204] The widespread adoption of the Common Arrangement structure has delivered a uniformity of approach that most parts of the construction industry have welcomed. For the specifier, the library of NBS work sections provides a valuable checklist, ensuring that most aspects of any project specification will be covered. Also, because the Common Arrangement imposes a particular *format* on specification, the construction industry now expects that specification documents will be produced to that format.

To make writing specifications a quicker and more assured business, the NBS has been available in a variety of *computerised* formats since the 1990s. But with today's IT, guidance notes can be viewed on screen alongside the relevant clauses, and the specification can be edited by clicking on tick boxes. Where there are areas of uncertainty, the user can skip a clause and go back to it later; but the software only recognises the work section as complete when a decision has been made on every clause.

The overview of the specification shows each work section as a pie chart which changes colour as the section is completed. Customers of the NBS welcome this because it reminds them that work still needs to be done, thus reducing the likelihood of omissions.

With the more recent NBS software, specifiers can create their own practice standard specifications based on the NBS libraries. These can be drafted with additional practice clauses and guidance, thus sharing knowledge between the NBS and specifying architectural studios, and speeding up the process of future specification. When the NBS updates are applied, the software automatically updates the office templates, ensuring that old material is not re-used.

In May 2003 the CPIC published a new code on production drawings, specifications and schedules of work.[205] Launched at the RIBA, this code develops earlier CPIC guidance to take into account advances made in computer-based aids. It aims to provide guidance on optimising

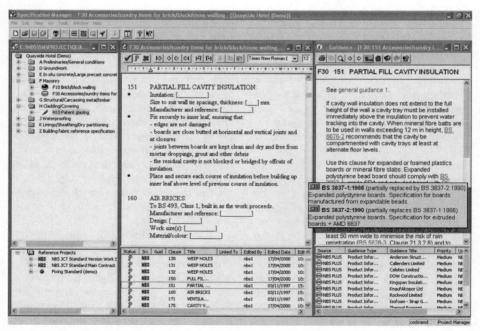

A screenshot of the current version of NBS Specification Manager

the use of widely adopted IT systems. With a view to establishing the sort of production discipline that the development of CAD into 3D Building Modelling is going to require, the code sets out to unify the writing of specifications with the structuring of project schedules.

The temptation to promote the widespread use of cutting-edge IT has been resisted, with CPIC considering that the greatest short-term benefit to the industry will come from the universal adoption of sound principles and basic technology. Because of this short-to-medium term focus, the 2003 code is seen as having a probable service life of around five years, after which it will need to be reviewed in the light of developments. The target readership for the 2003 CPIC code comprises four groups:

- clients of the industry who will be interested in better service and value for money for their projects and who will wish to encourage the changes in practice needed to achieve this;
- designers, be they consultant architects, structural, civil or service engineers, specialist constructors or component manufacturers;
- education and training establishments that prepare those professionals for a career in construction; and
- providers of continuous professional development.

The CPIC defines production information as that 'prepared by designers, which is passed to a construction team to enable a project to be constructed'. Such information is the means of communication between designers and constructors, either in separate organisations or the same organisation. It is independent of who employs the designers and which procurement route or form of contract is used. To emphasise this point, the contractually neutral term 'constructor' has been used throughout the CPIC code, rather than the term 'contractor'.

The CPIC is right to take a holistic view, for specification information has many different sources, from the client's design brief, through the process of cost planning, design drawings and submissions for statutory approval, and on to production documents and instructions to be issued to the contractor. As a result the specification document should be developed and changed over the life of the project design. Once more, IT is essential to this process.

Since 2002 a new managing director, Richard Waterhouse, has led NBS development. As a young architect-cum-CAD manager working in the early 1990s, Waterhouse was an early adopter of NBS software. He joined the NBS in 1993 to help increase the use of more productive software products by the provision of training to designers, moving into research and product development.

Talking to the *Architects' Journal*, Waterhouse commendably explained that 'at the end of the day the point is to spend less time doing specifications so that there is more time for design'. He emphasised that the NBS would welcome competition in the marketplace: 'it might save us from having to do all the R&D'.[206] Unable to wait for rivals to emerge, however, the NBS has been quick to see the potential of electronic information exchange and object-based software.

Waterhouse has been pivotal in the recent merging of the NBS with the Architectural Informatics Research Group of Newcastle University,[207] forming one of the most exciting informatics research and development teams in the construction industry. This is the consolidation of a collaborative partnership between Newcastle University and the NBS that spans more than a decade. That collaboration will now drive the development of a range of innovative software tools for UK construction professionals that builds on successful products from the NBS.

Box 29 SPECS IN CONTEXT   Clare Morris

As far back as 1846, the architect Alfred Bartholomew wrote:

> Almost solely from sufficient pains not being taken in drawing the specifications for buildings, and from want of proper foresight, may be traced, most of the disputes between the builder and the architect and the employer, which so often occur, and which lead to lawsuits and arbitrations, which are oft-times so excessively and even ruinously expensive, and though final, are unsatisfactory to all parties.[208]

Bartholomew's *Specifications for Practical Architecture* was a popular work: it was published in 1840, 1846, 1886 and again in 1893, if not more often.[209] Yet if problems with specifications are historic, they also exist worldwide. The International Construction Information Society (ICIS) groups together 16 national bodies from around the world whose job it is to publish master specifications for builders. Members of ICIS meet regularly to share news and to support initiatives in building information that lead to worthwhile international consensus and standards.[210]

The National Building Specification, Britain's own library of specification clauses, bases itself on proven practice rather than innovation. However, it is also part of the technical authors' brief to be aware of the innovative use of materials.

The technical investigation and subsequent clause-writing undertaken by NBS authors means that NBS users benefit from not having to start from scratch with each new specification they draft. A good selection of standard clauses reflecting common practice, and adhering to current legislation, has already been produced: for many projects, there will be little need to write additional clauses. The specifier simply builds the specification by selecting the appropriate clauses for the project, deleting those that are not relevant.

Since 1987 the NBS has been arranged in accordance with the Common Arrangement of Work Sections,[211] developed as part of the Construction Project Information Committee's initiative on coordinated project information.[212] Following CPIC guidance makes NBS compatible with the 1995 Standard Method of Measurement,[213] and enables easy cross-referencing between drawings, specifications and bills of quantities. The widespread adoption of the Common Arrangement structure has delivered a uniformity of approach that has been welcomed by most parts of the industry. For the specifier, the library of NBS work sections provides a valuable checklist, ensuring that most aspects of any project specification will be covered. Also, because the Common Arrangement imposes a particular structure, the construction industry now expects that specification documents will be produced in a standard structure.

Like other master specifications, the NBS has many advantages when used properly. It has, however, increased the occurrence of unwieldy specifications. Any system that offers a complete library of clauses for editing is open to abuse. When short of time or technically uncertain, the specifier may be tempted to include all the clauses applicable to a certain topic in the hope that the right information will be in there somewhere. However, one clause may contradict another, thus causing confusion and undermining the validity of the specification document.

To bring about good documentation, the NBS has always supplied extensive guidance notes to help specifiers select appropriate clauses for their projects. In the traditional version of NBS, supplied in the form of loose-leaf binders and word processing discs, the guidance is only printed on the paper reference copy. It was never intended that the word processing discs should be used without the paper reference, but in practice this does occur. As a result, some specifiers 'select all' with their word processing software and make specifications more voluminous than they are anyway.

These unwieldy specifications, containing irrelevant and often contradictory information, are less than useful as working documents. They become a hammer to hit the contractor with if things go wrong. Sadly, many professionals believe that specification documents are there primarily as a guard against litigation. Yet a massive document full of contradictory information protects nobody: should a dispute arise, it is only clear, concise and unambiguous documentation that will resolve the argument.

Box 30 **IT HELPS IN THE SCHEDULING OF REFURBISHMENT**

Clare Morris

The Common Arrangement structure of NBS is applicable to newbuild and larger projects, but is less suitable for use in refurbishment. There, schedules of work are more likely to be used. Research undertaken by the NBS in 1999 indicated that a wide variety of scheduling methods were being used, with no standardisation. This contributed to inefficiency and cut into the profit margins on smaller projects, which were already slim.

In 2002, therefore, the NBS launched NBS Scheduler. Scheduler works differently from the NBS. Instead of presenting a structured library of clauses for editing, it offers users the flexibility to create schedules from scratch or to set up a project template for frequent use. The schedule can be organised by cost element, trade, location, or to suit the job.

Users select from a menu of 'constructions' and 'work items', simply dragging and dropping them into the schedule. This can then be edited, if necessary. There is NBS guidance related to the work items, and 'property value lists' (drop-down lists of commonly used data) to help specifiers complete the document. The software allows the user automatically to split the schedule into trades, which is particularly helpful for subcontract tendering. As the schedule develops, a reference specification is automatically created, which provides supporting statements of quality.

NBS Scheduler software was built using Industry Foundation Classes (IFCs), which are a collection of definitions enabling properties to be attached to items in a standardised way. One ICIS project to which NBS is contributing is the further investigation of IFCs as a means by which a common software language could be understood by different applications, such as CAD and specification packages. In the future, there could be links created between the specification document and production drawings, so that changes need only to be made in one location, and cross-referencing is automatic. Until such time as automatic cross-referencing becomes a reality, manual effort will still very much be required.

The Coordinated Project Information conventions give clear advice about limiting the notes on drawings to specification reference numbers, materials, shapes, sizes and locations. It is important that the annotations on production drawings are limited to reference information only, and do not repeat detailed specification information. Drawings should identify different items of work, not specify them. If too much specification detail is added to drawings, there is a danger that the specification document will be ignored or, if the requirements change, that the process of updating the project documentation will be repetitive, more laborious and less likely to be completed successfully.

5.6.3 Electronic Document Management Systems

Today, new websites and extranets are opened up around every building project. That has changed how construction companies conduct their day-to-day site-based business. These systems promise to reduce paperwork, lower costs, improve communications and help people meet project deadlines. In construction they are a welcome development, since the cost of postal deliveries amounts to a small fortune, mistakes frequently result from use of outdated drawings, and projects typically involve participants who are scattered all over the country.

Many companies have for years used IT to manage and schedule projects. However today's project websites and extranets claim to provide more opportunities for consistent document reviews, multi-party collaboration and expanded communications – both on-site and in the office. Through Electronic Document Management Systems (EDMS), companies can post drawings and documents so that, in theory, everyone can easily access and share the latest changes and additions.

With many programs, users are expected to mark up documents on-line without changing the original drawings, allowing for resolution of design and engineering queries on-site. Some applications combine the interactive collaboration features with a workflow tracker that posts and records communications and other documents between architects, engineers, contractors and subcontractors. These systems are supposed to allow for quick responses to requests for information and change orders, streamlining site processes, preventing disputes and even bringing the project's deadlines forward. The website or extranet becomes a common depository for communications, creating an accurate and comprehensive virtual audit trail for the project.

However in reality EMDS have not delivered and cannot deliver either the paperless office or a just-in-time flow of uncontentious project and production information. As McCrea observes, in construction IT happens in a practical and legal context and is no panacea for the endless litigation that graces the backward building trade:

These systems create a record of all requests, orders, submittals and other communications during a project, the Web sites supposedly create a greater sense of accountability and reduce the risk of disputes. However, before project Web sites are embraced as a solution for some of the industry's problems, there are several significant legal and practical concerns to keep in mind.[214]

McCrea's concerns are as follows:

- ownership, control, and confidentiality of data;
- reliability problems requiring data back up and proper equipment housing;
- faults in software and hardware;
- bad software leading to needless bureaucracy;
- malicious attack from inside or outside the project;
- the viability of new service providers flooding the marketplace;
- adequate support staffing and user training;
- insurance for damage to or loss of data, information or program functions;
- professional indemnity insurance and quality assurance schemes require hard copy files; and
- cost, particularly if paperwork is duplicated electronically.[215]

The industry should expect project websites to go down or perform inadequately at some point during a project and should have contingency plans in place before that happens. All parties participating in the site should be aware of, and be expected to conform to, the contingency procedures to mitigate possible work interruptions and other problems. Allowing users to access and post information raises concerns about whether documents can be improperly or unwittingly changed by parties. If a legal dispute arises because of alleged changes or omissions in electronically published documents and drawings, the system itself may play a major role in resolving the final outcome of the issue.

Also, project-specific websites only perform at their fullest capacity if the team is committed to using it and using it properly. Some undercapitalised subcontractors and consultants decline to use IT applications, making it necessary for contractors to employ dual systems of both electronic and hard copy communications. This wasteful process significantly undermines the effectiveness of EDMS. Sometimes, and particularly when they are foisted onto subcontractors and consultants, there is good sense in refusing to use EDMS that make an already difficult job impossible to conduct diligently. Resistance may be futile – but sometimes it is justified.

For McCrea, EDMS make it 'easier for anybody with correct privileges to find and access the document they want'.[216] But EDMS fail to let project participants work on those documents together, as they would normally with red pen, hard copy and a table top. EDMS are a sophisticated postal system, but you can't see much through a letterbox. As a result, and in order to keep a grip on the progress of design development into production drawings and overall project management, there is often a need for dualism again – for both EDMS drawings and printed versions.

Poorly managed, IT can always produce more problems than it solves. EDMS are no different from other IT systems in this regard. They can frustrate design coordination, as project overviews are lost in an overload of documents. Construction managers, or their document controllers, can lose consultants by deluging them with documents through EDMS. This unprofessional conduct is entirely consistent with the construction sector's dilettante attitude to technology. We should be going 3D, in both CAD and prototypes (see Box 31).

5.6.4 Tablet PCs

Not so long ago, the mobile phone was the hot new device on the construction site. Now, it has become as common as a pencil or a tool belt. The next step may be the adoption of Tablet PCs.[220]

In 2002 Microsoft launched the Tablet PC as a pen based mobile computing platform, having the same level of functionality as other computers running Windows. But Microsoft's real innovation is the electromagnetic screen that allows users to write and draw with a digital pen. The screen digitises the pen's movements and displays them as handwritten text or drawn sketches. Handwriting recognition software can translate script into text. The user can draw at different scales or within a developing 3D model, whilst having an entire portfolio of documents available to cut and paste between. When working with a digital camera the potential is clear.

The mobile size, weight and pen-driven input of the Tablet PC makes it a tool that can be used everywhere. Tasks such as taking notes, sketching and commenting on drawings while walking around the construction site are all possible. As more and more software becomes web-based, construction practitioners may gradually adopt Tablet PCs and related construction software in the same way they have adopted the mobile phone. Most Tablet PCs include built-in wireless network connectivity, which enables users to stay connected while away from their desktops.

There are two types of Tablet PC: the slate tablet and the convertible. The slate is a Tablet PC in its purest form, minus both keyboard and mouse, with the pen being the only input device. Convertibles, on the other hand, offer the ability to convert between a Tablet PC and a standard laptop layout. Simply, the laptop screen swivels around and closes with the screen surface facing on the outside. In practice this means carrying the weight of the whole laptop-sized Tablet; but that can be a purely marginal

Box 31   IT ASSISTS IN THE 'PRINTING' OF 3D ARCHITECTURAL PROTOTYPE MODELS

In stereolithography, product designers turn out quick-fire prototype models by hitching digitised dimensional data to lasers directed at tanks full of photosensitive polymers. Machines typically cost well over $100,000. But in Burlington, Massachusetts, Z Corporation builds 3D printers that achieve similar results for prices as low as $32,000. Z Corp's machines are small and quiet enough for office use; they spray a water-based binder on to dirt-cheap powdered cornstarch to build up objects layer by layer.[217]

Chris Rand, editor of the on-line weekly newsletter *Engineering Talk*, believes that specially handcrafted prototype models of architectural components will, by 2007, be replaced by prototypes that are digitally 'printed' like this. Although CAD took 20 years to establish, take-up of such 3D printing promises to be more like that of the World Wide Web, which spent only about five years gaining mass popularity. But where will 3D printing leave us? Rand's guess is that, just as IT has led to a higher output of paper in the office, so the ability to knock out three-dimensional prototypes will leave such items strewn about throughout the construction milieu.[218] Prototypes, indeed, could be posted, in quantity, to architectural and engineering offices – almost as junk mail.

For exponents of the naturalistic perspective, in construction as elsewhere, such a resource-intensive use of IT would be anathema.[219] But for a relatively small number of construction professionals to receive junk mail full of prototypes is a small price to pay for faster time to market in the development of new building products.

Not only paper prototypes but also plastic and wax rapid prototyping are now possible, and with small batch casting being economic, it is possible for architects and engineers to develop replicable details for smaller and smaller projects. Rapid prototyping could make repeat detailing on buildings better, but it will bring much more notable productivity gains when it is applied to manufactured buildings.

Chris Rand

disadvantage compared to the benefits won in terms of functionality.

Using a mouse or a keyboard is fast and precise, but as input devices they have not replaced the use of pen and paper – especially for drawing or sketching. Using a digital pen and drawing directly on to a screen, however, feels quite similar to using paper. In meetings, too, one gets rid of the clacking of keyboards and the continual glancing at raised screens.

There seems to be little reason for the construction professional to buy a con-

ventional notebook PC when, for about the same price, a Tablet PC can be bought. But if the professional lacks the technical or creative capacity to specify or draw on the spot and on demand, such Tablet PCs will not help speed site-based construction. Competent and experienced professionals sensibly need time to consider the implications of a practical or contractual problem, away from the usual queue of expectant hard-hatted site operatives. Tablet PCs are wonderful automated clipboards; but though they might appeal to incompetent construction managers who work in a state of continual crisis, they will not replace the need for coordinated project information before work starts on-site.

There are three drawbacks with use of Tablet PCs for the processing of *drawings*:

- they cannot easily be gathered round, in the way that drawings on a table can;
- only one page can be viewed at any time – it is hard to see several drawings at once;
- electronic zoom capabilities help but tend to make their users lose the big picture.

We have already seen how boosters of mobile IT in urban space are adept at losing the big picture. Nevertheless, the future of construction lies with developments like Tablet PCs.

5.7 When teams model buildings in 3D

Richard McWilliams

5.7.1 Beyond flat

Information Technology is often said to be a key enabler of change in construction industry processes, but what specific tools are appropriate, and why are they not being used more than they are? The experience of IT in other industries suggests that the construction sector could become more efficient through the reform of the systems and methods used in the preparation of design information. On design development and coordination, current use of computer-aided design in two dimensions – 2D CAD – as the primary medium for collaboration between consultants and trade contractors is woefully inadequate.

No wonder that, when things get to site, they often do not fit together properly. Bespoke buildings designed in 2D

Physical models retain a place in the planning process, but if they are handmade, they can contribute nothing directly to the production of a building

are, after all, the first prototype of a production run of . . . one.

2D CAD offers no improvement on drawing in pencil or pen in the pursuit of a coordinated design. The reason is simple. From large general arrangement drawings to small-scale details, a building's plans, sections and elevations rely solely on the author to make sure they can all be properly put together in the right sequence and in the right place. Multiplied throughout teams that lack strong project management, 2D computer drawings can create an illusion of coordination.

Building modelling – the preparation of a virtual 3D prototype – presents a much more feasible way of achieving a step-change in the efficiency of project teams. Since all information is derived from a central model, it is inherently consistent and coordinated. Having a constant reference back to one 3D model greatly enhances clarity and reduces ambiguity. Among other things, information can also be added to improve planning of the construction sequence, the delivery of materials and other site logistics.

But why aren't building modelling methods used more, if they offer so much opportunity for generating value? Let's assess the progress made toward implementing shared building modelling in practice, and consider the hurdles that need to be overcome.

5.7.2 How far Building Modelling has come

Specialist steelwork contractors have been using CAD models for many years, taking 2D design information and generating a 3D prototype steel frame, complete with nuts, bolts, endplates and welds.[221] This prototype is used to direct the machine tools that cut and drill the stock steel sections, to administer ordering, fabrication and delivery, and to aid identification on site to speed the frame assembly. Whitby Bird and Partners, engineers, have sought to integrate steelwork contractors into the design process using both 2D and 3D CAD.[222] The experience suggests that savings of 10 to 20 per cent are achievable through building modelling devoted to computer aided manufacturing along the supply chain.[223]

Several contractors from other supply chains have responded to the challenge of 3D design coordination for production and are evolving similar methodologies to those now familiar in the steelwork sector. Drawing directly upon experience from the petrochemical and manufacturing industries, more and more building services pipework, ductwork and lift-equipment subcontractors can use CAD modelling to link together design, detailing and fabrication. Similarly, component-based structural systems manufacturers and installers, most notably

from the precast concrete and timber sectors, now use Computer Integrated Manufacturing.

Compared with shared building modelling, improvements in single supply chains are relatively easy to mobilise. But while CIM undoubtedly offers commercial benefits for individual trade contractors, project-wide savings will remain a

Juxson House, Paternoster Square, London, is a good example of the use of 3D building modelling in the effort to coordinate structural steel with stone-faced pre-cast concrete cladding

Junctions on the steel frame were detailed to interface with pre-cast concrete panels at connections designed to accommodate frame erection tolerances, and to allow for a sequence of operations to align heavy panels

mirage until shared building modelling is adopted throughout the construction industry. So long as there are clashes with other trade contractors still working in 2D, the full value to be had from building modelling will remain elusive. Client leadership and commercial commitment are required for everyone working in 3D to benefit from it.

By consolidating the advances made in single trade supply chains, and by bringing in third party building modelling expertise, clients such as Stanhope and BAA have led the effort to gain maximum project benefits from combined, multidisciplinary 3D models. Stanhope has suggested that such models can save as much as two per cent of the project cost

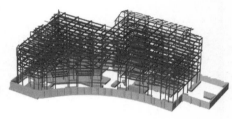

Clashes between structural frame and the cladding, or between adjacent precast panels, were identified in the model and designed out

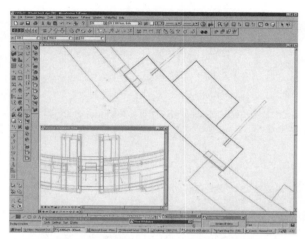

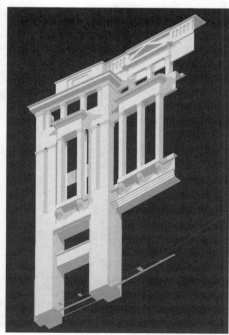

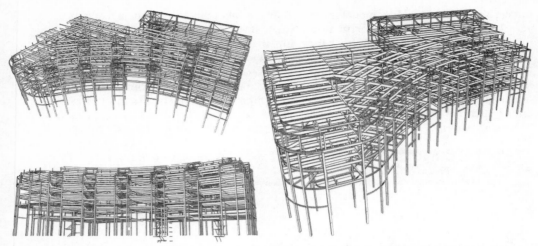

Hidden-line drawings of the steel frame can be created. Enlarged, it is clear that this is a model of steel sections only. The steel fabricator develops connection details from the consultant engineer's model of steel sections

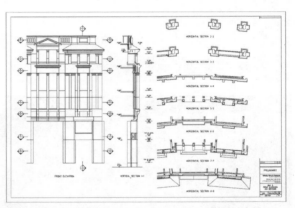

2D production drawings are extracted from the building model

Built next to St Pauls Cathedral, the Juxson House development was logistically difficult and depended for its success on the fit-first-time promise of building modelling

It was the anti-modernist intervention of Prince Charles in the early 1980s that led to the neo-classical masterplan for Paternoster Square, and the design of Juxson House – a development eventually designed by Sidell Gibson Architects, and one that was almost 20 years in the making[224]

As the scaffold is removed, the extent of remedial works required is revealed – work which is difficult to execute

Some defects are unresolveable, such as misalignment or distortion

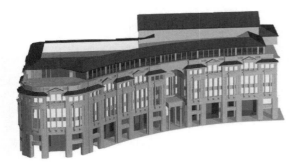

Poor precast panel-to-panel joints may be obscured by machining the stone facings on site. Such problems were made likely by efforts to install stone-faced pre-cast concrete cladding panels to tight joint widths and tolerances, in an attempt to give the illusion of ashlar stonework

Poor stone-to-stone tolerances from the placing of facings in moulds. The failure to reject these panels off-site results in a need for stone replacement or the spinning of the facings on site

Finely-finished capitals contrast with mouldings

Some geometric problems between arches and splayed
pilasters were not designed out. These could be meant as a
feature, but appear to be a mistake

Examples of panels further
damaged in the attempt to
build them in where they
did not fit

Juxson House is meant to look 'traditional', but is contemporary in technology. Also, expensive stone detailing at lower levels is offset in the budget at higher levels with a transition to reconstituted stone

Hand-laid lead-roll roofing is used in an effort to achieve the illusion of tradition . . .

. . . but what about drip moulds to avoid weather-staining on heavily articulated features? This is a level of detail that the building model never extended down to incorporate, but which depends on the appreciation of good practice in construction, whether afforded in stone or in concrete

through improvements in the management of materials that are made possible through the model.[225] By modelling every construction component and scheduling its planned construction, logistics planners can optimise both deliveries to site and on-site storage. Other benefits gained from this approach have included the identification of sequencing problems, the early detection of a lack of coordination, and improved briefing of site operatives. The absence of these services tends to keep project costs higher than they need be.

After its experience of Building Modelling at Stansted Airport (Box 32), BAA hopes that what it calls a 'common data environment' in IT will, by encouraging collaboration, deliver cost savings of 10 per cent in the construction of Terminal 5. There, BAA has brought together a number of trade supply chains to use standard systems and methods to contribute to, and benefit from, a collaorative building model. BAA directly employs its construction project team staff and runs project offices on site at which all managers, consultants and trade contractors are co-located in one office. Consequently a client like BAA can begin to overcome the silo mentality indulged in between consultants, each with their respective trade contractors. By co-locating to run a common building model, designers and specialist subcontractors are forced to work together very closely.[226]

With single supply chain savings of up to 20 per cent already being reported, BAA's target appears readily achievable. Soon more information will be available. So, the perceived value of collaborative working through a shared building model is beginning to be supported by hard figures from leading clients. But is there evidence that these encouraging signs are translating into a wider industry adoption of building modelling?

5.7.3 Signs of change

Cutting across the construction industry, small numbers of clients, architects, structural engineers, services engineers, building surveyors, contractors, specialist sub-contractors and manufacturers have started to try to use building modelling as their primary means for preparing design information. However, behind all the publicity generated, these pioneering companies represent a tiny portion of the industry. There are other signs of wider change beyond the boosterism.

Of those consultant companies that have been using building modelling techniques for sometime, a number have joined forces to pitch to clients as integrated teams, realising value by collaborating on multidisciplinary building models. Several groupings have gone so far as to form joint venture organisations, and to develop a branded approach so as to differentiate their design development and project implementation services to clients.

Part of the reason that groups of consultants can offer shared building model-

Interior, Stansted Airport

ling on normal projects is that CAD tools are more and more user-friendly, functional and affordable, as well as running on better and cheaper computing power than that which was available in the past. While previous CAD systems needed highly specialised operatives to run them, today's tools are becoming accessible to all but the most technophobic of construction team members. The use of CAD software tools is taught as a core component of most construction courses, so that many designers entering the industry are now not only familiar with building modelling but may also have some training in it.

Since 2000, not-for-profit organisations such as Teamwork have been established to encourage the more risk-averse to experiment with building modelling off-line.[228] This initiative helps to develop the necessary skills and experience to implement the move into 3D. Teamwork has attracted government, professional and commercial support, which is a good sign that the adoption of building modelling is about to become widespread.

In the spring of 2003, architects Lars Hesselgren of Kohn Pedersen Fox Associates, Hugh Whitehead of Foster and Partners and J Parrish of Arup Sport formed the SmartGeometry group.[229] Currently their development efforts are focused on the new forms of object-orientated software technology being created by Robert Aish at Bentley

Box 32 **IT-BASED DATA COORDINATION REDUCES STANSTED'S COSTS BY A TENTH**

Clare Morris

The new CPIC publication provides a case study detailing the advantages of 3D modelling as used on a £6m four-storey office building at Stansted Airport. This project was the third of six near-identical buildings commissioned by BAA in the mid 1990s.[227] During construction of the second office block at Gatwick airport, extra costs of £550,000 were incurred. These costs were directly related to the structural frame, building services and curtain-walling. Among the causes were a lack of spatial coordination and poor management of information flow.

On the third Stansted project, spatial coordination and integrity were achieved by preparing a 3D model from the 2D drawings provided by various designers on the project, building a virtual prototype of the development. By using a 3D CAD approach, discrepancies can be identified before a project goes on site. The cost and time savings can be considerable.

A common area for concern, over which disputes frequently occur, is the integration of building services with the building fabric. But at Stansted, the entire architectural model could be checked against the services model in less than two minutes. At one point, 2,500 'clashes' were identified. It is unlikely that all these clashes would have been found using traditional methods, and they would certainly not have been found so quickly.

As a result of using 3D modelling, and exchanging information over a project extranet, 10 per cent of the contract sum for Stansted was saved. This excellent result was due in no small part to the efforts made to ensure that everyone on the project team was equipped and trained to an optimum standard. Investment in IT led to savings across the project.

A detailed IT questionnaire was sent to all members of the team, requesting information on their operating systems, CAD packages, drawing standards, spreadsheet software and word processing packages. Using this information, a set of standard methods and protocols was set up at the beginning of the project. This enabled design team members to exchange data freely and re-use it, rather than having to re-create it. The approach facilitated the development of the project, ensuring that all team members were working to a recognised structure, and with the appropriate software tools to make timely contributions.

Systems.[230] This allows the designer to focus on geometric relationships and proportions rather than dimensioning, and is aimed, Hesselgren says, at 'liberating architects from the constraints imposed by the CAD industry'.[231]

The point is well made, because the constraints of CAD software can be an obstacle to designing buildings. Similarly, building modelling initiatives that are focused simply on design must remember that *building modelling is ultimately about construction*. It requires the discipline of dimensioning and an appreciation of the material reality of development.

As a result of the accessibility of 3D CAD tools, and the spread of practitioners keen to develop their use, building modellers exhibit growing confidence. Today many companies that usually avoid advanced CAD technologies actively pursue the 3D sort. Construction has approached the point at which a critical mass of senior technical and managerial staff understands and has experienced building modelling.

However, it would be wrong to ignore the difficulties being negotiated by pioneering teams – or the obstacles that may yet inhibit wider industry adoption.

5.7.4 The obstacles are real enough

A key element in any real vision for building modelling is that manufacturers must one day come to provide their information in catalogues that are held on the internet. The idea is that designers should be able to drag and drop products – and details of their specification and costings – into their building prototypes on-screen. This approach to design, with a direct view to product procurement, has been proven in a few cases.

BAA's on-line Washroom Product is a notable example (see Box 33). Similarly, the Anglo-Dutch steel firm Corus has been exemplary as suppliers in its efforts to streamline construction through building modelling.[232] It has made a number of their products available in a 3D object form that can be directly imported into a variety of CAD packages. Its approach is branded *Construction Parts*,[233] and is more than a mere 3D CAD library. The objects are real products that can be procured from Corus: each comes with a wealth of technical and sales knowledge, available by clicking on its CAD representation on-screen.

The more intractable problem is that although there are many examples where building modelling leads to tangible benefits, they are seldom realised without significant extra technical efforts to ensure that things actually function properly. This issue goes well beyond the need for virtual objects that work in the range of commonly used building modelling software applications.[238]

One domain into which enormous resources have been directed – fruitlessly, in most cases – is that of *model analysis*. It would appear straightforward to link a building model to analysis engines designed to consider structure, thermal performance, lighting, acoustics, air flow or patterns of building occupancy. There are already 3D systems for each. Yet the fact is that each analysis system makes simplifying assumptions, often about differing aspects of the space. As a consequence, integrating analysis software with spatial models is extremely difficult.

The need for standardisation is greater now than it has ever been. Interoperability through open standards, such as those presented by the International Alliance for Interoperability,[239] although 'nearly here', is still far from common and accessible for lay users. Using 'all AutoCAD' or 'all Microstation' systems is not a complete answer either.[240] There are many other non-CAD software systems, such as those used by quantity surveyors or facilities managers, which need to work through the model. Similarly, the differences in levels of detail and levels of association of objects required by different parties at differing stages of the building modelling are still by no means systematised in a consistently functional way. Many vendors claim their systems are already interoperable; but that is simply not yet the case.

When, for example, a project is still in the stage of being the subject of a feasibility study, a quantity surveyor will need spatial schedules for differing types of area-use, whereas a structural engineer may prefer discrete elemental models of various structural options. As more detail develops, some work, such as architectural visualisation, may merely require simplified models, whereas sub-contractors may wish to add layer upon layer of detail to ensure that every component and interface is fully prototyped. These multiple requirements have prompted the proliferation of duplicated modelling efforts on projects, in which several parties – sometimes, even within the same company – may individually model the same building for their own narrow purposes. They may not be aware of the other's efforts, and are often frustrated in attempts to serve their respective needs in one model.

The absence of interoperability is a real problem in practice, but is often exaggerated as the only issue to be resolved. As with many major IT developments, it is easy to lose sight of the fact that collaboration relies more on the calibre of the people involved and the way they work

Box 33 BAA WASHROOM PRODUCT

Richard McWilliams

The BAA Washroom Product was a proof-of-concept project to provide Web objects that would directly link design, specification and procurement.[234] The aim was to develop tools, compatible with CAD, that would allow users to configure a major product, such as a whole washroom or toilet block, using a Web-based software wizard. The design would be downloaded for use in the project building model, complete with each of the components such as doors, sink units and connection points. The associated schedule of components would then be registered in the shopping cart of the on-line procurement system Asite.[235]

The project based its information on the internationally recognised Industry Foundation Classes for CAD.[236] It was therefore possible to download the components into any major CAD package. Part of the testing phase of this project involved teams at Teamwork's 2002 event.[237] Teamworkers found that the BAA Washroom Product wizard removed much of the drudgery of specification, speeding the compilation of accurate production information. To clarify procurement and installation processes, the scheduled information associated with the web objects included details of supplier, price and weight.

This approach is client-led, is not product-, supplier- or CAD-platform specific, and as such may gain wide support from Industry. It also goes beyond the 'standard product' approach adopted by many component manufacturers who have understandably established web-based catalogues for their product ranges. BAA's Washroom Product creates bespoke designs of several interrelated but differently sourced packages, interfacing with the services, structure and construction of the developing building model.

This proof-of-concept project is now at the stage of needing to develop further functionality, and to expand the system to other configurable components. The images are far from photorealistic; but then all 2D production information is an abstraction too. As the system develops, a more realistic object will be achieved, bringing the building model toward an integration of presentation, production drawing and procurement. As this approach reaches maturity and wide availability, the design and procurement processes will become more like specifying the computer you want from Dell, or buying numerous products on Amazon.

However, few manufacturers have committed to providing product information in this way, not least because the number of designers and contractors that would make use of it is still small. It is a situation that can only improve with the adoption of building modelling.

than on the tools they use. There is no waiting for an IT fix for perfect project management and design.

Innovation is essential to develop CAD skills and refine the software; but the fact is that we will always be faced with IT tools that are less than perfect. Still, such tools are continuously being developed. Building modelling is no different in this regard. Anyway, the key issues that need to be addressed around it are often non-technical.

Even with the leadership of pioneering companies, the growing accessibility of software systems, the greater numbers of people able to use them, and the increasing evidence that building modelling adds value, construction companies will very often adopt a risk-averse position toward 3D design. Initiatives within the more adventurous companies may become derailed when differences between new and old approaches are neither recognised nor managed. It is necessary to consider how the evident momentum to adopt 3D can be built up and how the management issues surrounding 3D may be confronted.

5.7.5 Developing momentum

The inertia of individuals, teams or companies can stop attempts to get started in building modelling. Often, 'no action' appears to present the least effort and risk. Faced with a lack of tangible evidence to the contrary, the decision to advance into building modelling is something of a leap of faith.

At the same time, there is no shortage of 3D zealotry. If inertia doesn't obstruct take-up, those who try it frequently fall foul of the hype, whether it comes from external or internal sales pitches. As a result, the problem with 3D CAD can be one of *too much* momentum toward it – with the commitment to proceed based upon unrealistic targets for both programme and performance.

The reality of the benefits of building modelling is to be found between caution and hype, between backwardness and a doomed-to-failure abandonment of perfectly good current CAD practice. Nigel Davies, while CAD Development Manager at Whitby Bird and Partners, argued at the British Institute of Architectural Technologists[241] that studios in the construction sector need to get the most out of existing software and CAD staff before they move into building modelling. Davies pointed out that 'if you've got problems in your 2D CAD systems, you're going to get the same problems cubed in your 3D systems'.[242]

The greatest problem Davies identified is that CAD operatives from all the professions frequently don't have enough grasp of construction technology. In misleading style, 'Engineer warns against joining the 3D bandwagon' was how Davies was given a headline in *Building Design*, even though the magazine more accurately reminded its readers that, among users of CAD, no amount of IT or access to digital information can make up for a lack of competence and judgement.

While many companies are preoccupied with finding low-risk methods of implementing new information technologies, many still choose high-risk, fast-track strategies, often resulting in an outcome that is not perceived as successful. In such circumstances, the IT becomes a scapegoat for lack of proper planning, and anecdotal warnings that 3D CAD doesn't result in useful production information contribute significantly to the obstacles others face when seeking to implement building modelling. Those who succeed in developing the momentum to generalise building modelling have often fought for and struck a balance between expectation and innovation in their practices. Getting a meeting of minds between practices is another order of argument and persuasion altogether.

When companies have successfully implemented building modelling, they seek project team partners that work in the same way, agreeing to share information as part of their appointment and contract. Unfortunately, because of the differing fee agreements and scopes of work, teams working through a unified building model are a rarity. To reiterate, if some consultants or trade contractors are not willing or able to use building modelling, the gains are frustrated but not necessarily entirely lost.

On the other hand, during the course of projects the positive experience of building modelling from individual consultants or trade contractors can persuade others that they should also avail themselves of such services. A good example is provided by the Greater London Assembly headquarters designed by architects Foster and Partners and engineers Ove Arup and Partners. Warner Land Surveys were progressively engaged by the steel fabricator and following trades trying to cope with the detailing and setting out.[243] WLS supplemented the design model, developed the design, generated production information from the 3D data, set out the works with laser accuracy, checked the as-built structure and construction, updated the model to reflect achieved tolerances, and ended up with an accurate reflection of the reality of the finished building. Subsequent trades could then adjust their design to suit.

To make this possible, the critical construction detailing had to anticipate tolerances and adjustment. Rapid 3D surveying and buildable detailing ensured 'virtual fit' and 'fit-first-time' for the interfacing packages, but only to the extent that the trade contractors used WSL rather than another surveyor. Some construction managers decline to take responsibility for a centralised surveying service, and each trade contractor is expected to provide its own setting out, leading to multiple errors and interminable arguments. The possibility of a

shared building model reveals how backwardly risk-averse some construction management has become. At the same time the more forward thinking managers are asking for building modelling to cut out the potential for clashes, misfits and omissions.

Sharing building models with the specialist contractors is a key part of the overall vision of building modelling. However this is not as straightforward as issuing a model and expecting contractual responsibilities to end there. Issuing a model 'for information only' nullifies much of the potential value for the receiver, but issuers are rarely keen to take full responsibility for their design in model form. Their Professional Indemnity Insurers may even be advising against taking such risks, choosing to hide behind the imprecision of 2D 'design intent' drawings. Similarly many consultants produce physical models and 2D photorealistic or rendered images with which to persuade clients, obtain planning approvals or produce brochures.

There is obviously nothing wrong with physical models or graphics. These media have their own particular advantages. However presentational material could equally be delivered through a 3D building model that serves as the preliminary but precise design iteration, leading directly into design development and production drawing project phases, and ending as a 3D 'as-built' record.

Issues of responsibility are set to become more difficult where different team members 'own' different attributes of one component or assembly. These are issues that will be difficult to resolve quickly and generically. However, with clear agreements on liability involving regular 'back-ups' to track model changes, there should be solutions for specific circumstances. An alternative approach would be to adopt one of the emerging contracts that support project wide insurance and shared liability. Innovation in construction industry insurance is required, rather than ever more risk-averse restrictions justified as quality assurance procedures.

It is apparent that all parties need to have a common understanding of the 3D way of working, not only in principle but

To make steelwork for the Greater London Assembly headquarters, the fabricator had to use building modelling for production information, site surveying and the coordination of interfaces with other trade contractors. Details on the 'Cotton Reel' column head were developed to allow ample adjustment of the structural frame on site. Despite the use of 3D modelling, however, a lot of on-site welding and templating were required

also in practical detail. Teams should resolve the boundaries of responsibility and interdependencies of working on a shared model, rather than leave matters to outmoded contractual forms or partnering agreements. Such process analysis should be adopted proactively to manage production information flow, rather than simply contract for an apportionment of liability when information falters or fails. But explicit appointments or contracts are still required.

Non-orthogonal buildings are often best represented as 3D models

5.7.6 New management issues

As with the migration from manual drafting to 2D CAD, moving from 2D to building modelling can make some routines more difficult or time-consuming and others easier or quicker. This subtle yet significant shake-up must be understood if it is to be practically and actively managed.

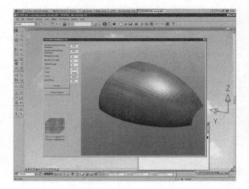

Complex geometries can be designed as compilations of discrete components

While modelling simple buildings is relatively straightforward, it is in spatially complex buildings that the greatest difference is evident between 2D and 3D processes. This is true even though – at first glance, at least – counter-intuitive. Non-orthogonal buildings are often easier to produce as 3D models rather than 2D drawings. In flat views, complexity of form is difficult to communicate to any purpose beyond presentation. Draw in three dimensions, however, and geometric or even random designs become much more intuitive to prepare, even if the same cannot always be said for the complex individual elements that may be part of this whole. Judgement is needed.

As part of an overall spatial model, it is a very quick affair to place, amend and manage both simple single items such as beams or columns, and more complicated compound elements available from application menus or libraries, such as windows, doors, lighting and furniture. Such elements can be dragged and dropped on-screen, and can be modified in their attributes or by menus of tools.

The stunning Great Court roof at the British Museum, by Foster and Partners, is a good example of building modelling[244]

Another example of building modelling is the gridshell of the Weald and Downland Museum Centre, by Edward Cullinan Architects[245] and Buro Happold Engineers[246]

Problems arise when components are needed that are not supported by the modelling application or are not available in 3D from manufacturers or suppliers. Complicated compound elements bespoke to a building design tend to come with no intelligence embedded in them: as a result, they do not allow easy and rapid modification when changes occur. Each design change requires the user to enter into a specific and potentially lengthy change process, likely to be far more involved than they would previously have undertaken in 2D.

When, during design development and before manufacturing detailing, 2D design drawings undergo an approvals process, red-lining those drawings – making comments upon them – often involves many changes to interrelated drawings. It is at this stage that secondary or tertiary impacts of design changes may not be spotted in 2D before problems are encountered on site. The problem is made all the more likely when commenting on-line through an irritating Document Control Management System forces users to view drawings on screen, as if through a keyhole.

In contrast, and for many discrete changes, managing a 3D model is much more efficient when drawing with the prospect of design development in mind. Moving an element in space will automatically update both plans and sections. Yet there often comes a point at which, if there are numerous changes, even of a minor nature, it is quicker to remodel the area affected by the design development rather than amend individual elements. But on flat drawings too there was, after enough revisions, always a moment when it became sensible to start afresh.

So where the design is evolving rapidly, it may be more effective to sketch in 2D and only prepare a model when the design is relatively stable, at each stage of its development. The attempt to manage a detailed model through numerous iterations can become onerous. Complex building modelling cannot satisfy the appetite bad managers have for asking for what they represent as a 'few' last-minute changes. Time to realise change in the model has to be planned for, with an appreciation of which changes are easy and quick and which are difficult and slow.

The big advantage brought about by building modelling is that all potential clashes and mismatches are immediately apparent. Clash detection software is getting better too. It is difficult to fudge early design on the sloppy assumption that interfaces can be resolved later in the project.

Designers, of course, still need a well-developed sense of spatial awareness. A 3D model is no magic bullet, so designers cannot rely on 3D to solve construction problems for them. However, building models greatly reduce the scope for self-delusion or deception that is endemic to 2D.

Another element of hype that is often accepted is that building modelling produces traditional 2D CAD drawings 'automatically'. Yet although extracting plan and section views of a building model is relatively automated, turning flat views of a model into design information that is specific and has a specific sytle about it still requires significant manual efforts: the addition of notes, labels and section marks, and the extraction of those further detailed views that are required to explain the design. As a result, nearly half the modellers' CAD time can be spent on annotation by hand.

Much more important than drawing style in building modelling is the quality of the information conveyed. Once something is placed in a building model,

3D modelling and clash detection software ease the integration of building services within structures below slabs and above suspended ceilings

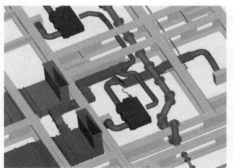

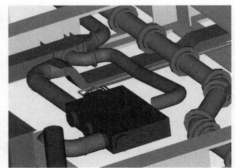

it is not a sketch line or ambiguous item that can await later clarification. It is always both precisely something and precisely somewhere. If the model is shared with the supply chain, and unless a design change intervenes, elements should be installed exactly as drawn.

The literal character of building modelling is the fundamental difference between 2D and building modelling processes, and is often held as a significant psychological and contractual barrier to change. As the past NASA Administrator Dan Golden has said:

We should build prototypes in the inexpensive virtual world, not the very expensive real world.[247]

Creating a virtual prototype of every element in the building enforces, on project teams, many changes – both technical and human – in the way they prepare their information. Provided that the need for such changes is recognised and a balanced approach to implementing them is adopted, the savings achieved by the pioneers of building modelling will be available to all.

5.7.7 Ring out the old

Beyond the hype it has prompted over the past five to ten years, and beyond the risk-averse industry postures that it has also brought to light, building modelling has become an accessible means of improving the way the best clients, consultants and contractors work together. More and more evidence is available to support the claims of pioneers that there are business benefits to be had. To improve their services and productivity generally, companies need to invest in, be committed to, and provide leadership over building modelling. It is the means to achieve coordinated project information.

The availability of intelligent configurable components, directly obtained from manufacturers and suppliers, is a sign of change. So is the broader maturation of the building modelling community. More and more, building modelling is seen as a mainstream activity.

As part of a robust approach, team leaders need to recognise and understand the new management and legal issues involved, appreciating where 2D and 3D methodologies diverge in subtle yet significant ways. With building modelling, teams will gain a level of precision and coordination in their work that is largely unachievable using 2D CAD. Teams will become more productive, designs more thoroughly considered, and construction phases more predictable as a result.

We will look back on these years in the same way we now look back on the time when other design tools went through a step-change. We no longer rely upon slide rules or pocket calculators; we should no longer rely on 2D CAD.

5.8 The cultural climate impeding technological innovation

For many, the downturn in the IT industry since the collapse of the dot.com bubble in March 2000 seems to underline the dangers of too great an investment – in both dollars and hopes – in new technology. In 2001 Michael Porter generalised from the negative experience of the dot.com era. Rightly observing that technology is no substitute for corporate strategy, he went on to attack 'the myth of the first mover'. In his view, it was a myth that those companies first to exploit a technology were best place to succeed.[248]

The failure of Sony's Betamax innovation is just one example among many that would seem to bear Porter out. But in attacking first movers, Porter was really arguing that nobody should dare to innovate ahead of anybody else – and especially not around the internet, which he regarded as a force for levelling down the necessary differentiation of the corporate world. In Porter's paean to strategy, there was a palpable contempt toward firms prepared to make aggresive technological bets.

The investment crisis in the West, with which this chapter opened, is therefore one both of practice and of ideas. But on top of this, therapeutic and naturalistic perspectives on construction combine to *shift the focus of architects and builders away from technology*. The growing weight of regulation compounds that shift; and so does today's media sycophancy toward bespoke, 'signature' buildings.

Altogether, investment crisis, irrational perspectives, regulatory constraint and cultural prejudice go to form an atmosphere in which technology, including IT and the technologies of construction and mass manufacture, gets a bad rap. In the same way that critics of mobile telephones still rush to ridicule Wireless Application Protocol software with the phrase 'WAP is crap', so it is fashionable to attack IT as a hyped-up solution looking for a problem. In May 2003, for example, the *Harvard Business Review* made waves with an article titled 'IT Doesn't Matter'. We had spent too much on it; the 'build-out' of infrastructure was more than half done; IT had become a commoditised utility; it could no longer deliver even the transient benefits it used to give companies seeking a technological edge; few industries now awaited transformation by it; the tasks with IT were to worry about what might go wrong with it. With breathtaking condescension, the article concluded:

If, like many executives, you've begun to take a more defensive posture toward IT in the last two years, spending more frugally and thinking more pragmatically, you're already on the right course.[249]

Disenchantment with technology goes further than Harvard's dismissive attitude toward IT. For more than a decade, enlightened authorities in the West have also inveighed against 'technology push' attempts to predict or control the future. Instead, the injunction is to remember that:

- 'marketing is everything',[250] or 'the customer is king';
- customers should be the ultimate partner of corporations, and be made

the subject of detailed anthropological research;[251]
- those who adopt irresponsible forms of consumption, energy use or transport should and will be taxed for their fecklessness. In Britain, those who use air transport are given a government White Paper that includes 'the economic instruments' for cutting their contribution to global warming, air pollution and noise.[252]

In consumer markets, including the market for residential housing, it is the management of demand, not the expansion of supply, which obsesses today's experts. Corporate 'technology push', the making of wealth in volume, and the unregulated individual pursuit of consumption are held in disrepute. Behind worldlywise cynicism about these things, however, is a wider distrust of human actions in general.

Technology is a series of human creations. In the anti-capitalist's knowing critique of technology, there is always a strong drive to reduce science and its application to avarice, secretiveness, and to absolute power corrupting absolutely.[253] The critique sounds radical. But by questioning all human motives as self-seeking it paralyses construction and, with it, architecture.

At present, UK construction:

- ignores prefabricated, robotised manufacture, despite the worldwide advances made in manufacturing technique;
- shows an excessively Green paranoia about materials and energy; and
- trivialises and obscures the potentially enormous contribution that IT could make to productivity.

Yet architects and building firms could work with prefabrication and new materials to make industrialised construction a reality – and they could do the same with the help of IT.

IT should be used to design well, and as quickly as possible, so that staff can go home early and enjoy their leisure. In 1994, at least, the productivity-raising potential inherent in the use of digital data was appreciated. Then, in Britain, it was officially recommended that:

paying a higher fee to the designers for such information will be repaid many times over if it ensures a well planned project which meets the client's aspirations. The establishment of common standards for the exchange of electronic data would be highly desirable and further consideration should be given to this issue.[254]

The use of IT and CAD in construction has improved since these words were written. But it has not improved nearly enough.

In his discredited attempts to reform the public sector, Tony Blair always attacks what he calls the old, 'one size fits all' tradition of service delivery. But to ridicule the mass production of buildings in the same tones is equally facile. In fact, architects could ensure that mass manufacturing techniques in construction avoid not only shoddy workmanship and pinched spaces but also uniformity of styling. With investment, construction could adapt, to its own purposes and to its own benefit, some of the key processes of volume manufacture.

There remain technological barriers to the rapid modernisation of building that is now so urgent. In terms of the penetration of IT, construction is a lagging sector in the UK economy (see Table 19).

However the bigger impediments to progress in construction are cultural more than they are technological or economic. They are to do with talking up branded buildings and branded architects. They are to do with eulogising 'virtual space' and playful, oh-so-mobile theories of IT, while ignoring both its gritty limitations and its future real potential.

The key task with IT in building is what Peter Goodwin, in an excellent

In 2001, Britain's National Audit Office noted the special backwardness of UK building in the development and application of IT

report, has characterised as *effective integration*.[256] For Goodwin there are six dimensions to the integration of IT on a building project. These dimensions, and the key issues that, in each case, mark progress in integration, are listed in Table 20.

As Goodwin also observes, the establishment of *common standards for the exchange of information* will be 'the core driver to IT integration' in the construction industry. Those standards will come with the advent of *web services*.

Web services use packets of XML code. They are based on a Simple Object Access Protocol, or SOAP, for the wrapping and encoding of objects and the issue of remote procedure calls. The key benefit of web services will be to allow information to be exchanged among a decentralised group of client computers and servers without regard to programming language or operating system.

TABLE 19 Along with manufacturing, transport, storage and communication, construction is poorly computerised

'Which of the following comes closest to the proportion of employees at your establishment over that you estimate are using a PC or other computerized equipment in their job?'

	100 per cent	75 per cent	50 per cent	25 per cent	0 per cent
Manufacturing/Construction	22.6	11.7	13.0	44.7	7.9
Wholesale/Retail	27.5	10.4	9.0	36.2	16.8
Transport, Storage, Communication	20.2	6.7	12.6	52.9	5.0
Financial and Business Services	74.0	9.5	4.0	10.3	1.6
Public Administration, Government, Health, Education	34.3	17.8	8.5	25.3	13.8
All establishments	36.3	12.3	9.0	31.2	10.8

Source: 30-minute telephone survey, July-September 2002, of 2,000 human resource or industrial relations managers in a nationally representative stratified random sample[255]

Apart from web services, the integration of IT is also inseparable from the development of *standard product and components*. As Goodwin dryly remarks:

In the UK building industry there are fewer standard products and components compared to the US building industry and the worldwide oil industry . . . Improvements in the range and availability of standard products and components will facilitate growth in the availability of a greater range of standard industry objects, which will then help further drive IT integration on projects.[258]

The cultural climate for technological innovation today means that good construction practice in IT, as in materials and energy, is as hard to come by as standard products and components. On the other hand, an undersupply of residential housing has been accompanied not only by an oversupply of office buildings and visitor attractions but also by an oversupply of architects.

The practical disciplines that surround the built environment disciplines are none too attractive to young people in Britain. For example, applications to become a planner fell by 7.1 per cent between 2001 and 2002. But students in Britain do sign up to read architecture, which registered an 8.9 per cent growth in applications in the same period.[259]

In Britain creativity is in, and maths, structural engineering, building services engineering, surveying and construction management are out. There was a 30 per cent decrease in A level passes in physics in the five years running up to 2002.[260] The percentage of UK academic engineers who are under 30 fell from 2.7 in 1995 to 1.5 in 2000.[261] Britain produces 20,000 graduate engineers a year; China produces 832,000.[262]

Clarity of thought is not required in today's youth-obsessed culture in Britain – a culture in which fashion is more important than fabrication. As Richard Saxon, chairman of the multidisciplinary Building Design Partnership, has cogently argued, architecture is appealing to students:

TABLE 20 The effective integration of IT

	Low integration	Medium integration	High integration
Information sharing and re-use	Paper documents – can only be re-used through photocopying or scanning	Electronic paper – can only be re-used if receiving systems can read the data transmitted	Two-way data exchange according to project information exchange standards – limited re-use of data becomes possible	Two-way data exchange with full project management control to track changes. Full re-use of data, production of audit trail	Multi-way data exchange; full re-use and audit trail
Building modelling	Paper drawings	Simple 2D CAD	Advanced 2D CAD: one single drawing of the project	3D CAD. Improved visualization reduces the clash of disciplines and helps test construction methods	Use of 3D objects speeds modelling, improves accuracy. Objects can contain manufacturer data on design and costs. Use of intelligent 3D objects – in the sense that each can relate to others so as to speed design
E-business	Basic web site/email	Integrated project tools: web-based applications that enable collaboration around project extranets, as well as the issue and receipt of electronic tenders	Intelligent transactions triggering manufacturing, invoicing, stock availability, delivery notification	Real-time trading communities for the automated negotiation of simple buy/sell contracts, buildability and the benefits of whole-life cost reduction. Full integration of the supply chain	
Team integration	Separate 'black box' units	Black box units with single-box-to-single-box coordination only	Integrated design teams	Design integrated with contracting. Design integrated with contracting and suppliers	
Design process	Sequential stages	Coordinated	Concurrent	Concurrent and interactive in the sense that design depends on the use of intelligent 3D objects	
Information management	Independent document management and reprographics	Central document management and reprographics	Project collaboration through extranets	Custom-managed data network and central hub	

Source: after Peter Goodwin, *Effective integration of IT in construction: final report*[257]

he rightly warned, there is no architecture without these other professions.

For Martin Pawley, this turn to dull and superficial imaginings was to be expected, because 'neither architecture nor fashion is routinely renewed by fresh thought and new discoveries: for the most part both survive by plagiarism and repetition. Indeed they rapidly lose their bearings when deprived of a steady diet of precedent and example'.[264] He rightly compares architects' obsession with unrepresentative masterpieces, from Mies van der Rohe's Farnsworth House to the Case Study 8 House by Charles and Ray Eames, to the elitism of *haute couture* in women's dressmaking.

The cultural climate today impedes technological innovation in building. The obsession with branded superstar architects of the past is only a further aspect of that with branded one-off offices and visitor attractions. These things are, all too comfortably, a million miles away from the real achievements of the car industry and their relevance to off-site manufacture. They are also a million miles away from what IT can do on-site.

In a fascinating study prepared for British Telecom, the IT research house Gartner Group defines what it calls *business agility* as:

The ability to demonstrate flexible, efficient and swift responses to changing circumstances by maximising physical and human resources.[265]

According to Gartner, the following information technologies contribute to business agility in property and construction:

because it is "creative" and teaches through simulation, a form of play. Engineering, surveying and construction degrees seem in comparison to be dry and stolid and associated with uncomfortable careers. Many of the scarce engineering graduates also fail to go into the profession, using their numeracy to go into management consultancy or financial services, for better pay and working conditions.[263]

As Saxon suggests, 'creative' means playing, not production, and those jobs that are seen to be about getting buildings built are perceived as too much like boring and repetitive hard work. However, as

- remote access to time-reporting web sites;
- equipment tracking;
- scheduling and management tools;
- personnel databases for resource allocation and availability; and

- bid, construction and calculation tools.

It concludes:

These technologies may all be accessed remotely over wireless connections to an enterprise's private intranet.[266]

Gartner is right about mobile intranets. Apart from its role in improving customer service and supply chain management, IT can make a big difference to productivity in building through mobile intranets hooked up to Tablet PCs.

In Japan, consumer electronics manufacturers such as Sony have created a situation where it is possible to get the same data coming to an individual whether he or she moves from a desktop PC and broadband line to a laptop, personal digital appliance or mobile phone hooked up to GSM or WiFi networks.

Such 'seamless roaming' isn't needed throughout construction. But the integration of fixed-line and mobile intranets around enterprise resource planning, building modelling and supply chain management – this would not be false innovation, but the real thing.

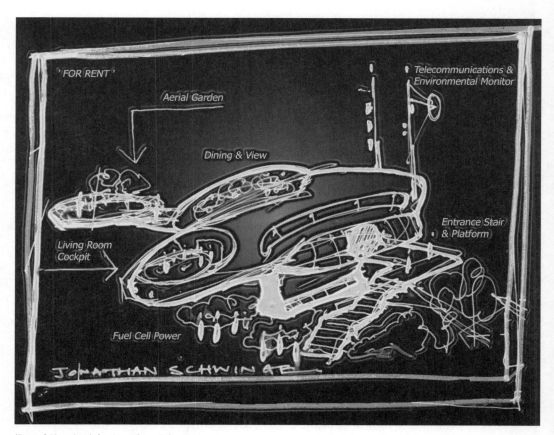

'Rental Housing', by Jonathan Schwinge

Box 34 A COMPUTER SCIENTIST SHOWS VISION

Ben Shneiderman is not an architect. He is a professor in computer science at the University of Maryland, and for years was one of America's top but lonely pioneers of improved user interfaces in IT. Yet it is Shneiderman, in his stimulating book *Leonardo's laptop*, who has evoked a picture of architecture in the future more vivid than even Rem Koolhaas has achieved. Shneiderman makes, in the opening of a lengthy passage:

> the revolutionary assumption that creativity support tools [in IT] would enable an architect to have a broader range of decision-making power, ranging from the initial setting of requirements to the supervision of construction. This reverses the fragmentary approach of contemporary architectural practice by restoring control and responsibility to one individual.[267]

Although he goes too far in believing that IT can fundamentally transform power relations in the building trade, Shneiderman's story of how an architect might one day design a modular hotel in a national park is entirely convincing – and worth quoting at length:

> To get ideas, she searches an architectural library for digital exemplars of thousands of hotels from around the world . . . She visualises the data in a two-dimensional scattergram that shows heating requirements, heat loss, and energy consumption patterns for these 300 possibilities. She uses the interface controls to find strategies that are energy efficient and low-cost . . .

> Susan chooses a log cabin design and pays the creator a fee, then wrestles with the problems of adding more windows, movable modules, and solar heating panels. Her composition tools allow her to manipulate the underlying architectural model so she can resize the building to accommodate the required number of rooms . . .

> Susan collaborates with specialists who confer over her plans for the electric wiring, plumbing, phones and Internet connections. The same groupware gets her rapid advice but preserves her control over wall decorations, flooring, and furniture styles . . .

> At this point, consultations begin with potential builders. Rather than having the park managers do this job, Susan gets them to accept the bold proposal that she handle it herself. Her knowledge of the design and her fluency with the technology make it possible. Susan meets resistance from the builders, but they eventually submit their capabilities report and then their detailed bids electronically to her. She generates bill-of-materials lists for suppliers and a construction schedule for discussion by all parties . . .

> Susan runs into more trouble as she supervises construction. A slow-working subcontractor has attempted to make changes to her designs to reduce construction costs, but Susan catches these problems quickly using her process model that checks against digital progress indicators at the construction site.[268]

Idyllic? Certainly. An impossible empowerment of the individual architect? Very probably. But if Shneiderman knows anything about computer science, his partial snapshot of a less backward construction industry is eminently achievable, and entirely worthy of approval.

NOTES

1 Michael Ball, *European Housing Market Review 2003* (London, Royal Institution of Chartered Surveyors, February 2003).

2 Scheherazade Daneshkhu and Lydia Adetunji, 'Investment slump casts new doubt on forecasts', *Financial Times*, 26 February, p 1.

3 'Exports fuel surge in China', *International Herald Tribune*, 1–2 March 2003, p 14.

4 James Steele, *Eames House: Charles and Ray Eames*, Architecture in Detail series (London, Phaidon, 1994).

5 'House at Highgate', *Architects' Journal*, 23 March 1966, p 763 to 776. 'Walter Segal's Houses', *Architects' Journal*, 30 September 1970, p 769 to 780. 'A basic satisfaction in building a shelter for oneself', *Architects' Journal*, 3 September 1975, p 458 to 461. 'Walter Segal: timber framed housing', *RIBA Journal*, July 1977, p 284 to 295. 'Do-it-yourself Vernacular', *Architects' Journal*, feature edition, 17 December 1980. Charlotte Ellis, 'Self-Build Selection', *Architects' Journal*, 25 January 1984, p 37 to 39. Charlotte Ellis, 'Walter Segal: 1907 to 1985', *Architects' Journal*, 6 November 1985, p 28 to 31.

6 'Housing: Lightweight Timber System', *Architects' Journal*, 26 November 1975, p 1121 to 1138. Bruce Martin, 'Architecture as the art of construction', *Architects' Journal*, 16 March 1983, p 59 to 74.

7 www.cambridge2000.com

8 Marcial Echenique, in correspondence with Ian Abley, 2 June 1983.

9 Sutherland Lyall, 'Beam me up Dunroamin', *Building*, 29 November 1985, p 36 to 38.

10 Patience Wheatcroft, 'Time for another property crash', *The Times*, 8 August 2002, p 22.

11 Norma Cohen, 'From boom to bust in London's office market', *Financial Times*, 13 March 2003, p 25.

12 John Gillott and Manjit Singh, *Science and the Retreat from Reason* (London, Merlin Press, 1995).

13 M&S spokesman, quoted in Indira Das-Gupta, 'M&S to open in India after cuts across Europe', *The Independent*, 27 August 2001, www.independent.co.uk

14 Michael Wines, 'Sea of ads swamps Russia: capitalist billboards blot out historic vistas', *International Herald Tribune*, 20 August 2001, p1.

15 Witold Rybczynski, *The Look of Architecture* (New York, Oxford University Press, 2001) p 41 to 42.

16 www.orourke.co.uk

17 www.geoffreyreidassociates.com

18 www.burohappold.com

19 www.franklinandrews.com

20 www.fpdsavills.co.uk

21 www.byl.co.uk

22 Gyula Sebestyén, *Construction Craft to Industry* (London, E&FN Spon, 1998) p 17.

23 Gerry Kermouch, 'The best global brands', *Business Week*, 5 August 2002, p 94 to 99.

24 Naomi Klein, *No Logo: Taking aim at the brand bullies* (London, Flamingo/HarperCollins, 2000) p xxi.

25 Naomi Klein, *No Logo: Taking aim at the brand bullies* (London, Flamingo/Harper Collins, 2000) p 15.

26 Anatole Kaletsky, 'Mood of consumers holds the key to investment', *The Times*, 14 August 2001, p 18.

27 Patience Wheatcroft, 'Commentary', *The Times*, 28 August 2001, p 51.

28 Philip Newman, 'Trial and Error', *Architects' Journal*, 3 April 2003, p 41.

29 Dominique Perrault, 'Tissus', *A+U*, April 2003, and posted on www.perraultarchitecte.com

30 Philip Kotler and others, *Principles of Marketing*, Second European Edition (Upper Saddle River, New Jersey, Prentice Hall, 1999) p 571 to 572.

31 *Architects' Journal*/British Council of Offices conference, *Commercial Offices: promise and performance*, 6 February 2003.

32 'Pride of Place', *Business Week*, 2 November 1998, p 60 to 81 and posted on www.businessweek.com

33 www.sheppardrobson.com

34 James Woudhuysen, *Cult IT* (London, Institute of Contemporary Arts, 1999).

35 Stephen Dingle, quoted in Norma Cohen, 'We're getting out of bricks and mortar', *Financial Times Survey: Corporate real estate*, 17 May 2002, p 12 and posted on http://surveys.ft.com/cre2002

36 Norma Cohen, 'We're getting out of bricks and mortar', *Financial Times Survey: Corporate real estate*, 17 May 2002, p 12 and posted on http://surveys.ft.com/cre 2002

37 John Stewart, 'Functional features in product strategy', *Harvard Business Review*, March-April 1959, and posted on http://harvardbusinessonline.hbsp.harvard.edu/b 01/en/hbr/hbr_home.jhtml

38 Theodore Levitt, 'Marketing myopia', *Harvard Business Review*, July-August 1960, and posted on http://harvardbusiness online.hbsp.harvard.edu/b01/en/hbr/hbr_ home.jhtml

39 Ralph Nader, *Unsafe at Any Speed: The designed-in dangers of the American automobile* (New York, Grossman Publishers, 1965).

40 Victor Papanek, *Design for the Real World: Human ecology and social change*, first published 1972 (London, Thames & Hudson, second edition, completely revised, 1980).

41 Theodore Levitt, 'Marketing success through differentiation – of anything', *Harvard Business Review*, January-February 1980, and posted on http://harvardbusinessonline. hbsp.harvard.edu/b01/en/hbr/hbr_home. jhtml

42 Theodore Levitt, *The Marketing Imagination*, first published 1983 (New York, Free Press, expanded edition 1986) p 128, 221.

43 Theodore Levitt, 'After the sale is over', *Harvard Business Review*, September-October 1983, and posted on http://harvardbusinessonline.hbsp.harvard.edu/b01/ en/hbr/hbr_home.jhtml

44 Theodore Levitt, 'The globalisation of markets', *Harvard Business Review*, May-June 1983 and posted on http://harvardbusiness online.hbsp.harvard.edu/b01/en/hbr/hbr_ home.jhtml

45 Erich Joachimsthaler and David A Aaker, 'Building brands without mass media', *Harvard Business Review*, January-February 1997, and posted on http://harvardbusiness online.hbsp.harvard.edu/b01/en/hbr/hbr_ home.jhtml

46 Kara Swisher, 'Kitchen renovation brings temptation' and Dagmar Aalund, 'Trends in European kitchens', *Wall Street Journal Europe*, 10–11 August 2001, p 29.

47 Rita Clifton, *The Future of Brands*, Macmillan, 2000, p xiii.

48 'The 100 top brands', *Business Week*, 5 August 2003, p 78.

49 Rem Koolhaas, Jens Hommert and Michael Kubo, Editors, *Projects for Prada Part 1* (Milan, Fondazione Prada Edizione, 2001) and available through www.fondazione prada.org

50 Rem Koolhaas, Jens Hommert and Michael Kubo, Editors, *Projects for Prada Part 1* (Milan, Fondazione Prada Edizione, 2001) and available through www.fondazione prada.org

51 Rem Koolhaas, Jens Hommert and Michael Kubo, Editors, *Projects for Prada Part 1*

(Milan, Fondazione Prada Edizione, 2001) and available through www.fondazione prada.org

52 Ole Bouman, quoted in 'Press gang', *RIBA Journal*, January 2000, p 94.

53 Susan Szenasy, quoted in 'Press gang', *RIBA Journal*, January 2000, p 94.

54 John Anthony, *An Illustrated Life of Sir Joseph Paxton*, 1803 to 1865, first published in 1973 (Princes Risborough, Shire Publications, 1992).

55 David M Gann, *Building Innovation: Complex constructs in a changing world* (London, Thomas Telford, 2000) p 26.

56 David M Gann, *Building Innovation: Complex constructs in a changing world* (London, Thomas Telford, 2000) p 29.

57 David M Gann, *Building Innovation: Complex constructs in a changing world* (London, Thomas Telford, 2000) p 141.

58 Gyula Sebestyén, *Construction Craft to Industry* (London, E&FN Spon, 1998) p 49.

59 Eric Kentley, 'A Turkish Prefab: The Renkioi Hospital', in Eric Kentley, Angie Hudson and James Peto, editors, *Isambard Kingdom Brunel: Recent Work* (London, Design Museum, 2000) p 78.

60 Jane Wernick, Project Assessment, 'A Turkish Prefab: The Renkioi Hospital', in Eric Kentley, Angie Hudson and James Peto, editors, *Isambard Kingdom Brunel: Recent Work* (London, Design Museum, 2000) p 82.

61 www.bbc.co.uk/history/programmes/great britons/final_topten.shtml

62 David M. Gann, *Building Innovation: Complex constructs in a changing world* (London, Thomas Telford, 2000) p 29.

63 David M Gann, *Building Innovation: Complex constructs in a changing world* (London, Thomas Telford, 2000) p 13.

64 David M Gann, *Building Innovation: Complex constructs in a changing world* (London, Thomas Telford, 2000) p 213.

65 David M Gann, *Building Innovation: Complex constructs in a changing world* (London, Thomas Telford, 2000) p 13 to 14.

66 David M Gann, *Building Innovation: Complex constructs in a changing world* (London, Thomas Telford, 2000) p 94.

67 www.jusoken.or.jp/english.htm

68 David M Gann, *Building Innovation: Complex constructs in a changing world* (London, Thomas Telford, 2000) p 150.

69 David M Gann, 'Construction as a manufacturing process? Similarities and differences between industrialised housing and car production in Japan', *Construction*

Management and Economics, Issue 14 1996, p 437 to 450.

70 Gyula Sebestyén, *Construction Craft to Industry* (London, E&FN Spon, 1998) p 51.

71 Vikras Agrawal, Luis D Arjona, Ron Lemmens, 'E-performance: The path to rational exuberance', *The McKinsey Quarterly*, 2001, No 1.

72 Martin Pawley, 'Lavish, visionary architecture puts the user in the driving seat', *Architects' Journal*, 1 March 2001, p 26.

73 Michael Trudgeon, 'Architecture as an anti-technological virus: the work of Michael Trudgeon' *World Architecture*, Issue 23, May 1993, quoted by Martin Pawley, *Terminal Architecture*, Reaktion Books, London, 1998, p 196.

74 James P Womack, Daniel Roos and Daniel T Jones, *The Machine that Changed the World: The Massachusetts Institute of Technology 5-million-dollar, 5-year Report on the Future of the Automobile Industry* (New York, Rawson Associates, 1990).

75 James P Womack and Daniel T Jones, *Lean Thinking: Banish Waste and Create Wealth in Your Corporation* (New York, Simon & Schuster, 1996).

76 James P Womack and Daniel T Jones, *Lean Thinking: Banish Waste and Create Wealth in Your Corporation* (New York, Simon & Schuster, 1996) p 51.

77 James P Womack and Daniel T Jones, *Lean Thinking: Banish Waste and Create Wealth in Your Corporation* (New York, Simon & Schuster, 1996) p 27.

78 *Rethinking Construction: The report of the Construction Task Force* (London, DETR, 1998) p 26.

79 *Rethinking Construction: The report of the Construction Task Force* (London, DETR, 1998) p 21.

80 James P Womack and Daniel T Jones, *Lean Thinking: Banish Waste and Create Wealth in Your Corporation* (New York, Simon & Schuster, 1996) p 292.

81 James Mackintosh, 'Japanese gather pace on their drive into the US', *FT Auto*, 4 March 2003 and posted on www.ft.com/auto march2003

82 James Mackintosh, 'GM says new system saves $1.5 bn a year', *Financial Times*, 30 December 2002, p 17.

83 www.boeing.com/commercial/initiatives/ lean/movingline.html

84 'Back to business', *Flight International* supplement on Boeing, 17 June 2003, p viii, x and posted on www.flightinternational.com

85 Peter Marsh, 'One size fits all: except for local preferences', *Financial Times*, 27 December 2002, p 9.

86 www.buildingcentretrust.org

87 Gyula Sebestyén, *Construction Craft to Industry* (London, E&FN Spon, 1998) p 180.

88 United Nations Economic Commission for Europe, *World Robotics 2003* (Geneva, United Nations Economic Commission for Europe, October 2003), p 1, and posted on www.unece.org/press/pr2003/03robots_in dex.htm

89 United Nations Economic Commission for Europe, *World Robotics 2003* (Geneva, United Nations Economic Commission for Europe, October 2003), p 5.

90 United Nations Economic Commission for Europe, *World Robotics 2003* (Geneva, United Nations Economic Commission for Europe, October 2003), p 3.

91 www.friendlymachines.com

92 James Mackintosh, 'Robots lose out to the human touch', *Financial Times*, 1 May 2003, p 11.

93 Byoung K Choi and Byung H Kim, 'MES architecture for FMS compatible to ERP', *International Journal of Computer Integrated Manufacturing*, Volume 15, Number 3, May/June 2002, p 274; J Michael Tarn, David C Yen and Marchus Beaumont, 'Exploring the rationales for ERP and SCM integration', *Industrial Management & Data Systems*, Volume 102, Number 1, 2002, p 26 to 34.

94 CWCT, *The Performance of Gaskets in Window and Cladding Systems: A 'state of the art' review* (Bath, Centre for Window and Cladding Technology, 1996) p 8.

95 *Homing in on Excellence – a commentary on the use of offsite fabrication methods for the UK housebuilding industry* (The Housing Forum, London, 2002) page 33.

96 *Homing in on Excellence – a commentary on the use of offsite fabrication methods for the UK housebuilding industry* (London, The Housing Forum, 2002) p 45.

97 John Miles, speaking at The Pre-Fabulous Home, and posted on www.audacity.org/ Activity.htm

98 *Homing in on Excellence – a commentary on the use of offsite fabrication methods for the UK housebuilding industry* (London, The Housing Forum, 2002) p 15.

99 Darren Richards, quoted by Josephine Smit, 'We're going to struggle', *Building*, 8 November 2002, p 50.

100 Adriaan Beukers and Ed van Hinte, *Lightness: the Inevitable Renaissance of Minimum Energy*

Structures (Uitgeverij, 010 Publishers, 1998) p 13 to 16.

101 Clive Cookson, 'Labs spin spider silk "tougher than steel"', *Financial Times*, 18 January 2002, p 6 and posted on www.nexiabiotech.com/en/01_tech/03.php

102 Juming Yao and Tetsuo Asakura, 'Synthesis and structural characterization of silk-like materials incorporated with an elastic motif', *The Journal of Biochemistry*. Vol 133, No 1, 2003, p 147 to 154 and posted on www.jb.oupjournals.org/cgi/content/full/133/1/147

103 Fiona Harvey, 'Building better concrete', *Financial Times*, 23 January 2003, and posted on www.spbstu.ru

104 K D Ross and R N Butlin, *BRE Report 141: Durability tests for building stone* (Watford, BRE, 1989).

105 *prEn 1469 Natural Stone: Finished products, slabs for cladding – Specifications* (Chiswick, British Standards Institution, 2000 and subsequent revisions)

106 *Construction Products Directive 89/106/EEC* (CPD) (Brussels, European Union, 1988) and posted on www.europa.eu.int

107 Construction Products Regulations 1991 (London, HMSO, 1991) and posted on www.legislation.hmso.gov.uk/si/si1991/Uksi_19911620_en_1.htm

108 *Department of the Environment Circular 13/91* (London, HMSO, 1991) and posted on www.safety.odpm.gov.uk/bregs/cpd/pdf/doecircular13.pdf

109 *Construction Products (Amendment) Regulations 1994* (London, HMSO, 1994) and posted on www.legislation.hmso.gov.uk/si/si1994/Uksi_19943051_en_1.htm

110 *Department of the Environment Circular 1/95* (London, HMSO, 1995) and posted on www.safety.odpm.gov.uk/bregs/cpd/pdf/doecircular1.pdf

111 'Trouble in nanoland', *The Economist*, 7 December 2002, p 107 to 108.

112 www.nanocom.org

113 www.molecularuniverse.com and www.accelrys.com

114 'Trouble in nanoland', *The Economist*, 7 December 2002, p 107 to 108.

115 Bill Joy, 'Why the future doesn't need us', *Wired*, April 2000, and posted on www.wired.com/wired/archive/8.04/joy.html

116 Michael Crichton, *Prey* (London, Harper Collins, 2002).

117 Bryan Appleyard, 'Countdown to catastrophe', *Sunday Times magazine*, 15 December 2002, p 35.

118 Quoted in Simon London, 'The high-tech rebels', *Financial Times*, 5 September 2002, and posted on www.ft.com

119 e-tagging 2002 – Special Briefing (London, Construction Products Association, 2002) and posted on www.constprod.org.uk

120 Anna McCrea, 'Handhelds – new fashion statement or useful tool for construction?', *ITCBP Intelligence*, 18 December 2002, and posted on www.itcbp.org.uk

121 Simon London, 'Radio ID tags spread waves of anger among privacy activists', *Financial Times*, 1 March 2003, and posted on www.ft.com

122 Simon London, 'Radio ID tags spread waves of anger among privacy activists', *Financial Times*, 1 March 2003. and posted on www.ft.com

123 'The best thing since the bar-code', *The Economist*, 8 February 2003, p 71 to 72.

124 Accenture, *Seize the Day: The silent commerce imperative*, 2002, p 17, and posted on www.accenture.com

125 www.mrfluid.com/news_room/press_releases

126 Ministry of Defence, *Better Defence Buildings* (Sutton Coldfield, Defence Estates, 2001) and posted on www.betterpublicbuildings.gov.uk/pdf_files/better_defence_buildings.pdf

127 DTI, *Our Energy Future – creating a low carbon economy*, February 2002, and posted on www.dti.gov.uk/energy/whitepaper/ourenergyfuture.pdf

128 DTI, *Our Energy Future – creating a low carbon economy*, February 2002, p 9, and posted on www.dti.gov.uk/energy/whitepaper/ourenergyfuture.pdf

129 DTI, *Our Energy Future – creating a low carbon economy*, February 2002, p 37, and posted on www.dti.gov.uk/energy/whitepaper/ourenergyfuture.pdf

130 DTI, *Our energy future – creating a low carbon economy*, February 2002, p 16, and posted on www.dti.gov.uk/energy/whitepaper/ourenergyfuture.pdf

131 Daniel Dombey and Tobias Buck, 'EU sets 2007 deadline for energy market liberalisation', *Financial Times*, 4 June 2003, and posted on www.ft.com

132 Royal Academy of Engineering, *An Engineering Appraisal of the Policy and Innovation Unit's Energy Review – Memorandum prepared by The Royal Academy of Engineering for Mr B. Wilson MP, Minister of State for Energy and Industry* (London, RAENG, 30 August 2002) and posted on www.raeng.org.uk

133 Jean Eaglesham, 'Blair stepped in to block plans for new nuclear power stations', *Financial Times*, 25 February 2003, p 3.

134 Andrew Jack and Christopher Adams, 'Blair and Putin put differences behind them', *Financial Times*, 27 June 2003, and posted on www.ft.com

135 Brian Wilson, interviewed by Jean Eaglesham, 'Green policy "could mean 10% price rise"', *Financial Times*, 28 April 2003, p 3.

136 'Hewitt announces biggest ever expansion in renewable energy', DTI press release, 14 July 2003, posted on www.gnn.gov.uk/gnn/national.nsf

137 Andrew Taylor, 'Green groups hail wind-farm growth', *Financial Times*, 15 July 2003, and posted on www.ft.com

138 Dr Vivian Moses, 'Fanning the flames', spiked online, 10 September 2002, and posted on www.spiked-online.com/Articles/00000006DA2C.htm

139 Nick Baker and Koen Steemers, *Energy and Environment in Architecture – A Technical Design Guide* (London, E & FN Spon, 2000) p 3.

140 Brian Edwards and Paul Hyett, *Rough Guide to Sustainability* (London, RIBA Publications, 2001) p 10.

141 Table 2.4, 'Contractor Output', *Office for National Statistics and the Department of Trade and Industry, Construction Statistics Annual 2002 edition* (London, The Stationery Office, 2002) and posted on www.dti.gov.uk/construction/stats/stats2002/pdf/constat2002.pdf.

142 Department of Transport, Local Government and the Regions, *The Building Regulations 2000: Approved Document L2 – Conservation of Fuel and Power in buildings other than dwellings*, 2002 edition (London, The Stationery Office, 2002).

143 www.saveenergy.co.uk/

144 Department of Transport, Local Government and the Regions, *The Building Regulations 2000: Approved Document L1 – Conservation of Fuel and Power in dwellings*, 2002 edition (London, The Stationery Office, 2002).

145 Department of Transport, Local Government and the Regions, *The Building Regulations 2000: Approved Document L2 – Conservation of Fuel and Power in buildings other than dwellings*, 2002 edition (London, The Stationery Office, 2002).

146 Ted King, 'Strategy behind the revised Building Regulations Parts L1 and L2', *Architects' Journal – Product Focus*, Spring 2002, p 3 to 4.

147 Helene Guldberg and Peter Sammonds, 'Design Tokenism', chapter 5 in Ian Abley and James Heartfield, editors, *Sustaining Architecture in the Anti-Machine Age* (Chichester, Wiley-Academy, 2001), p 72 to 83.

148 www.climatelaw.org/support

149 www.atelierten.com

150 Patrick Bellow, 'Special report – Energy', *Architects' Journal*, 20 January 2000, p 45.

151 www.sbp.de/en/fla/contact/download/The_Solar_Chimney.pdf

152 Peter F Smith, *Architecture in a Climate of Change: A guide to sustainable design* (Oxford, Architectural Press, 2001) p 136.

153 Nicholas D Kristof, 'The coolest car ever costs only $5 million', *International Herald Tribune*, 27 February 2003, p 9.

154 'Vehicle of Change: How Fuel-Cell Cars Could Revolutionize the World', *Scientific American*, October 2002, p 40 to 49, and posted on www.sciam.com

155 *Kyoto Protocol to the United Nations Framework Convention on Climate Change*, posted on http://unfccc.int/resource/docs/convkp/kpeng.pdf

156 Bjørn Lomborg, *The Skeptical Environmentalist – Measuring the Real State of the World* (Cambridge, Cambridge University Press, 2001) p 135.

157 Bjørn Lomborg, *The Skeptical Environmentalist – Measuring the Real State of the World* (Cambridge, Cambridge University Press, 2001) p 302.

158 Bjørn Lomborg, *The Skeptical Environmentalist – Measuring the Real State of the World* (Cambridge, Cambridge University Press, 2001) p 304.

159 Bjørn Lomborg, *The Skeptical Environmentalist – Measuring the Real State of the World* (Cambridge, Cambridge University Press, 2001) p 318.

160 Bjørn Lomborg, *The Skeptical Environmentalist – Measuring the Real State of the World* (Cambridge, Cambridge University Press, 2001) p 322.

161 Helene Guldberg, 'The Lomborg Inquisition', spiked online, 16 January 2003 and posted on www.spiked-online.com/Articles/00000006DBEB.htm

162 Josie Appleton, 'I'm right because . . . you're a Nazi', spiked online, 24 January 2002 and posted on www.spiked-online.com/Printable/00000002D3C6.htm

163 Bjørn Lomborg, *The Skeptical Environmentalist – Measuring the Real State of the World* (Cambridge, Cambridge University Press, 2001) p 321.

164 DTI Retail Logistics Task Force, @ your service: future models of retail logistics, Department of Trade and Industry, 2000, p 21 to 22, and posted on www.foresight.gov.uk

165 James Woudhuysen, 'Management speak in IT', Critical Quarterly, Vol. 44, No 4 December 2002, p 1 to 10.

166 William J Mitchell, e-topia: Urban Life, Jim – But Not As We Know It (Cambridge, Massachussetts, The MIT Press, 2000) p142.

167 Jeremy Rifkin, The Age of Access (New York, NY, Tarcher/Putnam, 2000) p 252 to 253.

168 Joel Kotkin, The New Geography: How the digital revolution is reshaping the American landscape (New York, Random House, 2000) p 6.

169 Charles Handy, 'The workers' revolution', The Times Magazine, 28 April 2001, and posted on www.the–times.co.uk

170 David Brooks, 'Time to do everything except think', Newsweek, 30 April 2001, and posted on www.newsweek.com

171 Manuel Castells, 'High technology, economic restructuring, and the urban regional process in the United States', in Manuel Castells, editor, High Technology, Space and Society (London, Sage Publications, 1985) p 33.

172 James Crabtree, 'The cult of Castells', Prospect, February 2002, p 50 to 54.

173 Manuel Castells, The Internet Galaxy: Reflections on the Internet, business, and society (Oxford, Oxford University Press, 2001).

174 Manuel Castells, The Internet Galaxy: Reflections on the Internet, business, and society (Oxford, Oxford University Press, 2001) p 5.

175 John David Bolter, Turing's Man: Western culture in the computer age (London, Duckworth, 1984).

176 Manuel Castells, The Internet Galaxy: Reflections on the internet, business, and society (Oxford, Oxford University Press, 2001), p 3.

177 Manuel Castells, The Rise of the Network Society, Volume 1 of The information Age: Economy, Society and Culture (Oxford, Blackwell Publishers, 1996) p 477.

178 Playing Together, The Teamwork 2002 Conference, Royal Institute of British Architects, London, 21 November 2002, and posted on www.itcbp.org.uk

179 James Harkin, Mobilisation: The growing public interest in mobile technology (London, Demos in association with O₂, July 2003) and posted on www.demos.co.uk/catalogue/mobilisation_page274.aspx

180 www.helsinkivirtualvillage.fi/Resource.phx/adc/inenglish/arealnetwork.htx

181 William Shaw, 'In Helsinki Virtual Village', Wired, Issue 9.03, March 2001 and posted on www.wired.com/wired/archive/9.03/helsinki.html.

182 Howard Rheingold, Virtual Reality: the revolutionary technology of computer-generated artificial worlds – and how it promises to transform society (New York, Summit Books, 1991).

183 Howard Rheingold, The Virtual Community: Finding connection in a computerized world (London, Secker & Warburg, 1994).

184 Howard Rheingold, Smart Mobs: The Next Social Revolution – Transforming Cultures and Communities in the Age of Internet Access (Cambridge, Massachusetts, Perseus Publishing, 2002).

185 Howard Rheingold, Smart Mobs: The Next Social Revolution – Transforming Cultures and Communities in the Age of Internet Access (Cambridge, Massachussetts, Perseus Publishing, 2002), p2.

186 William Mitchell, Me++: The Cyborg Self and the Networked City (Cambridge, Massachusetts, The MIT Press, 2003).

187 Terry Schmidt and Anthony Townsend, 'Why Wi-Fi wants to be free', Source Communications of the ACM, Volume 46, Issue 5, special issue on wireless networking security, ACM Press, New York, NY, May 2003, p 48, and posted on http://portal.acm.org/citation.cfm?doid=769800.769825

188 Terry Schmidt and Anthony Townsend, 'Why Wi-Fi wants to be free', Source Communications of the ACM, Volume 46, Issue 5, special issue on wireless networking security, ACM Press, New York, NY, May 2003, p 49, and posted on http://portal.acm.org/citation.cfm?doid=769800.769825

189 Terry Schmidt and Anthony Townsend, 'Why Wi-Fi wants to be free', Source Communications of the ACM, Volume 46, Issue 5, special issue on wireless networking security, ACM Press, New York, NY, May 2003, p 52, and posted on http://portal.acm.org/citation.cfm?doid=769800.769825

190 Anthony M Townsend, 'Life in the real-time city: mobile phones and urban metabolism', Journal of Urban Geography, Vol 7 No 2 (2000, pp85–104, quoted in James Harkin, Mobilisation: the growing public interest in mobile technology (London, Demos in association with O₂, July 2003) and posted on

www.demos.co.uk/catalogue/mobilisa-tion_page274.aspx

191 Anna McCrea, 'Broadband demystified', *ITCBP Intelligence*, 23 October 2002, and posted on www.itcbp.org.uk

192 *Making IT Work in Construction – A framework for business improvement* (London, Construction Confederation, 2001) p 31, and posted on www.itcbp.org.uk

193 Marcus Fairs, Leader, 'What's a computer for?', *Building*, 25 October 2002, p 3.

194 Movement for Innovation and Waterloo Air Management, *The Why, What and How of Partnering the Supply Chain* (London, Rethinking Construction, 2001) p 5.

195 Quoted in Susanne Hertz, Johny Johansson and Flip de Jager, 'Customer-oriented cost cutting: process management at Volvo', *Supply Chain Management*, Vol 6, No 3, 2001, p 140.

196 Matthew Symonds, 'The next revolution', *Economist Survey on Government and the Internet*, 22 June 2000.

197 James Woudhuysen, 'Don't believe e-procurement hype', *IT Week*, 14 May 2002, available on www.itweek.co.uk/Analysis/1131745

198 Anna McCrea, 'Tender, bid, auction, and all online – should construction industry embrace or reject?', *ITCBP Intelligence*, 8 October 2002, and posted on www.itcbp.org.uk

199 Anna McCrea, 'Online bidding – controversy or welcome practice?', *ITCBP Intelligence*, 16 October 2002, and posted on www.itcbp.org.uk

200 'A moving story', *The Economist*, 7 December 2002, p 93

201 'A moving story', *The Economist*, 7 December 2002, p 94.

202 www.theNBS.com

203 www.productioninformation.org

204 Royal Institution of Building Surveyors and the Construction Confederation, *Standard Method of Measurement of Building Works* (London, Royal Institution of Chartered Surveyors, seventh edition 1995) and posted on www.rics.org.uk

205 Construction Project Information Committee, *Production Information – a code of procedure for the construction industry* (London, CPIC, 2003) and posted on www.productioninformation.org

206 Richard Waterhouse, quoted in 'Standard – Bearer', *Architects' Journal*, 10 October 2002, p 25.

207 www.apl.ncl.ac.uk/ai/

208 Alfred Bartholomew, quoted in John Gelder, *Specifying Architecture* (Milsons Point, New South Wales, Australia, Construction Information Systems, 2001).

209 Alfred Bartholomew, *Specifications for Practical Architecture* (London, John Williams & Co., 1840).

210 www.icis.org

211 Construction Project Information Committee, *Common Arrangement of Work Sections for Building Works* (London, RIBA Publications, second edition 2001).

212 www.productioninformation.org

213 Royal Institution of Building Surveyors and the Construction Confederation, *Standard Method of Measurement of Building Works* (London, Royal Institution of Chartered Surveyors, seventh edition 1995) and posted on www.rics.org.uk

214 Anna McCrea, 'Project Collaboration Online – Part 1', *ITCBP Intelligence*, 18 September 2002, and posted on www.itcbp.org.uk

215 Anna McCrea, 'Project Collaboration Online – Part 2', *ITCBP Intelligence*, 26 September 2002, and posted on www.itcbp.org.uk

216 Anna McCrea, 'Paperless office or still sifting documents?', *ITCBP Intelligence*, 29 January 2003, and posted on www.itcbp.org.uk

217 www.zcorp.com

218 Chris Rand, Editorial, *Engineering Talk*, 26 September 2002, and posted on www.engineeringtalk.com

219 www.forumforthefuture.org.uk

220 Anna McCrea, 'Keyboard lost – welcome Tablet PC', *ITCBP Intelligence*, 8 January 2003, and posted on www.itcbp.org.uk

221 www.Tekla.com

222 www.whitbybird.com

223 Richard McWilliams and Mark Whitby, 'Establishing business benefits through CIMsteel', *The Structural Engineer*, Volume 76, No 3, 3 February 1998, p 56 to 58. Nigel Davies, 'To 3D or not 3D – That is the question', posted on www.audacity.org/Research.htm

224 www.sidellgibson.co.uk

225 Marcus Fairs, 'Logistics', *Building*, 28 June 2002, and posted on www.building.co.uk

226 Mervyn Richards, speaking at the EMAP Priceless Objects conference, London, 27 February 2002.

227 www.baa.co.uk

228 www.teamwork2002.org

229 www.smartgeometry.com

230 www.bentley.com

231 Lars Hesselgren, quoted in 'Model Pupils', *Building Design*, 21 March 2003, p 20.

232 www.corus.com

233 www.corusconstruction.com/construction parts

234 Marcus Fairs, 'What the talking toilet has to tell us', *Building*, 14 June 2002, and posted on www.building.co.uk

235 www.asite.com

236 www.iai.org.uk

237 www.teamwork2002.org

238 Rami Al-Yazjee, 'Developments in Building Modelling', posted on www.audacity.org/Research.htm

239 www.iai.org.uk

240 www.autodesk.com
www.bentley.com

241 Nigel Davies, 'To 3D or not 3D – That is the question', posted on www.audacity.org/Research.htm

242 Nigel Davies, quoted in 'Engineer warns against joining 3D bandwagon', *Building Design*, 21 February 2003, p 20.

243 www.warnerlandsurveys.com

244 www.fosterandpartners.com

245 www.edwardcullinanarchitects.com

246 www.burohappold.com

247 Dan Golden, past NASA Administrator, quoted by Richard McWilliams.

248 Michael Porter, 'Strategy and the Internet', *Harvard Business Review*, March 2001.

249 Nicholas G Carr 'IT Doesn't Matter', *Harvard Business Review*, May 2003, and posted on http://harvardbusinessonline.hbsp.harvard.edu/b01/en/hbr/hbr_home.jhtml

250 Regis McKenna, 'Marketing is everything', *Harvard Business Review*, January-February 1991, and posted on http://harvardbusinessonline.hbsp.harvard.edu/b01/en/hbr/hbr_home.jhtml

251 John Seely Brown, 'Research that reinvents the corporation', *Harvard Business Review*, January-February 1991, and posted on http://harvardbusinessonline.hbsp.harvard.edu/b01/en/hbr/hbr_home.jhtml

252 Department of Transport, *The Future of Air Transport*, 16 December 2003, Chapter 3 and Annex B, and posted on http://www.dft.gov.uk/aviation/whitepaper/main/index.htm

253 Penny Lewis, Vicky Richardson and James Woudhuysen, *In Defence of the Dome: The case for human agency in the new millennium* (London, Adam Smith Institute, 1999) p 10.

254 *Constructing the Team: Joint review of procurement and contractual arrangements in the United Kingdom construction industry, Final Report* (London, HMSO, 1994) p 25.

255 Robert Taylor, *Managing Workplace Change* (Swindon, Economic and Social Research Council, 2002), Table One, p 13.

256 Peter Goodwin, *Effective Integration of IT In Construction: Final Report* (London, Information Technology Construction Best Practice, October 2001).

257 Peter Goodwin, *Effective Integration of IT In Construction: Final Report* (London, Information Technology Construction Best Practice, October 2001) p 15.

258 Peter Goodwin, *Effective Integration of IT In Construction: Final Report* (London, Information Technology Construction Best Practice, October 2001) p 18.

259 Martin Spring, 'Pulling the leavers', *Building*, 6 September 2002, p 42.

260 Martin Spring, 'Pulling the leavers', *Building*, 6 September 2002, p 42.

261 Royal Academy of Engineering, 'News Release', 6 November 2002, and posted on http://www.raeng.org.uk/

262 Digby Jones, Director General of the Confederation of British Industry, reported in Jim Kelly, 'Business feels graduates lack awareness of world of work', *Financial Times*, 11 April 2003, p 10.

263 Richard Saxon, 'Design Rules', *Building Design*, 4 April 2003, page 9.

264 Martin Pawley, *Twentieth Century Architecture – a readers' guide* (Oxford, Architectural Press, 2000) p 4.

265 Gartner Consulting, *The Age of Agility*, report prepared for BT, 2002, p 4.

266 Gartner Consulting, *The Age of Agility*, report prepared for BT, 2002, p 34.

267 Ben Schneiderman, *Leonardo's Laptop: Human needs and the new computing technologies* (Cambridge, Massachusetts, The MIT Press, 2002, p 227 to 228.

268 Ben Schneiderman, *Leonardo's Laptop: Human needs and the new computing technologies* (Cambridge, Massachusetts, The MIT Press, 2002, p 228 to 229.

6 To take human achievement seriously

6.1 Holding the line against the reaction to 9–11

6.1.1 Daniel Libeskind and the triumph of the emotions

On both sides of the Atlantic, his domination of America's media became, itself, the subject of media commentary. The *Wall Street Journal* intervened to attack his chief architectural rival as a collaborator of brutal Argentinian generals. In the *London Review of Books*, a perceptive professor from Princeton warned that he had mixed an obeisance to the demands of the families of the victims of 9–11 with today's cult of monuments: the result, Hal Foster wrote, could mean that people today 'monumentalise only identity politics'.[1]

So when Daniel Libeskind, the architect of the new World Trade Centre, Manhattan, said that 'from now on architecture will never be the same', it is worth considering the significance of his remark.[2]

The decision in favour of Libeskind was hailed as a blow against the architectural establishment and a victory for the avant-garde. What is it about his ideas that so captured the mood in New York? Libeskind's design, which he calls 'Memory Foundations', epitomises American society's morbid focus on death and conflict.

The proposal takes as its starting point the empty pit – nicknamed the 'bathtub' – where the Twin Towers once stood and where fires raged for days after the attacks. A section of the pit's bleak concrete walls, of the type that can be seen in the early stages of any construction project, will be left exposed as a permanent reminder of the horror of 11 September 2001. This part of Libeskind's design was especially well received by many survivors of 9–11 and many victims' families. They argued that the site was 'sacred', or 'hallowed ground', and so should be preserved.

Every aspect of Libeskind's design pulls at the heartstrings. A Park of Heroes will have markings in the pavements

Daniel Libeskind

One foggy Saturday morning in July 1945, an American two-engine, 10-ton B-25 bomber crashed into the North wall of the 1931 Empire State Building between the 78th and 79th floors, killing 14 people. No fire had ever before broken out at this height in such a building

Although damaged, the structure of the Empire State was resilient enough for the building to open for business the Monday after the crash. Partly because of this, perhaps, the incident never led New Yorkers to fear work in buildings over 70 storeys high

By contrast the devastation of, and much larger loss of life at, the World Trade Centre on 11 September 2001 was followed by real reluctance to use or develop accommodation higher than 70 floors up

containing the names of the fire and rescue companies that responded to the attack, with each name set on an axis between the centre of Ground Zero and the rescue company's home. In a Wedge of Light, buildings are to be angled so that,   on 11 September of each and every year, the intersection of Fulton and Greenwich streets will be flooded with sunlight from 8.46am to 10.28am – the time period between the strike of the first plane and the collapse of the second tower. The final flourish is an observation tower that stands at exactly 1776 ft high.

Such devices will be familiar to those who have visited Libeskind's two completed buildings in Europe: the Jewish Museum, in Berlin, and the Imperial War Museum North, in Manchester. These buildings, characterised by their fractured plans, angular walls and jagged edges, have more in common with war memorials than with conventional works of architecture. For Libeskind, however, the task of building on Ground Zero represented the opportunity to take his emotional approach to the extreme.

The winning design represents a triumph of what Richard Patterson calls *trauma architecture*.[3] It is the highest and, at the same time, the lowest expression of the therapeutic perspective. As Libeskind has said in an interview:

The design and the rebuilding of the World Trade Centre site has to be a spiritual process, not only an architectural one. It's not only finding the visible angles, but the angles in the soul. It's not only finding the external skin, but the internal equivalent to that experience.[4]

Libeskind both expressed and found a deep link with American and Western society's privileging of emotional reactions over rational ones. For 20 years now, and especially since Daniel Goleman brought it to a mass audience, the concept of emotional intelligence (EI) has gained wider and wider approval.[5] EI is now the fashion in parenting, schooling, children's play, everyday life and, significantly, in management discussions of leadership. These discussions are very relevant to a top architect like Libeskind.

The best leaders, UCLA professor Warren Bennis and Accenture's Robert Thomas have discovered, have generally suffered 'intense, often traumatic, always unplanned' experiences in the past – experiences that confer upon them 'an almost magical ability to transcend adversity'. They also retain juvenile characteristics into adulthood.[6] In a similar vein, Goleman, Richard Boyatzis and Annie McKee call on leaders to exert 'primal' leadership, in the sense of the emotional ability to 'prime good feeling in those they lead'. A leader, they write, 'creates *resonance* – a reservoir of positivity that frees the best in people'. Among senior leaders, about 85 per cent of the difference between star performers and average ones is attributable to EI rather than technical expertise, they say.[7]

At Barcelona, the business school Esade

John Tauranac, The Empire State Building – The Making of a Landmark, New York, St Martin's Griffin, 1995

employs Boyatzis to teach Emotional Intelligence to MBA students. With the zeal of the convert, its head asserts that 'more than 90 per cent of management is about having relationships with others'.[8]

After 9–11, Goleman and his colleagues argued, aspirant leaders had a proper desire to take stock. If they felt trapped or bored by their work, they had to reawaken their passion for it by . . . taking a sabbatical. They had to find, and had to help their employees find:

- an executive coach;
- a meaningful cause; and
- a few hours a day or week for self-examination.[9]

These are the priorities in 'leadership development' today. They mark a triumph for EI, despite the fact that it:

remains to be seen whether there is anything to EI that researchers in the fields of personality, intelligence and applied psychology do not already know.[10]

By putting his own feelings about 9–11 at the heart of his design, Libeskind took advantage of today's climate of emotionalism. For every opponent, he was able to find an ally or three. When the *New York Times* architecture critic Herbert Muschamp dared to ask why a large piece of Manhattan had to be permanently dedicated to an artistic representation of an enemy assault, the city's trendy *Metropolis* magazine ran an editorial entitled 'Why the *NY Times* needs a new architecture critic'. But as the British architecture critic Deyan Sudjic properly pointed out:

The troubling issue for Libeskind now is whether he is an architect, in the widest sense, or one who has focussed entirely on the idea of commemorating tragedy in one form or another.[11]

The commemoration of tragedy does mark a departure for architecture. In inviting designs for the World Trade Centre site, the $2.5 billion Lower Manhattan Development Corporation asked respondents to present examples of work that were indicative of:

Risk-taking
Not accepting received wisdom but starting with fundamentals to go beyond easy and safe design solutions.

Inspiration
Creating buildings, urban districts, plazas and parks that are extraordinary in their ability to elevate people's everyday experience.

Understanding
Synthesizing disparate or contradictory information in an energetic way so that the whole is greater than the sum or the product of the parts.[12]

But Libeskind's design is the opposite of risk-taking. It is, as *The Times*'s man in New York has observed, 'closer to a curse than a prayer'.[13] It is a curse on the twin Towers' architect, the ill-fated Minoru Yamasaki, and what the British architect Will Alsop has called the 'financial penis' of America.[14]

After 9–11, an aide to the prime minister of Japan said:

We Japanese saw the World Trade Center as a symbol of strength. The WTC was considered one of the strongest New York corporate brands.[15]

But as the editor of the UK construction magazine *Building* argued in the wake of 9–11, 'the glory of symbolising your commercial prowess with the tallest building in the city has evaporated'.[16] In its place, Libeskind has designed a shattered and shattering indictment of the Fall of Man.

Libeskind is the authorised monumental mason for a new millennium of emotionalism. Not perhaps for him, but certainly for more than a few of his admirers, man's inhumanity to man has become something intrinsic, eternal and immutable, while – just as significantly – human achievement is regarded as flawed from the start.

In this sense, perhaps, Libeskind was right. Perhaps, from now on, architecture will indeed never be the same.

6.1.2 Self-loathing and the end of ambition in architecture

Like vultures fighting over a dead carcass, architects and architectural critics began a still raging debate about which architects and what designs would best serve the World Trade Center site . . . unconcerned with the larger issues and focused entirely on the issue of architecture itself.[17]

In *The Architectural Review*, Edward Robbins felt that rival architects for the World Trade Centre were vultures unconcerned with the larger issues. But Libeskind's victory shows that this was far from the case. As we have seen, architects prefer therapeutic social engineering to real engineering. Their professional embarrassment about the World Trade Centre competition, if any were needed, should lie neither in their rivalry for work nor in the desire to create great architecture from the devastation of Ground Zero. It should lie, rather, in being caught believing that the proper business of architecture should not be sharply focused on architecture.

The question of New York building at scale once again, raised by James Sanders in the *New York Times*, is however part of the business of architects. So is the question of symbolising human achievement, which was raised by the prominent New York architect, Robert Stern. Respectively, they wrote:

Can New York City, which for more than a century led the world in the construction of major public works, only to repudiate the practice some 30 years ago, somehow learn to build on a grand scale again?[18]

We must rebuild the Towers. They are a symbol of our achievement as New Yorkers and Americans and to put them back says that we cannot be defeated.[19]

We can address their concerns, first, by a glance at New York's historical record.

Before and after the Second World War, New York's master builder, Robert Moses, conceived and executed many large-scale projects. Immense political and financial resources were devoted to these projects, which meant the wholesale disruption of people's lives. Earlier generations of New Yorkers accepted the discomfort – and the exercise of immense power by a handful of often unelected individuals – as the price of spectacular and innovative public improvements.

By the 1960s, as Sanders points out, that calculus no longer held.[20] Post-war projects offered little of the imagination or style that had gone before. Their phys-

ical and human cost had grown too high – certainly for those who suspected that professional urban planners didn't necessarily know best. Very properly, Sanders dates the doubt and disenchantment from the early 1960s, the time not only of Jane Jacobs, but also of successful community opposition to a high-rise housing project for Greenwich Village and an eight-lane expressway across Lower Manhattan.

Robert Caro's monumental biography of Moses was published in 1975.[21] *The Power Broker* revealed the brutal and undemocratic means by which New York City's master builder got things done. Yet, for all his criticism, Caro acknowledged that an autocratic, unelected figure like Moses solved a crucial dilemma for modern democratic societies: when public officials fear alienating the electorate over costs and disruptions, how can society ever build the large public works that are essential to modern urban life?

In the mid-1970s, New York community organisations, through an elaborate review process, gained a say in major works – at the expense of the autocratic planners of the past. The rise of the environmental movement gave civic groups another powerful tool against large-scale construction: legal challenges that could tie up projects for years, effectively killing them. The system of

Robert Moses. Photo by Long Island State Park Region Photo Archive

consultation made it far easier to reject than approve any large public project, whatever its merit.

Then, *since 11 September 2001, popular fears about risk have been generalised, making for a social context that is even more profoundly hostile to ambition in architecture. Grand constructions, it is now held, make us more vulnerable – like grand technology, or big brands.* Thus in Britain in the summer of 2002, MI5 announced that 350 major buildings and equipment installations in the UK were potential targets. Equally, Swiss Re argued:

the size, complexity and vulnerability of certain targets – such as densely overbuilt downtown areas or economic centres – enable perpetrators to achieve staggering consequences with relatively simple but concentrated attacks.[22]

To impose one's will upon the environment is the very premise of architecture. Yet today, impact on the environment invites what Vicky Richardson describes, but also rightly questions, as 'resistance to the homogenizing force of global capitalism, sometimes known as "global-blanding"'.[23] Impact on the environment is culpable because it seems a rather American, and thus a rather reckless, exercise. In their post 9–11 *Why do people hate America?*, Ziauddin Sardar and Merryl Wyn Davies, two anti-capitalists writing from Britain, insist:

America is taking over the lives of ordinary people in the rest of the world and shrinking their cultural space – their space to be themselves, to be different, to be other than America.[24]

A great amount of self-doubt, and in some places a lot of self-loathing, now accompanies the achievements of Western civilisation. When Silvio Berlusconi and Pim Fortuyn dared venture the observation that Islam was a backward religion, they were vilified for their old-fashioned upholding of Western values. In Europe and elsewhere, America is widely hated for being a machine-age culture. Yet in a world that sees nothing good in capitalism, but no social alternative to it, this feeling is not confined to America's foreign critics. Many Americans indulge in self-loathing. As Chris Rand noted of the Johannesburg conference on sustainable development in 2002:

The delegates at the World Summit yesterday who jeered and heckled US Secretary of State Colin Powell as he defended America's record on the environment turned out to be mainly Americans too, but millions of people throughout the so-called 'developed' world were with them in spirit, it seems.[25]

In the latter decades of the 20th century, at the very moment America confirmed its status as the leading world power, the idea of the superiority of the American way of life was called into question at home. Confidence evaporated in the power of science and technology to benefit humanity, and in the idea that nature is there to be developed for humanity's advantage. On campuses and also way beyond them, every other cornerstone of US cultural orthodoxy crumbled. The consequence, as Johannesburg showed, has been the establishment of a debilitating loss of nerve. To their credit, Sardar and Wyn Davies recognise this:

For America, the multicultural debate seems like a fight for survival, and that's the essence of the problem. If freedom, liberty and justice have not been pure, perfect and good in practice – either in history or in contemporary society – then America is not innocent and virtuous, neither special nor different, not the last best hope but just like all other societies, another flawed human endeavour saddled with imperfections that has to face up to the challenge of change.[26]

America itself has become a case of capitalism in denial. As the conduct of the Gulf War in 2003 showed, the US elite can win a military campaign, but goes into every new one having lost a whole series of wars beforehand – the culture wars of the 1990s.

Ray Anderson is a Georgia state engineer, as well as chairman and founder of the giant US carpet manufacturer Interface. In Britain his company won, in 2002, the Queen's Award for Enterprise in the category of Sustainable Development. Yet Anderson says, of Interface's record on environmental matters:

In the future, people like us will go to prison.[27]

He believes that he should be arrested if Interface is unable to prove itself sustainable.

Anderson is no extremist. But in ideology, more youthful and more radical anti-capitalist figures than he have much in common with the Saudi Arabian playboys who executed 9–11. Kenan Malik writes that, on the surface:

Kenan Malik

the two seem poles apart: fundamentalists loathe Western decadence, Western radicals fear Islamic presumptions of certainty. But what unites the two is that both are rooted in contemporary nihilistic multiculturalism; both express, at best, ambivalence about, at worst outright rejection of, the ideas of modernity, universality, and progress. And both see no real alternative to Western power.[28]

Malik is right. Modernity, universality and progress are not being held in check just by capitalism. Capitalism both develops wealth and restrains wealth creation: that has long been true. *What is new is that, especially since 9–11, modernity, universality and progress are held in check by new forces – those who, because their dismissal of capitalism is so inchoate, in the process dismiss ambition and human achievement itself.* That is one of the reasons that the long-term future of the overall World Trade Centre site, in terms of the balance between Good housing and Evil commercial development, still remains so unclear. It is also why, in the first round of the competition to redesign the towers, the simple task of replacing the lost commercial space there – 1,022,000 square metres of offices, 56,000

square metres for retailing and 56,000 square metres for a hotel – proved too much for everyone, leading to six designs rejected for their blandness and ridiculed for their inattention to residential space.

Yet progress in the scale and ambition of building, like innovation in the design and production methods associated with it, must not now fall victim to the self-hatred that has broken out since 9–11. Development cannot be held hostage by impulsive reactions to groups like Al Qaeda. After all, today's febrile mood, it has been observed, 'can lead some states to terrorise themselves far better than the terrorists'.[29] The first step toward an adequate mechanised architecture for tomorrow is to challenge this mood today.

One of the ways of doing this is to uphold the general principle, if not every individual practice, of the skyscraper.

In March 2003 it was announced that British Telecom's BT Tower, off London's Tottenham Court Road, was to gain listed status. Ken Livingstone and Richard Rogers favour the skyscraper through their commercial and environmentalist weakness for high-density urban development. In curating a Royal Academy exhibition on the history of the sky-scraper, Norman Foster went so far as to say that 'the challenge for all cities across the planet is how we achieve higher densities of population'.[30] Rem Koolhaas has designed an 80-storey tower in Beijing for China Central Television; the Shanghai World Financial Centre will dwarf Kuala Lumpur's twin Petronas Towers as the world's tallest building; and another eight of the world's tallest buildings are under construction in the Far East.[31]

Yet the principle of skyscrapers still needs defending for the right reasons – for if the wrong reasons are advanced, we may yet see some kind of freeze on sky-scrapers. It is vital, for instance, to support Renzo Piano's 'vertical city' at London Bridge. Why? If only because, in the proper contemporary manner, the distinguished architect himself is so defensive about it. He proclaims:

Symbols are dangerous. Often tall buildings are aggressive and arrogant symbols of power and ego, selfish and hermetic. The tower is designed to be a sharp and light presence in the London skyline. Architecture is about telling stories and expressing visions, and memory is part of it.

Our memory is permeated by history.[32]

Renzo Piano

While the naturalistic perspective seems to favour building upward rather than outward in cities, those who maintain the perspective still want to put limits on the energy, working floorspace and height made over to buildings. They want deep chimney wells for natural ventilation, plants everywhere, gardens on every roof, and unobstructed urban views. The result is skyscrapers whose conception and goals are stunted from the start – buildings which apologise for human achievement from their design onwards.

But there is also a newer force restraining the development of skyscrapers. Since 9–11, the view has grown that the task of architecture is not just to save the planet, but also to save everyone against a terrorist attack – from whatever quarter. The task of skyscrapers, then, is to provide something that, paradoxically, is both unambitious and impossible: guaranteed *business continuity*.

6.1.3 Architecture as business continuity

We saw in Chapter 3 how legal innovation around business continuity is on the rise. However, the idea that architects should now step forth as physical protectors of the people is not just something that enthralls lawyers: it is an idea attractive to architects and, obviously, to the users of buildings. The provision of business continuity represents merely one of a series of redefinitions of architecture away from technology, and toward the much dodgier business of *reassurance*. Let's look first at the technicalities of 9–11.

At the old World Trade Centre, one Boeing 767 hit the North tower first between floors 94 and 98. Another struck the South tower between floors 78 and 84. Both airliners were loaded with enough fuel to reach Los Angeles. One had 92 people on board; the other, 65. Along with the passengers, 2,830 building occupants and 343 emergency services workers lost their lives. The total loss of life was 3330. About 58,000 people were at the WTC complex at the time, mostly in stations and concourse areas. In total, 10 major buildings experienced total or partial collapse and about 2,790,000 square metres of commercial office space was removed from service-able use, of which 1,115,000 m² belonged to the WTC towers.

In its massive *World Trade Center Building Performance Study*, the Federal Emergency Management Agency (FEMA) found, of the WTC, no specific structural features that could be regarded as sub-standard. In fact, it found many struc-tural and fire protection features of the WTC's design and construction to be superior to the minimum code require-ments. The FEMA observed:

The structural damage sustained by each of the two buildings as a result of the terrorist attacks was massive. The fact that the structures were able to sustain this level of damage and remain standing for an extended period of time is remarkable and is the reason that most build-ing occupants were able to evacuate safely.[33]

The reason the WTC collapsed had lit-tle to do with architecture. According to the FEMA, it was because the WTC was:

subjected to a second, simultaneous severe loading event in the form of the fires caused by the aircraft impacts . . . as the burning jet fuel spread across several floors of the build-ings, it ignited much of the buildings' contents . . . this heat induced additional stresses into the damaged structural frames while simulta-neously softening and weakening these frames. This additional loading and the result-ing damage were sufficient to induce the col-lapse of both structures.[34]

It went on:

depending on the size of the aircraft, it may not be technically feasible to develop design provisions that would enable all structures to be designed and constructed to resist the effects of impacts by rapidly moving aircraft, and the ensuing fires, without collapse.[35]

In London, the Institution of Structural Engineers (IStructE) came to a similar view. After convening a working group, it found that 'solutions to reducing the probability of a recurrence of extreme events such as occurred on 11 September do not lie within the gift of building own-ers, operators and construction profes-sionals'.[36] But both the FEMA and the IStructE wanted developers and others *to proof many of tomorrow's major buildings against every eventuality*. The FEMA wrote:

the attacks on the World Trade Center are a reason to question design philosophies . . . [although] there are insufficient data to deter-mine whether there is reasonable threat of attacks on specific buildings to recommend inclusion of such requirements in building codes . . . However, individual building devel-opers may wish to consider design provisions for improving redundancy and robustness for such unforeseen events, particularly for struc-tures that, by nature of their design or occu-pancy, may be susceptible to such incidents.[37]

The IStructE wrote:

Decisions need to be made by owners, opera-tors, designers and building managers based on an understanding of all the issues . . . Overall strategies involving the design of the building, its management and the relationships with emergency services are required in order to maximise protection of building occupants for a wide range of possible extreme events.[38]

After vast exercises in research, both the FEMA and the IStructE told clients and their consultants to carry out risk assessments based on their own worst fears – or those of their insurers.

When, in the wake of 9–11, New Labour decided not to strengthen the Building Regulations on fire safety, after so much advice to the contrary, it was considered reckless.[39] Every kind of risk, it is held, must now be imagined and pre-pared for. *The Precautionary Principle now extends from saving the planet through sus-tainable architecture to saving office workers from future terrorist attack.*

This new, expanded Precautionary Principle threatens architects with an explosion of legal claims. In the past, the common law in Britain considered them, like other professional people, to be reasonable individuals among their peers – people whom Lord Bowen, a 19th century peer, famously conceptualised as 'the man on the Clapham Omnibus'.[40] As ubiquitous, reasonable men and women, they were not thought clairvoyant, but were expected to have learnt from experience, possibly acquiring a level of expertise. Nearly 50 years ago, the test of professionalism was, according to English courts:

the standard of the ordinary skilled man exercising and professing to have that special skill. A man need not possess the highest expert skill; it is well established law that it is sufficient if he exercises the ordinary skill of an ordinary competent man exercising that particular art.[41]

Just a little more than a decade ago, in his *Negligence in Building Law*, the lawyer Jon Holyoak added only this:

It is self-evident that building owners expect their buildings to be designed and built with something more than the skill of the ordinary man, and so it is necessary to adapt the test accordingly; the basic approach is to compare the acts of the professional or skilled defendant with the approach of the reasonable practitioner of the particular profession or skill in question.[42]

The law required professionals to show such skill and judgement as their fellow professionals routinely demonstrated in contemporary practice. This temporal component was essential, because each generation finds its predecessor ignorant, and there is a steady rise in the standards of competence expected of professionals.

Well: to work properly, the law of negligence must be restricted to narrow technicalities. Nobody can ever have all the competence to deal with every imaginable scenario. Nor should it matter

whether architects or engineers wish to improve the environment or protect occupants from terrorists: the law has sought to discourage negligent acts or omissions that betray a wilful disregard for others, but has not previously encouraged the reasonable man to act for others. The matter was clarified just a few years before 9–11:

It is one thing for the law to say that a person who undertakes some activity shall take reasonable care not to cause damage to others. It is another thing for the law to require that a person who is doing nothing in particular shall take steps to prevent another from suffering harm from the acts of third parties . . . or natural causes.[43]

Architects used not to be held responsible for what others did. Yet, since the WTC attack, a growing consensus has it that buildings should not only protect the environment for future generations, but protect life and limb from suicide bombers. That is a tall order.

Forgotten in the new, ultra-precautionary stance is the fact that *terrorists are responsible for deaths through terrorism, not architects or engineers*. But architects and engineers must ask whether saving lives from a putative terrorist strike is really the criterion on which they want to be measured. Are business continuity and 'defence' really to become the highest form of architectural achievement?

While obsession with the extreme possibilities of fire, evacuation and security may make the individual consultant feel morally upright, it may be against the general interest of society. Since 9–11 the Precautionary Principle, pursued equally through self-regulation and the statutory kind, promises to distract designers still further from the task of industrialising architecture.

Cars are not safe against terrorism, but we do not demand that automotive designers make them so. However, as mass-produced products, cars have been engineered to higher and higher levels of safety. Only by mass-producing high-quality constructions can safer buildings be made without spiralling costs. Fire protection is a case in point here (see Box 34).

Fully volumetric prefabrication remains a distant prospect for skyscrapers. We have yet to see the production of whole floors: in high rise, prefabrication has only extended to the components and sub-assemblies of façade, raised floor and suspended ceiling construction, the services they contain, and to toilet pods, plant rooms, stairs and lifts. But if, in airships, German and British attempts to commercialise lifts and cranes also come to fruition, some skyscrapers may one day be built in totally different ways to those that are in use at present. Whole blocks of prefabricated flats just might be deliverable by air.

The alternative is a stark one. It is to reach new depths of human self-abasement rather than achievement: to pile more and more work into spurious protections for one-off buildings that will always have more imponderables about them than the mass-produced sort.

Cargo Lifter was an audacious German attempt to develop a 'go-anywhere-direct' system for delivering structures weighing up to 160 tonnes. After developing an astonishing hangar, and experimenting with a few smaller vehicles, the under-funded venture collapsed into insolvency. Nobody with the required capital has yet had the courage to invest in it

Box 35 PREFABRICATION IS THE BEST PROTECTION AGAINST FIRE

Diligent consultants already spend a lot of time on site conducting spot checks to ensure that smoke-seal-
ing, fire compartmentation and structural protection have been installed to the manufacturer's recommendations. It is most definitely not the architect's responsibility to supervise all works on site. Assuming
that design consultants have specified and detailed a consistently practical solution, the battle is often
against construction managers trying to change arrangements for the routing of services (heat, light, power,
IT, air and drainage), or against sloppy workmanship on the part of the different trades that work on site.

Officials charged with ensuring the safety of buildings face similar problems. Generally, they are only
able to check the active fire safety systems, smoke vents, and provision of fire doors. Afterward, the
prospect always remains that those who install services may destroy protections against fire out of either
unfamiliarity or contempt. After all, fit-out contractors vary from the expert to the cheapest tenderer on
the fastest programme.

Off-site fabrication is the way to make sure that buildings have the fabric and functionality to be safe from
fire. Naturally, some residual building management and maintenance issues will always remain; yet it is
flawed site practices that are to blame for most ordinary fire situations, and it is these that need addressing.

6.2 How construction can catch up

The crisis of backwardness in British con-
struction has reached such a pitch, even
New Labour ministers have noticed it.
Housing minister Keith Hill has observed:

When the rest of industry zealously minimises
processes to cut down costs and minimise the
risk of mistakes, it is curious that housebuilders
remain . . . welded to the technology of the
past.[44]

Yet for every rhetorical outburst, New
Labour makes new, highly practical but-
tresses to backwardness. It plans to force
homeowners to pay up to £1,000 to
provide buyers with information on their
property.[45] It may raise stamp duty on
the sale of homes, and has already raised
lease duties on business property.[46]

In a special December 2003 report to
Gordon Brown on how to boost housing
supply, Bank of England monetary policy
committee member Kate Barker favoured
a modest relaxation of Britain's planning
system.[47] Yet such tinkerings are not the
way to make construction catch up.
Below we present a six-point manifesto as
an alternative to New Labour paralysis.

6.2.1 Anticipate a new architectural division of labour

To take themselves and human achievement seriously, architects must face up to
some realities. Tough to encounter at first,
these realities are, if grasped in a tena-
cious style over a period of years, nevertheless likely to pay exhilarating rewards.
The most important reality to confront
first is *the vested interest that architecture
has in construction remaining backward.*

If construction was mechanised, relied
on decent supplier relationships and was
pursued with lightweight structures,
some architects might expect to be out of
work. The manufacture of buildings, the
integration of their services and the simplification of their ground works might
well mean that society needed, in aggregate, fewer architects. But might those
that remained not enjoy higher public
regard, if construction was finally to
catch up with other industries – and,
indeed, with the 21st century?

There is lots of work for architects to
do, but not every architectural student
can be Norman Foster. The architectural
profession in the UK has lost talent over
the boom and bust cycles for which the
construction industry used to be famous.

However, such a shake-out is not unique to architecture. What does seem unique to the profession is its inability to sustain new talent.

In architecture there are branded superstar architects, but no durable schools of innovators. And there is a lesson in this for architects. It is not a slower attrition of professional numbers that should bother them, so much as the need for innovation in building.

In a lengthy and unconscious rearguard action against innovation in general and prefabrication in particular, architects have retreated into a multitude of small practices. They are enormously reluctant to abandon their exalted, apparently timeless, role of seeing everything, whether stadium or hospital, through from initial concept design to practical completion. Each has been prepared for such a Renaissance role, after all, by two degrees over five years of British higher education.

Many small bespoke projects, done by knowing but actually rather parochial small studios, allow scores of would-be great artist-architects to enjoy themselves – even if they are rarely paid for resolving projects that go wrong, or for dealing with awkward clients. The architectural profession has thus become bloated with mediocrities. Many architects are neither great artistic generalists, nor usefully employable specialists.

It is, however, exactly a division of labour between generalist leaders and specialist integrators that will accompany the capitalisation of an off-site manufacturing industry in Britain. To achieve things, architects must be clear about which of two kinds of professionals they want to be:

Generalist leaders

A leader in architecture is not simply someone who has a developed design talent and the vocabulary of the science, technology, history, management, commerce, law and users that surround buildings. He or she is someone who is able to combine real technical knowledge and insight in these disciplines into a rational vision of progress. A leader gains the right to lead neither by trying to transform society through a bespoke building, nor by exhibiting emotional intelligence, but through a succession of real and ever more adept achievements on the ground. Some leaders may stick to bespoke buildings if they can secure the clients. Others will continue to do some vestigial work in that field, but will form much more ambitious collaborations with discerning building manufacturers. A few of this latter group will form an elite of building product designers.

Specialist integrators

An integrator in architecture is someone who, whether in bespoke or manufactured buildings, has a diligent, penetrating and sceptical drive to deepen and make more practical a particular field of expertise. A specialist may have the aspiration and potential to become a leader but these qualities are not required of a specialist. The qualities that are vital are a preparedness to work with colleagues as directed by a good leader, a determination to sharpen that endeavour through a personal responsibility for a narrow field of enquiry, and an ambition to be among the best of specialists in the science, technology, history, management, commerce, law or patterns of user behaviour that surround buildings. Some specialists will concentrate on bespoke buildings and others will become employees in manufacturing enterprises.

The common title of architect might differentiate between the required elite of generalist leaders and a body of specialist integrators. It would not matter if that difference were legally or institutionally formalised or not: architects already recognise it intuitively, when they distinguish the principals of an architectural studio from its employees. Much more important would be any trend, in tendering for architectural work, for mass prefabrication to mean that *architectural competence* trumped *personal and business contacts* as the chief criterion for winning a design job. Competition would be intensified, because better designers would be required.

It would, however, matter if the role of a specialist architect were not formally recognised as the equivalent to the architectural technologist or technician, engineer, surveyor or construction manager. Specialist integrators should square up as the equivalent to every construction professional now serving the bespoke building industry, together with all those new specialisms that will only cohere once architecture is manufactured. That will not preclude those who are more gifted than their peers being recognised for their greater potential; this is the case in any walk of life. Nor, if the volume of construction output can be raised enough, does our proposal necessarily preclude an overall expansion in the number of architects. What it does challenge is the continued delusion among architects that smallness guarantees only integrity, and not backwardness.

It is no good bemoaning the way architects have drifted from positions of influence with the client. Like other trades and professions, architects must outline clear ways of working that afford economies of scale. Bespoke landmark developments require substantial fees if the architectural visions behind them are to be realised. All other building types, however, are broadly susceptible to being systematised as mass-produced and, if necessary, branded products that are continually improved upon over time.

6.2.2 Assert independence from unbridled client power and partnership fudge

In arrogant style, architects delude themselves when they imagine that they are right, in the 21st century, to remain in the realm of bespoke buildings and backward practices. But in Chapter 3, in our concluding discussion of power in the building trade, we saw that the prevailing consensus in favour of more state regulation makes for circumstances in which the state-backed Good Adviser saves the Helpless Client not just from the Naughty Builder, but from the Wicked Consultant too. So when they are not persuading themselves that they, too, can be branded superstars, architects frequently grovel in the face of the market power that, in all their helplessness before the state, clients still wield. In the process, architects open themselves up to legal liabilities that are unprecedented.

Nobody likes contracts in construction contracting, and particularly not contractors. The only good thing about contracts is that they are supposed to allocate responsibilities clearly. Nevertheless the 'wishes' of clients, Sir Michael Latham insisted in 1994, 'must be paramount for all construction participants – subject only to planning and development control and the wider public interest'.[48]

For a decade or more, clients and also main contractors have come second only to the state in their domination of all other parties to a building project. But both clients and main contractors need to know that they cannot always get what they want. Of course any party to a contract tries to off-load responsibilities on to others. Yet architects seem particularly unable to *say no* to the demands made of them. Again and again, they agree to more legal liabilities for less design and lower fees.

Latham recommended that architects go 'signing off of the various stages of design when they have been achieved, but with sufficient flexibility to accommodate the commercial wishes of clients'. By that process 'the lead manager and/or design leader should then take responsibility for coordinating the work of all the consultants'.[49] It all sounds easy enough; but it is not the real world of specifying and coordinating trade contractors' drawings and test certificates in time to avoid design development becoming a sequence of crises, delays and *fait accomplis* on-site.

To ensure quality results, Latham's mysterious 'lead designer' – the architect – must assert independence from unbridled client power. In bespoke buildings, architects are under extreme commercial pressure to *say yes* when their professional conscience *screams no*. All design consultants face that dilemma, of course. But when the generalist leaders of tomorrow's architectural profession establish themselves and close ranks, will they be able to *say no* for good reasons – including aesthetic ones – and make it stick?

At the moment just the opposite situation holds: far from being independent, the 'lead designer' is liable for more and more faults. The construction industry has forgotten Latham's sensible point – that it should begin:

taking all reasonable steps to avoid changes to pre-planned works information. But, where variations do occur, they should be priced in advance, with provision for independent adjudication if agreement cannot be reached.[50]

Instead, clients have been encouraged to believe that they can ask for almost anything, at any time, and at no cost to them. And consultants of all kinds, not just architects, indulge them in this. Meanwhile main contractors, acting more and more just as paid managerial bureaucrats of the client, pass on down every outrageous request from on high. The result is that architects, surveyors and others, anxious to avoid the courts, work more unpaid hours and lay out more and more of their fees on professional indemnity insurance – for the avoidance of risk.

This is grovelling which cannot go on. At the same time, to try to dissolve 'adversarial relationships' in the building trade in the emollient fudge of 'partnership' is not the solution either. As *The Economist* asserted as early as 1995:

More and more companies are forming cosy partnerships with their suppliers. Such relationships can be risky . . . Trust is good. But for many companies, hostility may still be more profitable.[51]

Just as it is silly to believe that contracting is the problem with construction, so it is silly to believe that partnering is a new and trendy idea. Nobody can be against partnership, of course; but perhaps now is the time. In fact it was in 1964 that the Banwell report suggested that there was, in certain circumstances, scope for clients to award a contract to a contractor without competition if the contractor had turned in a particularly good performance on their behalf. Such serial contracting, or negotiation, Banwell felt especially suitable where the contractor could move on from a contract to its next stage, whether on an adjoining site or as a logical sequence to it.[52]

Partnering agreements, however, often represent commitments to high standards that are only rhetorical. In practice, this kind of collaborative working can serve to diffuse and thus confuse the reality of legal responsibilities.

Architecture does not need more branded prima donnas. But architects do need to assert their business, technological, political and legal independence from clients and main contractors. If that means the odd 'adversarial' moment, so be it. From clashes of professional viewpoint, there can come light. From subordination to client fiat and from the cloying embrace of partnership, there can come only darkness.

6.2.3 Radically reform Britain's planning system

The most shocking thing I find as a novice to politics is that 20 years under-investment doesn't mean 20 years but 30 years to rectify.[53]

These remarks, made by Richard Rogers late in 2002, speak volumes. In Chapter 4 we saw how, in Britain in the 1960s, no serious systems building revolution was ever really envisaged. It now appears that, in British building as much as on Britain's railways, no serious programme of remedial investment is in prospect. Rogers, chief policy adviser to Britain's Deputy Prime Minister, would rather not press him to get £22 billion out of the Treasury every year from now on, rather than just over 2004–6; he would rather not insist that expenditure go on new homes instead of bureaucracy. No. He would rather carp about the situation being 'shocking' – until, perhaps, he gets a telegram from the monarch.

After years of New Labour, the lengthy time horizon that Rogers sets for an urban renaissance ought to suggest that he and the government have pursued the wrong policy. Rogers complains that he has been sidelined. But it was always intended that he help the government blur and evade its immediate responsibility to confront the planning context in which British cities operate.

In Britain, cities have their elected local planning committee freedoms restricted by national guidelines that are set by elected central government ministers. Ministers must also decide what kind and scale of investment urban development deserves – just like health care, or education, or defence. But that is not how Lord Richard Rogers, Britain's unelected Chief Planner, sees it:

I don't think that ministers can possibly address the state of our streets, the crap paving, the dog shit, the appalling urban furniture, the ghastly road fatalities. They can only look at national policy, and cities don't respond to national policy . . . Cities have got to be given greater freedom, even to make mistakes.[54]

This libertarian, bottom-up, do-your-own-thing approach to planning sounds great. But, through the numerous recommendations of his Urban Task Force, Rogers himself hastened the centralisation of British planning policy. New Labour will not and does not want to let local councillors have the power to ignore planning guidance from the centre or their planning officers to be allowed to do a professional job. After all, they might think Rogers and Prescott wrong! Nor does government want to find the funds to overcome the backwardness of construction; and the private sector will not step in to reconstruct dilapidating cities any more than at the continuing level of make-do-and-mend.

Whatever Rogers may say, Britain has no plans for urban development in the 21st century. When he publishes his *State of the City* report in 2005, it will merely repeat the idea that our cities are still in a state, and that we are all to blame for not rallying to compact, high-density, mixed-use, socially cohesive and environmentally sustainable urban non-growth.

Yet in fact planning need not be like this. There are two radical reforms that are urgent.

Denationalise the right to develop land

Britain's planning system ensures that land must nearly always be protected, building must nearly always be bespoke, and that prefabrication is a non-starter. But before 1947, those who owned land had the freedom to design and build on it, subject only to bye-laws imposed by elected local authorities, legal covenants on freehold, or agreements – of any kind – negotiated between individuals.

It is time to bring Clement Attlee's experiment in nationalised development rights to an end. Of course, Britain has national standards of *Building Control*. This is a system made statutory and developed since 1965, requiring local authority approval of building designs, backed with inspection of works on-site to basic structural and technical standards. These standards – improved through periodic revisions as construction develops or public policy changes – should be retained and advanced, but rescued from their naturalistic perspective about energy use and climate change.

For the rest, however, the right to develop land should be immediately returned to those who own freehold. The possibility that such a free-for-all might create some aesthetic monstrosities is a small risk to take for ending half a century of planning paralysis, with a capacity for monstrosities all its own. Freehold should only be subject to meeting the socially-minded technicalities of the Building Control approval system – so that buildings do not fall down, allow fires to spread, or have walls that the neighbours can hear through. Otherwise, within that social context, a freehold should be what it says it is: the freedom to hold land and develop it.

Extend the Type Approvals approach from Building Control

If an architect regularly uses a particular design, building system or construction feature, it can be checked for compliance with Building Control. Type Approvals can be for:

- house types;
- building systems;
- standard garages;
- standard specifications;
- standard details;
- foundations;
- building elements; and
- individual flat layouts and common stacking arrangements in blocks of flats – even though the elevations need not be pre-determined.

Once agreed, the resulting Type Approval is accepted by local authorities throughout England and Wales, and by Britain's National House Building Council. Result: a significant saving of time and money, because less information is required with any subsequent site applications made.

Already, throughout England and Wales, the Local Authority National Type Approval Confederation offers fast-track Approvals for both public and private sector *building systems* and *building types*.[55] It is entirely possible, given the political will, to extend something like LANTAC from *building control* to *planning*. After full public debate, *different types of architecture – at first bespoke, but soon manufactured* – could be given Type Approvals as an executive planning license to consultants, contractors, developers and whole building manufacturers, so that landowners would be unimpeded by the need to have further planning permission or public consultation.

That would immediately allow off-site manufacturing for stock, rather than to order. It would enable manufacturers to plan their production and improve their productivity subject only to being able to secure market share for their product. It would mean off-the-shelf homes for anyone with the land on which to site them. It would make history.

The extension of Type Approvals may be a more preferable reform than the denationalisation of the right to develop land. With it, planning specialists would retain a degree of aesthetic control, whether they were locally or regionally based. The Type Approvals could also be geographically specific, to allow for regional preferences and habits.

But by adopting either approach, Britain's housing shortage could be solved in years, not decades.

Returning development rights or granting Type Approvals would each spur the development of manufactured homes. Customers for these would be free of the delays and uncertainties of planning, as well as of the compromises that come out of consultation. Our proposals would start to cut through the volume of planning applications processed each year, and free planning officers and committees to think more strategically.

Everyone knows that planners are struggling. The Office for National Statistics and the DTI publish a *Construction Statistics Annual*, which gives a good indication of the inertia in the development control or planning system.[56] In the 2002 edition, Table 11.2, *Planning Decisions by District Planning Authorities by Speed of Decision, Region and Type of Authority*, shows that:

- about half a million planning applications for bespoke designs, large and small, are lodged each year;
- more than 85 per cent are approved;
- about two thirds are approved within eight weeks; and
- more than 10 per cent drag on beyond 13 weeks.

Britain's planning labyrinth is vast. Much of the work within it consists of rubber-stamping uncontentious and uncontested proposals, but a third of cases are considered controversial, and become protracted. Worse still, in the statistics *Annual*, Table 11.3, *Planning Decisions by District Planning Authorities by Speed of Decision and Type and Size of Development*, shows that it is major housing developments which take the longest time to be processed through consultation and controversy. Less than a fifth of all major schemes get through within eight weeks.

Housing needs planning reforms. The approaches of returning development rights and granting Type Approvals work for both urban and rural land. Of course, planning exclusions – of countryside, prime farmland or historic centres – could still be argued through. But by making either of these two reforms and sticking to them, Britain could bring its construction industry out of backwardness.

6.2.4 Dismiss opponents of prefabrication as utopians

Better to look at the pattern books of identical terraces that successfully created our cities in the 19th century and rethink them for the 21st century, than to pursue the architectural utopia where every building looks different but in its high cost and inflexibility turns out to be exactly the same.[57]

Alex Lifschutz, a sociologist, psychologist and a man who trained at the Architectural Association, has ably hit back at the cynics. As our discussion of technological possibilities in Chapter 5 confirms, it is the defenders of the status quo who are the utopians, in imagining that Victorian methods of specifying, pricing and building bespoke architecture, along with chronic housing shortages, can and should persist right into the 21st century. The one thing that should be reinvented from the Victorian and Georgian eras is the pattern-book of house plans. Equally, other repetitive building types could be systematised as a catalogue.

In June 1998, a British adult on average earnings had to work for more than 30

weeks to be able to afford an average car. By October 2002, the time needed to accumulate the funds necessary had fallen to 21 weeks.[58] What is more, the quality and functionality of cars – cars that are still made in Britain, as well as in Eastern Europe and the Far East – keeps on improving. What is utopian, then, is the view that architects can simply ignore all this progress in the real world and instead continue sticking their colours, and their egos, to the backwardness of bespoke buildings.

As we have remarked, most of Britain's tiny proportion of prefabricated houses is destined for 'social' housing. But off-site fabrication needs to leave the safety and the limitations of the social housing sector. It may adopt the heavyweight, concrete-based approach promoted by John Miles,[59] or the lightweight housing modules preferred by John Prewer.[60] But whatever shape its products take, prefabrication will have to deliver housing as a consumer good, in various forms, for any condition of site. Cheap at its price, spacious and packed with energy systems and IT, such housing will be upgraded through the kind of after-sales service we expect from car manufacturers.

It will be the same with corporate buildings. In the future, clients for these, it has been remarked:

will not want to select the type of ducting or window locks. They will tell their contractors that they want to accommodate 500 high tech workers and pay £X for the building. The rest is left to the contractor and the army of specialists and product suppliers. This requires the construction industry to marshal teams of companies to solve the problem.[61]

At the seminar on the *Prefabulous Home*, however, the architect Simon Allford, of Allford Hall Monaghan and Morris, made a very fair point about too narrow an advocacy of prefabrication. The danger, he argued, is that 'thinking about the making takes over from the quality of the product'.[62] Yet if we change the way we make housing, we can *also* improve its quality.

It is possible and necessary, not utopian, to change both process and, with it, the product. What needs to be done is as follows:

1 Use a preliminary unit as a design tool, for training, and as a control sample.
2 Raise customer expectations about landscaping and urban design.
3 Push the performance and functionality of units to extremes unbeatable on site.
4 Simplify foundations and utilities conduits so as to achieve fit-first-time accuracy.
5 Make all building services accessible and upgradeable over the life of the structure.
6 Minimise the interfaces between components but maximise choice in ranges available.
7 Maximise the use of IT in the cyclical process of product and service improvement.
8 Design out maintenance and reduce running costs.
9 Avoid scaffolding and site based construction by pre-finishing as far as possible.
10 Reduce circulation space by careful planning of the volumes and how they stack.

11 Build modules as long, wide and high as simple road delivery and craneage allow.
12 Anticipate damage and the need for periodic refitting and refurbishment.
13 Offer supporting customer services, including financing, furnishing and upgrades.

Heavy concrete modules

Light steel modules

In *Homing in on Excellence*, John Miles says that we need factories:

designed to meet the twin (and sometimes conflicting) demands of "lean" and "agile" production, with systems that are carefully balanced to deliver the following characteristics:

- Flexibility of product (allowing different house types to be delivered against unpredictable demand)
- Elasticity of production (allowing the plant to cope with the peaks and troughs of demand)
- Low capital cost (recognising that even the entire national demand at 180,000 units a year is a small volume over which to amortise the investment).

Only the simultaneous achievement of these three goals will allow cost-effective products to flow into the market place and become widely accepted by the housebuilders. This is a very significant challenge for production engineers and factory process designers. Very few manufacturing systems currently boast the simultaneous achievement of these objectives and a successful outcome cannot be guaranteed.[63]

But as Miles himself points out, in housing, new products will not appear without high capital investment. Still:

- 'flexibility of product' – customisation – need not be a Holy Grail if space standards and servicing, high functionality and great design allow for considerable standardisation;
- elasticity of production would be little needed if Britain's inane planning system was reformed to one of Type Approvals, assuming freehold is unlikely to be reinvigorated; and
- to replace the UK's ageing housing stock and reverse long-term undersupply, the annual target need only exceed the peak of house production in 1968 – when new completions in Britain reached *413,700*.

From this point, the mathematics of British housing is not difficult to summarise:

1 The 4 million additional households that are expected in the two decades to 2021 require 200,000 new homes to be built each year.
2 Assuming homes can be designed and built to last an average of 100 years, the 28 million households that Britain will have in 2021 will require 280,000 homes a year to replace the stock on a 100 year cycle.
3 Therefore *Britain needs 480,000, 100-year-homes a year now*, each year, even before catching up with year-on-year accumulation of historically low levels of building replacement that has resulted in an ageing stock reliant on extended refurbishment.
4 Yet, since 1990, the annual output of new homes in the UK has failed to reach 200,000, and today has fallen *below 160,000*.

There is a massive backlog of housing that needs replacing, and the low level of replacement means that new houses will have to last more than 100 years, when they should be designed and built to be replaced with better quality development at 50, or even 25 years.

The key to raising the quality of construction is a greater quantity of development that is intended to be rendered technically or socially obsolete at a faster pace. But that will take investment in production. As Latham said of the backwardness of British construction in 1994:

it is too easy to set up in business as a general contractor. No qualifications are required, no experience and virtually no capital. While market forces ultimately remove incompetent firms by depriving them of work, the existence of such unskilled producers is a threat to responsible firms, bad for consumers and highly damaging to the wider reputation of the industry.[60]

In a new millennium, the only way the better firms are ever going to escape the gravitational commercial pull of the incompetent is to capitalise their production methods. They need to secure market share out of the reach of those

The patching up and extending of Georgian, Victorian, and 20th century housing cannot go on indefinitely; but at the current rate of housing stock replacement it will have to. The low rate of replacement is surely why DIY has become such a widespread and almost desperate obsession in the UK. It is also why the construction industry is based on so many small businesses, not all of which are incompetent

who can invest in shovels, but not factories. Training will come as standard when production has been highly capitalised. Regulation, where it is needed at all, can be managed in-house, with minimal independent certification. The changed business model for off-site construction should allow it to escape scores of arbitrators, adjudicators, mediators and construction lawyers.

What critics of prefabrication miss is that, in Britain, as in most of the Western world, the money is around for the capitalisation of construction. What is lacking is the cultural and political will.

Detractors also miss the benefits that mass-produced housing could provide once it is installed:

- Stacking systems could allow any volumetric unit of housing to be changed for upgrading at any time.
- Fixtures, fittings and finishes should be much easier to upgrade – and so,

The man who played with blocks

importantly, should utilities. Most of Britain's housing stock was built for fossil fuels and the National Grid. Where successive occupants have not expensively refurbished it at great expense, such site-built stock is now obsolete. There are now many more technological options for building services today, and there is much more technology to service.

- Just as a manufactured building can be taken back if the customer defaults, the customer for mass-produced housing should be able to stop paying for it if it is faulty. Manufactured architecture will have to be complete in every regard and without patent defects. If latent defects do materialise after an extensive R&D effort has been invested, products should be called in.

In the face of these benefits, it is just utopian to carry on in the old way.

For John Prescott matters stand differently. For him one merit of prefabrication is that it assures tied microflats for key workers – 'I want key-worker housing but I'm not convinced we're doing it fast enough yet', he told *Housing Today*.[65] The other merit is cheapness. About 'prefabs', he told a Commons Select Committee:

They lasted an awful long time. At the end of the day, I think offsite manufacturing gives you a better chance of building some better design more efficiently and more effectively and that is why we have set up this £150 million in the Challenge Fund to the Housing Corporation to have something like 25 per cent of it done by these new types of production and I think design does allow you . . . I think John Egan made it absolutely clear in this report which we commissioned him to do on construction. It is like a car. You get the basic design of the house; it is basically the same for most of them. However, you can do a number of feature changes to the outside to meet these design requirements and that is what CABE is giving us advice about.[66]

The Prescott case for prefabrication is vulgar and philistine. For prefabrication could bring better houses, to all kinds of workers – and it would not just be the outsides of these houses that would be capable of a number of feature changes.

6.2.5 Uphold Ford Dagenham, or something like it, to end the UK's housing shortage

Stretching from London's Tower Bridge to Thurrock and Dartford, beyond to Southend-on-Sea, and South of the river into Kent, the Thames Gateway is the biggest development challenge facing Britain, as well as Europe's largest and most ambitious regeneration effort.[67] It will be the testing ground for the plan to create New Labour's sustainable communities. The Thames Gateway will be the measure of the popularity and affordability of new housing. Yet Prescott only talks of 200,000 homes being built in the vast Gateway area, when it could be a city the size of Tokyo.

No funding was officially discussed, except for the millions to set up the administrative architecture of development agencies and consortia. Nor has any funding for infrastructure, and especially transport infrastructure, been announced, even though battle has been joined on the subject.[68] Yet the world needs an unprecedented architectural, engineering and infrastructural achievement east of London just as much as it needs all of these things in lower Manhattan.

Within the Thames Gateway, the London Development Agency is charged with facilitating the vision for an eastward expansion of London as a city where design matters. One component of that initiative is to encourage the prefabrication of 21st century housing. This is necessary to meet changing demography and aspirational needs in London and the South East.

However, as we discussed in Chapter 4, Britain has seen prefabs and system building before and rejected that kind of housing for suburban forms of development. If design is to matter in the Thames Gateway, prefabrication must deliver an urbanism that people will prefer over patterns of development from the past. Housing must be designed for prefabrication so as to be:

- larger – in floor area and ceiling height;
- better – in manufacture and servicing;
- sharper – in design and finish;
- cheaper – in volume and method of production;
- faster – in approval and delivery;
- smarter – in IT and flexibility; and
- easier – in operation and maintenance.

If, using inappropriate technology, prefabricated housing in the Thames Gateway becomes *microflats for families*, it will certainly be unpopular. It will be even more unpopular if it is unsophisticated, in need of subsidy, made in volumes that are too low, fraught with planning problems, badly serviced, or a maintenance burden.

The economies of scale that are possible through the Thames Gateway are the key to manufacturing much of the future of Britain's housing. That future must be one of homes as spacious, well-made, affordable, available, functional and convenient industrial products – products that can be chosen from a range of designs that are approved in open competition and consultation. Thames Gateway housing should not be built on site, at a time of labour shortages and rising land prices, at insufficient quantities and to a low level of quality.

People will demand more – and rightly so. But it is possible to deliver more, given the will. At the heart of the Thames Gateway is Ford of Dagenham (see Box 36). The continuing history of Ford is lesson enough for would-be manufacturers of prefabricated housing. But Ford also knows quite well, perhaps, that prefabricated housing was the missed opportunity of the 20th century. In 1991, the Henry Ford Museum, Dearborn, Michigan, bought the parts to the only surviving prototype of Buckminster Fuller's 1945 Dymaxion House. After research and the restoration of its 3000 components, the Museum opened the Dymaxion House to the public in 2001.[69]

The significance of Ford's effort to bring the Dymaxion House back to life is that the House was Fuller's solution to the need for mass-produced, affordable, easily transportable and environmentally efficient homes. The name came from three of his favourite words: *dynamic*, *maximum* and *tension*. The House, which was meant to sell at about the price of a Cadillac, used tension suspension from a central column or mast, and could be shipped worldwide in its own metal tube. Toward the end of the Second World War, Fuller persuaded Beech Aircraft, a plane maker in Wichita, Kansas, to work with him to take it to market. Then, as Martin Pawley shows in *Buckminster Fuller: How much does the building weigh?*, Fuller eventually seemed to lose his

nerve. He refused to go into production, missing the opportunity to improve his design over time.

The Dymaxion House was a single house type for low-density housing; but while the semi-rural fringes of the Thames Gateway may offer sites for homes of this type, it is higher density urbanism that must predominate. Nevertheless, *the coincidence of massive UK demand for housing, the Thames Gateway project, Dagenham's historic role in world manufacturing and Ford's interest in the Dymaxion House raises the prospect of an historic technological advance: high-density but spacious housing, built in lean production factories for sale as stock and aided by a Type Approval system as a new, tough but accessible kind of planning approval.*

The factories might be centred on Ford land at Dagenham, once the industrial and transport infrastructure there had been readied for renewed productive activity. A pipe dream? It is a concept that the London Development Agency has begun to discuss with the Ford Motor Company.

After its opening in May 1929, Ford's South Dagenham changed both manufacturing and development planning in Britain irrevocably. Now it has the chance to do the same again. Today Ford, or a company like it, is faced with one of the greatest opportunities in British architectural history: to return to Dagenham, not to make cars, but to mass-produce Thames Gateway architecture – both for stand-alone, low-density sites, and for stacking at high densities.

More than 80 hectares of development land have become available in Dagenham as a result of the drastic restructurings that Ford has had to make.[71] There are plans to use this Thames Gateway land as merely another brownfield site on which to build series of bespoke, sustainable housing estates, like BedZed in Wallington, Sutton or the Greenwich Millennium Village. But why not use it to manufacture volumetric housing – not only for the entire Thames Gateway but also for transport by road, rail or sea to any market where orders can be lined up?

That would put a lot of builders and consultants, developers and agents out of business; but it would transform construction. It would turn clients into customers, designers into generalist leaders and specialist integrators, and tradesmen into factory workers. Though there would be redundancies in such a consolidation, the best of those who did not want to leave site-based building would still find jobs in the continuing market for bespoke landmark developments. And until Britain boasted several Dagenhams

Box 36 DAGENHAM: RISE AND FALL

Planned as a near self-contained manufacturing facility, Dagenham had its own power station, foundry, gas plants, coke ovens and blast furnace. It was the largest private wharf on the Thames, and had Europe's largest unloading cranes. From docking ships, Dagenham grabbed coal for its ovens and iron ore and limestone for its furnace. Nor did the cars that rolled out of its other end just move directly on to Britain's railways and its developing network of roads. In the 1930s, 1950s and 1960s, Dagenham's output gave large parts of the middle classes and the skilled working class the wherewithal to move to suburban living space.

Dagenham showed lean thinking long before the phrase was invented. Nothing was wasted. Burning London rubbish, the power station generated enough electricity to satisfy a town of 180,000 inhabitants. The foundry provided all the iron needed to make castings, while the rolling mills streamed steel bars and steel-strip in every 8-hour shift. Gases produced in the process of turning coal into coke were stored in a special gas-holder and converted in a separate plant devoted to by-products. The slag from the furnace was converted into tarmacadam to surface new roads. Outside customers bought the electricity, pig-iron, coke, and gas that were surplus to the factory's needs.

Over the years, significant improvements were made to manufacturing at Dagenham. Consequently employment fell from 40,000 in 1963 to just 8000 in 1996, when the site assembled its 20 millionth vehicle. By February 2000, Ford had to axe 1500 jobs, and daily output fell from 1200 to 560 units. In May that same year, the company announced that car production would move to Cologne in 2002 and that Dagenham's paint, trim and assembly plant would close with the loss of 1900 jobs. In place of the vehicle assembly plant, the company plans a diesel engine complex.[70]

The old foundry site is now a heritage centre – an ignominious fate. Dagenham deserves better than this.

BedZed, a zero-emissions living and working development designed by Bill Dunster. The brightly-coloured ventilation cowls and sedum-covered roofs make for great publicity images. The real building materials, however, were scavenged from local demolition sites. Here back-to-back housing is boosted as something to celebrate

making other architectural product ranges, there would be a healthy amount of site-based work around to ease the transition for construction industry professionals and tradesmen. Indeed, the current stock of British buildings will need considerable repair and maintenance before it is completely written off.

Manufacturers will need to consolidate a market for their increased and repetitive architectural output. They will need to beat any competition. And they will need to put both professional practitioners and site-based contractors out of business on a considerable scale. Such seismic shifts in employment have happened in other sectors before now; even in construction, the knowledge base and subdisciplines of the industry have gone through many changes.

It is time to face up to the further changes that are necessary. To delay mechanising construction would be to make a mistake for which future generations would not thank us. And when prefabricated homes are eventually built as a routine matter, at rapid rates of building stock replacement, future generations will want macroflats, not microflats, and macro-houses with gardens everywhere.

There is every reason to make the backwardness of the construction industry just a passing phase.

6.3 Conclusion

'Housebuilding techniques', Sir Stuart Lipton told the world in August 2003, 'have not changed much since Roman

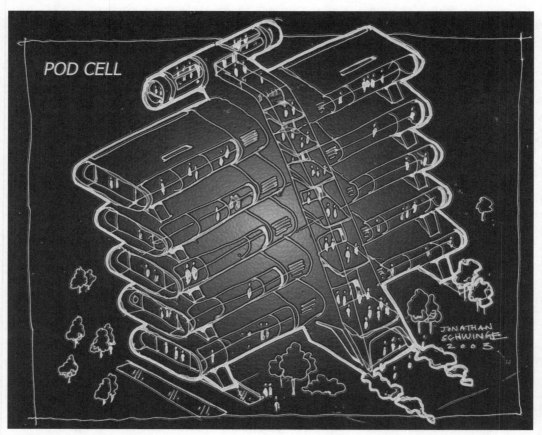

'Pod Cell', by Jonathan Schwinge

times'.[72] This book has tried to explain why, and what can be done about the broader backwardness of the construction industry.

In Britain, America and elsewhere, housing, workplaces, government buildings and samey cultural destinations have joined the financial sector as the subject of society's investments and its attention. Behind this trend of the past two decades lies a broader atrophy of capitalism. Innovation has, since the 1970s in the US, turned out to be an uphill struggle. By contrast construction and finance, and especially housing finance, have so far proved an easier path.

Construction, like capitalism, is not in its essence about money, speculation, corruption, the annexation of land or the plunder of the earth. What construction shares with the rest of capitalism is a great difficulty in introducing fundamental innovations. Nor is this merely an economic matter. Capital can still bring us progressive advances, such as the Internet; but, *to skirt round risk,* it has downplayed not only construction and manufacturing but also, since 2001, the stock market itself. Corporations are not what they were. Born of a lengthy slowdown in its productive parts, capital's general liquidity has shifted out of many shares and pensions and into houses. In a risk-averse climate, houses appear the safer bet – the more secure refuge.

Governments have favoured the emergence of housing as one of the central financial instruments of our times. In Britain and America they have allowed interest rates to fall. Through housing, governments have seen the whole apparatus of consumer credit massively expanded, and a social 'feelgood factor' also expanded.

In Britain, too, New Labour has used a 50-year-old planning system to restrict housing supply. To avoid building new houses, and instead buy old ones in order to let them out, can hardly be described as speculation any more.

Some of the backwardness of construction in Britain reflects British traits. The low productivity and supercillious class attitudes of the UK building trade, and the sermons aimed at countering these; the hypocrisy about immigrant building workers; the romanticisation of the countryside; the shop, town, museum and stage as emblematic of civility, not class struggle; obviously, the home as castle – all these things have a strongly British flavour. But the overall backwardness and atomisation of the construction sector is a global phenomenon. More important, the predilection for architectural objects, rather than great ideas and social movements, now characterises the whole of the West.

We live in an era defined by what the American critic Russell Jacoby has called *The end of utopia.*[73] Widely-held visions of the future, whether right-wing or left-wing, have lost adherents. In the place of these visions have come individual attempts to create unique personal identities and narratives. So when they search for the ideal architectural home, people don't just seek an economic refuge. Nor do they just seek a physical haven from the outside world, and, indeed from Al Qaeda. In addition to these things, *people all over the West look to houses to help them recover a sense of who they are.* They see, in houses, a means to end some of the insecurity and vulnerability that the past 20 years of capitalism have done so much to encourage.

On the television shows dedicated to makeovers of residential interiors, the congratulations are commoditised thus: 'Fantastic! You have really created a space that reflects your personality'. With this approach, born of anxiety, it is not surprising that today's as-seen-on-TV DIY and interior design solutions tend to be tentative, twee or conservative. For when people are allowed simply to express simply what risks and fears they would like architecture quickly to deal with, and when they are not led carefully to innovations they might in the future desire, the results will always be modest.

It could be argued that, since there is only one Earth, architecture and construction are forever set to be a suppliers', rather than a buyers', market. In this framework, much of the blame for the backwardness of construction can be laid at the door of bull-necked builders, know-all surveyors and arrogant architects. Yet as we have just seen, the dynamics of the housing market are not just a narrow question of supply and demand. Whether people in construction are rapacious, avaricious, self-centred, effete or just obsessed with getting photographs of their buildings into glossy magazines, none of these descriptions explains why construction is backward.

An alternative explanation for backwardness, and in particular the site-based nature of 21st century building work, is that the world's sites themselves are all different and, therefore, will always be peculiarly intractable. But everything about the world's sites is known, or can be known. Satellites and IT, climatology, geology and many other sciences allow human beings to master space, divide it in grids, build upon it with stilts. The mastery is by no means complete; but it is, despite all the backwardness of construction, increasing.

Like bits of stone, every site is different. But in the same way that humans have for centuries worked with stone, we can – within certain limits – fashion the world's differentiated sites the way we want to. And we should still be able to take delight in the ensuing combinations of nature and artifice.

To harp on the variegated range of the world's sites is to reveal a basic unwillingness ambitiously to grapple with the conditions that surround us. 'Every site is diferent' is often only the preface to the unquestioning adoption of a vernacular style – one that looks not toward a transformed future, but rather a preserved past of local, regional or 'national' character.

Neither universal client power, then, nor the idiosyncratic powers of space really stand up as explanations for the backwardness of building. Yet if the Victorian promise of houses as kits of parts has not been realised, that is not because such kits are technically a bad idea. Across Britain, swathes of land wait to be developed on an industrial basis. Once dilapidated Victorian terraced streets are demolished, large modular homes could be slotted in over their standard plot-widths and depths. The same could be done with the standard semi-detached and detached plots that characterise the building stock of 1930s suburbs. With a bit of typological thought, and some rudimentary preparing of foundations and services to take the delivery of new superstructures, Britain's decrepit accommodation could be replaced with a series of type-approved products based on the legacy of previous periods of development. Meanwhile, completely novel house typologies could be developed for sites that are already cleared, or on redundant farmland.

The backwardness of building does not follow from intrinsic defects with the kit-of-parts approach. The problem lies rather with the state. So long as the right to develop land is not denationalised, and so long as the masses are not allowed to exercise freehold, kit manufacturers will be condemned to go, cap in hand, to the planner, to win approval for the sensitivity they have showed toward the sites they want to build on.

The denationalisation of development rights, the emergence of a new architectural division of labour and the drawing of clear lines of demarcation between architects and the people with whom they do business – these things, like the falling of the Berlin Wall, form an abrasive destruction of the old order in architecture. There will be many scrapes if our agenda for audacity is adopted; but it represents a better shot than carrying on with the old backward methods.

It is ironic that New Labour, its tame environmentalists and the anti-capitalists should still see state bodies and quangos as the best arbiters of construction and urban development. After all, government buildings, which New Labour hopes will set an example to us all in their therapeutic and naturalistic virtue, are better renowned for their poor planning. Scotland's parliament building in Edinburgh, costed at £40 million before the 1997 referendum on devolution, will cost £400 million by the time of its fit-out in May 2004. The New Home Office headquarters, designed by Sir Terry Farrell on the site of London's old Department of the Environment HQ, will be ready in 2004 at a cost of £311 million. It is designed for 3450 staff; but Gordon Brown's programme of recruitment to the public sector has already ensured that its capacity will not be adequate.[74]

New Labour refuses to learn anything new. On 30 July 2003, Tony Blair and John Prescott launched the first of a series of updates on their plan for creating sustainable communities. They introduced two new Urban Development Corporations (UDCs) for Thurrock and East London, as well as a London Thames Gateway Partnership Board to 'develop Thames Gateway delivery and investment strategies in London'. In inimitable prose and punctuation, their update continued:

Board members have been drawn from the London Development Agency, Transport for London, Local Authorities, Housing Corporation, English Partnerships, the London UDC Chair (when appointed) the private sector and Lord Rogers. Meetings will take place around six times a year, the first of which took place in July.[75]

At Thames Gateway, then, the usual suspects remain in charge. With their Holy Trinity of measurement, the therapeutic perspective and the naturalistic perspective, they will arrange for lowlier types to install, on brownfield sites, through teamwork and with the help of a non-adversarial manner, long-life microflats for London's key workers. New Gateway office buildings will be entered for innumerable competitions as fantastic places to work. Some kind of 'Dagenham Experience', a memorial to the tragic lives of Ford Dagenham workers, may also be built as part of Gateway's cultural strategy.

It is neither utopian nor illiberal to resist the dead hand of the state when it retards construction. Demand for construction makes a new course necessary; new technologies make such a course possible. It is a time to strike out, not for a few penny-pinching microflats, but for the mass prefabrication of macroflats. It is a time for homes with gardens in the countryside and for a whole new generation of skyscrapers.

To break from past traditions in architecture will be tough. But nothing less must be done if torpor is ever to be ended and progress finally begun.

NOTES

1 Hal Foster, 'In New York', *London Review of Books*, 20 March 2003, p 17.
2 Daniel Libeskind, quoted in Hal Foster, 'In New York', *London Review of Books*, 20 March 2003, p 17.
3 Richard Patterson, 'The Tragic in Architecture', *Architectural Design*, Vol 70, No 5, Wiley-Academy, October 2000.
4 www.lowermanhattan.info/rebuild/plans/studio_daniel_libeskind.asp
5 Daniel Goleman, *Emotional Intelligence*, first published 1995 (London, Bloomsbury, 1996).
6 Warren G Bennis and Robert J Thomas, *Geeks and Geezers: How era, values and defining moments shape leaders* (Boston, Harvard Business School Press, 2002).
7 Richard Boyatzis, Annie McKee and Daniel Goleman, *The New Leaders: Transforming the art of leadership into the science of results* (New York, Little Brown, 2002) p IX, 250.
8 Carlos Losada, quoted in Della Bradshaw, 'Softer skills move to the centre', *Financial Times*, 16 December 2002.
9 Richard Boyatzis, Annie McKee and Daniel Goleman, 'Reawakening your passion for work', *Harvard Business Review*, April 2002, p 90 to 91.
10 Gerald Matthews, Moshe Zeidner, Richard D Roberts, *Emotional Intelligence: Science and Myth* (Boston, The MIT Press, 2003).
11 Deyan Sudjic, 'Towering ambition', *The Observer*, 2 March 2003, p 27.
12 Lower Manhattan Development Corporation, *Request for Qualifications – Innovative Designs for the World Trade Center Site*, LMDC, 19 August 2002, p 5, and posted on www.renewnyc.com

13   Ben Macintyre, 'Out of the inferno, a towering symbol of New York', *The Times*, 1 March 2003, p 28.

14   Will Alsop, quoted in 'The aftermath', *Building*, 21 September 2001, p 14.

15   'Assault on America: the Story', *Financial Times*, 15 September 2001.

16   Adrian Barrick, Leader, 'Everything's different now', *Building*, 21 September 2001, p 3.

17   Edward Robbins, 'After the Cataclysm', *The Architectural Review*, November 2002, p 21.

18   James Sanders, 'Thinking Big in New York – Seeking a Grand Vision of Public Works', *The New York Times*, 3 September 2002, and posted on www.nytimes.com

19   'To Rebuild or Not: Architects Respond', *The New York Times*, 23 September 2001.

20   James Sanders, 'Thinking Big in New York – Seeking a Grand Vision of Public Works', *The New York Times*, 3 September 2002, and posted on www.nytimes.com

21   Robert A Caro, *The Power Broker: Robert Moses and the Fall of New York* (New York, Random House, 1975).

22   Swiss Re, 'Natural catastrophes and man-made disasters in 2001: man-made losses take on a new dimension', *Sigma*, No 1, 2002, p 17, quoted in Frank Furedi, *Refusing to be Terrorised: Managing risk after September 11th* (Global Futures, 2002), available as a pdf on www.futureproof.org

23   Vicky Richardson, *New Vernacular Architecture* (London, Laurence King, 2001) p 16.

24   Ziauddin Sardar and Merryl Wyn Davies, *Why Do People Hate America?* (Cambridge, Icon Books, 2002) p 104 to 105.

25   Chris Rand, editorial, *engineering talk*, 5 September 2002, and posted on www.engineeringtalk.com

26   Ziauddin Sardar and Merryl Wyn Davies, *Why Do People Hate America?* (Cambridge, Icon Books, 2002) p 142.

27   Ray Anderson, quoted on the cover of *Interface – A journey into sustainability* (Interface, 2002) and posted on www.interfacesustainability.com

28   Kenan Malik, 'All Cultures are not Equal', spiked, 28 May 2002, and posted on www.spiked-online.com

29   John Gearson, 'Superterrorism: Policy Responses', a special issue of *The Political Quarterly*, Blackwell Publishing, 2002, p 8.

30   Quoted in Robert Winnett, 'Foster plans "tower towns" housing 55,000', *The Sunday Times*, 25 May 2003, p6.

31   Edwin Heathcote, 'The only way is up', *Weekend FT*, 25 January 2003, p VI.

32   www.londonbridgetower.com

33   Federal Emergency Management Agency, *World Trade Center Building Performance Study – Data Collection, preliminary Observations, and Recommendations* (New York, FEMA, 2002) p 2.

34   Federal Emergency Management Agency, *World Trade Center Building Performance Study – Data Collection, preliminary Observations, and Recommendations* (New York, FEMA, 2002) p 2.

35   Federal Emergency Management Agency, *World Trade Center Building Performance Study – Data Collection, preliminary Observations, and Recommendations* (New York, FEMA, 2002) p 3.

36   International Working Group of the Institute of Structural Engineers, *Safety in Tall Buildings and Other Buildings with Large Occupancy* (London, Institute of Structural Engineers, 2002) p 13.

37   Federal Emergency Management Agency, *World Trade Center Building Performance Study – Data Collection, preliminary Observations, and Recommendations* (New York, FEMA, 2002) p 3.

38   International Working Group of the Institute of Structural Engineers, *Safety in Tall Buildings and Other Buildings with Large Occupancy* (London, Institute of Structural Engineers, 2002) p 11.

39   Headline, 'Ministers reject 9–11 safety review', *Building Design*, 8 November 2002, p 1.

40   Lord Bowen, *McQuire v Western Morning News Co* (1903) 2 KB 100.

41   Justice McNair, *Bolam v. Friern Hospital Management Committee* (1957) 1 WLR 582 at 586.

42   Jon Holyoak, *Negligence in Building Law: Cases and Commentary* (Oxford, Blackwell Scientific Publications, 1992) p 36.

43   Lord Hoffman, *Stovin v. Wise* (1996) A.C. 923.

44   Quoted in Roger Blitz, 'Builders have "held back" use of modern technology', *Financial Times*, 9 October 2003, p 2.

45   Patrick Barkham and Melissa Kite, 'Ministers insist on home sale packs', *The Times*, 11 November 2003, p 7.

46   Susanna Voyle, 'Companies face large rise in stamp duty bills', *Financial Times*, 15 November 2003, p 4.

47   Kate Barker, *Review of Housing Supply – Securing Our Future Housing Needs: Interim*

Report Analysis, HM Treasury, 10 December 2003 and posted on www.hm-treasury. gov.uk/consultations–and–legislations/bark er/consult_barker_index.cfm#interim

48 Constructing the Team: Joint review of pro-curement and contractual arrangements in the United Kingdom construction industry, Final Report (London, HMSO, 1994) p 19.

49 Constructing the Team: Joint review of pro-curement and contractual arrangements in the United Kingdom construction industry, Final Report (London, HMSO, 1994) p 23 to 24.

50 Constructing the Team: Joint review of pro-curement and contractual arrangements in the United Kingdom construction industry, Final Report (London, HMSO, 1994) p 37.

51 'Holding the hand that feeds', The Eco-nomist, 9 September 1995, and posted on www.economist.com

52 Sir Harold Banwell, chair, Report of the Committee on the Placing and Management of Contracts for Building and Civil Engineering work (London, HMSO, 1964), quoted in Constructing the Team: Joint review of pro-curement and contractual arrangements in the United Kingdom construction industry – Final Report (London, HMSO, 1994) p 61.

53 Richard Rogers, quoted in Robert Booth, 'Rogers fears Brown stance', Building Design, 8 November 2002, p 5.

54 Richard Rogers, quoted by Marcus Fairs, 'Power to the people', Building, 18 October 2002, p 30.

55 www.labc–services.co.uk

56 Office for National Statistics and the Department of Trade and Industry, Construction Statistics Annual 2002 Edition (London, The Stationery Office, 2002) Tables 11.2 and 11.3, and posted on www.dti.gov.uk/construction/stats/stats2002/pdf/constat2002.pdf

57 Alex Lifschutz, 'Rewind and Repeat', Building Design, 4 April 2003, page 9.

58 'News from CEBR – Issue 4', Centre for Economics and Business Research, December 2002, and posted on www.cebr.com

59 John Miles, Homing in on Excellence – a com-mentary on the use of offsite fabrication methods for the UK housebuilding industry (London, The Housing Forum, 2002).

60 John Prewer, RM Lawson, PJ Grubb and PJ Trebilcock, Modular Construction using Light Steel Framing – An Architect's Guide (Ascot, Steel Construction Institute, 1999).

61 Movement for Innovation and Waterloo Air Management, The Why, What and How of Partnering the Supply Chain (London, Rethinking Construction, 2001) p 5.

62 Simon Allford, speaking at The Pre-Fabulous Home and posted on www.audacity.org/Activity.htm

63 John Miles, Homing in on Excellence – a com-mentary on the use of offsite fabrication methods for the UK housebuilding industry (The Housing Forum, London, 2002) p 61.

64 Constructing the Team: Joint Review of Procurement and Contractual Arrangements in the United Kingdom Construction Industry, Final Report (London, HMSO, 1994) p 66.

65 Stuart Macdonald, 'Hurry up on prefab, Prescott tells sector', Housing Today, 30 May 2003, and posted on www.housing–today.co.uk

66 John Prescott, Question 722, Select Commi-ttee on Office of the Deputy Prime Minister – Housing, Planning, Local Government and the Regions, Minutes of Evidence – Examina-tion of Witnesses (Questions 720 – 739), 25 February 2003, and posted on www.publications.parliament.uk

67 www.thames–gateway.org.uk

68 'Battle over Thames Gateway site', Building, 8 November 2002, p 15.

69 www.hfmgv.org/dymaxion/contents.html

70 An Ambition for South Dagenham: Intro-duction of the task for consultants (London, London Borough of Barking and Dagenham and London Borough of Havering, 2001).

71 An Ambition for South Dagenham: Intro-duction of the task for consultants (London, London Borough of Barking and Dagenham and London Borough of Havering, 2001).

72 Norma Cohen, 'Lipton plots UK construc-tion shake-up', Financial Times, 26 August 2003, p19.

73 Russell Jacoby, The End of Utopia: politics and culture in an age of apathy (New York, Basic Books, 1999).

74 Comptroller and Auditor General, PFI: The New Headquarters for the Home Office, National Audit Office,15 July 2003, and posted on www.nao.gov.uk/pn/02–03/0203954.htm

75 Office of the Deputy Prime Minister, Creating Sustainable Communities: making it happen, 30 July 2003, p 3, and posted on www.odpm.gov.uk/stellent/groups/odpm_communities/documents/page/odpm_comm_023714.pdf

7 Biographies

7.1 Ian Abley

Ian Abley trained as an architect at Newcastle University between 1980 and 1987, but immediately entered business as a housebuilder registered by the National House Building Council. After 10 years and a move to London, he

Ian and Alex Abley. Photo by Caroline Irby

qualified and registered as an architect in 1998.

Ian currently works as a senior façade architect at Whitby Bird and Partners Façade Engineering. Though he can draw, his work has always largely been technical, rather than focused on design: he likes being a specialist integrator in the architectural profession.

He was the prime mover in organising the first event held by Audacity Ltd, in July 2000. Ian was co-editor, with James Heartfield, of *Sustaining Architecture in the Anti-Machine Age*, a collection of 18 essays variously advocating and critical of sustainability, and published by Wiley-Academy in 2001. He is also the driving force behind the audacity.org website, and is always on the look-out for new, high-quality contributions that, like everything else to do with the website, are volunteered to raise a level of debate.

Ian may be contacted at abley@ audacity.org, or visit www.audacity.org.

7.2 Miles Glendinning

Miles Glendinning is a historian and writer based at the Royal Commission on the Ancient and Historical Monuments of Scotland – Scotland's national survey of the built environment. Miles may be contacted at Milesg@rcahms.gov.uk or visit www.rcahms.gov.uk.

For over two decades, Miles has specialised in the history of post-war mass housing – at first, out of zeal for an epoch of high ideals that had been damned for reasons that seemed largely unfair or frivolous. During the 1980s and early 1990s he collaborated with Stefan Muthesius in researching and writing what would hopefully be a definitive rebuttal of this torrent of invective: *Tower Block*. Its preparation involved him, among other things, in personally visiting and researching every council tower block in the UK, and interviewing a vast range of people who were actually involved in the great housing drive – including well-known characters such as T Dan Smith and Sir Keith Joseph. The records generated from the research were housed in a specially-bought flat on the 20th floor of Edinburgh's tallest tower block, Martello Court, built in 1964.

More recently, Miles has specialised in the architectural and urban history of Scotland, and has co-authored and edited numerous books and other publications on this subject – including *Home Builders*, 1999, with colleague Diane M Watters, a history of the 20th-century housebuilding industry in Scotland; *History of*

Scottish Architecture, 1996, with Aonghus MacKechnie; and a forthcoming book on Scottish architecture in the Thames & Hudson World of Art series, also with MacKechnie.

He has played a prominent role in the affairs of DOCOMOMO, the international working group for the documentation and conservation of Modern Movement buildings and sites. He has also intervened in current Scottish debates concerning architecture and the city in the new era of home rule, most notably through the book *Clone City: Crisis and Renewal in Contemporary Scottish Architecture*, 1999, co-authored with the architect David Page. The authors pleaded for a modern, Geddesian, regionalist response to the challenge of globalisation, and attacked the meretricious national-identity image-making approach symbolised by Enric Miralles's design for the new Scottish Parliament.

7.3 Richard McWilliams

Richard McWilliams joined Symonds Group, London, in the spring of 2003 as a senior consultant. His brief is to establish

Miles Glendinning

Richard McWilliams

a new line of business in IT consultancy, specialising in the practical application of emerging technologies in the construction industry.

Prior to that, Richard formed and led the Whitby Bird and Partners Technology Group and the consultancy 'the-e-shop', having pioneered the use of 3D project modelling and project extranets. Richard acknowledges the experience and expertise gained at Whitby Bird and Partners from 1994 and 2002, working with Gareth Griffiths and the CAD Development Team.

As a doubly chartered engineer, Richard is a member of Council for the Steel Construction Institute, a member of the Information Advisory Panel for the Institution of Structural Engineers, and chairs the Teamwork 2002 Steering Group.[1]

He may be contacted at Richard. Mcwilliams@symonds–group.com or visit www.symonds–group.com.

7.4 Clare Morris

Clare Morris has worked in UK construction industry marketing for 15 years, the past 10 of which have been spent with the NBS, publisher of the industry standard National Building Specification. Clare may be contacted at info@theNBS. com, or visit www.theNBS.com.

Through its involvement with the Construction Project Information Committee[2] and the International Construction Information Society,[3] the NBS is a major contributor to industry best practice initiatives. Based in Newcastle upon Tyne with about 100 staff, the NBS is committed to developing innovative software that enables specifiers to improve the quality and production of project documentation. The NBS recognises that its development is dependent on feedback from NBS users, and that relationship is one that Clare aims to strengthen.

7.5 Stefan Muthesius

Stefan Muthesius is an architectural and design historian who trained in the 1960s in Germany, and then in London under Nikolaus Pevsner. He joined the rising Victorian Society in its new enthusiasm for 'rogue' High Victorian church architecture, and, as a result, wrote *The High Victorian Movement in Architecture 1850–1870*, which was published by

Clare Morris

The NBS, The Old Post Office, St Nicholas Street, Newcastle upon Tyne, NE1 1RH
Telephone 0845 456 9594

Routledge & Kegan Paul in 1972. That was followed by *Das Englische Volbild* (Munich, Prestel, 1974), in which he investigated the impact of 'model England' in German architecture and design during the second half of the 19th century.

From 1968 onwards Stefan has taught at the University of East Anglia in Norwich. His recognition that Foster's Sainsbury Centre and Denys Lasdun's campus constituted milestones in 20th century architecture grew; but the lure of Victorian Architecture proved stronger. *Victorian Architecture*, written with Roger Dixon, was published by Thames & Hudson in 1978. In 1982 *The English Terraced House*, which also went to a German edition, was published by Yale University Press, and extended the confines of polite architecture.

Those confines were, one might say, extended in a different direction with work on post-war British council housing, sparked by Miles Glendinning's excitement with height in 1983, and researched in cooperation with him throughout. *Provincial Mixed Development*, a modest tome on Norwich hand-produced by the authors in 1986, was followed by the doorstopper *Tower Block*

(Yale University Press, 1994). This investigated all aspects of the production of high council blocks in the whole of the UK so thoroughly that, in 1994, it gained the 1994 Society of Architectural Historians' Hitchcock Medallion.

Stefan's interest then turned in a completely different direction. *Art, Architecture and Design in Poland* (Koenigstein im Taunus, 1994) followed. Work on the 1960s campus at UEA with Peter Dormer led to *Concrete and Open Skies: Architecture at the University of East Anglia 1962–2000* (Unicorn Press, 2001). He then researched more broadly *The Postwar University – Utopianist College and Campus* (Yale, 2000). His recent interest has returned to the 19th century in the *Poetic Home: Nineteenth century Interior Décor to Interior Design* (Reaktion Books, forthcoming).

Stefan may be contacted at s.muthesius @uea.ac.uk, or visit www.uea.ac.uk.

7.6 Vicky Richardson

Vicky Richardson has a degree in architecture from Westminster University and writes about architecture and design. Her articles have been widely published in

Stefan Muthesius

Vicky Richardson and May

national, international and professional magazines including *Dazed & Confused*, *Housing Today*, *Blueprint* and *World of Interiors*. Until 2002 she was deputy editor of *RIBA Journal*, and before that editor of *Public Service & Local Government* magazine and assistant editor of *Public Sector Building*. She remains Practice editor of *RIBA Journal* and author of its monthly column 'The Office'. Her book *New Vernacular Architecture* was published by Laurence King in 2001.

Vicky is the recipient of an Arts Council grant to explore ways of communicating about architecture, resulting in the publication in August 2003 of the Dungeness Box, an assemblage of materials, found objects and words about a house on the south coast of England.

Current writing projects include an essay on globalisation and regionalism for the German Architecture Museum's exhibition 'Post-Modernism Revisited', scheduled for opening in Frankfurt in 2004. Vicky may be contacted at vicky@foundling.net.

7.7 James Woudhuysen

James Woudhuysen is professor of forecasting and innovation at De Montfort University, and a director of Audacity Ltd. He may be contacted at james@woudhuysen.com or visit www.audacity.org.

A physics graduate, he helped install Britain's first computer-controlled car park in 1968, wrote about chemical weapons for *The Economist* in 1978, drafted a word processor instruction manual in 1983, led a multi-client study of e-commerce in 1988 and, in 1993, proposed that the internet be delivered over TV. He has worked with 50 of the world's top corporations, including AT&T, BT, Ford, Hewlett-Packard, IBM, Microsoft, Motorola, Orange, Renault, Unilever and Whirlpool.

Each month, he contributes to *IT Week*. In the 1980s James was editor of *Design* magazine and a co-founder of *Blueprint*, before heading research at the international designers Fitch. In the 1990s he led consulting in urban strategy for the Henley Centre, London, where he advised London, Birmingham, Glasgow and Manchester on economic and technological development. He established Henley's consulting in IT, as well as working with Ahrend NV, BAA, London Underground and Milliken in Facilities Management.

Next, James headed worldwide market intelligence for Philips consumer electronics in the Netherlands, before returning to the UK as a director of product designers Seymour Powell. In this

James Woudhuyse

www.audacity.org

position, he worked on the future of technology users with Casio, Mars, McDonalds, Nokia and Yamaha Motor Europe.

James has written for *Applied Ergonomics*, *Demos Quarterly*, *The Economist*, Guardian Unlimited, *Institute of Mechanical Engineers Journal*, *Long Range Planning*, *Marketing* and *The Times*. He is the author of *Cult IT*, published by the Institute of Contemporary Arts in 1999, and of 'Play as the Main Event in International and UK Culture', in *Cultural Trends*.

NOTES

1   www.teamwork2002.org
2   www.productioninformation.org
3   www.icis.org

Index